HOLT SCIENCE & TECHNOLOGY

Forces, Motion, and Energy

ANNOTATED TEACHER'S EDITION

HOLT, RINEHART AND WINSTON

A Harcourt Classroom Education Company

Austin · New York · Orlando · Atlanta · San Francisco · Boston · Dallas · Toronto · London

Acknowledgments

Chapter Writers

Christie Borgford, Ph.D.
Professor of Chemistry
University of Alabama
Birmingham, Alabama

Andrew Champagne
Former Physics Teacher
Ashland High School
Ashland, Massachusetts

Mapi Cuevas, Ph.D.
Professor of Chemistry
Santa Fe Community College
Gainesville, Florida

Leila Dumas
Former Physics Teacher
LBJ Science Academy
Austin, Texas

William G. Lamb, Ph.D.
Science Teacher and Dept. Chair
Oregon Episcopal School
Portland, Oregon

Sally Ann Vonderbrink, Ph.D.
Chemistry Teacher
St. Xavier High School
Cincinnati, Ohio

Lab Writers

Phillip G. Bunce
Former Physics Teacher
Bowie High School
Austin, Texas

Kenneth E. Creese
Science Teacher
White Mountain Junior High
   School
Rock Springs, Wyoming

William G. Lamb, Ph.D.
Science Teacher and Dept. Chair
Oregon Episcopal School
Portland, Oregon

Alyson Mike
Science Teacher
East Valley Middle School
East Helena, Montana

Joseph W. Price
Science Teacher and Dept. Chair
H. M. Browne Junior High
   School
Washington, D.C.

Denice Lee Sandefur
Science Teacher and Dept. Chair
Nucla High School
Nucla, Colorado

John Spadafino
Mathematics and Physics Teacher
Hackensack High School
Hackensack, New Jersey

Walter Woolbaugh
Science Teacher
Manhattan Junior High School
Manhattan, Montana

Academic Reviewers

Paul R. Berman, Ph.D.
Professor of Physics
University of Michigan
Ann Arbor, Michigan

Russell M. Brengelman, Ph.D.
Professor of Physics
Morehead State University
Morehead, Kentucky

John A. Brockhaus, Ph.D.
*Director, Mapping, Charting and
   Geodesy Program*
Department of Geography and
   Environmental Engineering
United States Military Academy
West Point, New York

Walter Bron, Ph.D.
Professor of Physics
University of California
Irvine, California

Andrew J. Davis, Ph.D.
Manager, ACE Science Center
Department of Physics
California Institute of
   Technology
Pasadena, California

Peter E. Demmin, Ed.D.
*Former Science Teacher and
   Department Chair*
Amherst Central High School
Amherst, New York

Roger Falcone, Ph.D.
*Professor of Physics and
   Department Chair*
University of California
Berkeley, California

Cassandra A. Fraser, Ph.D.
Assistant Professor of Chemistry
University of Virginia
Charlottesville, Virginia

L. John Gagliardi, Ph.D.
*Associate Professor of Physics and
   Department Chair*
Rutgers University
Camden, New Jersey

Gabriele F. Giuliani, Ph.D.
Professor of Physics
Purdue University
West Lafayette, Indiana

Roy W. Hann, Jr., Ph.D.
Professor of Civil Engineering
Texas A&M University
College Station, Texas

John L. Hubisz, Ph.D.
Professor of Physics
North Carolina State University
Raleigh, North Carolina

Samuel P. Kounaves, Ph.D.
Professor of Chemistry
Tufts University
Medford, Massachusetts

Karol Lang, Ph.D.
Associate Professor of Physics
The University of Texas
Austin, Texas

Gloria Langer, Ph.D.
Professor of Physics
University of Colorado
Boulder, Colorado

Phillip LaRoe
Professor
Helena College of Technology
Helena, Montana

Joseph A. McClure, Ph.D.
Associate Professor of Physics
Georgetown University
Washington, D.C.

LaMoine L. Motz, Ph.D.
Coordinator of Science Education
Department of Learning
   Services
Oakland County Schools
Waterford, Michigan

R. Thomas Myers, Ph.D.
Professor of Chemistry, Emeritus
Kent State University
Kent, Ohio

Hillary Clement Olson, Ph.D.
Research Associate
Institute for Geophysics
The University of Texas
Austin, Texas

David P. Richardson, Ph.D.
Professor of Chemistry
Thompson Chemical
   Laboratory
Williams College
Williamstown, Massachusetts

John Rigden, Ph.D.
Director of Special Projects
American Institute of Physics
Colchester, Vermont

Acknowledgments (cont.)

Peter Sheridan, Ph.D.
Professor of Chemistry
Colgate University
Hamilton, New York

Vederaman Sriraman, Ph.D.
*Associate Professor of
    Technology*
Southwest Texas State
    University
San Marcos, Texas

Jack B. Swift, Ph.D.
Professor of Physics
The University of Texas
Austin, Texas

Atiq Syed, Ph.D.
*Master Instructor of
    Mathematics and Science*
Texas State Technical College
Harlingen, Texas

Leonard Taylor, Ph.D.
Professor Emeritus
Department of Electrical
    Engineering
University of Maryland
College Park, Maryland

Virginia L. Trimble, Ph.D.
*Professor of Physics and
    Astronomy*
University of California
Irvine, California

Martin VanDyke, Ph.D.
Professor of Chemistry, Emeritus
Front Range Community
    College
Westminster, Colorado

Gabriela Waschewsky, Ph.D.
Science and Math Teacher
Emery High School
Emeryville, California

Safety Reviewer

Jack A. Gerlovich, Ph.D.
Associate Professor
School of Education
Drake University
Des Moines, Iowa

Teacher Reviewers

Barry L. Bishop
Science Teacher and Dept. Chair
San Rafael Junior High
    School
Ferron, Utah

Paul Boyle
Science Teacher
Perry Heights Middle School
Evansville, Indiana

Kenneth Creese
Science Teacher
White Mountain Junior High
    School
Rock Springs, Wyoming

Vicky Farland
Science Teacher and Dept. Chair
Centennial Middle School
Yuma, Arizona

Rebecca Ferguson
Science Teacher
North Ridge Middle School
North Richland Hills, Texas

Laura Fleet
Science Teacher
Alice B. Landrum Middle
    School
Ponte Vedra Beach, Florida

Jennifer Ford
Science Teacher and Dept. Chair
North Ridge Middle School
North Richland Hills, Texas

Susan Gorman
Science Teacher
North Ridge Middle School
North Richland Hills, Texas

C. John Graves
Science Teacher
Monforton Middle School
Bozeman, Montana

Dennis Hanson
Science Teacher and Dept. Chair
Big Bear Middle School
Big Bear Lake, California

David A. Harris
Science Teacher and Dept. Chair
The Thacher School
Ojai, California

Norman E. Holcomb
Science Teacher
Marion Local Schools
Maria Stein, Ohio

Kenneth J. Horn
Science Teacher and Dept. Chair
Fallston Middle School
Fallston, Maryland

Tracy Jahn
Science Teacher
Berkshire Junior-Senior High
    School
Canaan, New York

Kerry A. Johnson
Science Teacher
Isbell Middle School
Santa Paula, California

Drew E. Kirian
Science Teacher
Solon Middle School
Solon, Ohio

Harriet Knops
Science Teacher and Dept. Chair
Rolling Hills Middle School
El Dorado, California

Scott Mandel, Ph.D.
*Director and Educational
    Consultant*
Teachers Helping Teachers
Los Angeles, California

Thomas Manerchia
Former Science Teacher
Archmere Academy
Claymont, Delaware

Edith McAlanis
Science Teacher and Dept. Chair
Socorro Middle School
El Paso, Texas

Kevin McCurdy, Ph.D.
Science Teacher
Elmwood Junior High School
Rogers, Arkansas

Alyson Mike
Science Teacher
East Valley Middle School
East Helena, Montana

Donna Norwood
Science Teacher and Dept. Chair
Monroe Middle School
Charlotte, North Carolina

Joseph W. Price
Science Teacher and Dept. Chair
H. M. Browne Junior High
    School
Washington, D.C.

Terry J. Rakes
Science Teacher
Elmwood Junior High School
Rogers, Arkansas

Beth Richards
Science Teacher
North Middle School
Crystal Lake, Illinois

Elizabeth J. Rustad
Science Teacher
Crane Middle School
Yuma, Arizona

Kerry A. Johnson

Rodney A. Sandefur
Science Teacher
Naturita Middle School
Naturita, Colorado

Helen Schiller
Science Teacher
Northwood Middle School
Taylors, South Carolina

Bert J. Sherwood
Science Teacher
Socorro Middle School
El Paso, Texas

Patricia McFarlane Soto
Science Teacher and Dept. Chair
G. W. Carver Middle School
Miami, Florida

David M. Sparks
Science Teacher
Redwater Junior High School
Redwater, Texas

Larry Tackett
Science Teacher and Dept. Chair
Andrew Jackson Middle
    School
Cross Lanes, West Virginia

Elsie N. Waynes
Science Teacher and Dept. Chair
R. H. Terrell Junior High
    School
Washington, D.C.

Sharon L. Woolf
Science Teacher
Langston Hughes Middle
    School
Reston, Virginia

Alexis S. Wright
*Middle School Science
    Coordinator*
Rye Country Day School
Rye, New York

Lee Yassinski
Science Teacher
Sun Valley Middle School
Sun Valley, California

John Zambo
Science Teacher
Elizabeth Ustach Middle
    School
Modesto, California

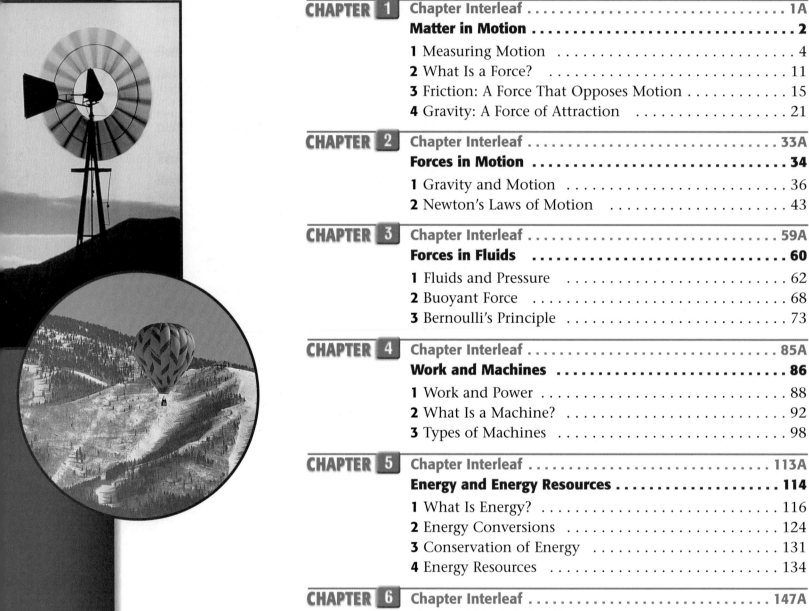

M Forces, Motion, and Energy

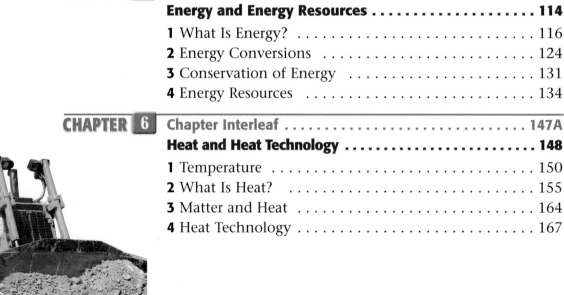

Skills Development

Process Skills

QuickLabs

Chapter Labs

Skills Development *(continued)*

Research and Critical Thinking Skills

Apply

Feature Articles

Connections

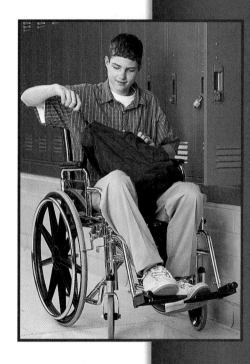

Program Scope and Sequence

Selecting the right books for your course is easy. Just review the topics presented in each book to determine the best match to your district curriculum.

	A MICROORGANISMS, FUNGI, AND PLANTS	**B** ANIMALS
CHAPTER 1	**It's Alive!! Or, Is It?** ❑ Characteristics of living things ❑ Homeostasis ❑ Heredity and DNA ❑ Producers, consumers, and decomposers ❑ Biomolecules	**Animals and Behavior** ❑ Characteristics of animals ❑ Classification of animals ❑ Animal behavior ❑ Hibernation and estivation ❑ The biological clock ❑ Animal communication ❑ Living in groups
CHAPTER 2	**Bacteria and Viruses** ❑ Binary fission ❑ Characteristics of bacteria ❑ Nitrogen-fixing bacteria ❑ Antibiotics ❑ Pathogenic bacteria ❑ Characteristics of viruses ❑ Lytic cycle	**Invertebrates** ❑ General characteristics of invertebrates ❑ Types of symmetry ❑ Characteristics of sponges, cnidarians, arthropods, and echinoderms ❑ Flatworms versus roundworms ❑ Types of circulatory systems
CHAPTER 3	**Protists and Fungi** ❑ Characteristics of protists ❑ Types of algae ❑ Types of protozoa ❑ Protist reproduction ❑ Characteristics of fungi and lichens	**Fishes, Amphibians, and Reptiles** ❑ Characteristics of vertebrates ❑ Structure and kinds of fishes ❑ Development of lungs ❑ Structure and kinds of amphibians and reptiles ❑ Function of the amniotic egg
CHAPTER 4	**Introduction to Plants** ❑ Characteristics of plants and seeds ❑ Reproduction and classification ❑ Angiosperms versus gymnosperms ❑ Monocots versus dicots ❑ Structure and functions of roots, stems, leaves, and flowers	**Birds and Mammals** ❑ Structure and kinds of birds ❑ Types of feathers ❑ Adaptations for flight ❑ Structure and kinds of mammals ❑ Function of the placenta
CHAPTER 5	**Plant Processes** ❑ Pollination and fertilization ❑ Dormancy ❑ Photosynthesis ❑ Plant tropisms ❑ Seasonal responses of plants	
CHAPTER 6		
CHAPTER 7		

Life Science

C CELLS, HEREDITY, & CLASSIFICATION

Cells: The Basic Units of Life
- ❑ Cells, tissues, and organs
- ❑ Populations, communities, and ecosystems
- ❑ Cell theory
- ❑ Surface-to-volume ratio
- ❑ Prokaryotic versus eukaryotic cells
- ❑ Cell organelles

The Cell in Action
- ❑ Diffusion and osmosis
- ❑ Passive versus active transport
- ❑ Endocytosis versus exocytosis
- ❑ Photosynthesis
- ❑ Cellular respiration and fermentation
- ❑ Cell cycle

Heredity
- ❑ Dominant versus recessive traits
- ❑ Genes and alleles
- ❑ Genotype, phenotype, the Punnett square and probability
- ❑ Meiosis
- ❑ Determination of sex

Genes and Gene Technology
- ❑ Structure of DNA
- ❑ Protein synthesis
- ❑ Mutations
- ❑ Heredity disorders and genetic counseling

The Evolution of Living Things
- ❑ Adaptations and species
- ❑ Evidence for evolution
- ❑ Darwin's work and natural selection
- ❑ Formation of new species

The History of Life on Earth
- ❑ Geologic time scale and extinctions
- ❑ Plate tectonics
- ❑ Human evolution

Classification
- ❑ Levels of classification
- ❑ Cladistic diagrams
- ❑ Dichotomous keys
- ❑ Characteristics of the six kingdoms

D HUMAN BODY SYSTEMS & HEALTH

Body Organization and Structure
- ❑ Homeostasis
- ❑ Types of tissue
- ❑ Organ systems
- ❑ Structure and function of the skeletal system, muscular system, and integumentary system

Circulation and Respiration
- ❑ Structure and function of the cardiovascular system, lymphatic system, and respiratory system
- ❑ Respiratory disorders

The Digestive and Urinary Systems
- ❑ Structure and function of the digestive system
- ❑ Structure and function of the urinary system

Communication and Control
- ❑ Structure and function of the nervous system and endocrine system
- ❑ The senses
- ❑ Structure and function of the eye and ear

Reproduction and Development
- ❑ Asexual versus sexual reproduction
- ❑ Internal versus external fertilization
- ❑ Structure and function of the human male and female reproductive systems
- ❑ Fertilization, placental development, and embryo growth
- ❑ Stages of human life

Body Defenses and Disease
- ❑ Types of diseases
- ❑ Vaccines and immunity
- ❑ Structure and function of the immune system
- ❑ Autoimmune diseases, cancer, and AIDS

Staying Healthy
- ❑ Nutrition and reading food labels
- ❑ Alcohol and drug effects on the body
- ❑ Hygiene, exercise, and first aid

E ENVIRONMENTAL SCIENCE

Interactions of Living Things
- ❑ Biotic versus abiotic parts of the environment
- ❑ Producers, consumers, and decomposers
- ❑ Food chains and food webs
- ❑ Factors limiting population growth
- ❑ Predator-prey relationships
- ❑ Symbiosis and coevolution

Cycles in Nature
- ❑ Water cycle
- ❑ Carbon cycle
- ❑ Nitrogen cycle
- ❑ Ecological succession

The Earth's Ecosystems
- ❑ Kinds of land and water biomes
- ❑ Marine ecosystems
- ❑ Freshwater ecosystems

Environmental Problems and Solutions
- ❑ Types of pollutants
- ❑ Types of resources
- ❑ Conservation practices
- ❑ Species protection

Energy Resources
- ❑ Types of resources
- ❑ Energy resources and pollution
- ❑ Alternative energy resources

Scope and Sequence (continued)

		F INSIDE THE RESTLESS EARTH	**G** EARTH'S CHANGING SURFACE
CHAPTER	**1**	**Minerals of the Earth's Crust** ❑ Mineral composition and structure ❑ Types of minerals ❑ Mineral identification ❑ Mineral formation and mining	**Maps as Models of the Earth** ❑ Structure of a map ❑ Cardinal directions ❑ Latitude, longitude, and the equator ❑ Magnetic declination and true north ❑ Types of projections ❑ Aerial photographs ❑ Remote sensing ❑ Topographic maps
CHAPTER	**2**	**Rocks: Mineral Mixtures** ❑ Rock cycle and types of rocks ❑ Rock classification ❑ Characteristics of igneous, sedimentary, and metamorphic rocks	**Weathering and Soil Formation** ❑ Types of weathering ❑ Factors affecting the rate of weathering ❑ Composition of soil ❑ Soil conservation and erosion prevention
CHAPTER	**3**	**The Rock and Fossil Record** ❑ Uniformitarianism versus catastrophism ❑ Superposition ❑ The geologic column and unconformities ❑ Absolute dating and radiometric dating ❑ Characteristics and types of fossils ❑ Geologic time scale	**Agents of Erosion and Deposition** ❑ Shoreline erosion and deposition ❑ Wind erosion and deposition ❑ Erosion and deposition by ice ❑ Gravity's effect on erosion and deposition
CHAPTER	**4**	**Plate Tectonics** ❑ Structure of the Earth ❑ Continental drifts and sea floor spreading ❑ Plate tectonics theory ❑ Types of boundaries ❑ Types of crust deformities	
CHAPTER	**5**	**Earthquakes** ❑ Seismology ❑ Features of earthquakes ❑ P and S waves ❑ Gap hypothesis ❑ Earthquake safety	
CHAPTER	**6**	**Volcanoes** ❑ Types of volcanoes and eruptions ❑ Types of lava and pyroclastic material ❑ Craters versus calderas ❑ Sites and conditions for volcano formation ❑ Predicting eruptions	

Earth Science

H WATER ON EARTH

The Flow of Fresh Water
❏ Water cycle
❏ River systems
❏ Stream erosion
❏ Life cycle of rivers
❏ Deposition
❏ Aquifers, springs, and wells
❏ Ground water
❏ Water treatment and pollution

Exploring the Oceans
❏ Properties and characteristics of the oceans
❏ Features of the ocean floor
❏ Ocean ecology
❏ Ocean resources and pollution

The Movement of Ocean Water
❏ Types of currents
❏ Characteristics of waves
❏ Types of ocean waves
❏ Tides

I WEATHER AND CLIMATE

The Atmosphere
❏ Structure of the atmosphere
❏ Air pressure
❏ Radiation, convection, and conduction
❏ Greenhouse effect and global warming
❏ Characteristics of winds
❏ Types of winds
❏ Air pollution

Understanding Weather
❏ Water cycle
❏ Humidity
❏ Types of clouds
❏ Types of precipitation
❏ Air masses and fronts
❏ Storms, tornadoes, and hurricanes
❏ Weather forecasting
❏ Weather maps

Climate
❏ Weather versus climate
❏ Seasons and latitude
❏ Prevailing winds
❏ Earth's biomes
❏ Earth's climate zones
❏ Ice ages
❏ Global warming
❏ Greenhouse effect

J ASTRONOMY

Observing the Sky
❏ Astronomy
❏ Keeping time
❏ Mapping the stars
❏ Scales of the universe
❏ Types of telescope
❏ Radioastronomy

Formation of the Solar System
❏ Birth of the solar system
❏ Planetary motion
❏ Newton's Law of Universal Gravitation
❏ Structure of the sun
❏ Fusion
❏ Earth's structure and atmosphere

A Family of Planets
❏ Properties and characteristics of the planets
❏ Properties and characteristics of moons
❏ Comets, asteroids, and meteoroids

The Universe Beyond
❏ Composition of stars
❏ Classification of stars
❏ Star brightness, distance, and motions
❏ H-R diagram
❏ Life cycle of stars
❏ Types of galaxies
❏ Theories on the formation of the universe

Exploring Space
❏ Rocketry and artificial satellites
❏ Types of Earth orbit
❏ Space probes and space exploration

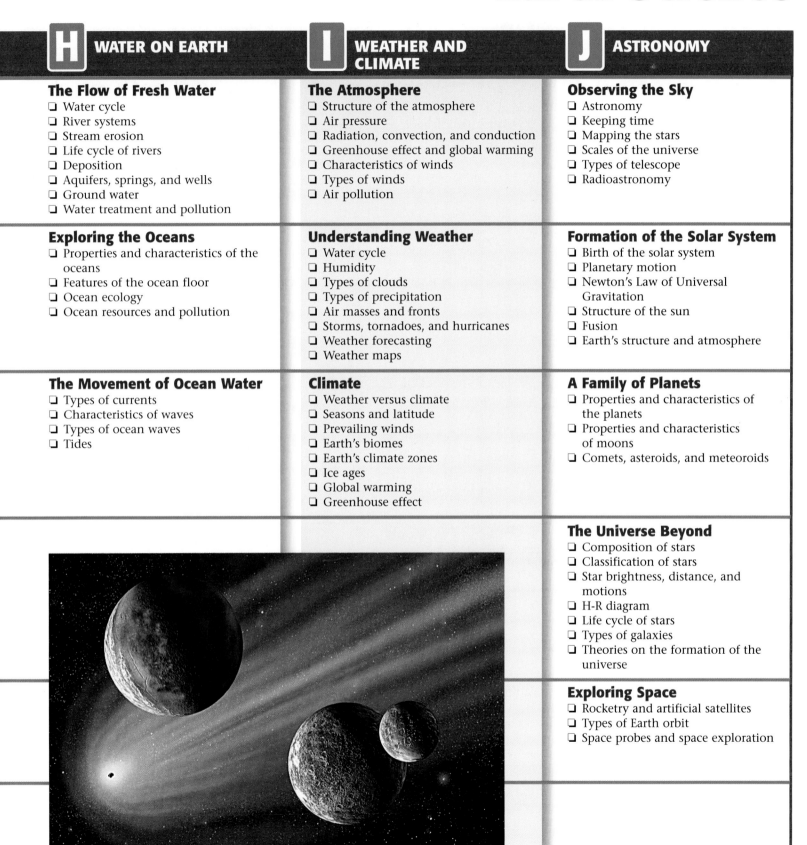

Scope and Sequence *(continued)*

	K INTRODUCTION TO MATTER	**L** INTERACTIONS OF MATTER
CHAPTER 1	**The Properties of Matter** ❏ Definition of matter ❏ Mass and weight ❏ Physical and chemical properties ❏ Physical and chemical change ❏ Density	**Chemical Bonding** ❏ Types of chemical bonds ❏ Valence electrons ❏ Ions versus molecules ❏ Crystal lattice
CHAPTER 2	**States of Matter** ❏ States of matter and their properties ❏ Boyle's and Charles's laws ❏ Changes of state	**Chemical Reactions** ❏ Writing chemical formulas and equations ❏ Law of conservation of mass ❏ Types of reactions ❏ Endothermic versus exothermic reactions ❏ Law of conservation of energy ❏ Activation energy ❏ Catalysts and inhibitors
CHAPTER 3	**Elements, Compounds, and Mixtures** ❏ Elements and compounds ❏ Metals, nonmetals, and metalloids (semiconductors) ❏ Properties of mixtures ❏ Properties of solutions, suspensions, and colloids	**Chemical Compounds** ❏ Ionic versus covalent compounds ❏ Acids, bases, and salts ❏ pH ❏ Organic compounds ❏ Biomolecules
CHAPTER 4	**Introduction to Atoms** ❏ Atomic theory ❏ Atomic model and structure ❏ Isotopes ❏ Atomic mass and mass number	**Atomic Energy** ❏ Properties of radioactive substances ❏ Types of decay ❏ Half-life ❏ Fission, fusion, and chain reactions
CHAPTER 5	**The Periodic Table** ❏ Structure of the periodic table ❏ Periodic law ❏ Properties of alkali metals, alkaline-earth metals, halogens, and noble gases	
CHAPTER 6		

Physical Science

M FORCES, MOTION, AND ENERGY

Matter in Motion
- Speed, velocity, and acceleration
- Measuring force
- Friction
- Mass versus weight

Forces in Motion
- Terminal velocity and free fall
- Projectile motion
- Inertia
- Momentum

Forces in Fluids
- Properties in fluids
- Atmospheric pressure
- Density
- Pascal's principle
- Buoyant force
- Archimedes' principle
- Bernoulli's principle

Work and Machines
- Measuring work
- Measuring power
- Types of machines
- Mechanical advantage
- Mechanical efficiency

Energy and Energy Resources
- Forms of energy
- Energy conversions
- Law of conservation of energy
- Energy resources

Heat and Heat Technology
- Heat versus temperature
- Thermal expansion
- Absolute zero
- Conduction, convection, radiation
- Conductors versus insulators
- Specific heat capacity
- Changes of state
- Heat engines
- Thermal pollution

N ELECTRICITY AND MAGNETISM

Introduction to Electricity
- Law of electric charges
- Conduction versus induction
- Static electricity
- Potential difference
- Cells, batteries, and photocells
- Thermocouples
- Voltage, current, and resistance
- Electric power
- Types of circuits

Electromagnetism
- Properties of magnets
- Magnetic force
- Electromagnetism
- Solenoids and electric motors
- Electromagnetic induction
- Generators and transformers

Electronic Technology
- Properties of semiconductors
- Integrated circuits
- Diodes and transistors
- Analog versus digital signals
- Microprocessors
- Features of computers

O SOUND AND LIGHT

The Energy of Waves
- Properties of waves
- Types of waves
- Reflection and refraction
- Diffraction and interference
- Standing waves and resonance

The Nature of Sound
- Properties of sound waves
- Structure of the human ear
- Pitch and the Doppler effect
- Infrasonic versus ultrasonic sound
- Sound reflection and echolocation
- Sound barrier
- Interference, resonance, diffraction, and standing waves
- Sound quality of instruments

The Nature of Light
- Electromagnetic waves
- Electromagnetic spectrum
- Law of reflection
- Absorption and scattering
- Reflection and refraction
- Diffraction and interference

Light and Our World
- Luminosity
- Types of lighting
- Types of mirrors and lenses
- Focal point
- Structure of the human eye
- Lasers and holograms

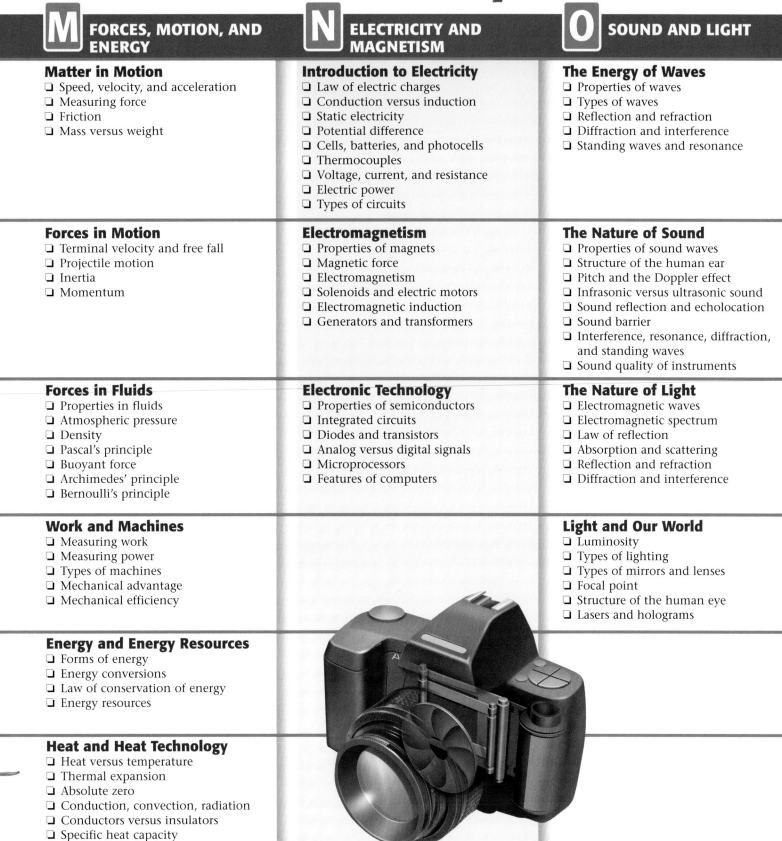

Components Listing

Effective planning starts with all the resources you need in an easy-to-use package for each short course.

Directed Reading Worksheets Help students develop and practice fundamental reading comprehension skills and provide a comprehensive review tool for students to use when studying for an exam.

Study Guide Vocabulary & Notes Worksheets and Chapter Review Worksheets are reproductions of the Chapter Highlights and Chapter Review sections that follow each chapter in the textbook.

Science Puzzlers, Twisters & Teasers Use vocabulary and concepts from each chapter of the Pupil's Editions as elements of rebuses, anagrams, logic puzzles, daffy definitions, riddle poems, word jumbles, and other types of puzzles.

Reinforcement and Vocabulary Review Worksheets Approach a chapter topic from a different angle with an emphasis on different learning modalities to help students that are frustrated by traditional methods.

Critical Thinking & Problem Solving Worksheets Develop the following skills: distinguishing fact from opinion, predicting consequences, analyzing information, and drawing conclusions. Problem Solving Worksheets develop a step-by-step process of problem analysis including gathering information, asking critical questions, identifying alternatives, and making comparisons.

Math Skills for Science Worksheets Each activity gives a brief introduction to a relevant math skill, a step-by-step explanation of the math process, one or more example problems, and a variety of practice problems.

Science Skills Worksheets Help your students focus specifically on skills such as measuring, graphing, using logic, understanding statistics, organizing research papers, and critical thinking options.

LAB ACTIVITIES

ALL LABS ARE CLASSROOM TESTED & APPROVED

Datasheets for Labs These worksheets are the labs found in the *Holt Science & Technology* textbook. Charts, tables, and graphs are included to make data collection and analysis easier, and space is provided to write observations and conclusions.

Whiz-Bang Demonstrations Discovery or Making Models experiences label each demo as one in which students discover an answer or use a scientific model.

Calculator-Based Labs Give students the opportunity to use graphing-calculator probes and sensors to collect data using a TI graphing calculator, Vernier sensors, and a TI CBL 2™ or Vernier Lab Pro interface.

EcoLabs and Field Activities Focus on educational outdoor projects, such as wildlife observation, nature surveys, or natural history.

Inquiry Labs Use the scientific method to help students find their own path in solving a real-world problem.

Long-Term Projects and Research Ideas Provide students with the opportunity to go beyond library and Internet resources to explore science topics.

ASSESSMENT

Chapter Tests Each four-page chapter test consists of a variety of item types including Multiple Choice, Using Vocabulary, Short Answer, Critical Thinking, Math in Science, Interpreting Graphics, and Concept Mapping.

Performance-Based Assessments Evaluate students' abilities to solve problems using the tools, equipment, and techniques of science. Rubrics included for each assessment make it easy to evaluate student performance.

TEACHER RESOURCES

Lesson Plans Integrate all of the great resources in the *Holt Science & Technology* program into your daily teaching. Each lesson plan includes a correlation of the lesson activities to the National Science Education Standards.

Teaching Transparencies Each transparency is correlated to a particular lesson in the Chapter Organizer.

Concept Mapping Transparencies, Worksheets, and Answer Key

Give students an opportunity to complete their own concept maps to study the concepts within each chapter and form logical connections. Student worksheets contain a blank concept map with linking phrases and a list of terms to be used by the student to complete the map.

TECHNOLOGY RESOURCES

 One-Stop Planner CD-ROM

Finding the right resources is easy with the One-Stop Planner CD-ROM. You can view and print any resource with just the click of a mouse. Customize the suggested lesson plans to match your daily or weekly calendar and your district's requirements. Powerful test generator software allows you to create customized assessments using a databank of items.

The One-Stop Planner for each level includes the following:

- All materials from the Teaching Resources
- Bellringer Transparency Masters
- Block Scheduling Tools
- Standards Correlations
- Lab Inventory Checklist
- Safety Information
- Science Fair Guide
- Parent Involvement Tools
- Spanish Audio Scripts
- Spanish Glossary
- Assessment Item Listing
- Assessment Checklists and Rubrics
- Test Generator

 sciLINKS

sciLINKS numbers throughout the text take you and your students to some of the best on-line resources available. Sites are constantly reviewed and updated by the National Science Teachers Association. Special "teacher only" sites are available to you once you register with the service.

go.hrw.com

To access Holt, Rinehart and Winston Web resources, use the home page codes for each level found on page 1 of the Pupil's Editions. The codes shown on the Chapter Organizers for each chapter in the Annotated Teacher's Edition take you to chapter-specific resources.

Smithsonian Institution

Find lesson plans, activities, interviews, virtual exhibits, and just general information on a wide variety of topics relevant to middle school science.

CNNfyi.com

Find the latest in late-breaking science news for students. Featured news stories are supported with lesson plans and activities.

CNN Presents Science in the News Video Library

Bring relevant science news stories into the classroom. Each video comes with a Teacher's Guide and set of Critical Thinking Worksheets that develop listening and media analysis skills. Tapes in the series include:

- Eye on the Environment
- Multicultural Connections
- Scientists in Action
- Science, Technology & Society

 Guided Reading Audio CD Program

Students can listen to a direct read of each chapter and follow along in the text. Use the program as a content bridge for struggling readers and students for whom English is not their native language.

Interactive Explorations CD-ROM

Turn a computer into a virtual laboratory. Students act as lab assistants helping Dr. Crystal Labcoat solve real-world problems. Activities develop students' inquiry, analysis, and decision-making skills.

Interactive Science Encyclopedia CD-ROM

Give your students access to more than 3,000 cross-referenced scientific definitions, in-depth articles, science fair project ideas, activities, and more.

ADDITIONAL COMPONENTS

Holt Anthology of Science Fiction
Science Fiction features in the Pupil's Edition preview the stories found in the anthology. Each story begins with a Reading Prep guide and closes with Think About It questions.

Professional Reference for Teachers
Articles written by leading educators help you learn more about the National Science Education Standards, block scheduling, classroom management techniques, and more. A bibliography of professional references is included.

Holt Science Posters
Seven wall posters highlight interesting topics, such as the Physics of Sports, or useful reference material, such as the Scientific Method.

 Holt Science Skills Workshop: Reading in the Content Area
Use a variety of in-depth skills exercises to help students learn to read science materials strategically.

> **Key**
>
> These materials are blackline masters.
>
> ■ All titles shown in green are found in the *Teaching Resources* booklets for each course.

Science & Math Skills Worksheets

The *Holt Science and Technology* program helps you meet the needs of a wide variety of students, regardless of their skill level. The following pages provide examples of the worksheets available to improve your students' science and math skills, whether they already have a strong science and math background or are weak in these areas. Samples of assessment checklists and rubrics are also provided.

In addition to the skills worksheets represented here, *Holt Science and Technology* provides a variety of worksheets that are correlated directly with each chapter of the program. Representations of these worksheets are found at the beginning of each chapter in this Annotated Teacher's Edition. Specific worksheets related to each chapter are listed in the Chapter Organizer. Worksheets and transparencies are found in the softcover *Teaching Resources* for each course.

Many worksheets are also available on the HRW Web site. The address is **go.hrw.com.**

Science Skills Worksheets: Thinking Skills

BEING FLEXIBLE
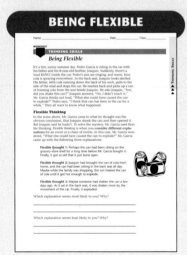

USING YOUR SENSES

THINKING OBJECTIVELY
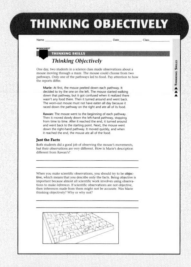

UNDERSTANDING BIAS
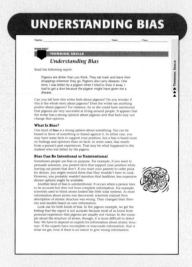

USING LOGIC

BOOSTING YOUR MEMORY
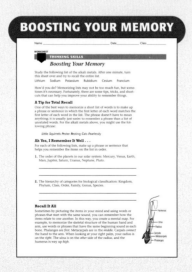

IMPROVING YOUR STUDY HABITS

READING A SCIENCE TEXTBOOK
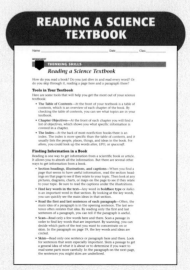

Science Skills Worksheets: Experimenting Skills

SAFETY RULES!

DOING A LAB WRITE-UP
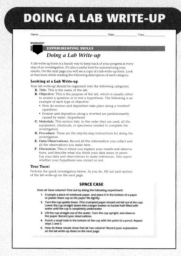

UNDERSTANDING VARIABLES
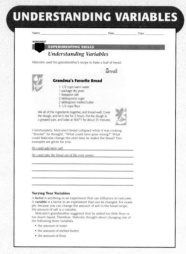

WORKING WITH HYPOTHESES
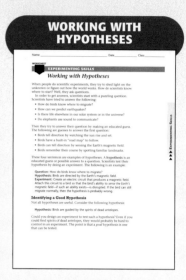

DESIGNING AN EXPERIMENT
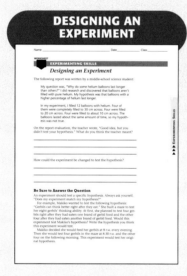

USING THE INTERNATIONAL SYSTEM OF UNITS (SI)
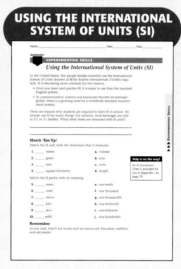

MEASURING
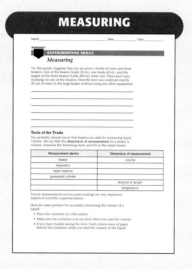

Science Skills Worksheets: Researching Skills

CHOOSING YOUR TOPIC
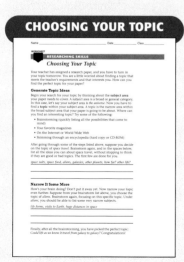

ORGANIZING YOUR RESEARCH

FINDING USEFUL SOURCES
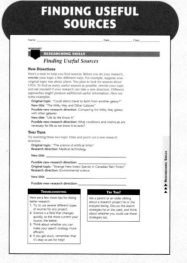

RESEARCHING ON THE WEB

Science Skills Worksheets: Researching Skills (continued)

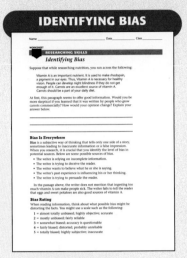

IDENTIFYING BIAS

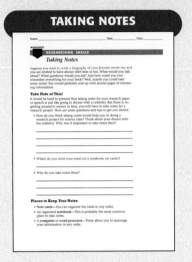

TAKING NOTES

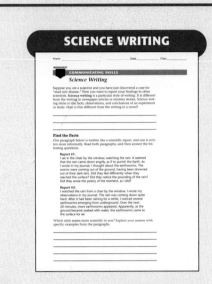

SCIENCE WRITING

Science Skills Worksheets: Communicating Skills

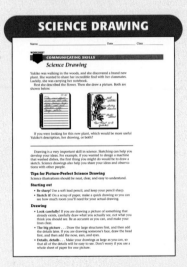

SCIENCE DRAWING

USING MODELS TO COMMUNICATE

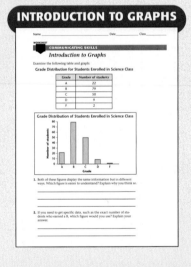

INTRODUCTION TO GRAPHS

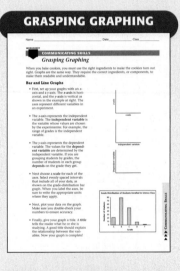

GRASPING GRAPHING

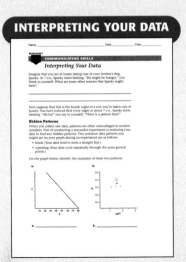

INTERPRETING YOUR DATA

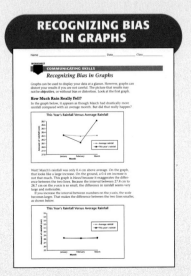

RECOGNIZING BIAS IN GRAPHS

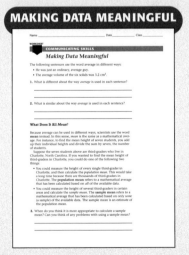

MAKING DATA MEANINGFUL

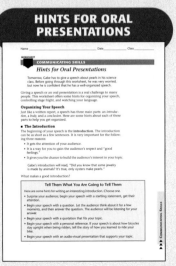

HINTS FOR ORAL PRESENTATIONS

Math Skills for Science

ADDITION AND SUBTRACTION

Addition Review

Addition is used to find the total of two or more quantities. The answer to an addition problem is known as the sum.

PROCEDURE: To find the sum of a set of numbers, align the numbers vertically so that the ones digits are in the same column. Add each column, working from right to left.

SAMPLE PROBLEM: Find the sum of 317, 435, and 92.

Step 1: Add the ones. Don't forget to carry your numbers.	Step 2: Add the tens.	Step 3: Add the hundreds.
317 435 + 92 4	317 435 + 92 44	317 435 + 92 844

The sum is **844**.

Add It Up!
1. Find the sum of the following problems:
   a. 348 + 23   b. 98,125 + 233   c. 593 + 386   d. 36,186 + 27,309

2. Your doctor advises you to take 60 mg of vitamin C, 20 mg of niacin, and 15 mg of zinc every day. How many milligrams of nutrients will you take?

3. A chemistry experiment calls for 356 mL of water, 197 mL of saline solution, and 55 mL of vinegar. How much liquid is needed in all?

Subtraction Review

Subtraction is used to take one number from another number. The answer to a subtraction problem is known as the difference. The difference is how much larger or smaller one number is than the other.

PROCEDURE: To find the difference between two numbers, first align the numbers vertically so that the ones digits are in the same column, with the larger number above the smaller number. Subtract, working from right to left, one column at a time. Remember to borrow when necessary.

SAMPLE PROBLEM: Find the difference between 622 and 348.

Step 1: Subtract the ones, borrowing when necessary.	Step 2: Subtract the tens, borrowing when necessary.	Step 3: Subtract the hundreds.
622 −348 4	622 −348 74	622 −348 274

The difference of the numbers is **274**.

Take It Away!
1. Find the difference in the following problems:
   a. 88 − 36   b. 1695 − 352   c. 47,220 − 36,193   d. 6048 − 3724

2. 571 − 338 =   3. 8317 − 211 =

4. Mars has a diameter of 6790 km. The diameter of Jupiter is 142,984 km. How much larger is the diameter of Jupiter than the diameter of Mars?

5. A horse is born with a mass of 36 kg. It is expected to have a mass of 495 kg when fully grown. How much mass will it gain?

6. Traveling with the wind, a plane reaches a speed of 212 m/s. On the return trip, the same plane flies into the wind and achieves a speed of only 179 m/s. How much faster does the plane fly with the wind?

MULTIPLICATION

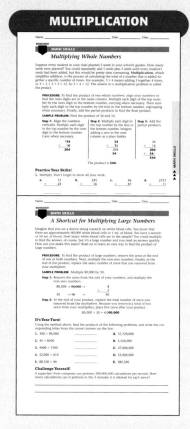

Multiplying Whole Numbers

A Shortcut for Multiplying Large Numbers

Practice Your Skills!
1. Multiply. Don't forget to show all your work.

It's Your Turn!

DIVISION

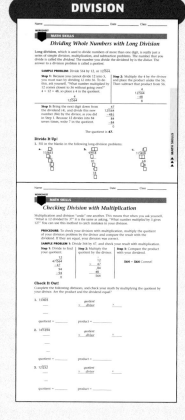

Dividing Whole Numbers with Long Division

Checking Division with Multiplication

Divide It Up!

Check It Out!

AVERAGES

What Is an Average?

Average, Mode, and Median

Practice Your Skills!

Get in the Mode!

POSITIVE AND NEGATIVE NUMBERS

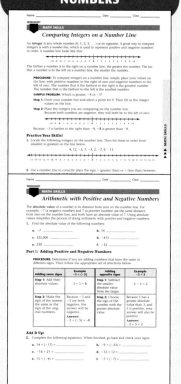

Comparing Integers on a Number Line

An integer is any whole number (0, 1, 2, 3, . . .) or its opposite. A good way to compare integers is with a number line, which is used to represent positive and negative numbers in order. A number line looks like this:

The farther a number is to the right on a number line, the greater the number. The farther a number is to the left on a number line, the smaller the number.

PROCEDURE: To compare integers on a number line, first place your values on the line, with positive numbers to the right of zero and negative numbers to the left of zero. The number that is the farthest to the right is the greatest number. The number that is the farthest to the left is the smallest number.

SAMPLE PROBLEM: Which is greater, −8 or −3?

Step 1: Draw your number line and select a point for 0. Then fill in the integer values on first.

Step 2: Place the integers you are comparing on the number line. Because both numbers are negative, they will both be to the left of zero.

Because −3 is farther to the right than −8, −3 is greater than −8.

Practice Your Skills!
1. Locate the following integers on the number line. Then list them in order from smallest to greatest on the line below.

4, 12, −2, 7, −5, 2, −7, 9, −13

Arithmetic with Positive and Negative Numbers

The absolute value of a number is its distance from zero on the number line. For example, −7 is a negative number and 7 is a positive number, but both have an absolute value of 7. Using absolute values simplifies the process of doing arithmetic with positive and negative numbers.

1. Write the absolute value of the following numbers.
   a. −7   b. 45
   c. 325,000   d. −475
   e. 250   f. −52

Part 1: Adding Positive and Negative Numbers

PROCEDURE: Determine if you are adding numbers that have the same or different signs. Then follow the appropriate set of directions below.

	Example −3 + (−5)	Adding opposite signs	Example −8 + 5
Adding same signs			
Step 1: Add their absolute values.	3 + 5 = 8	Step 1: Subtract the smaller absolute value from the larger.	5 − 3 = 2
Step 2: Make the sign of the answer the same as the sign of the original numbers.	Because −3 and −5 are both negative, the sign will be negative. Answer: −3 + (−5) = −8	Step 2: Choose the sign of the number with the greater absolute value.	Because 8 has a greater absolute value than 3 and 5 is positive, your answer will also be positive. Answer: −3 + 5 = 2

Add It Up!
2. Complete the following equations. When finished, go back and check your signs.
   a. 14 + (−17) =   b. −9 + (−23) =
   c. −16 + 21 =   d. −12 + (−5) =
   e. 15 + (−4) =   f. 7 + (−7) =

FRACTIONS

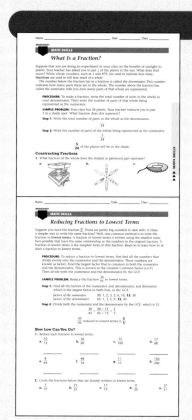

What Is a Fraction?

Suppose that you are doing research on white blood cells. You know that there are approximately 80,000 white blood cells in 1 mL of blood. You have a sample of 50 mL of blood. How many white blood cells are in the sample?

The number below the fraction bar is called the denominator. The number above the fraction bar, called the numerator, tells you how many parts of the whole are represented.

PROCEDURE: To change a fraction, write the total number of units in the whole as your denominator. Then write the number of parts of that whole being represented as the numerator.

Constructing Fractions
1. What fraction of the whole does the shaded or patterned part represent?

1. Write True or False next to each equation.

Reducing Fractions to Lowest Terms

How Low Can You Go?
1. Reduce each fraction to lowest terms.

Improper Fractions and Mixed Numbers

Adding and Subtracting Fractions

Part 1: Adding and Subtracting Fractions with the Same Denominator

Practice What You've Learned!

Part 2: Adding and Subtracting Fractions with Different Denominators

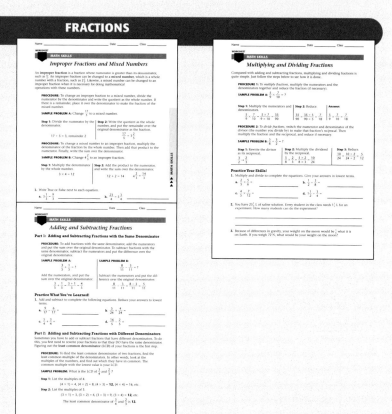

Multiplying and Dividing Fractions

Practice Your Skills!

Math Skills for Science (continued)

RATIOS AND PROPORTIONS

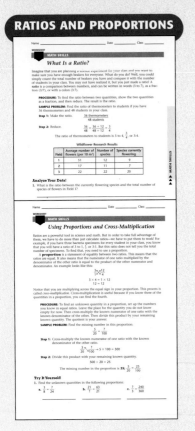

DECIMALS

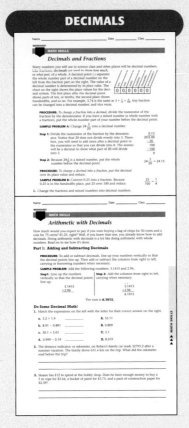

PERCENTAGES

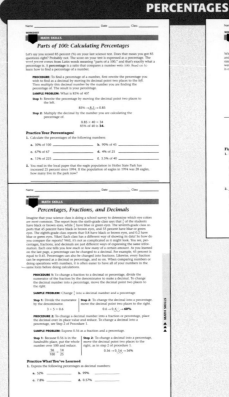

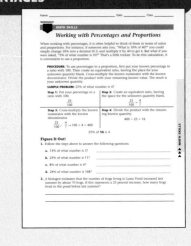

POWERS OF 10

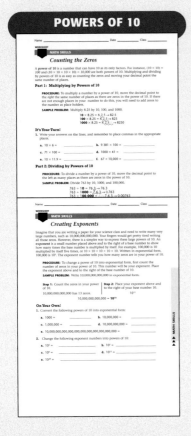

SCIENTIFIC NOTATION

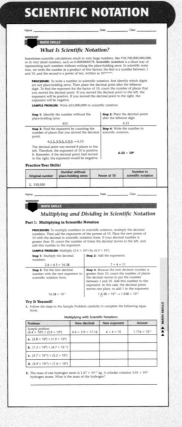

SI MEASUREMENT AND CONVERSION

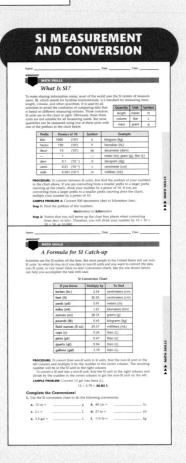

Math Skills for Science (continued)

GEOMETRY

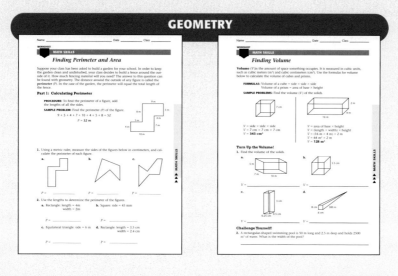

WORKSHEET — MATH SKILLS

Finding Perimeter and Area

Suppose your class has been asked to build a garden for your school. In order to keep the garden clean and undisturbed, your class decides to build a fence around the outside of it. How much fencing material will you need? The answer to this question can be found with geometry. The distance around the outside of any figure is called the **perimeter** (P). In the case of the garden, the perimeter will equal the total length of the fence.

Part 1: Calculating Perimeter

PROCEDURE: To find the perimeter of a figure, add the lengths of all the sides.

SAMPLE PROBLEM: Find the perimeter (P) of the figure.

$9 + 5 + 4 + 7 + 10 + 4 + 5 + 8 = 52$

$P = 52$ m

1. Using a metric ruler, measure the sides of the figures below in centimeters, and calculate the perimeter of each figure.

   a.   b.   c.

   P =   P =   P =

2. Use the lengths to determine the perimeter of the figures.
   a. Rectangle: length = 4 m, width = 2m
   b. Square: side = 45 mm

   P =   P =

   c. Equilateral triangle: side = 6 m
   d. Rectangle: length = 3.5 cm, width = 2.4 cm

   P =   P =

WORKSHEET — MATH SKILLS

Finding Volume

Volume (V) is the amount of space something occupies. It is measured in cubic units, such as cubic meters (m³) and cubic centimeters (cm³). Use the formulas for volume below to calculate the volume of cubes and prisms.

FORMULAS: Volume of a cube = side × side × side
Volume of a prism = area of base × height

SAMPLE PROBLEMS: Find the volume (V) of the solids.

$V = side \times side \times side$
$V = 7 cm \times 7 cm \times 7 cm$
$V = 343 cm^3$

$V = area of base \times height$
$V = (length \times width) \times height$
$V = (16 m \times 4 m) \times 2 m$
$V = 64 m^2 \times 2 m$
$V = 128 m^3$

Turn Up the Volume!

1. Find the volume of the solids.
   a.   b.

   V =   V =

   c.   d.

Challenge Yourself!

2. A rectangular-shaped swimming pool is 50 m long and 2.5 m deep and holds 2500 m³ of water. What is the width of the pool?

THE UNIT FACTOR AND DIMENSIONAL ANALYSIS

WORKSHEET — MATH SKILLS

The Unit Factor and Dimensional Analysis

The measurements you take in science class, whether for time, mass, weight, or distance, are more than just numbers—they are also units. To make comparisons between measurements, it is convenient to have your measurements in the same units. A mathematical tool called a **unit factor** is used to convert back and forth between different kinds of units. A unit factor is a ratio that is equal to 1. Because it is equal to 1, multiplying a measurement by a unit factor changes the measurement's units but does not change its value. The skill of converting with a unit factor is known as **dimensional analysis**. Read on to see how it works.

Part 1: Converting with a Unit Factor

PROCEDURE: To convert units with a unit factor, determine the conversion factor between the units you have and the units you want to convert to. Then create the unit factor by making a ratio, in the form of a fraction, between the units you want to convert to in the numerator and the units you already have in the denominator. Finally, multiply your measurement by this unit factor to convert to the new units.

SAMPLE PROBLEM A: Convert 1.5 km to millimeters.

Step 1: Determine the conversion factor between kilometers and millimeters.
1 km = 1,000,000 mm

Step 2: Create the unit factor. Put the units you want to convert to in the numerator and the units you already have in the denominator.
$\frac{1,000,000 \ mm}{1 \ km} = 1$

Step 3: Multiply the unit factor by the measurement. Notice that the original unit of the measurement cancels out with the unit in the denominator of the unit factor, leaving the units you are converting to.
$1.5 \ km \times \frac{1,000,000 \ mm}{1 \ km} = 3,500,000 \ mm$

On Your Own!

1. Convert the following measurements using a unit factor.

Conversion	Unit factor	Answer
a. 2.34 cm = ? mm		
b. 54.6 mL = ? L		
c. 12 kg = ? g		

MATH IN SCIENCE: INTEGRATED SCIENCE

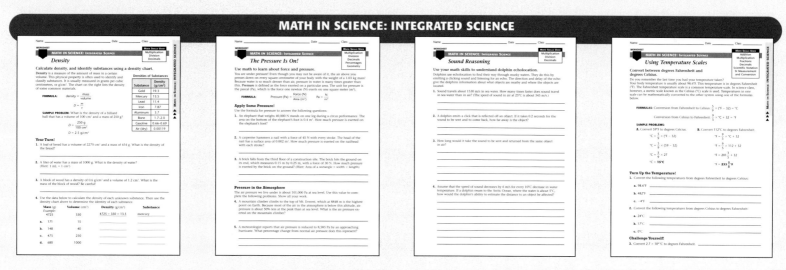

WORKSHEET — MATH IN SCIENCE: INTEGRATED SCIENCE

Density

Math Skills Used: Multiplication, Division, Decimals

Calculate density, and identify substances using a density chart.

Density is a measure of the amount of mass in a certain volume. This physical property is often used to identify and classify substances. It is usually measured in grams per cubic centimeters, or g/cm³. The chart on the right lists the density of some common materials.

FORMULA: $density = \frac{mass}{volume}$

$D = \frac{m}{v}$

SAMPLE PROBLEM: What is the density of a billiard ball that has a volume of 100 cm³ and a mass of 250 g?

$D = \frac{250 \ g}{100 \ cm^3}$

$D = 2.5 \ g/cm^3$

Densities of Substances

Substance	Density (g/cm³)
Gold	19.3
Mercury	13.5
Lead	11.4
Iron	7.87
Aluminum	3.7
Bone	1.7–2.0
Gasoline	0.66–0.69
Air (dry)	0.00119

Your Turn!

1. A loaf of bread has a volume of 2270 cm³ and a mass of 454 g. What is the density of the bread?

2. A liter of water has a mass of 1000 g. What is the density of water? (Hint: 1 mL = 1 cm³)

3. A block of wood has a density of 0.6 g/cm³ and a volume of 1.2 cm³. What is the mass of the block of wood? Be careful!

4. Use the data below to calculate the density of each unknown substance. Then use the density chart above to determine the identity of each substance.

Mass (g)	Volume (cm³)	Density (g/cm³)	Substance
Example: 4725	350	4725 ÷ 350 = 13.5	mercury
a. 171	15		
b. 148	40		
c. 475	250		
d. 680	1000		

WORKSHEET — MATH IN SCIENCE: INTEGRATED SCIENCE

The Pressure Is On!

Math Skills Used: Multiplication, Division, Decimals, Percentages, Geometry

Use math to learn about force and pressure.

You are under pressure! Even though you may not be aware of it, the air above you presses down on every square centimeter of your body with the weight of a 1.03 kg mass! Because water is much denser than air, pressure in water is many times greater than this. **Pressure** is defined as the force exerted on a particular area. The unit for pressure is the pascal (Pa), which is the force one newton (N) exerts on one square meter (m²).

Apply Some Pressure!

Use the formula for pressure to answer the following questions.

$Pressure (Pa) = \frac{Force (N)}{Area (m^2)}$ $Pa = \frac{N}{m^2}$

1. An elephant that weighs 40,000 N stands on one leg during a circus performance. The area on the bottom of the elephant's foot is 0.4 m². How much pressure is exerted on the elephant's foot?

2. A carpenter hammers a nail with a force of 45 N with every stroke. The head of the nail has a surface area of 0.002 m². How much pressure is exerted on the nailhead with each stroke?

3. A brick falls from the third floor of a construction site. The brick hits the ground on its end, which measures 0.15 m by 0.25 m, with a force of 30 N. How much pressure is exerted by the brick on the ground? (Hint: Area of a rectangle = width × length)

Pressure in the Atmosphere

The air pressure we live under is about 101,000 Pa at sea level. Use this value to complete the following problems. Show all work.

4. A mountain climber climbs to the top of Mt. Everest, which at 8848 m is the highest point on Earth. Because most of the air in the atmosphere is below this altitude, air pressure is about 30% less at the peak than at sea level. What is the air pressure exerted on the mountain climber?

5. A meteorologist reports that air pressure is reduced to 8,585 Pa by an approaching hurricane. What percentage change from normal air pressure does this represent?

WORKSHEET — MATH IN SCIENCE: INTEGRATED SCIENCE

Sound Reasoning

Math Skills Used: Multiplication, Division, Decimals

Use your math skills to understand dolphin echolocation.

Dolphins use echolocation to find their way through murky waters. They do this by emitting a clicking sound and listening for an echo. The direction and delay of the echo give the dolphins information about what objects are nearby and where the objects are located.

1. Sound travels about 1530 m/s in sea water. How many times faster does sound travel in sea water than in air? (The speed of sound in air at 25°C is about 345 m/s.)

2. A dolphin emits a click that is reflected off an object. If it takes 0.2 seconds for the sound to be sent and to come back, how far away is the object?

3. How long would it take the sound to be sent and returned from the same object in air?

4. Assume that the speed of sound decreases by 6 m/s for every 10°C decrease in water temperature. If a dolphin swam to the Arctic Ocean, where the water is about 5°C, how would the dolphin's ability to estimate the distance to an object be affected?

WORKSHEET — MATH IN SCIENCE: INTEGRATED SCIENCE

Using Temperature Scales

Math Skills Used: Addition, Multiplication, Fractions, Decimals, Scientific Notation, SI Measurement and Conversion

Convert between degrees Fahrenheit and degrees Celsius.

Do you remember the last time you had your temperature taken? Your body temperature is usually about 98.6°F. This temperature is in degrees Fahrenheit (°F). The Fahrenheit temperature scale is a common temperature scale. In science class, however, a metric scale known as the Celsius (°C) scale is used. Temperatures in one system can be mathematically converted to the other system using one of the formulas below.

FORMULAS: Conversion from Fahrenheit to Celsius: $\frac{5}{9} \times (°F - 12) = °C$

Conversion from Celsius to Fahrenheit: $\frac{9}{5} \times °C + 32 = °F$

SAMPLE PROBLEMS:
A. Convert 59°F to degrees Celsius.
$°C = \frac{5}{9} \times (°F - 12)$
$°C = \frac{5}{9} \times (59 - 12)$
$°C = \frac{5}{9} \times 27$
$°C = 15°C$

B. Convert 112°C to degrees Fahrenheit.
$°F = \frac{9}{5} \times °C + 32$
$°F = \frac{9}{5} \times 112 + 32$
$°F = 201\frac{3}{5} + 32$
$°F = 233\frac{3}{5}°F$

Turn Up the Temperature!

1. Convert the following temperatures from degrees Fahrenheit to degrees Celsius:
   a. 98.6°F
   b. 68.2°F
   c. -4°F

2. Convert the following temperatures from degrees Celsius to degrees Fahrenheit:
   a. 24°C
   b. 17°C
   c. 0°C

Challenge Yourself!

3. Convert 2.7 × 10⁴ °C to degrees Fahrenheit.

WORKSHEET — MATH IN SCIENCE: INTEGRATED SCIENCE

Radioactive Decay and the Half-life

Math Skills Used: Multiplication, Division, Fractions, Decimals, Percentages, Scientific Notation

Use the half-lives of elements to learn about radioactive dating.

Most elements found in nature are stable; they do not change over time. Some elements, however, are unstable—that is, they slowly change into a different element over time. Elements that go through this process of change are called **radioactive**, and the process of transformation is called **radioactive decay**. Because radioactive decay happens very steadily, scientists can use radioactive elements like clocks to measure the passage of time. By looking at how much of a certain element remains in an object and how much of it has decayed, scientists can determine an approximate age for the object.

So why use scientists interested in learning the ages of objects? By looking at very old things, such as rocks and fossils, and determining when they were formed, scientists learn about the history of the Earth and the plants and animals that have lived here. Radioactive dating makes this history lesson possible! A **half-life** is the time that it takes for half a certain amount of a radioactive material to decay, and it can range from less than a second to billions of years. The chart below lists the half-lives of some radioactive elements.

Table of Half-lives

Element	Half-life	Element	Half-life
Bismuth-212	60.5 minutes	Phosphorus-24	14.3 days
Carbon-14	5730 years	Polonium-215	0.0018 seconds
Chlorine-36	400,000 years	Radium-226	1600 years
Cobalt-60	5.26 years	Sodium-24	15 hours
Iodine-131	8.07 days	Uranium-238	4.5 billion years

1. Use the data in the table above to complete the following chart.

Table of Remaining Radium

Number of years after formation	0	1600	3200	6400	12,800
Percent of radium-226 remaining	100%	50%			

2. If 1 g of sodium-24 has decayed from a sample that was originally 2 g, how old is the sample?

3. What fraction of chlorine-36 remains undecayed after 200,000 years?

WORKSHEET — MATH IN SCIENCE: INTEGRATED SCIENCE

Rain-Forest Math

Math Skills Used: Multiplication, Decimals, Percentages, Scientific Notation, The Unit Factor and Dimensional Analysis

Calculate the damage to the world's rain forests.

Tropical rain forests now cover about 7 percent of the Earth's land surface; however, about half the original forests have been cut during the last 50 years. An additional 2 percent of the total remaining tropical rain forest is being cut each year.

The Damage Done

1. Approximately what percentage of the earth's surface was covered by rain forest 50 years ago?

2. The land surface of the Earth is approximately 1.49 × 10⁸ km². How many square kilometers of that is rain forest today? Give your answer in scientific notation.

3. Suppose a certain rain forest consists of 500,000 km². The amount of rainfall per square meter per day is 20 L. If 2 percent of this rain forest is cut this year, how much water will be lost to next year's water cycle? Show all your work.

MATH IN SCIENCE: PHYSICAL SCIENCE

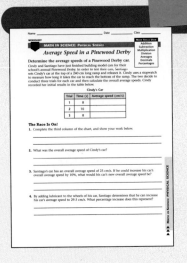

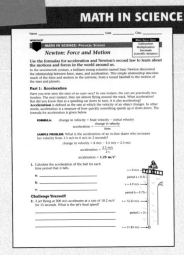

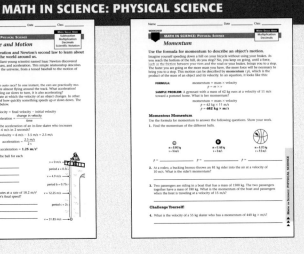

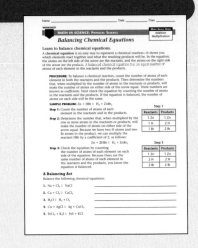

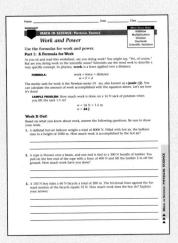

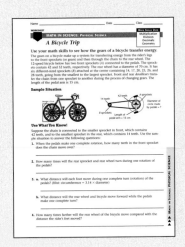

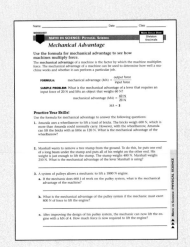

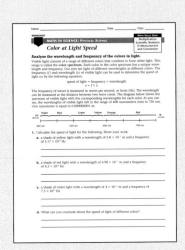

Assessment Checklist & Rubrics

The following is just a sample of over 50 checklists and rubrics contained in this booklet.

RUBRICS FOR WRITTEN WORK

RUBRIC FOR EXPERIMENTS

TEACHER EVALUATION OF COOPERATIVE LEARNING

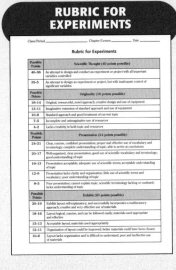

TEACHER EVALUATION OF STUDENT PROGRESS

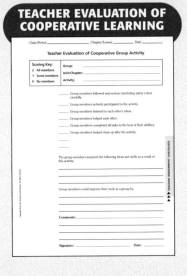

PHYSICAL SCIENCE NATIONAL SCIENCE EDUCATION STANDARDS CORRELATIONS

The following lists show the chapter correlation of **Holt Science and Technology: Forces, Motion, and Energy** with the *National Science Education Standards* (grades 5-8)

UNIFYING CONCEPTS AND PROCESSES

Standard	Chapter Correlation	
Systems, order, and organization Code: UCP 1	Chapter 1 Chapter 5 Chapter 6	1.1, 1.2, 1.4 5.3 6.1
Evidence, models, and explanation Code: UCP 2	Chapter 6	6.1, 6.2, 6.3
Change, constancy, and measurement Code: UCP 3	Chapter 1 Chapter 2 Chapter 4 Chapter 5 Chapter 6	1.1, 1.3, 1.4 2.1, 2.2 4.1, 4.2, 4.3 5.1, 5.3 6.1, 6.2, 6.3
Evolution and equilibrium Code: UCP 4	Chapter 1 Chapter 2 Chapter 3	1.2 2.2 3.2
Form and function Code: UCP 5	Chapter 3 Chapter 4	3.3 4.3

SCIENCE IN PERSONAL AND SOCIAL PERSPECTIVES

Standard	Chapter Correlation	
Populations, resources, and environments Code: SPSP 2	Chapter 6	6.2, 6.4
Risks and benefits Code: SPSP 4	Chapter 5	5.4
Science and technology in society Code: SPSP 5	Chapter 1 Chapter 4 Chapter 5 Chapter 6	1.2, 1.4 4.2, 4.3 5.2 6.1, 6.2, 6.3, 6.4

SCIENCE AS INQUIRY

Standard	Chapter Correlation	
Abilities necessary to do scientific inquiry Code: SAI 1	Chapter 1 Chapter 2 Chapter 3 Chapter 4 Chapter 5 Chapter 6	1.1, 1.3, 1.4 2.1, 2.2 3.1, 3.2, 3.3 4.1, 4.3 5.2 6.2
Understandings about scientific inquiry Code: SAI 2	Chapter 1 Chapter 2 Chapter 3 Chapter 6	1.1, 1.3 2.2 3.1 6.1

SCIENCE AND TECHNOLOGY

Standard	Chapter Correlation	
Abilities of technological design Code: ST 1	Chapter 2 Chapter 4 Chapter 5 Chapter 6	2.1 4.3 5.3 6.2
Understandings about science and technology Code: ST 2	Chapter 1 Chapter 3 Chapter 4 Chapter 5	1.4 3.1, 3.2, 3.3 4.2, 4.3 5.2, 5.3, 5.4

HISTORY AND NATURE OF SCIENCE

Standard	Chapter Correlation	
Science as a human endeavor Code: HNS 1	Chapter 1 Chapter 2 Chapter 4 Chapter 5	1.4 2.1 4.2 5.4
History of science Code: HNS 3	Chapter 1	1.4

PHYSICAL SCIENCE National Science Education Content Standards

PROPERTIES AND CHANGES OF PROPERTIES IN MATTER

Standard	Chapter Correlation
A substance has characteristic properties, such as density, a boiling point, and solubility, all of which are independent of the amount of the sample. A mixture of substances often can be separated into the original substances using one or more of the characteristic properties. Code: PS 1a	**Chapter 6** 6.3
Substances react chemically in characteristic ways with other substances to form new substances (compounds) with different characteristic properties. In chemical reactions, the total mass is conserved. Substances often are placed in categories or groups if they react in similar ways; metals is an example of such a group. Code: PS 1b	**Chapter 6** 6.3

MOTIONS AND FORCES

Standard	Chapter Correlation
The motion of an object can be described by its position, direction of motion, and speed. That motion can be measured and represented on a graph. Code: PS 2a	**Chapter 1** 1.1
An object that is not being subjected to a force will continue to move at a constant speed and in a straight line. Code: PS 2b	**Chapter 1** 1.2 **Chapter 2** 2.2
If more than one force acts on an object along a straight line, then the forces will reinforce or cancel one another, depending on their direction and magnitude. Unbalanced forces will cause changes in the speed or direction of an object's motion. Code: PS 2c	**Chapter 2** 2.2

TRANSFER OF ENERGY

Standard	Chapter Correlation	
Energy is a property of many substances and is associated with heat, light, electricity, mechanical motion, sound, nuclei, and the nature of a chemical. Energy is transferred in many ways. Code: PS 3a	**Chapter 5** **Chapter 6**	5.1, 5.2 6.1, 6.2, 6.4
Heat moves in predictable ways, flowing from warmer objects to cooler ones, until both reach the same temperature. Code: PS 3b	**Chapter 6**	6.1, 6.2, 6.4
Electrical circuits provide a means of transferring electrical energy when heat, light, sound, and chemical changes are produced. Code: PS 3d	**Chapter 5**	5.1
In most chemical and nuclear reactions, energy is transferred into or out of a system. Heat, light, mechanical motion, or electricity might all be involved in such transfers. Code: PS 3e	**Chapter 5**	5.1, 5.4
The sun is a major source of energy for changes on the earth's surface. The sun loses energy by emitting light. A tiny fraction of that light reaches the earth, transferring energy from the sun to the earth. The sun's energy arrives as light with a range of wavelengths, consisting of visible light, infrared, and ultraviolet radiation. Code: PS 3f	**Chapter 5** **Chapter 6**	5.1, 5.2, 5.4 6.2

Master Materials List

For added convenience, Science Kit® provides materials-ordering software on CD-ROM designed specifically for *Holt Science and Technology*. Using this software, you can order complete kits or individual items, quickly and efficiently.

CONSUMABLE MATERIALS	AMOUNT	PAGE
Bag, sealable plastic	1	200
Balloon, long, 12 in.	1	189
Cardboard, 10 x 15 cm	3	190
Cardboard, approx. 60 x 30 cm	1	16, 195
Carton, empty milk, 1/2 pint	1	199, 200
Carton, empty milk, 1 qt	1	193
Clay, modeling	1 stick	26, 71, 195
Craft stick	1	195
Cup, paper	1	35, 189
Cup, plastic-foam, large	1	201
Cup, plastic-foam	2	174
Cup, plastic-foam with lid, small	1	201
Egg, hard-boiled	1	52
Egg, raw	1	52, 199
Glue, white	1 bottle	190, 195
Ice cube	1	200
Marker, permanent, black	1	198
Marshmallow, miniature	2	188
Paper, graphing	1 sheet	157, 187, 194

CONSUMABLE MATERIALS	AMOUNT	PAGE
Rubber band	1–2	122, 174, 190, 195
Sandpaper, medium, 9 x 11 in. or cloth	1 sheet	16
Shoe box	1	195
Spoon, plastic	1	188
Straw, jumbo	1–6	189, 190, 195
String, 15 cm	2	115, 189
String, approx. 10 cm	1	190
String, approx. 30–50 cm	1	174, 196
String, approx. 1–2 m	1	91, 187, 194, 195, 198
Tape, duct, 20–30 cm	1	188
Tape, masking, 20–30 cm	1	140, 186, 193, 195
Tape, transparent, 20–30 cm	1	189
Thread	1 spool	52
Twist tie	1	189
Wax paper	1 sheet	122

NONCONSUMABLE EQUIPMENT	AMOUNT	PAGE
Balance, metric	1	78, 140, 174, 187, 200
Ball, styrene, 2–3 cm diam.	1	26
Beaker, 250 mL	1	157
Block, wood, 3.5 x 3.5 x 1 cm	1	188
Block, wood, approx. 10 x 5 x 5 cm	10	194
Board, wood, 1 m x 30 cm	1	140, 194
Bottle, 2 L soda	1	66, 192
Bottle, plastic, 1 L, with lid	1	26
Bottle caps	30	195
Bucket, rectangular (or fish tank)	1	78
Can, coffee	1	122
Car, toy	1	16, 186
Card, index, 3 x 5 in.	1	52
Cardboard, 10 x 10 cm	1	149
Clamp, C	2	196
Cork	1	26
Cup, clear plastic	1–2	45, 52, 200
Domino	25	3
Dowel, wood, 0.5 in. diam.	1 ea. (10 cm, 15 cm, 20 cm, 25 cm)	196
Dowel, wood, 1 in. diam.	30 cm	196
Dropper, medicine	1	192
Eraser, pink rubber	1	87
Film canister	1	157
Fishing line, 3 m	1	189
Graduated cylinder, 100 mL	1	174, 201
Hot plate	1	200, 201
Marble	1	190
Mass, 1 kg	1	52, 196
Mass, hooked, 100 g	1	115, 198
Mass set	1	78

NONCONSUMABLE EQUIPMENT	AMOUNT	PAGE
Metal, small piece	1	149
Meterstick	1	3, 16, 52, 140 186, 188, 189 190, 194, 196, 198
Nail, approx. 2 in.	12	174
Pan, rectangular baking	1	78
Pan or bucket, approx. 45 x 60 cm	1	35, 71, 193
Pan or bucket, plastic	3	151
Penny	1–3	42, 201
Penny	100	189
Pipe, PVC, 1.5 in.	1	196
Plastic, small piece	1	149
Plastic foam, small piece	1	149
Protractor	1	188
Pushpin	1–3	26, 190
Quarter	1	52
Rock, small	1	149
Rolling cart	1	140
Ruler, metric	1	42, 78, 91 87, 91, 106
Scissors	1	26, 52, 187, 190, 195
Screw, small	1	196
Spools, empty thread	30	195
Spring scale	1	91, 187, 194, 196
Stones	30	195
Stopwatch	1	3, 91, 106, 140 186, 201
Thermometer	1	174, 201
Thermometer	2	157
Thermometer, LCD strip	1	149
Tongs, crucible	1	201
Wheel	1	196
Wood, small piece	1	149

Answers to Concept Mapping Questions

The following pages contain sample answers to all of the concept mapping questions that appear in the Chapter Reviews. Because there is more than one way to do a concept map, your students' answers may vary.

CHAPTER 1 Matter in Motion

14.

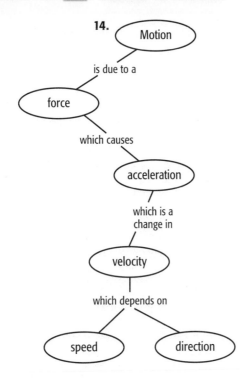

CHAPTER 2 Forces in Motion

15.

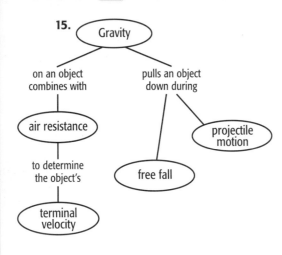

CHAPTER 3 Forces in Fluids

16.

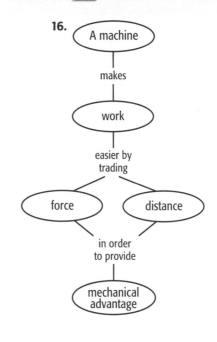

CHAPTER 4 Work and Machines

16.

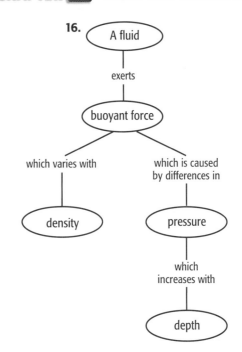

CHAPTER 5 Energy and Energy Resources

18.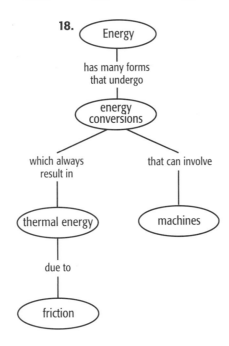

CHAPTER 6 Heat and Heat Technology

17.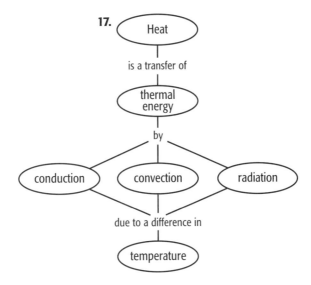

To the Student

This book was created to make your science experience interesting, exciting, and fun!

Go for It!

Science is a process of discovery, a trek into the unknown. The skills you develop using *Holt Science & Technology*— such as observing, experimenting, and explaining observations and ideas— are the skills you will need for the future. There is a universe of exploration and discovery awaiting those who accept the challenges of science.

Science & Technology

You see the interaction between science and technology every day. Science makes technology possible. On the other hand, some of the products of technology, such as computers, are used to make further scientific discoveries. In fact, much of the scientific work that is done today has become so technically complicated and expensive that no one person can do it entirely alone. But make no mistake, the creative ideas for even the most highly technical and expensive scientific work still come from individuals.

Activities and Labs

The activities and labs in this book will allow you to make some basic but important scientific discoveries on your own. You can even do some exploring on your own at home! Here's your chance to use your imagination and curiosity as you investigate your world.

Keep a ScienceLog

In this book, you will be asked to keep a type of journal called a ScienceLog to record your thoughts, observations, experiments, and conclusions. As you develop your ScienceLog, you will see your own ideas taking shape over time. You'll have a written record of how your ideas have changed as you learn about and explore interesting topics in science.

Know "What You'll Do"

The "What You'll Do" list at the beginning of each section is your built-in guide to what you need to learn in each chapter. When you can answer the questions in the Section Review and Chapter Review, you know you are ready for a test.

Check Out the Internet

You will see this  logo throughout the book. You'll be using *sci*LINKS as your gateway to the Internet. Once you log on to *sci*LINKS using your computer's Internet link, type in the *sci*LINKS address. When asked for the keyword code, type in the keyword for that topic. A wealth of resources is now at your disposal to help you learn more about that topic.

In addition to *sci*LINKS you can log on to some other great resources to go with your text. The addresses shown below will take you to the home page of each site.

internet**connect**

This textbook contains the following on-line resources to help you make the most of your science experience.

Visit **go.hrw.com** for extra help and study aids matched to your textbook. Just type in the keyword HB2 HOME.

Visit **www.scilinks.org** to find resources specific to topics in your textbook. Keywords appear throughout your book to take you further.

 Smithsonian Institution®
Internet Connections

Visit **www.si.edu/hrw** for specifically chosen on-line materials from one of our nation's premier science museums.

Visit **www.cnnfyi.com** for late-breaking news and current events stories selected just for you.

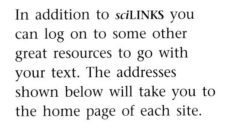

To the Student   1

Chapter Organizer

CHAPTER ORGANIZATION	TIME MINUTES	OBJECTIVES	LABS, INVESTIGATIONS, AND DEMONSTRATIONS
Chapter Opener pp. 2–3	45	National Standards: UCP 3, SAI 1, PS 2a	**Start-Up Activity,** The Domino Derby, p. 3
Section 1 **Measuring Motion**	120	▶ Identify the relationship between motion and a reference point. ▶ Identify the two factors that speed depends on. ▶ Determine the difference between speed and velocity. ▶ Analyze the relationship of velocity to acceleration. ▶ Interpret a graph showing acceleration. UCP 1, UCP 3, PS 2a; Labs UCP 3, SAI 1–2, PS 2a	**Demonstration,** Models, p. 4 in ATE **Interactive Explorations CD-ROM,** Force in the Forest A **Worksheet** is also available in the **Interactive Explorations Teacher's Edition.** **Design Your Own,** Built for Speed, p. 186 **Datasheets for LabBook,** Built for Speed **Skill Builder,** Detecting Acceleration, p. 26 **Datasheets for LabBook,** Detecting Acceleration **Calculator-Based Labs,** The Fast Track
Section 2 **What Is a Force?**	120	▶ Give examples of different kinds of forces. ▶ Determine the net force on an object. ▶ Compare balanced and unbalanced forces. UCP 1, UCP 4, SPSP 5, PS 2b, PS 2c	**Demonstration,** p. 13 in ATE
Section 3 **Friction: A Force That Opposes Motion**	120	▶ Explain why friction occurs. ▶ List the types of friction, and give examples of each. ▶ Explain how friction can be both harmful and helpful. UCP 3, SAI 1, PS 2c; Labs SAI 1–2	**Demonstration,** p. 15 in ATE **QuickLab,** The Friction 500, p. 16 **Interactive Explorations CD-ROM,** Stranger Than Friction
Section 4 **Gravity: A Force of Attraction**	120	▶ Define *gravity.* ▶ State the law of universal gravitation. ▶ Describe the difference between mass and weight. UCP 1, UCP 3, ST 2, SPSP 5, HNS 1, HNS 3, PS 2c; Labs UCP 3, SAI 1	**Demonstration,** p. 21 in ATE **Skill Builder,** Relating Mass and Weight, p. 187 **Datasheets for LabBook,** Relating Mass and Weight **Long-Term Projects & Research Ideas,** Tiny Troubles

*See page **T23** for a complete correlation of this book with the*

NATIONAL SCIENCE EDUCATION STANDARDS.

TECHNOLOGY RESOURCES

 Guided Reading Audio CD
English or Spanish, Chapter 1

 Interactive Explorations CD-ROM
CD 2, Exploration 4, Force in the Forest
CD 3, Exploration 3, Stranger Than Friction

 One-Stop Planner CD-ROM with Test Generator

  CNN. Science, Technology & Society,
The Science of Bowling, Segment 7

Scientists in Action, Segments 16 and 25

 Science Discovery Videodiscs
Image and Activity Bank with Lesson Plans:
Friction Finder, Name That Structure

Science Sleuths: The Collapsing Bleachers

CLASSROOM WORKSHEETS, TRANSPARENCIES, AND RESOURCES	SCIENCE INTEGRATION AND CONNECTIONS	REVIEW AND ASSESSMENT
Directed Reading Worksheet **Science Puzzlers, Twisters & Teasers**		
Directed Reading Worksheet, Section 1 **Math Skills for Science Worksheet,** Average Speed in a Pinewood Derby **Transparency 213,** A Graph Showing Speed **Math Skills for Science Worksheet,** The Unit Factor and Dimensional Analysis **Science Skills Worksheet,** Organizing Your Research **Transparency 214,** Determining Resultant Velocity **Transparency 215,** Calculating Acceleration **Transparency 216,** A Graph Showing Acceleration **Reinforcement Worksheet,** Bug Race	**MathBreak,** Calculating Average Speed, p. 5 **Math and More,** p. 5 in ATE **MathBreak,** Calculating Acceleration, p. 9 **Math and More,** p. 9 in ATE **Holt Anthology of Science Fiction,** *Direction of the Road*	**Homework,** pp. 5, 8 in ATE **Self-Check,** p. 6 **Section Review,** p. 7 **Section Review,** p. 10 **Quiz,** p. 10 in ATE **Alternative Assessment,** p. 10 in ATE
Directed Reading Worksheet, Section 2 **Transparency 217,** Forces in the Same Direction **Transparency 217,** Forces in Different Directions	**Science Connection,** p. 13 **Science, Technology, and Society:** Is It Real . . . or Is It Virtual? p. 32 **Across the Sciences:** The Golden Gate Bridge, p. 33	**Self-Check,** p. 13 **Section Review,** p. 14 **Quiz,** p. 14 in ATE **Alternative Assessment,** p. 14 in ATE
Directed Reading Worksheet, Section 3 **Transparency 218,** Force and Friction **Transparency 219,** Static Friction **Reinforcement Worksheet,** Friction Action	**Connect to Life Science,** p. 15 in ATE **Real-World Connection,** p. 17 in ATE **Cross-Disciplinary Focus,** p. 17 in ATE **Apply,** p. 20	**Self-Check,** p. 18 **Homework,** pp. 18, 19 in ATE **Section Review,** p. 20 **Quiz,** p. 20 in ATE **Alternative Assessment,** p. 20 in ATE
Directed Reading Worksheet, Section 4 **Transparency 161,** Tidal Variations **Transparency 220,** The Law of Universal Gravitation **Reinforcement Worksheet,** A Weighty Problem **Critical Thinking Worksheet,** A Mission in Motion **Transparency 221,** Weight and Mass Are Different	**Biology Connection,** p. 21 **Connect to Earth Science,** p. 22 in ATE **Astronomy Connection,** p. 23 **Connect to Earth Science,** p. 23 in ATE **Real-World Connection,** p. 23 in ATE	**Self-Check,** p. 22 **Homework,** p. 23 in ATE **Section Review,** p. 25 **Quiz,** p. 25 in ATE **Alternative Assessment,** p. 25 in ATE

  internet connect

go. hrw .com **Holt, Rinehart and Winston On-line Resources**

go.hrw.com

For worksheets and other teaching aids related to this chapter, visit the HRW Web site and type in the keyword: **HSTMOT**

 National Science Teachers Association

www.scilinks.org

Encourage students to use the *sci*LINKS numbers listed in the internet connect boxes to access information and resources on the **NSTA** Web site.

END-OF-CHAPTER REVIEW AND ASSESSMENT

Chapter Review in Study Guide

Vocabulary and Notes in Study Guide

Chapter Tests with Performance-Based Assessment, Chapter 1 Test

Chapter Tests with Performance-Based Assessment, Performance-Based Assessment 1

Concept Mapping Transparency 5

Chapter Resources & Worksheets

Visual Resources

TEACHING TRANSPARENCIES

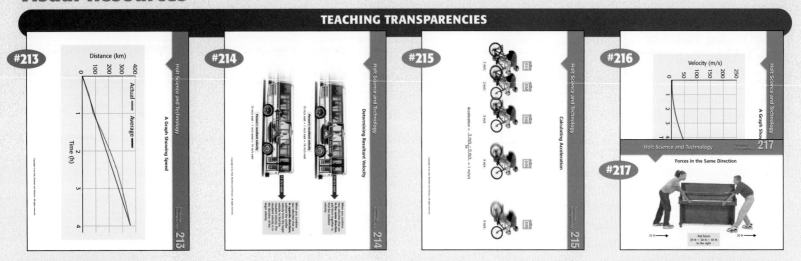

#213 — A Graph Showing Speed

#214 — Determining Resultant Velocity

#215 — Calculating Acceleration

#216 — A Graph Showing Velocity

#217 — Forces in the Same Direction

TEACHING TRANSPARENCIES

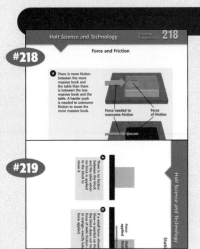

#218 — Force and Friction

#219

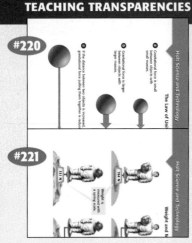

#220 — The Law of Universal Gravitation

#221 — Weight and Mass

#161 — Tidal Variations

LINK TO EARTH SCIENCE

CONCEPT MAPPING TRANSPARENCY

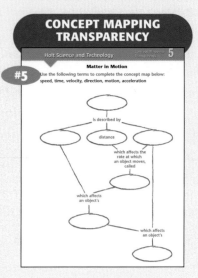

#5 — Matter in Motion

Use the following terms to complete the concept map below: speed, time, velocity, direction, motion, acceleration

Meeting Individual Needs

DIRECTED READING

#1 — DIRECTED READING WORKSHEET

Matter in Motion

Chapter Introduction

As you begin this chapter, answer the following.

1. Read the title of the chapter. List three things that you already know about this subject.

2. Write two questions about this subject that you would like answered by the time you finish this chapter.

3. How does the title of the Start-Up Activity relate to the subject of the chapter?

Section 1: Measuring Motion (p. 4)

4. Name something in motion that you can't see moving.

Observing Motion (p. 4)

5. To determine if an object is in motion, compare its position over time to a _____ point.

REINFORCEMENT & VOCABULARY REVIEW

#1 — REINFORCEMENT WORKSHEET

Bug Race

Complete this worksheet after you finish reading Chapter 5, Section 1.

You and a friend are having a bug race. You measure the distance your pet bugs travel along a straight race track and record their time as they race. The results are plotted in the graphs below. Take a look at the two graphs. Then answer the questions that follow.

Your Bug

Your Friend's Bug

To determine your bug's velocity at a given moment, you must divide the distance it has traveled by the amount of time it takes to travel that distance. For example, at Point A your bug has traveled 20 centimeters in 3.5 seconds. 20 divided by 3.5 is about 5.7, so your bug is traveling at a velocity of 5.7 cm/s.

1. What is the velocity of your bug at Point B?

2. Is your bug's graph a graph of acceleration? Explain.

3. What is the velocity of your friend's bug at Point C?

4. What is the velocity of your friend's bug at Point D?

5. Why is your friend's bug's graph a graph of acceleration?

6. Is the acceleration in your friend's graph positive or negative? Explain.

#1 — VOCABULARY REVIEW WORKSHEET

Penny's Puns

After you finish Chapter 5, give this puzzle a try!

Oh no! Penny Punster's computer mixed up her physical science dictionary with her dictionary of puns. The computer paired the terms related to forces with her goofy definitions, and it paired her pun-related terms with the real definitions. Help Penny unscramble the mismatched pairs and get her dictionaries back in order. The first one has been done for you!

___ 1. farce: a push or pull
___ 2. grubby tea: force of attraction between objects with mass
___ 3. freak shore: force opposing motion between touching surfaces
___ 4. fellow's city: speed in a particular direction
___ 5. sty tic: friction that disappears when an object starts moving
___ 6. exhilaration: rate at which velocity changes
___ 7. mow shun: changing position over time
___ 8. speed: rate at which an object moves
___ 9. bell lanced: forces producing a net force of zero
___ 10. net for us: result of combined forces on an object
___ 11. wade: measure of the force of gravity on an object
___ 12. mace: amount of matter in an object
___ 13. roe link: friction between wheels and the floor
___ 14. Libra can't: reduces friction
___ 15. flu ad: friction that slows down a swimmer
___ 16. now ten: unit used to measure force
___ 17. sly ding: friction that makes brakes work

a. balanced: a ringer on a stick
b. newton: used to be nine
c. force: slapstick
d. fluid: influenza commercial
e. motion: lawn-cutting avoidance
f. gravity: dirty English drink
g. velocity: guy's town
h. net force: mesh that's ours
i. static: pigpen twitch
j. mass: spiked medieval war club
k. friction: weird shimminess
l. acceleration: thrill
m. weight: slowly walk into the water
n. speed: played secret agent
o. sliding: sneaky dent
p. lubricant: the sign between Virgo and Scorpio won't work
q. rolling: fish egg connection

SCIENCE PUZZLERS, TWISTERS & TEASERS

#1 — SCIENCE PUZZLERS, TWISTERS & TEASERS

Matter in Motion

Daffy Definitions

1. Below are some really silly definitions for words found in the chapter. The number after each word shows the number of letters in the answer. See how many you can solve!

a. A very weighty subject (7)
b. Opposite of a lubricant (9)
c. Web propulsion (8)
d. Roman "five," low metropolis (8)
e. Presently falling forward, also forces (10)
f. The weight of 2,000 frics (8)
g. Playground pastime; type of friction (7)
h. 2,000 pounds never seen before (6)

A-maze-ing

2. Follow the maze below in the proper order to spell out a word from the chapter.

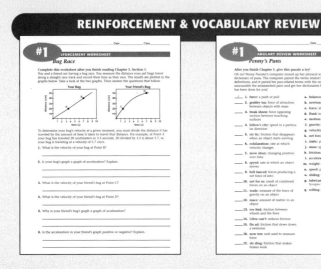

Start   Finish

word: _____

Chapter 1 • Matter in Motion

Review & Assessment

STUDY GUIDE

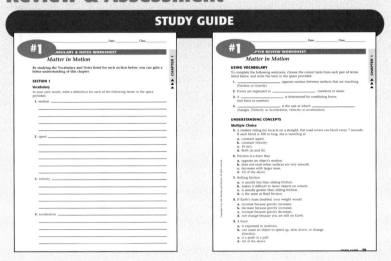

CHAPTER TESTS WITH PERFORMANCE-BASED ASSESSMENT

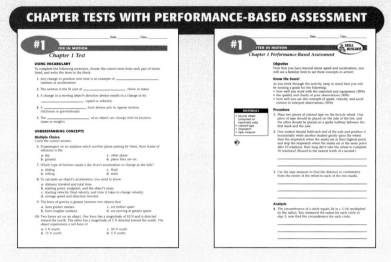

Lab Worksheets

LONG-TERM PROJECTS & RESEARCH IDEAS

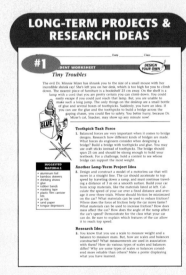

DATASHEETS FOR LABBOOK

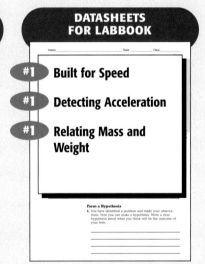

Built for Speed

Detecting Acceleration

Relating Mass and Weight

Applications & Extensions

CRITICAL THINKING & PROBLEM SOLVING

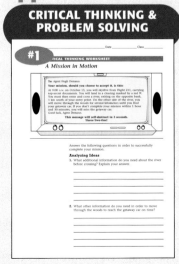

SCIENCE TECHNOLOGY

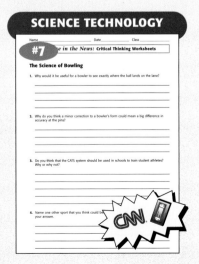

SCIENTISTS IN ACTION

INTERACTIVE EXPLORATIONS

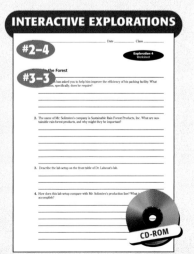

SECTION 1

Measuring Motion

▶ The Scientific Revolution

The movement now called the Scientific Revolution took place between the sixteenth and eighteenth centuries. Mainstream science of the time still taught the classical Aristotelian view of the universe. With the translation of Greek, Roman, and Arabic texts and the improvement of the printing press, ideas that are now the basis of modern science first became available to a large number of people.

- In astronomy, the theory that the sun is the center of the solar system was established by Copernicus. Galileo laid the foundations of the principles of mechanics and first turned a telescope toward the sky. Philosophers such as Descartes began to develop the idea of nature as a complicated system of particles in motion.

▶ Sir Isaac Newton (1642–1727)

Sir Isaac Newton was a central figure in the Scientific Revolution during the seventeenth century. He was born in 1642, the year Galileo died.

▶ Acceleration

Remember that acceleration, just like velocity, always includes direction. However, the relationship between acceleration and motion is different from the relationship between velocity and motion. An object's motion is always in the same direction as its velocity. An object's motion is not always in the same direction as its acceleration.

▶ Lacrosse and Physics

The sport lacrosse takes advantage of the physics of circular motion, and skilled lacrosse players can use a lacrosse stick to send the ball flying at speeds approaching 42 m/s, or about as fast as a typical fastball in Major League Baseball.

- Think of a line of students in a marching band making a turn. One student serves as the pivot point around which the others turn (similar to the bottom of the handle of the lacrosse stick). The far end of the line (or the web end of the stick) is moving very fast compared with the pivot. In lacrosse, some of that speed is imparted to the ball.

IS THAT A FACT!

- A fast runner can reach a speed of 32 km/h. The highest speed a person can attain when swimming, however, is only about 8 km/h.

SECTION 2

What Is a Force?

▶ Basic Forces of Nature

Scientists believe that the interactions of only four basic forces can describe all the physical properties and relationships in nature. These forces are:

- the gravitational force, which acts on all matter that has mass and on light, which has no mass

- the electromagnetic force, which is responsible for the attraction and repulsion of certain kinds of matter (including the electrical and magnetic forces)

- the strong nuclear force, which binds the protons and neutrons of atoms together in the nucleus

- the weak nuclear force, which describes some interactions between subatomic particles

IS THAT A FACT!

- Gravitational force and electromagnetic force were discovered long before nuclear forces because we can observe their effects on ordinary matter. The strong and weak nuclear forces were not discovered until the twentieth century, when we were able to probe the structure of atoms.

▶ Tug-of-War and Force
In a tug-of-war contest, the losing team always moves in the direction of the net force.

SECTION 3

Friction: A Force That Opposes Motion

▶ Sports and Friction
Many sports participants want to reduce friction as much as possible. Downhill skiers wax their skis to reduce friction between the skis and the snow. Surfers wax their boards to reduce friction between the boards and the water. However, in some sports, increased friction is what the athlete wants. A runner in the 100 m dash wants maximum friction between his or her shoes and the running track.

▶ Wheels
A wheel makes movement easier by reducing friction. Yet without friction between the wheel and the ground, the wheel would just spin around and the object to which the wheel is attached would go nowhere. Rolling friction usually dissipates much less energy than sliding friction.

IS THAT A FACT!

- Because friction can increase the temperature of objects, the space shuttle glows bright pink as it reenters the thick atmosphere of Earth. One astronaut reported that reentry is like riding in a neon tube.

- Athletic shoes come in so many varieties because they are designed to provide the proper amount of friction for maximum performance in each sport.

SECTION 4

Gravity: A Force of Attraction

▶ Gravity
Every object in the universe is constantly subject to the pull of gravity. The gravitational force acting on the object may be extremely small, but it is always present.

▶ Newton's Universal Law of Gravitation
The gravitational force exists between two objects anywhere in the universe. It exists regardless of the mass of the objects, the medium they are in, their composition, or the distance between them.

Newton's universal law of gravitation is $F_g = G\dfrac{m_1 m_2}{d^2}$, which means that the gravitational force
(F_g) = constant of universal gravitation ×
$\left(\dfrac{\text{mass}_1 \times \text{mass}_2}{(\text{distance between the centers of mass})^2}\right)$.

The size of the gravitational force is related to the masses of the objects and the distance between them.

IS THAT A FACT!

- When the gravitational force of the moon and sun pull together on the same side of Earth or pull on opposite sides of Earth, ocean tides are highest.

- If a person could hover at a distance of 6,400 km above Earth, twice Earth's radius, he or she would weigh only one-fourth his or her weight on Earth.

For background information about teaching strategies and issues, refer to the *Professional Reference for Teachers*.

CHAPTER 1

Matter in Motion

Pre-Reading Questions

Students may not know the answers to these questions before reading the chapter, so accept any reasonable response.

Suggested Answers

1. Motion is measured with speed (distance divided by time), velocity (speed in a given direction), and acceleration (the rate of change of velocity).

2. A force is a push or pull.

3. Friction opposes motion.

4. Gravity, a force of attraction, causes objects to be pulled toward each other.

Sections

Pre-Reading Questions

1. How is motion measured?
2. What is a force?
3. How does friction affect motion?
4. How does gravity affect objects?

2

SWOOSH!!

Have you ever watched a speed skating race during the Winter Olympics? Speed skaters are extremely fast. In fact, some speed skaters have been known to skate at a rate of 12 meters per second! Speed skaters, like the one you see in this photograph, must have a great deal of athletic skill and ability. First of all, they have to be very strong in order to exert the force needed to move so fast. Secondly, speed skaters skate on ice, which is very slippery. These athletes must be able to overcome the lack of friction between their skates and the ice—so they won't fall during the race! In this chapter, you will learn more about motion, including speed and acceleration, and the forces that affect motion, such as friction and gravity.

internet connect

HRW On-line Resources

go.hrw.com

For worksheets and other teaching aids, visit the HRW Web site and type in the keyword: **HSTMOT**

www.scilinks.com

Use the *sci*LINKS numbers at the end of each chapter for additional resources on the **NSTA** Web site.

Smithsonian Institution®

www.si.edu/hrw

Visit the Smithsonian Institution Web site for related on-line resources.

www.cnnfyi.com

Visit the CNN Web site for current events coverage and classroom resources.

THE DOMINO DERBY

Speed is the rate at which an object moves. In this activity, you will determine the factors that affect the speed of falling dominoes.

Procedure

1. Set up **25 dominoes** in a straight line. Try to keep equal spacing between the dominoes.

2. Using a **meterstick,** measure the total length of your row of dominoes, and write it down.

3. Using a **stopwatch,** time how long it takes for the entire row of dominoes to fall. Record this measurement.

4. Repeat steps 2 and 3 several times, using distances between the dominoes that are smaller and larger than the distance used in your first setup.

Analysis

5. Calculate the average speed for each trial by dividing the total distance (the length of the domino row) by the time taken to fall.

6. How did the spacing between dominoes affect the average speed? Is this result what you expected? If not, explain.

3

Focus

Measuring Motion

This section introduces students to the concept of motion. It introduces the idea of a *reference point* as a necessary starting point to observe motion. Students learn about average speed, velocity, and acceleration, and learn to calculate all three.

Bellringer

Have students describe their position in the classroom using a reference point and a set of reference directions. For example, a student might say, "I sit three desks behind Ahmed's desk," or "I sit 2 m east of the vent hood and 10 m north of the emergency shower."

1 Motivate

DEMONSTRATION

Models Place two identical wind-up toys on a table, one wound, the other not wound, so that one toy moves across the table while the other one remains motionless. Ask students to explain the difference between the toys. Help students understand that the difference is movement. Ask students to define motion in their own terms. Explain that in this section they will learn how to identify and measure different quantities related to motion.

Thur.
Read
4 + 5

Terms to Learn

motion	velocity
speed	acceleration

What You'll Do

- Identify the relationship between motion and a reference point.
- Identify the two factors that speed depends on.
- Determine the difference between speed and velocity.
- Analyze the relationship of velocity to acceleration.
- Interpret a graph showing acceleration.

Measuring Motion

Look around you—you're likely to see something in motion. Your teacher may be walking across the room, or perhaps a bird is flying outside a window. Even if you don't see anything moving, motion is still occurring all around you. Tiny air particles are whizzing around, the moon is circling the Earth, and blood is traveling through your veins and arteries!

Observing Motion

You might think that the motion of an object is easy to detect—you just observe the object. But you actually must observe the object in relation to another object that appears to stay in place. The object that appears to stay in place is a *reference point*. When an object changes position over time when compared with a reference point, the object is in **motion**. When an object is in motion, you can describe the direction of its motion with a reference direction, such as north, south, east, west, or up and down.

Common Reference Points The Earth's surface is a common reference point for determining position and motion. Nonmoving objects on Earth's surface, such as buildings, trees, and mountains, are also useful reference points, as shown in **Figure 1.**

A moving object can also be used as a reference point. For example, if you were on the hot-air balloon shown below, you could watch a bird fly by and see that it was changing position in relation to your moving balloon. Furthermore, Earth itself is a moving reference point—it is moving around the sun.

4

Figure 1 *During the time it took for these pictures to be taken, the hot-air balloon changed position compared with a reference point—the mountain.*

MISCONCEPTION /// ALERT \\\

The text defines *motion* as an object's change in position over time when compared with a reference point. Remind students that an object's *position* can be described in terms of a reference point and a set of reference directions. Common reference directions are compass directions (such as south and west) and relative directions (such as left of, just beyond, and in front of).

Speed Depends on Distance and Time

The rate at which an object moves is its **speed.** Speed depends on the distance traveled and the time taken to travel that distance. Look back at Figure 1. Suppose the time interval between the pictures was 10 seconds and the balloon traveled 50 m in that time. The speed (distance divided by time) of the balloon is 50 m/10 s, or 5 m/s.

The SI unit for speed is meters per second (m/s). Kilometers per hour, feet per second, and miles per hour are other units commonly used to express speed.

Determining Average Speed Most of the time, objects do not travel at a constant speed. For example, you probably do not walk at a constant speed from one class to the next. Therefore, it is very useful to calculate *average speed* using the following equation:

$$\text{Average speed} = \frac{\text{total distance}}{\text{total time}}$$

Recognizing Speed on a Graph Suppose a person drives from one city to another. The blue line in the graph below shows the distance traveled every hour. Notice that the distance traveled every hour is different. This is because the speed (distance/time) is not constant—the driver changes speed often because of weather, traffic, or varying speed limits. The average speed can be calculated by adding up the total distance and dividing it by the total time:

$$\text{Average speed} = \frac{360 \text{ km}}{4 \text{ h}} = 90 \text{ km/h}$$

The red line shows the average distance traveled each hour. The slope of this line is the average speed.

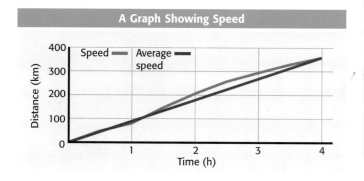

A Graph Showing Speed

The list below shows a comparison of some interesting speeds:

Cockroach . . . . . . 1.25 m/s

Kangaroo . . . . 15 m/s

Cheetah (the fastest land animal). . . . . . . 27 m/s

Sound (in air) . . . . . 343 m/s

Space shuttle . . . 10,000 m/s

Light . . . . . 300,000,000 m/s

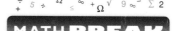

MATH **BREAK**

Calculating Average Speed

Practice calculating average speed in the problems listed below:

1. If you walk for 1.5 hours and travel 7.5 km, what is your average speed?

2. A bird flies at a speed of 15 m/s for 10 s, 20 m/s for 10 s, and 25 m/s for 5 s. What is the bird's average speed?

In the fig. . . . . . owing **Speed,** th . . . . . straight line) on t . . . . . that the average s . . . . . for the entire trip . . . . . linear curve (cr . . . . . ates that the s . . . . . changed several ti . . . . . rip.

Answers to MATHBREAK

1. 5 km/h

2. 19 m/s

Item 2 requires dimensional analysis.

LabBook **PG 186**

Built for Speed

MATH and **MORE**

Give students the following problems to solve:

- What is your average speed if you take 0.5 hour to walk 4,000 m? (8,000 m/h)

- If the average speed of a car is 110 km/h, how long will it take the car to travel 715 km? (6.5 hours)

 Math Skills Worksheet "Average Speed in a Pinewood Derby"

Homework

Obtain bus, train, or airplane schedules that list departure and arrival times. Help students plan a trip with at least four segments.

Using a map of the route, have students estimate the distance between points on the route as accurately as possible. Have them calculate the average speed of the vehicle between checkpoints and compare the average speed for each segment. Does the average speed remain constant or does it change? What might account for any differences?

 Teaching Transparency 213 "A Graph Showing Speed"

 Math Skills Worksheet "The Unit Factor and Dimensional Analysis"

② Teach, continued

READING 📖 STRATEGY

Writing **Writing Activity** After students have read about velocity, have them write a paragraph in their ScienceLog that gives examples of when it is sufficient to know only the speed of something and when it is important to know the velocity.

MEETING INDIVIDUAL NEEDS

Advanced Learners Have students research the history of the measurement of the speed of light. Have them focus on the calculations involving distance and time. What were the difficulties in making these calculations? What factors improved their accuracy? How did the evolution of the definitions of lengths and time periods affect the measurement of the speed of light?

Answers to Self-Check

Numbers 1 and 3 are examples of velocity.

INDEPENDENT PRACTICE

Have students research navigational terminology referring to speed and velocity. What are the terms used in sailing, aviation, and rocketry to describe speed and velocity? Compare and contrast the usages. Focus particularly on the importance placed on direction in the terminology.

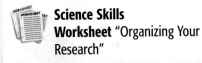

Science Skills Worksheet "Organizing Your Research"

Velocity: Direction Matters

Here's a riddle for you: Two birds leave the same tree at the same time. They both fly at 10 km/h for 1 hour, 15 km/h for 30 minutes, and 5 km/h for 1 hour. Why don't they end up at the same destination?

Have you figured it out? The birds traveled at the same speeds for the same amounts of time, but they did not end up at the same place because they went in different directions. In other words, they had different velocities. The speed of an object in a particular direction is the object's **velocity** (vuh LAHS uh tee).

Be careful not to confuse the terms *speed* and *velocity*; they do not mean the same thing. Because velocity must include direction, it would not be correct to say that an airplane's velocity is 600 km/h. However, you could say the plane's velocity is 600 km/h south. Velocity always includes a reference direction. **Figure 2** further illustrates the difference between speed and velocity.

Figure 2 *The speeds of these cars may be similar, but their velocities are different because they are going in different directions.*

Velocity Changes as Speed or Direction Changes You can think of velocity as the rate of change of an object's position. An object's velocity is constant only if its speed and direction don't change. Therefore, constant velocity is always along a straight line. An object's velocity will change if either its speed or direction changes. For example, if a bus traveling at 15 m/s south speeds up to 20 m/s, a change in velocity has occurred. But a change in velocity also occurs if the bus continues to travel at the same speed but changes direction to travel east.

> ✓ **Self-Check**
>
> Which of the following are examples of velocity?
> 1. 25 m/s forward   3. 55 m/h south
> 2. 1,500 km/h   4. all of the above
>
> *(See page 232 to check your answer.)*

IS THAT A FACT!

A 14-year-old land-speed record was broken in 1997 when the jet-powered *ThrustSSC* traveled faster than the speed of sound. The vehicle reached a speed of 1,230 km/h. The speed of sound in air at 0°C is about 1,192 km/h.

Combining Velocities If you're riding in a bus traveling east at 15 m/s, you and all the other passengers are also traveling at a velocity of 15 m/s east. But suppose you stand up and walk down the bus's aisle while it is moving. Are you still moving at the same velocity as the bus? No! **Figure 3** shows how you can combine velocities to determine the *resultant velocity.*

Figure 3 Determining Resultant Velocity

1 m/s east   15 m/s east

Person's resultant velocity

15 m/s east + 1 m/s east = 16 m/s east

When you combine two velocities that are **in the same direction**, add them together to find the resultant velocity.

1 m/s west   15 m/s east

Person's resultant velocity

15 m/s east – 1 m/s west = 14 m/s east

When you combine two velocities that are **in opposite directions**, subtract the smaller velocity from the larger velocity to find the resultant velocity. The resultant velocity is in the direction of the larger velocity.

SECTION REVIEW

1. What is a reference point?
2. What two things must you know to determine speed?
3. What is the difference between speed and velocity?
4. **Applying Concepts** Explain why it is important to know a tornado's velocity and not just its speed.

BRAIN FOOD

The space shuttle is always launched in the same direction that the Earth rotates, thus taking advantage of the Earth's rotational velocity (over 1,500 km/h east). This allows the shuttle to use less fuel to reach space than if it had to achieve such a great velocity on its own.

7

Prediction Guide Before reading about acceleration, ask students to predict whether the following sentences are true or false:

- If you slow down on your bicycle, you accelerate. (true)
- If you ride your bicycle at a constant speed, you cannot accelerate. (false)
- Changing the speed and changing the direction of your bicycle are both examples of acceleration. (true)

MEETING INDIVIDUAL NEEDS

Learners Having Difficulty Read aloud each of the following situations. Diagram them on the board or overhead projector. Then discuss with students whether or not acceleration occurred and why.

- You are riding your bike at 9 km/h. Ten minutes later, your speed is 6 km/h. (Acceleration occurred because speed decreased.)
- You ride your bike around the block at a constant speed of 11 km/h. (Acceleration occurred because direction changed.)
- You ride your bike in a straight line at a constant speed of 10 km/h. (No acceleration occurred because neither speed nor direction changed.) **Sheltered English**

Acceleration: The Rate at Which Velocity Changes

Imagine that you are in-line skating and you see a large rock in your path. You slow down and swerve to avoid the rock. A neighbor sees you and exclaims, "That was great acceleration! I'm amazed that you could slow down and turn so quickly!" You're puzzled. Doesn't *accelerate* mean to speed up? But you didn't speed up—you slowed down and turned. So how could you have accelerated?

Defining Acceleration Although the word *accelerate* is commonly used to mean "speed up," there's more to its meaning scientifically. **Acceleration** (ak SEL uhr AY shuhn) is the rate at which velocity changes. To *accelerate* means to change velocity. You just learned that velocity changes if speed changes, direction changes, or both. So your neighbor was right! Your speed and direction changed, so you accelerated.

Keep in mind that acceleration is not just how much velocity changes. It is also *how fast* velocity changes. The faster velocity changes, the greater the acceleration is.

Calculating Acceleration You can calculate acceleration by using the following equation:

$$\text{Acceleration} = \frac{\text{final velocity} - \text{starting velocity}}{\text{time it takes to change velocity}}$$

Velocity is expressed in meters per second (m/s), and time is expressed in seconds (s). Therefore, acceleration is expressed in meters per second per second (m/s/s).

Suppose you get on your bicycle and accelerate southward at a rate of 1 m/s/s. (Like velocity, acceleration has size and direction.) This means that every second, your southward velocity increases by 1 m/s, as shown in **Figure 4** on the next page.

Homework

Have students record examples of acceleration that they observe around their homes. Ask them to make a chart like the one at the bottom of page 9 to include each example of acceleration and to show how velocity changed in each example.

MISCONCEPTION
ALERT

The unit for acceleration is often written m/s², not m/s/s. This section uses m/s/s because many students lack experience with exponents. You may wish to use m/s² in this section if your students are familiar with exponents.

Figure 4 Acceleration at 1 m/s/s South

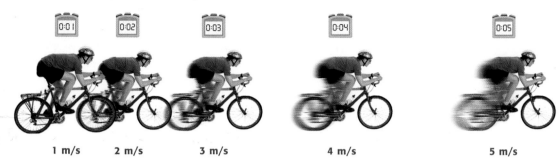

1 m/s   2 m/s   3 m/s   4 m/s   5 m/s

After 1 second, you have a velocity of 1 m/s south, as shown in Figure 4. After 2 seconds, you have a velocity of 2 m/s south. After 3 seconds, you have a velocity of 3 m/s south, and so on. If your final velocity after 5 seconds is 5 m/s south, your acceleration can be calculated as follows:

$$\text{Acceleration} = \frac{5 \text{ m/s} - 0 \text{ m/s}}{5 \text{ s}} = 1 \text{ m/s/s south}$$

You can practice calculating acceleration by doing the MathBreak shown here.

Examples of Acceleration   In the example above, your velocity was originally zero and then it increased. Because your velocity changed, you accelerated. Acceleration in which velocity increases is sometimes called *positive acceleration*.

Acceleration also occurs when velocity decreases. In the skating example, you accelerated because you slowed down. Acceleration in which velocity decreases is sometimes called *negative acceleration* or *deceleration*.

Remember that velocity has direction, so velocity will change if your direction changes. Therefore, a change in direction is acceleration, even if there is no change in speed. Some more examples of acceleration are shown in the chart below.

Example of Acceleration	How Velocity Changes
A plane taking off	Increase in speed
A car stopping at a stop sign	Decrease in speed
Jogging on a winding trail	Change in direction
Driving around a corner	Change in direction
Standing at Earth's equator	Change in direction

MATH BREAK

Calculating Acceleration

Use the equation shown on the previous page to do the following problems. Be sure to express your answers in m/s/s and include direction.

1. A plane passes over Point A with a velocity of 8,000 m/s north. Forty seconds later it passes over Point B at a velocity of 10,000 m/s north. What is the plane's acceleration from A to B?

2. A coconut falls from the top of a tree and reaches a velocity of 19.6 m/s when it hits the ground. It takes 2 seconds to reach the ground. What is the coconut's acceleration?

RESEARCH

Have small groups of students apply the idea of acceleration to the design of roller coasters. Have them research a particular roller coaster and create a drawing or diagram of its features. Have them describe the motion of the roller coaster in terms of velocity and acceleration.

MATH and MORE

Practice calculating acceleration with the following problems:

1. At point A, a runner is jogging at 3 m/s. Forty seconds later, at point B —on a hill—the jogger's velocity is only 1 m/s. What is the jogger's acceleration from point A to point B? (–0.05 m/s/s up)

2. In a summer storm, the wind is blowing with a velocity of 8 m/s north. Suddenly, in 3 seconds, the wind's velocity is 23 m/s north. What is the acceleration in the wind? (5 m/s/s north)

USING SCIENCE FICTION

Have students read the story "Direction of the Road" by Ursula K. LeGuin in the *Holt Anthology of Science Fiction*. As you discuss the story, ask students to describe the importance of identifying reference points.

9

Answers to MATHBREAK

1. 50 m/s/s north
2. 9.8 m/s/s downward (Note: Some students may recognize this answer as the acceleration due to gravity. Take this opportunity to set the tone for Section 4, "Gravity: A Force of Attraction," and for the next chapter, "Forces in Motion.")

Teaching Transparency 215 "Calculating Acceleration"

Interactive Explorations CD-ROM "Force in the Forest"

Quiz

1. What distinguishes the measurement of speed from that of velocity and acceleration? (Speed does not involve direction, as both velocity and acceleration do.)

2. What is centripetal acceleration? (acceleration that occurs in circular motion)

3. How do you calculate speed? velocity? acceleration? (divide the distance traveled by the time; divide the distance and direction traveled by the time; subtract the starting velocity from the final velocity, and divide by the time it takes to change velocity)

ALTERNATIVE ASSESSMENT

Ask students to draw two pictures of rolling balls as they would appear at 1 second intervals that would illustrate the difference between a ball rolling at a constant speed and a ball that is accelerating.

Teaching Transparency 216 "A Graph Showing Acceleration"

Reinforcement Worksheet "Bug Race"

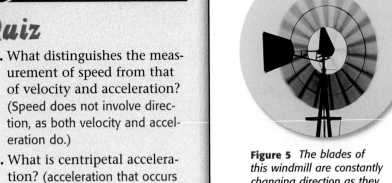

Figure 5 *The blades of this windmill are constantly changing direction as they travel in a circle. Thus, centripetal acceleration is occurring.*

internet**connect**

SCi*LINKS*
NSTA

TOPIC: Measuring Motion
GO TO: www.scilinks.org
*sci*LINKS NUMBER: HSTP105

Circular Motion: Continuous Acceleration   Does it surprise you to find out that standing at Earth's equator is an example of acceleration? After all, you're not changing speed, and you're not changing direction . . . or are you? In fact, you are traveling in a circle as the Earth rotates. An object traveling in a circular motion is always changing its direction. Therefore, its velocity is always changing, so acceleration is occurring. The acceleration that occurs in circular motion is known as *centripetal* (sen TRIP uht uhl) *acceleration.* Another example of centripetal acceleration is shown in **Figure 5.**

Recognizing Acceleration on a Graph   Suppose that you have just gotten on a roller coaster. The roller coaster moves slowly up the first hill until it stops at the top. Then you're off, racing down the hill! The graph below shows your acceleration for the 10 seconds coming down the hill. You can tell from this graph that your acceleration is positive because your velocity increases as time passes. Because the graph is not a straight line, you can also tell that your acceleration is not constant for each second.

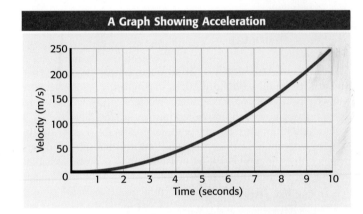

SECTION REVIEW

1. What is acceleration?

2. Does a change in direction affect acceleration? Explain your answer.

3. **Interpreting Graphics** How do you think a graph of deceleration would differ from the graph shown above? Explain your reasoning.

internet**connect**

SCi*LINKS*
NSTA

TOPIC: Measuring Motion
GO TO: www.scilinks.org
*sci*LINKS NUMBER: HSTP105

▼ *Answers to Section Review*

1. Acceleration is the rate at which velocity changes.

2. Yes, a change in direction does affect acceleration. Acceleration is a measure of velocity change. Velocity is speed in a given direction, and velocity changes if direction changes.

3. The graph showing acceleration has a positive slope. A graph showing deceleration would have a negative slope. The graph would take this shape because velocity would be decreasing as time passes.

Terms to Learn

force   net force
newton

What You'll Do

◆ Give examples of different kinds of forces.
◆ Determine the net force on an object.
◆ Compare balanced and unbalanced forces.

What Is a Force?

You often hear the word *force* in everyday conversation:

"That storm had a lot of force!"
"Our basketball team is a force to be reckoned with."
"A flat tire forced me to stop riding my bicycle."
"The inning ended with a force-out at second base."

But what exactly is a force? In science, a **force** is simply a push or a pull. All forces have both size and direction.

Forces are everywhere. In fact, any time you see something moving, you can be sure that its motion was created by a force. Scientists express force using a unit called the **newton (N).** The more newtons, the greater the force.

Forces Act on Objects

All forces are exerted by one object on another object. For any push to occur, something has to receive the push. You can't push nothing! The same is true for any pull. When doing schoolwork, you use your fingers to pull open books or to push the buttons on a computer keyboard. In these examples, your fingers are exerting forces on the books and the keys. However, just because a force is being exerted by one object on another doesn't mean that motion will occur. For example, you are probably sitting on a chair as you read this. But the force you are exerting on the chair does not cause the chair to move. That's because the Earth is also exerting a force on the chair. In most cases, it is easy to determine where the push or pull is coming from, as shown in **Figure 6.**

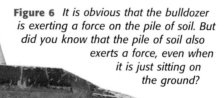

Figure 6 *It is obvious that the bulldozer is exerting a force on the pile of soil. But did you know that the pile of soil also exerts a force, even when it is just sitting on the ground?*

11

internet**connect**

SCI LINKS
NSTA

TOPIC: Forces
GO TO: www.scilinks.org
*sci*LINKS **NUMBER:** HSTP107

Focus

What Is a Force?

This section defines *force* and gives examples of different kinds of forces. Students learn to determine the net force on an object and to compare balanced and unbalanced forces.

🔊 Bellringer

Have students look around the room and think about the objects they see in terms of force. Remind them that a force is always exerted by one object on another object. Ask them the following question:

Where do you see a force happening in the room right now? Which object is exerting the force, and which is receiving it?

1 Motivate

DISCUSSION

Forces Every Day Using objects in the room or situations with which students are familiar (like riding a bicycle), discuss with students the forces that are operating on them. Ask students in each case to identify which object is exerting the force and which is receiving it. Continue the discussion by asking them to identify other types of daily activities that involve forces.

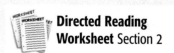

Directed Reading Worksheet Section 2

READING 📖 STRATEGY

Prediction Guide Before reading about forces in combination, have students look at **Figures 8** and **9**. While they are looking at these pictures, ask students to predict what happens when forces are exerted in the same direction and when forces are exerted in opposite directions.

BRAIN FOOD

Some people confuse *force* and *pressure* because they are related to each other.

Magicians depend on this difference when they lie down on a bed of nails. The **force**—the magician's weight—is fairly large, but because there are hundreds or even thousands of nails, the **pressure** (the amount of force exerted on a given area) from each nail is not enough to break the magician's skin.

Ask students for other examples of spreading force over a wide area to reduce pressure.

Teaching Transparency 217
"Forces in the Same Direction"

Figure 7
Something unseen exerts a force that makes your socks cling together when they come out of the dryer. You have to exert a force to separate the socks.

It is not always so easy to tell what is exerting a force or what is receiving a force, as shown in **Figure 7.** You cannot see what exerts the force that pulls magnets to refrigerators, and the air you breathe is an unseen receiver of a force called *gravity.* You will learn more about gravity later in this chapter.

Forces in Combination

Often more than one force is exerted on an object at the same time. The **net force** is the force that results from combining all the forces exerted on an object. So how do you determine the net force? The examples below can help you answer this question.

Forces in the Same Direction Suppose you and a friend are asked to move a piano for the music teacher. To do this, you pull on one end of the piano, and your friend pushes on the other end. Together, your forces add up to enough force to move the piano. This is because your forces are in the same direction. **Figure 8** shows this situation. Because the forces are in the same direction, they can be added together to determine the net force. In this case, the net force is 45 N, which is plenty to move a piano—if it is on wheels, that is!

Figure 8 *When the forces are in the same direction, you add the forces together to determine the net force.*

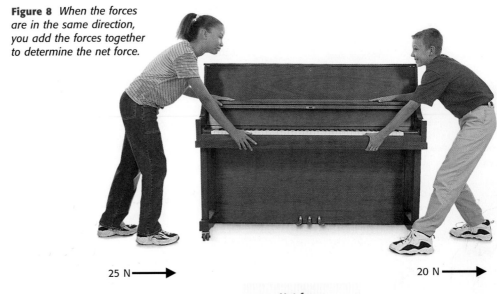

25 N ➡

20 N ➡

Net force
25 N + 20 N = 45 N
to the right

12

IS THAT A FACT!

Some trains are too massive to be moved by one locomotive. To compensate for the larger mass, extra locomotives are added until the net force of all the locomotives is large enough to move the train.

Forces in Different Directions Consider two dogs playing tug of war with a short piece of rope. Each is exerting a force, but in opposite directions. **Figure 9** shows this scene. Notice that the dog on the left is pulling with a force of 10 N and the dog on the right is pulling with a force of 12 N. Which dog do you think will win the tug of war?

Because the forces are in opposite directions, the net force is determined by subtracting the smaller force from the larger one. In this case, the net force is 2 N in the direction of the dog on the right. Give that dog a dog biscuit!

Science
CONNECTION

Every moment, forces in several directions are exerted on the Golden Gate Bridge. For example, Earth exerts a powerful downward force on the bridge while elastic forces pull and push portions of the bridge up and down. To learn how the bridge stands up to these forces, turn to page 33.

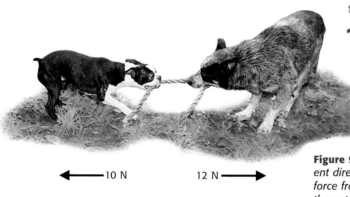

10 N   **12 N**

Net force
12 N − 10 N = 2 N
to the right

Figure 9 *When the forces are in different directions, you subtract the smaller force from the larger force to determine the net force.*

Unbalanced and Balanced Forces

If you know the net force on an object, you can determine the effect the force will have on the object's motion. Why? The net force tells you whether the forces on the object are balanced or unbalanced.

Unbalanced Forces Produce a Change in Motion In the examples shown in Figures 8 and 9, the net force on the object is greater than zero. When the net force on an object is not zero, the forces on the object are *unbalanced*. Unbalanced forces produce a change in motion (acceleration). In the two previous examples, the receivers of the forces—the piano and the rope—move. Unbalanced forces are necessary to cause a non-moving object to start moving.

✓ Self-Check

What is the net force when you combine a force of 7 N north with a force of 5 N south? *(See page 232 to check your answer.)*

13

Teaching Transparency 217 "Forces in Different Directions"

③ Extend

ACTIVITY

MATERIALS

FOR EACH STUDENT:
- toothpicks
- string and glue
- gumdrops
- cardboard

Making Models Students work in small groups to research, design, and build a bridge that spans a 60 cm gap and that is wide enough to accommodate a model car. The goal is to construct the strongest bridge that meets these requirements. Bridges will be rated according to the mass they can support without collapsing. Students should identify the forces acting on their bridge. A good place to start is the feature about the Golden Gate Bridge on page 33.

④ Close

Quiz

1. What is a net force? (the sum of all the forces acting on an object)
2. Are the forces on a kicked soccer ball balanced or unbalanced? How do you know? (Unbalanced; because the ball changes speed and/or direction.)

ALTERNATIVE ASSESSMENT

Poster Project Have students make a poster that shows an example of balanced forces (such as an elevator at rest or a gymnast motionless on a balance beam). The poster should show all forces acting on the object and should show what happens to the object if the forces become unbalanced.

Unbalanced forces are also necessary to change the motion of moving objects. For example, consider a soccer game. The soccer ball is already moving when it is passed from one player to another. When the ball reaches the second player, the player exerts an unbalanced force—a kick—on the ball. After the kick, the ball moves in a new direction and with a new speed.

Keep in mind that an object can continue to move even when the unbalanced forces are removed. A soccer ball, for example, receives an unbalanced force when it is kicked. However, the ball continues to roll along the ground long after the force of the kick has ended.

Balanced Forces Produce No Change in Motion When the forces applied to an object produce a net force of zero, the forces are *balanced*. Balanced forces do not cause a nonmoving object to start moving. Furthermore, balanced forces will not cause a change in the motion of a moving object.

Many objects around you have only balanced forces acting on them. For example, a light hanging from the ceiling does not move because the force of gravity pulling down on the light is balanced by an elastic force due to tension that pulls the light up. A bird's nest in a tree and a hat resting on your head are also examples of objects with only balanced forces acting on them. **Figure 10** shows another case where the forces on an object are balanced. Because all the forces are balanced, the house of cards does not move.

Figure 10 *The forces on this house of cards are balanced. An unbalanced force on one of the cards would cause motion—and probably a mess!*

SECTION REVIEW

1. Give four examples of a force being exerted.
2. Explain the difference between balanced and unbalanced forces and how each affects the motion of an object.
3. **Interpreting Graphics** In the picture at left, two bighorn sheep push on each other's horns. The arrow shows the direction the two sheep are moving. Describe the forces the sheep are exerting and how the forces combine to produce the sheep's motion.

Answers to Section Review

1. Accept all reasonable answers. Examples include: kicking a ball, writing with a pencil, pulling a rope, and pushing a stalled car.
2. Unbalanced forces occur when the net force on an object is not zero; balanced forces occur when the net force equals zero. Unbalanced forces cause a change in an object's motion; balanced forces cause no change.
3. Because the sheep are moving (as indicated by the arrow), the forces they are exerting on each other are unbalanced. The sheep on the left is exerting a larger force, so the total net force is in the direction it is pushing.

Terms to Learn

friction

What You'll Do

- ◆ Explain why friction occurs.
- ◆ List the types of friction, and give examples of each.
- ◆ Explain how friction can be both harmful and helpful.

Friction: A Force That Opposes Motion

Picture a warm summer day. You are enjoying the day by wearing shorts and tossing a ball with your friends. By accident, one of your friends tosses the ball just out of your reach. You have to make a split-second decision to dive for it or not. You look down and notice that if you dove for it, you would most likely slide across pavement rather than the surrounding grass. What would you decide?

Unless you enjoy scraped knees, you probably would not want to slide on the pavement. The painful difference between sliding on grass and sliding on pavement has to do with friction. **Friction** is a force that opposes motion between two surfaces that are touching.

The Source of Friction

Friction occurs because the surface of any object is rough. Even surfaces that look or feel very smooth are actually covered with microscopic hills and valleys. When two surfaces are in contact, the hills and valleys of one surface stick to the hills and valleys of the other surface, as shown in **Figure 11.** This contact causes friction even when the surfaces appear smooth.

The amount of friction between two surfaces depends on many factors, including the roughness of the surfaces and the force pushing the surfaces together.

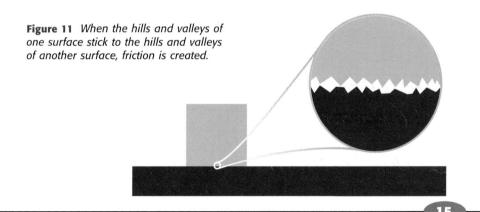

Figure 11 *When the hills and valleys of one surface stick to the hills and valleys of another surface, friction is created.*

15

Humans have tiny ridges in the skin of their hands and feet. These ridges increase friction between the skin and objects the hands or feet touch. This friction helps humans grasp objects with their hands and avoid slipping with their feet.

Directed Reading Worksheet Section 3

Focus

Friction: A Force That Opposes Motion

This section introduces and describes friction. Students explore the types of friction and study examples of each. Finally, students learn the role of friction in everyday life.

Bellringer

Have students answer the following question in their ScienceLog:

Suppose you and a younger sister or brother are swimming at a neighborhood pool. Your sister or brother asks why there are signs everywhere that say "NO RUNNING." What would be your answer?

1 Motivate

DEMONSTRATION

MATERIALS
• new, unopened paint can
• 6 marbles
• 4 heavy books

Place the can upright on a table. Balance all four books on top of the can. Then try to spin the books on top of the can.

Next, remove the books and place the six marbles evenly around the rim of the can.

Balance the books on top of the marbles and again try to spin the books. Have students record their observations and hypothesize about what forces were involved before and after adding the marbles.

MISCONCEPTION ALERT

The roughness of an object is not the only contributor to friction. Frictional forces are also influenced by the electrical attraction between the molecules of substances. The attraction makes it more difficult to slide the surfaces past one another.

QuickLab

MATERIALS

FOR EACH GROUP:
- cardboard (corrugated is best)
- 2 books
- toy car
- meterstick
- sandpaper or cloth (sandpaper should be very coarse; cloth should be fuzzy or nappy)

Teacher Notes: You can substitute pieces of plywood or several metersticks for the corrugated cardboard.

If your classroom is carpeted, you can move the ramp to the floor for one of the trials.

Answers to QuickLab

5. The covered surface had the most friction because it is the roughest. A heavier car would result in even more friction between the car and the surface because the force pushing the surfaces together would be increased.

Teaching Transparency 218
"Force and Friction"

QuickLab

The Friction 500

1. Make a short ramp out of a **piece of cardboard** and **one or two books** on a table.

2. Put a **toy car** at the top of the ramp and let go. If necessary, adjust the ramp height so that your car does not roll off the table.

3. Put the car at the top of the ramp again and let go. Record the distance the car travels after leaving the ramp. Do this three times, and calculate the average for your results.

4. Change the surface of the table by covering it with **sandpaper** or **cloth.** Repeat step 3. Change the surface one more time, and repeat step 3 again.

5. Which surface had the most friction? Why? What do you predict would happen if the car were heavier? Record your results and answers in your ScienceLog.

TRY at HOME

16

Rougher Surfaces Create More Friction Rougher surfaces have more microscopic hills and valleys. Thus, the rougher the surface, the greater the friction. Think back to the example on the previous page. Pavement is much rougher than grass. Therefore, more friction is produced when you slide on the pavement than when you slide on grass. This increased friction is more effective at stopping your sliding, but it is also more painful! On the other hand, if the surfaces are smooth, there is less friction. If you were to slide on ice instead of on grass, your landing would be even more comfortable—but also much colder!

Greater Force Creates More Friction The amount of friction also depends on the force pushing the surfaces together. If this force is increased, the hills and valleys of the surfaces can come into closer contact. This causes the friction between the surfaces to increase. Less massive objects exert less force on surfaces than more massive objects do, as illustrated in **Figure 12.** However, changing the amounts of the surfaces that touch does not change the amount of friction.

Figure 12 Force and Friction

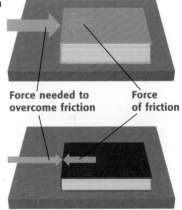

ⓐ There is more friction between the more massive book and the table than there is between the less massive book and the table. A harder push is needed to overcome friction to move the more massive book.

Force needed to overcome friction

Force of friction

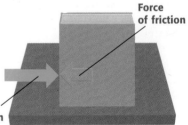

ⓑ Turning the more massive book on its edge does not change the amount of friction between the table and the book.

Force of friction

Force needed to overcome friction

Agent - the object that is having a noticeable effect on the other object (Receiver)

cuestick - cue ball

SCIENCE HUMOR

Tom: This match won't light.

Jerry: What's the matter with it?

Tom: I don't know; it worked a minute ago.

WEIRD SCIENCE

Air hockey is challenging because the puck floats on a very thin layer of air. Tiny holes in the table surface allow pressurized air to escape from underneath. The puck moves with very little friction.

Types of Friction

The friction you observe when sliding books across a tabletop is called sliding friction. Other types of friction include rolling friction, fluid friction, and static friction. As you will learn, the name of each type of friction is a big clue as to the conditions where it can be found.

Sliding Friction If you push an eraser across your desk, the eraser will move for a short distance and then stop. This is an example of *sliding friction*. Sliding friction is very effective at opposing the movement of objects and is the force that causes the eraser to stop moving. You can feel the effect of sliding friction when you try to move a heavy dresser by pushing it along the floor. You must exert a lot of force to overcome the sliding friction, as shown in **Figure 13.**

You use sliding friction when you go sledding, when you apply the brakes on a bicycle or a car, or when you write with a piece of chalk.

Rolling Friction If the same heavy dresser were on wheels, you would have an easier time moving it. The friction between the wheels and the floor is an example of *rolling friction.* The force of rolling friction is usually less than the force of sliding friction. Therefore, it is generally easier to move objects on wheels than it is to slide them along the floor, as shown at right.

Rolling friction is an important part of almost all means of transportation. Anything with wheels—bicycles, in-line skates, cars, trains, and planes—uses rolling friction between the wheels and the ground to move forward.

Figure 13 Comparing Sliding Friction and Rolling Friction

Moving a heavy piece of furniture in your room can be hard work because **the force of sliding friction is large.**

It is easier to move a heavy piece of furniture if you put it on wheels. **The force of rolling friction is smaller** and easier to overcome.

17

SYNTHESIS

When two very smooth surfaces move past each other, friction is mostly caused by "stickiness"—chemical bonding between the moving surfaces. When you picture friction between very smooth surfaces, don't think about hills and valleys sticking together. A better image is that of trying to drag very sticky tape along a surface. When there is a lot of friction, you may see pieces of one surface sticking onto the other surface.

MISCONCEPTION ALERT

Rolling friction is usually smaller than sliding friction, but it really depends on the situation. If both surfaces are hard, rolling friction is smaller. But if one of the surfaces is soft, such as deep snow, the sliding friction of skis or a sled might be a lot smaller than the rolling friction of a loaded wagon. Friction depends on several characteristics of both surfaces.

REAL-WORLD CONNECTION

PORTFOLIO Vehicle tires are designed to use friction to increase grip. Have students find information on as many different kinds of tires, tire compounds, and tread designs as they can. Have them do a poster or other project showing some of the types of tires and treads they have learned about. Sheltered English

---

CROSS-DISCIPLINARY FOCUS

History Scientists believe that the first wheeled vehicles were used in ancient Mesopotamia sometime between 3500 and 3000 B.C. Before wheels, people used a plank or a sled dragged along the ground to carry loads. With the invention of wheels, sleds were replaced with carts. The invention of the wheel is considered a major step in the advancement of human civilization. Ask students to write a short story about a day in their lives if wheels did not exist.

internet**connect**

SCi LINKS
NSTA

TOPIC: Force and Friction
GO TO: www.scilinks.org
*sci*LINKS NUMBER: HSTP110

2 Teach, *continued*

SYNTHESIS

Some competitive swimmers try to imitate the swimming style of marine mammals. Many swimmers shave off all of their body hair before a competition. Ask students to hypothesize how this relates to friction and to predict whether shaving might be helpful to a competitive swimmer. Ask students what other things might help a swimmer reduce friction and increase speed. (Studies seem to show that body shaving has no effect on swimmers' performance. It does seem to give swimmers a psychological boost, but it is hard to tell if that reduces a swimmer's time.)

Homework

Ask students to experiment with friction at home. Show them how to make a ramp using a piece of cardboard that has been covered tightly with plastic wrap. Have students select three or four different common objects they think might have different amounts of friction. Students can experiment by placing objects on the ramp while it is flat then lifting one end until each object slides down. Have them use a ruler to measure how high the ramp must be lifted before each object slides down. Ask them to record their observations in a chart or table and then write an explanation for their findings.
  Sheltered English

Answer to Self-Check

sliding friction

Figure 14 *Swimming provides a good workout because you must exert force to overcome fluid friction.*

Fluid Friction Why is it harder to walk on a freshly mopped floor than on a dry floor? The reason is that on the wet floor the sliding friction between your feet and the floor is replaced by *fluid friction* between your feet and the water. In this case, fluid friction is less than sliding friction, so the floor is slippery. The term *fluid* includes liquids, such as water and milk, and gases, such as air and helium.

  Fluid friction opposes the motion of objects traveling through a fluid, as illustrated in **Figure 14.** For example, fluid friction between air and a fast moving car is the largest force opposing the motion of the car. You can observe this friction by holding your hand out the window of a moving car.

Static Friction When a force is applied to an object but does not cause the object to move, *static friction* occurs. The object does not move because the force of static friction balances the force applied. Static friction disappears as soon as an object starts moving, and then another type of friction immediately occurs. Look at **Figure 15** to understand when static friction affects an object.

Figure 15 Static Friction

a There is no friction between the block and the table when no force is applied to the block to move it.

b If a small force—shown in blue—is exerted on the block, the block does not move. The force of static friction—shown in orange—exactly balances the force applied.

c When the force exerted on the block is greater than the force of static friction, the block starts moving. Once the block starts moving, all static friction is gone, and the force applied opposes sliding friction—shown in green.

✔ Self-Check

What type of friction was involved in the imaginary situation at the beginning of this section? *(See page 232 to check your answer.)*

Teaching Transparency 219 "Static Friction"

Interactive Explorations CD-ROM "Stranger Than Friction"

SCIENCE HUMOR

An impatient young girl named Lenore
Tried to run on a freshly waxed floor.
Since the friction was less,
She made quite a mess
As she slid right under the door.

Friction Can Be Harmful or Helpful

Think about how friction affects a car. Without friction, the tires could not push against the ground to move the car forward and the brakes could not stop the car. Without friction, a car is useless. However, friction can cause problems in a car too. Friction between moving engine parts increases their temperature and causes the parts to wear down. A liquid coolant is added to the engine to keep it from overheating, and engine parts need to be changed as they wear out.

Friction is both harmful and helpful to you and the world around you. Friction can cause holes in your socks and in the knees of your jeans. Friction by wind and water can cause erosion of the topsoil that nourishes plants. On the other hand, friction between your pencil and your paper is necessary for the pencil to leave a mark. Without friction, you would just slip and fall when you tried to walk. Because friction can be both harmful and helpful, it is sometimes necessary to reduce or increase friction.

Some Ways to Reduce Friction   One way to reduce friction is to use lubricants. *Lubricants* (LOO bri kuhnts) are substances that are applied to surfaces to reduce the friction between them. Some examples of common lubricants are motor oil, wax, and grease. **Figure 16** shows why lubricants are important to maintaining car parts.

Friction can also be reduced by switching from sliding friction to rolling friction. Ball bearings are placed between the wheels and axles of in-line skates and bicycles to make it easier for the wheels to turn by reducing friction.

FRI pgs 19 + 20

 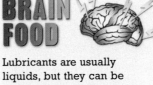
BRAIN FOOD

Lubricants are usually liquids, but they can be solids or gases too. Graphite is a shiny black solid that is used in pencils. Graphite dust is very slippery and is often used as a lubricant for ball bearings in bicycle and skate wheels. An example of a gas lubricant is the air that comes out of the tiny holes of an air-hockey table.

Figure 16 *Motor oil is used as a lubricant in car engines. Without oil, engine parts would wear down quickly, as the connecting rod on the bottom has.*

19

---

4) Close

Quiz

1. Which of the following would NOT help you move a heavy object across a concrete floor?

    water, ball bearings, oil, soapsuds, steel rods, foam rubber (foam rubber)

2. Name three common items you might use to increase friction. (Possible answers: sticky tape, sand, work gloves)

3. Name three common items you might use to reduce friction. (Possible answers: oil, water, wax, grease)

ALTERNATIVE ASSESSMENT

Ask students to imagine that they have been asked to design a bowling alley. Have them describe the areas where they would try to reduce friction and the areas where they would try to increase friction. Have them describe what materials they would use and why.

Answers to APPLY

Friction caused the treads (the raised surfaces that grip the road) to wear away, making the tire very smooth. Rolling friction is mainly responsible for the tire's appearance. Car owners should change their tires after several thousand kilometers because the tire surfaces are worn smooth by rolling friction. This decreases the friction between the tires and the road, which could cause the car to slide or skid when the brakes are applied.

Reinforcement Worksheet
"Friction Action"

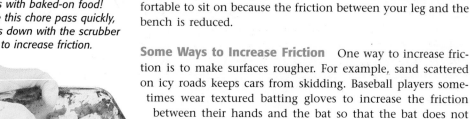

Figure 17 *No one enjoys cleaning pans with baked-on food! To make this chore pass quickly, press down with the scrubber to increase friction.*

Another way to reduce friction is to make surfaces that rub against each other smoother. For example, rough wood on a park bench is painful to slide across because there is a large amount of friction between your leg and the bench. Rubbing the bench with sandpaper makes it smoother and more comfortable to sit on because the friction between your leg and the bench is reduced.

Some Ways to Increase Friction One way to increase friction is to make surfaces rougher. For example, sand scattered on icy roads keeps cars from skidding. Baseball players sometimes wear textured batting gloves to increase the friction between their hands and the bat so that the bat does not fly out of their hands.

Another way to increase friction is to increase the force pushing the surfaces together. For example, you can ensure that your magazine will not blow away at the park by putting a heavy rock on it. The added mass of the rock increases the friction between the magazine and the ground. Or if you are sanding a piece of wood, you can sand the wood faster by pressing harder on the sandpaper. **Figure 17** shows another situation where friction is increased by pushing on an object.

APPLY

Friction and Tires

The tire shown here was used for more than 80,000 km. What effect did friction have on the rubber? What kind of friction is mainly responsible for the tire's appearance? Why are car owners warned to change their car tires after using them for several thousand kilometers?

internetconnect

SCLINKS.
NSTA

TOPIC: Force and Friction
GO TO: www.scilinks.org
*sci*LINKS NUMBER: HSTP110

SECTION REVIEW

1. Explain why friction occurs.

2. Name two ways in which friction can be increased.

3. Give an example of each of the following types of friction: sliding, rolling, and fluid.

4. **Applying Concepts** Name two ways that friction is harmful and two ways that friction is helpful to you when riding a bicycle.

▼ **Answers to Section Review**

1. Friction occurs because the microscopic hills and valleys of two touching surfaces "stick" to each other.

2. Friction can be increased by making surfaces rougher and by increasing the force pushing the surfaces together.

3. Answers will vary; accept all reasonable answers. Examples: sliding—skiing and writing with a pencil; rolling—riding a bicycle and pushing a handcart; fluid—swimming and throwing a softball.

4. Accept all reasonable answers. Sample answer: harmful—it causes tire tread to wear down and the wind can slow you down; helpful—the wheels grip the road, and your feet and hands stay on the pedals and handlebars.

Terms to Learn

gravity   mass
weight

What You'll Do

◆ Define gravity.
◆ State the law of universal gravitation.
◆ Describe the difference between mass and weight.

Gravity: A Force of Attraction

If you watch videotape of astronauts on the moon, you will notice that when the astronauts tried to walk on the lunar surface, they bounced around like beach balls instead.

Why did the astronauts—who were wearing heavy spacesuits—bounce so easily on the moon (as shown in **Figure 18**), while you must exert effort to jump a few centimeters off Earth's surface? The answer has to do with gravity. **Gravity** is a force of attraction between objects that is due to their masses. In this section, you will learn about gravity and the effects it has on objects.

Figure 18 *Because gravity is less on the moon than on Earth, walking on the moon's surface was a very bouncy experience for the Apollo astronauts.*

Biology CONNECTION

Scientists think seeds can "sense" gravity. The ability to sense gravity is what causes seeds to always send roots down and the green shoot up. But scientists do not understand just *how* seeds do this. Astronauts have grown seedlings during space shuttle missions to see how seeds respond to changes in gravity. So far, there are no definite answers from the results of these experiments.

All Matter Is Affected by Gravity

All matter has mass. Gravity is a result of mass. Therefore, all matter experiences gravity. That is, all objects experience an attraction toward all other objects. This gravitational force "pulls" objects toward each other. Right now, because of gravity, you are being pulled toward this book, your pencil, and every other object around you.

These objects are also being pulled toward you and toward each other because of gravity. So why don't you see the effects of this attraction? In other words, why don't you notice objects moving toward each other? The reason is that the mass of most objects is too small to cause an attraction large enough to move objects toward each other. However, you are familiar with one object that is massive enough to cause a noticeable attraction—the Earth.

21

Directed Reading Worksheet Section 4

Focus

Gravity: A Force of Attraction

This section describes gravity and the relationship between gravity, mass, and distance. It distinguishes between weight and mass.

Bellringer

Significantly decreased gravity gives astronauts the sensation of being weightless and forces astronauts to make many adjustments in their activities. Ask students to write a paragraph explaining what they would like and dislike about living with reduced gravity and some of the adjustments they would have to make if gravity disappeared.

1 Motivate

DEMONSTRATION

MATERIALS
• string
• sock
• toilet-paper tube
• beanbag

Safety Caution: Everyone should wear safety goggles during this demonstration.

Cut a length of string about 2 m long. Ball up the sock, and tie one end of the string around it. Pull the free end of the string through the tube, then tie it around the beanbag. Hold the tube, and twirl the beanbag in a circle. The sock represents the sun, and the beanbag represents Earth. Explain that the string represents the gravitational attraction between Earth and the sun.

READING 📖 STRATEGY

Prediction Guide Before students read this section, ask them to predict whether the following statements are true or false:

- Objects of any size exert a gravitational force. (true)
- The planets are held in their orbits by unbalanced forces. (true)
- If you traveled to Jupiter and you neither gained nor lost mass, your weight on Jupiter would be much greater than your weight on Earth. (true)

Answer to Self-Check

Gravity is a force of attraction between objects that is due to the masses of the objects.

MISCONCEPTION ///ALERT\\\

Although the gravitational attraction of an object toward Earth does decrease with altitude, this difference is very small. For all practical purposes, Earth's gravitational force on any object remains essentially the same anywhere in the atmosphere.

CONNECT TO
EARTH SCIENCE

Use Teaching Transparency 161 to help students understand the effects the moon's gravitational force has on Earth's tides.

Teaching Transparency 161
"Tidal Variations"

LINK TO EARTH SCIENCE

> **✓ Self-Check**
>
> What is gravity? *(See page 232 to check your answer.)*

Earth's Gravitational Force Is Large Compared with all the objects around you, Earth has an enormous mass. Therefore, Earth's gravitational force is very large. You must apply forces to overcome Earth's gravitational force any time you lift objects or even parts of your body.

Earth's gravitational force pulls everything toward the center of Earth. Because of this, the books, tables, and chairs in the room stay in place, and dropped objects fall to Earth rather than moving together or toward you.

The Law of Universal Gravitation

For thousands of years, two very puzzling questions were "Why do objects fall toward Earth?" and "What keeps the planets in motion in the sky?" The two questions were treated as separate topics until a British scientist named Sir Isaac Newton (1642–1727) realized that they were two parts of the same question.

The Core of an Idea Legend has it that Newton made the connection when he observed a falling apple during a summer night, as shown in **Figure 19**. He knew that unbalanced forces are necessary to move or change the motion of objects. He concluded that there had to be an unbalanced force on the apple to make it fall, just as there had to be an unbalanced force on the moon to keep it moving around Earth. He realized that these two forces are actually the same force—a force of attraction called gravity.

A Law Is Born Newton generalized his observations on gravity in a law now known as the *law of universal gravitation.* This law describes the relationships between gravitational force, mass, and distance. It is called universal because it applies to all objects in the universe.

Figure 19
Newton Makes the Connection

22

IS THAT A FACT!

In the reduced gravity of space, astronauts lose bone and muscle mass, even after a very short period of time. Sleep patterns may be affected and so may cardiovascular strength and the immune response. These same effects happen more gradually as people age on Earth. Scientists are interested in studying the effects of microgravity so they can find ways to counteract them in space and here on Earth.

The law of universal gravitation states the following: All objects in the universe attract each other through gravitational force. The size of the force depends on the masses of the objects and the distance between them. The examples in **Figure 20** show the effects of the law of universal gravitation. It is easier to understand the law if you consider it in two parts.

a Gravitational force is small between objects with small masses.

Figure 20 *The arrows indicate the gravitational force between the objects. The width of the arrows indicates the strength of the force.*

b Gravitational force is larger between objects with larger masses.

c If the distance between two objects is increased, the gravitational force pulling them together is reduced.

Part 1: Gravitational Force Increases as Mass Increases
Imagine an elephant and a cat. Because an elephant has a larger mass than a cat, the amount of gravity between an elephant and Earth is greater than the amount of gravity between a cat and Earth. That is why a cat is much easier to pick up than an elephant! There is gravity between the cat and the elephant, but it is very small because the cat's mass and the elephant's mass are so much smaller than Earth's mass.

The moon has less mass than Earth. Therefore, the moon's gravitational force is less than Earth's. Remember the astronauts on the moon? They bounced around as they walked because they were not being pulled down with as much force as they would have been on Earth.

Astronomy

CONNECTION

Black holes are formed when massive stars collapse. Black holes are 10 times to 1 billion times more massive than our sun. Thus, their gravitational force is incredibly large. The gravity of a black hole is so large that an object that enters a black hole can never get out. Even light cannot escape from a black hole. Because black holes do not emit light, they cannot be seen—hence their name.

23

MEETING INDIVIDUAL NEEDS

Advanced Learners Have students read H. G. Wells's 1901 story "The First Men in the Moon." Take one class to discuss the story and Wells's use of "Cavorite." Discuss how well the story fits with current scientific knowledge of the moon and gravity. How might the story be different if it were written today?

Answer to Activity

Accept all reasonable answers. Generally, students should demonstrate an understanding that increasing gravitational force would make things weigh more on Earth and make them harder to pick up; decreasing gravitational force would have the opposite effect.

③ Extend

DEBATE

Some scientists argue that the planet Pluto should not be called a planet. Other scientists believe that Pluto is a perfectly good planet. Help students research the issue and conduct a class debate about what is a planet and what isn't.

LabBook **PG 187**
Relating Mass and Weight

Reinforcement Worksheet
"A Weighty Problem"

Critical Thinking Worksheet
"A Mission in Motion"

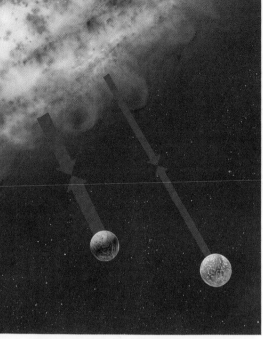

Figure 21 *Venus and Earth have approximately the same mass. However, Venus is closer to the sun. Thus, the gravity between Venus and the sun is greater than the gravity between Earth and the sun.*

Part 2: Gravitational Force Decreases as Distance Increases The gravity between you and Earth is large. Whenever you jump up, you are pulled back down by Earth's gravitational force. On the other hand, the sun is more than 300,000 times more massive than Earth. So why doesn't the sun's gravitational force affect you more than Earth's does? The reason is that the sun is so far away.

You are approximately 150 million kilometers away from the sun. At this distance, the gravity between you and the sun is very small. If there were some way you could stand on the sun (and not burn up), you would find it impossible to jump or even walk. The gravitational force acting on you would be so great that your muscles could not lift any part of your body!

Although the sun's gravitational force does not have much of an effect on your body here, it does have a big effect on Earth itself and the other planets, as shown in **Figure 21.** The gravity between the sun and the planets is large because the objects have large masses. If the sun's gravitational force did not have such an effect on the planets, the planets would not stay in orbit around the sun.

Weight Is a Measure of Gravitational Force

You have learned that gravity is a force of attraction between objects that is due to their masses. **Weight** is a measure of the gravitational force exerted on an object. When you see or hear the word *weight,* it usually refers to Earth's gravitational force on an object. But weight can also be a measure of the gravitational force exerted on objects by the moon or other planets.

You have learned that the unit of force is a newton. Because gravity is a force and weight is a measure of gravity, weight is also expressed in newtons (N). On Earth, a 100 g object, such as a medium-sized apple, weighs approximately 1 N.

Activity

Suppose you had a device that could increase or decrease the gravitational force of objects around you (including small sections of Earth). In your ScienceLog, describe what you might do with the device, what you would expect to see, and what effect the device would have on the weight of objects.

TRY at HOME

Science Bloopers

The moon used to be blamed for some strange behaviors in humans and animals (the word *lunatic* comes from the Latin word *luna,* meaning "moon"). Scientists once thought the moon affected the human body's fluids the same way it affects ocean tides. Women's menstrual cycles reinforced this belief. Today, scientists know that there is no evidence to support these beliefs.

Weight and Mass Are Different Weight is related to mass, but the two are not the same. Weight changes when gravitational force changes. **Mass** is the amount of matter in an object, and its value does not change. If an object is moved to a place with a greater gravitational force—like Jupiter—its weight will increase, but its mass will remain the same. **Figure 22** shows the weight and mass of an object on Earth and a place with about one-sixth the gravitational force—the moon.

Gravitational force is about the same everywhere on Earth, so the weight of any object is about the same everywhere. Because mass and weight are constant on Earth, the terms are often used to mean the same thing. This can lead to confusion. Be sure you understand the difference!

Figure 22 The astronaut's weight on the moon is about one-sixth of his weight on Earth, but his mass remains constant.

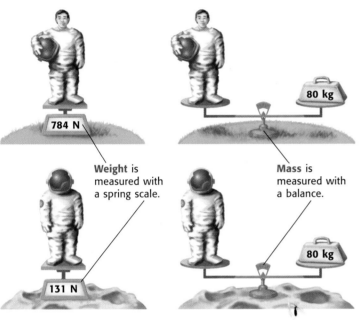

Weight is measured with a spring scale.

Mass is measured with a balance.

SECTION REVIEW

1. How does the mass of an object relate to the gravitational force the object exerts on other objects?

2. How does the distance between objects affect the gravity between them?

3. **Comparing Concepts** Explain why your weight would change if you orbited Earth in the space shuttle but your mass would not.

internetconnect

SCiLINKS
NSTA

TOPIC: Matter and Gravity
GO TO: www.scilinks.org
*sci*LINKS NUMBER: HSTP115

25

▼ **Answers to Section Review**

1. The greater an object's mass, the larger the gravitational force it exerts on other objects.

2. As the distance between objects increases, the gravitational force between them decreases; as the distance between objects decreases, the gravitational force between them increases.

3. A person's weight decreases in orbit because the distance between the person and the Earth would increase. But the person's mass would remain constant, because mass is the amount of matter in an object, and it does not depend on gravitational force.

GOING FURTHER

Help students find out what the gravitational force on other planets is compared with the gravitational force on Earth. Then have them write a short story or make a poster about what life would be like with different gravitational force acting on their bodies. Read Clifford Simak's science-fiction short story "Desertion" for one approach. **Sheltered English**

4) Close

Quiz

1. What is the difference between mass and weight? (Mass is the amount of matter in an object; weight is a measure of the gravitational force on an object.)

2. What must you know in order to determine the gravitational force between two objects? (their masses and the distance between them)

3. Where would you weigh the most, on a boat, on the space shuttle, or on the moon? (on a boat)

ALTERNATIVE ASSESSMENT

Poster Project Have students make a diagram or poster showing the motion of the solar system. Students should use the ideas presented in the chapter, including gravity, mass, centripetal force, velocity, and acceleration.

Teaching Transparency 221 "Weight and Mass Are Different"

Skill Builder Lab

Detecting Acceleration
Teacher's Notes

Time Required

One or two 45-minute class periods

Lab Ratings

EASY ———————→ HARD

TEACHER PREP 🜒
STUDENT SET-UP 🜒🜒
CONCEPT LEVEL 🜒🜒🜒
CLEAN UP 🜒🜒

MATERIALS

The materials listed are for each student or each small group of 2–3 students. Instead of using modeling clay to secure the thread to the bottle cap, students can cut the thread long enough so that it hangs out while the lid is screwed on tightly.

Safety Caution

Remind students to review all safety cautions and icons before beginning this lab activity.

Preparation Notes

You may wish to build an accelerometer before class to show students.

Elsie Waynes
Terrell Junior High
Washington, D.C.

Detecting Acceleration

Have you ever noticed that you can "feel" acceleration? In a car or in an elevator, you notice the change in speed or direction—even with your eyes closed! Inside your ears are tiny hair cells. These cells can detect the movement of fluid in your inner ear. When you accelerate, the fluid does, too. The hair cells detect this acceleration in the fluid and send a message to your brain. This message allows you to sense acceleration. In this activity you will build a device that detects acceleration.

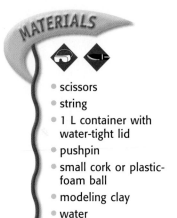

MATERIALS

* scissors
* string
* 1 L container with water-tight lid
* pushpin
* small cork or plastic-foam ball
* modeling clay
* water

Procedure

1. Cut a piece of string that is just long enough to reach three-quarters of the way inside the container.

2. Use a pushpin to attach one end of the string to the cork or plastic-foam ball.

3. Use modeling clay to attach the other end of the string to the center of the inside of the container lid. Be careful not to use too much string—the cork (or ball) should hang no farther than three-quarters of the way into the container.

4. Fill the container to the top with water.

5. Put the lid tightly on the container with the string and cork (or ball) on the inside.

6. Turn the container upside down (lid on the bottom). The cork should float about three-quarters of the way up inside the container, as shown at right. You are now ready to use your accelerometer to detect acceleration by following the steps on the next page.

26

📄 **Datasheets for LabBook**

7 Put the accelerometer lid side down on a tabletop. Notice that the cork floats straight up in the water.

8 Now gently start pushing the accelerometer across the table at a constant speed. Notice that the cork quickly moves in the direction you are pushing and then swings backward. If you did not see this motion, try the same thing again until you are sure you can see the first movement of the cork.

9 Once you are familiar with how to use your accelerometer, try the following changes in motion. Record your observations of the cork's first motion for each change in your ScienceLog.

a. While moving the device across the table, push a little faster.

b. While moving the device across the table, slow down.

c. While moving the device across the table, change the direction that you are pushing. (Try changing both to the left and to the right.)

d. Make any other changes in motion you can think of. You should only change one part of the motion at a time.

Analysis

10 The cork moves forward (in the direction you were pushing the bottle) when you speed up but backward when you slow down. Explain why. (Hint: Think about the direction of acceleration.)

11 When you push the bottle at a constant speed, why does the cork quickly swing back after it shows you the direction of acceleration?

12 Imagine you are standing on a corner and watching a car that is waiting at a stoplight. A passenger inside the car is holding some helium balloons. Based on what you observed with your accelerometer, what do you think will happen to the balloons when the car begins moving?

Going Further

If you move the bottle in a circle at a constant speed, what do you predict the cork will do? Try it, and check your answer.

Answers

10. The cork will move opposite to the motion of the water. As the bottle accelerates forward, the water sloshes backward, which makes the cork move forward. The cork will always move in the direction of acceleration.

11. The bottle stops accelerating (it is moving with a constant speed), so the cork shows zero acceleration.

12. As the car begins accelerating forward, the balloons will move forward because the air in the car moves backward. When the car reaches a steady speed, the balloons will move back to stand straight up.

Going Further

The cork will also travel in a circle, staying closest to the side of the bottle nearest the center of the circle.

27

Chapter Highlights

Chapter Highlights

VOCABULARY DEFINITIONS

SECTION 1

motion an object's change in position over time when compared with a reference point

speed the rate at which an object moves; speed depends on the distance traveled and the time taken to travel that distance

velocity the speed of an object in a particular direction

acceleration the rate at which velocity changes; an object accelerates if its speed changes, if its direction changes, or if both its speed and its direction change

SECTION 2

force a push or a pull; all forces have both size and direction

newton the SI unit of force

net force the force that results from combining all the forces exerted on an object

---

SECTION 1

Vocabulary

motion (p. 4)
speed (p. 5)
velocity (p. 6)
acceleration (p. 8)

Section Notes

- An object is in motion if it changes position over time when compared with a reference point.

- The speed of a moving object depends on the distance traveled by the object and the time taken to travel that distance.

- Speed and velocity are not the same thing. Velocity is speed in a given direction.

- Acceleration is the rate at which velocity changes.

- An object can accelerate by changing speed, changing direction, or both.

- Acceleration is calculated by subtracting starting velocity from final velocity, then dividing by the time required to change velocity.

Labs

Built for Speed (p. 186)

SECTION 2

Vocabulary

force (p. 11)
newton (p. 11)
net force (p. 12)

Section Notes

- A force is a push or a pull.

- Forces are expressed in newtons.

- Force is always exerted by one object on another object.

- Net force is determined by combining forces.

- Unbalanced forces produce a change in motion. Balanced forces produce no change in motion.

☑ Skills Check

Math Concepts

ACCELERATION An object's acceleration can be determined using the following equation:

$$\text{Acceleration} = \frac{\text{final velocity} - \text{starting velocity}}{\text{time it takes to change velocity}}$$

For example, suppose a cheetah running at a velocity of 27 m/s east slows down. After 15 seconds, the cheetah has stopped.

$$\frac{0 \text{ m/s} - 27 \text{ m/s}}{15 \text{ s}} = -1.8 \text{ m/s/s east}$$

Visual Understanding

THE SOURCE OF FRICTION Even surfaces that look or feel very smooth are actually rough at the microscopic level. To understand how this roughness causes friction, review Figure 11 on page 15.

THE LAW OF UNIVERSAL GRAVITATION This law explains that the gravity between objects depends on their masses and the distance between them. Review the effects of this law by looking at Figure 20 on page 23.

Lab and Activity Highlights

Detecting Acceleration `PG 26`

Built for Speed `PG 186`

Relating Mass and Weight `PG 187`

Datasheets for LabBook
(blackline masters for these labs)

SECTION 3

Vocabulary

friction *(p. 15)*

Section Notes

- Friction is a force that opposes motion.

- Friction is caused by "hills and valleys" touching on the surfaces of two objects.

- The amount of friction depends on factors such as the roughness of the surfaces and the force pushing the surfaces together.

- Four kinds of friction that affect your life are sliding friction, rolling friction, fluid friction, and static friction.

- Friction can be harmful or helpful.

SECTION 4

Vocabulary

gravity *(p. 21)*

weight *(p. 24)*

mass *(p. 25)*

Section Notes

- Gravity is a force of attraction between objects that is due to their masses.

- The law of universal gravitation states that all objects in the universe attract each other through gravitational force. The size of the force depends on the masses of the objects and the distance between them.

- Weight and mass are not the same. Mass is the amount of matter in an object; weight is a measure of the gravitational force on an object.

Labs

Relating Mass and Weight *(p. 187)*

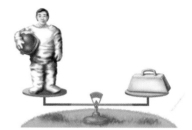

VOCABULARY DEFINITIONS, *continued*

SECTION 3

friction a force that opposes motion between two surfaces that are touching

SECTION 4

gravity a force of attraction between objects that is due to their masses

weight a measure of the gravitational force exerted on an object, usually by the Earth

mass the amount of matter that something is made of; its value does not change with the object's location

 Vocabulary Review Worksheet

 Blackline masters of these Chapter Highlights can be found in the **Study Guide.**

🔲 internet**connect**

GO TO: go.hrw.com

Visit the **HRW** Web site for a variety of learning tools related to this chapter. Just type in the keyword:

KEYWORD: HSTMOT

SCILINKS℠

NSTA

GO TO: www.scilinks.org

Visit the **National Science Teachers Association** on-line Web site for Internet resources related to this chapter. Just type in the *sci*LINKS number for more information about the topic:

TOPIC: Measuring Motion	*sci*LINKS NUMBER: HSTP105
TOPIC: Forces	*sci*LINKS NUMBER: HSTP107
TOPIC: Force and Friction	*sci*LINKS NUMBER: HSTP110
TOPIC: Matter and Gravity	*sci*LINKS NUMBER: HSTP115
TOPIC: The Science of Bridges	*sci*LINKS NUMBER: HSTP125

29

Lab and Activity Highlights

LabBank

 Calculator-Based Labs, The Fast Track

Long-Term Projects & Research Ideas, Tiny Troubles

Interactive Explorations CD-ROM

 CD 2, Exploration 4, "Force in the Forest"

CD 3, Exploration 3, "Stranger Than Friction"

USING VOCABULARY

1. Friction
2. newtons
3. net force
4. Acceleration, velocity

UNDERSTANDING CONCEPTS

Multiple Choice

5. d
6. a
7. a
8. a
9. d
10. c

Short Answer

11. Motion occurs when an object changes position over time when compared with a reference point (an object that appears to stay in place).

12. Acceleration can occur simply by a change in direction. Thus, no change in speed is necessary for acceleration.

13. Mass is the amount of matter in an object, and its value does not change with the object's location. Weight measures the gravitational force on an object, so it can change as the amount of gravitational force changes.

Chapter Review

USING VOCABULARY

To complete the following sentences, choose the correct term from each pair of terms listed below:

1. ___?___ opposes motion between surfaces that are touching. (*Friction* or *Gravity*)

2. Forces are expressed in ___?___. (*newtons* or *mass*)

3. A ___?___ is determined by combining forces. (*net force* or *newton*)

4. ___?___ is the rate at which ___?___ changes. (*Velocity* or *Acceleration/velocity* or *acceleration*)

UNDERSTANDING CONCEPTS

Multiple Choice

5. A student riding her bicycle on a straight, flat road covers one block every 7 seconds. If each block is 100 m long, she is traveling at
   a. constant speed.
   b. constant velocity.
   c. 10 m/s.
   d. Both (a) and (b)

6. Friction is a force that
   a. opposes an object's motion.
   b. does not exist when surfaces are very smooth.
   c. decreases with larger mass.
   d. All of the above

7. Rolling friction
   a. is usually less than sliding friction.
   b. makes it difficult to move objects on wheels.
   c. is usually greater than sliding friction.
   d. is the same as fluid friction.

8. If Earth's mass doubled, your weight would
   a. increase because gravity increases.
   b. decrease because gravity increases.
   c. increase because gravity decreases.
   d. not change because you are still on Earth.

9. A force
   a. is expressed in newtons.
   b. can cause an object to speed up, slow down, or change direction.
   c. is a push or a pull.
   d. All of the above

10. The amount of gravity between 1 kg of lead and Earth is _____ the amount of gravity between 1 kg of marshmallows and Earth.
    a. greater than   c. the same as
    b. less than   d. none of the above

Short Answer

11. Describe the relationship between motion and a reference point.

12. How is it possible to be accelerating and traveling at a constant speed?

13. Explain the difference between mass and weight.

Concept Mapping

14. Use the following terms to create a concept map: speed, velocity, acceleration, force, direction, motion.

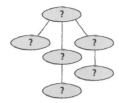

15. Your family is moving, and you are asked to help move some boxes. One box is so heavy that you must push it across the room rather than lift it. What are some ways you could reduce friction to make moving the box easier?

16. Explain how using the term *accelerator* when talking about a car's gas pedal can lead to confusion, considering the scientific meaning of the word *acceleration*.

17. Explain why it is important for airplane pilots to know wind velocity, not just wind speed, during a flight.

MATH IN SCIENCE

18. A kangaroo hops 60 m to the east in 5 seconds.

    a. What is the kangaroo's speed?

    b. What is the kangaroo's velocity?

    c. The kangaroo stops at a lake for a drink of water, then starts hopping again to the south. Every second, the kangaroo's velocity increases 2.5 m/s. What is the kangaroo's acceleration after 5 seconds?

INTERPRETING GRAPHICS

19. Is this a graph of positive or negative acceleration? How can you tell?

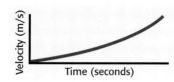

20. You know how to combine two forces that act in one or two directions. The same method you learned can be used to combine several forces acting in several directions. Examine the diagrams below, and predict with how much force and in what direction the object will move.

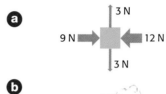

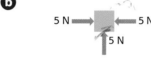

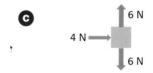

Reading Check-up

Take a minute to review your answers to the Pre-Reading Questions found at the bottom of page 2. Have your answers changed? If necessary, revise your answers based on what you have learned since you began this chapter.

31

Concept Mapping Transparency 5

Blackline masters of this Chapter Review can be found in the **Study Guide**.

Concept Mapping

14. An answer to this exercise can be found at the front of this book.

CRITICAL THINKING AND PROBLEM SOLVING

15. Accept all reasonable answers. Examples include using a hand-cart or dolly to take advantage of rolling friction and polishing the floor to reduce sliding friction.

16. The car's gas pedal is pressed by the driver to increase the car's velocity. Since the scientific meaning of the term *acceleration* can include slowing down and even changing direction, accelerator is not an accurate term for this device.

17. It is helpful for pilots to know wind velocity because velocity includes direction. Pilots need to know the wind's speed and direction so that they will know whether the wind is blowing in the same direction as the plane (which could increase the plane's resultant velocity and lead to an earlier arrival time) or in a different direction than the plane (which might lead to a later arrival).

MATH IN SCIENCE

18. a. 12 m/s
    b. 12 m/s east
    c. 2.5 m/s/s south

INTERPRETING GRAPHICS

19. Positive, because velocity increases as time passes.

20. a. 3 N to the left
    b. 5 N up
    c. 4 N to the right

Background

- Flight simulators have been popular computer applications for many years, but now powerful computers have brought motion simulation to a far more common experience—driving.

- VR machines can imitate the experience of driving many makes and models of cars for potential buyers to sample.

- Engineers might use driving simulators to test different features of a car or to test the design of intersections and roads before they are built.

- Golfers can practice in VR. They hit a real ball with a real club. The ball hits a vinyl screen, and sensors determine how the ball would fare on the course shown on the screen.

- Surgeons at the Virtual Reality in Medicine Laboratory at the University of Illinois at Chicago have created a virtual tour of the human ear, and they use the display (on a 6 m screen!) to learn their way around the inner ear.

- Scientists are working on a semi-transparent helmet for surgeons performing delicate operations, such as brain surgery. With this see-through helmet, a computer-generated three-dimensional image of a brain tumor, for example, is added to the surgeon's own view of the operation.

Science, Technology, and Society

Is It Real . . . or Is It Virtual?

You stand in the center of a darkened room and put on a helmet. The helmet covers your head and face, making it impossible for you to see or hear anything from outside. Wires run from the helmet to a series of computers, carrying information about how your head is positioned and where you are looking. Other wires carry back to you the sights and sounds the computer wants you to "see" and "hear." All of a sudden you find yourself driving a race car around a tricky course at 300 km/h. Then in another instant, you are in the middle of a rain forest staring at a live snake!

It's All an Illusion

Such simulated-reality experiences were once thought the stuff of science fiction alone. But today devices called motion simulators can stimulate the senses of sight and sound to create illusions of movement.

Virtual-reality devices, as these motion simulators are called, were first used during World War II to train pilots. Mock-ups of fighter-plane cockpits, films of simulated terrain, and a joystick that manipulated large hydraulic arms simulated the plane in "virtual flight." Today's jet pilots train with similar equipment, except the simulators use extremely sophisticated computer graphics instead of films.

Fooled You!

Virtual-reality hoods and gloves take people into a variety of "realities." Inside the hood, two small television cameras or computer-graphic images fool the wearer's sense of vision. The brain perceives the image as three-dimensional because one image is placed in front of each eye. As the images change, the computer adjusts the scene's perspective so that it appears to the viewer as though he or she is

moving through the scene. When the position of the head changes, the computer adjusts the scene to account for the movement. All the while, sounds coming through the headphones trick the wearer's ears into thinking he or she is moving too.

In addition to hoods, gloves, and images, virtual-reality devices may have other types of sensors. Driving simulators, for instance, often have a steering wheel, a gas pedal, and a brake so that the participant has the sensation of driving. So whether you want spine-tingling excitement or on-the-job training, virtual reality could very well take *you* places!

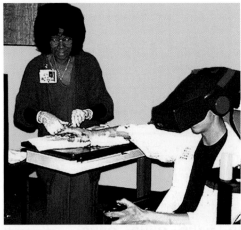

▲ *Wearing a virtual-reality helmet helps to lessen the pain this burn patient feels while his dressings are changed.*

Explore New Realities

▶ What other activities or skills could be learned or practiced with virtual reality? What are some problems with relying on this technology? Record your ideas in your ScienceLog.

32

Suggestions for Explore New Realities

Other activities in which virtual reality might be useful are hitting a baseball, operating complicated machinery, shopping, learning to dance, and practicing self-defense. Some problems with VR are its expense, the fact that what you learn through VR practice may not easily transfer to the real world, and that VR equipment may cause disorientation and discomfort in some users.

PHYSICAL SCIENCE • EARTH SCIENCE

The Golden Gate Bridge

Have you ever relaxed in a hammock? If so, you may have noticed how tense the strings got when the hammock supported your weight. Now imagine a hammock 1,965 m long supporting a 20-ton roadway with more than 100,000 cars traveling along its length each day. That describes the Golden Gate Bridge! Because of the way the bridge is built, it is very much like a giant hammock.

Tug of War

The bridge's roadway is suspended from main cables 2.33 km long that sweep from one end of the bridge to the other and that are anchored at each end. Smaller cables called *hangers* connect the main cables to the roadway. Tension, the force of being pulled apart, is created as the cables are pulled down by the weight of the roadway while being pulled up by their attachment to the top of each tower.

▲ *The Golden Gate Bridge spans the San Francisco Bay.*

Towering Above

Towers 227 m tall support the cables over the long distance across San Francisco Bay, making the Golden Gate the tallest bridge in the world. The towers receive a force that is the exact opposite of tension—compression. Compression is the force of being pushed together. The main cables holding the weight of the roadway push down on the top of the towers while Earth pushes up on the bottom.

Stretching the Limits

Tension and compression are elastic forces, which means they are dependent on elasticity, the ability of an object to return to its original shape after being stretched or compressed. If an object is not very elastic, it breaks easily or becomes permanently deformed when subjected to an elastic force. The cables and towers of the Golden Gate Bridge are made of steel, a material with great elastic strength. A single steel wire 2.54 mm thick can support over half a ton without breaking!

On the Road

The roadway of the Golden Gate Bridge is subjected to multiple forces at the same time, including friction, gravity, and elastic forces. Rolling friction is caused by the wheels of each vehicle moving across the roadway's surface. Gravity pulls down on the roadway but is counteracted by the support of the towers and cables. This causes each roadway span to bend slightly and experience both tension and compression. The bottom of each span is under tension because the cables and towers pull up along the road's sides, while gravity pulls down at its center. These same forces cause compression of the top of each span. Did you ever imagine that so many forces were at work on a bridge?

Bridge the Gap

▶ Find out more about another type of bridge, such as an arch, a beam, or a cable-stayed bridge. How do forces such as friction, gravity, tension, and compression affect these types of bridges?

33

Teaching Strategies

Build a people bridge. Students lean toward each other with palms touching. Have them move their feet back until they can't back up without falling. Where do they feel tension and compression? How about friction and gravity? Repeat the exercise with students facing each other and standing with their feet close to their partner's. Have them then hold hands and lean back.

internetconnect

SCiLINKS
NSTA

TOPIC: The Science of Bridges
GO TO: www.scilinks.org
sciLINKS NUMBER: HSTP125

Background

- The Golden Gate Bridge took 4 years to build and was completed in 1937. It was the longest suspension bridge (1,280 m) in the world for 27 years.

- 128,720 km of wire was used to create each main cable. Each cable contains 27,572 wires bundled into 61 strands and will support a mass of 90,718,000 kg.

- The longest suspension bridge, the Akashi Kaikyo Bridge, opened in Japan in 1998 with a center span of 1,990 m.

Answers to Bridge the Gap

All of the bridge types are affected by gravity. All the bridges are exposed to rolling friction from vehicles traveling across them.

- Arch: The weight of an arch bridge is carried out along the arch to the abutments at each end. When supporting its own weight and the weight of traffic, the entire arch is under compression.

- Beam: A beam bridge is a horizontal beam supported by piers at each end. The beam's weight pushes straight down, placing the bottom of the beam under tension and the top under compression. The strength of a beam bridge decreases with length.

- Cable-stayed: A cable-stayed bridge hangs the roadway from cables that extend from single towers to the deck. No cable anchorage is used, so the towers in compression bear the entire load from the cables, which are in tension.

Chapter Organizer

CHAPTER ORGANIZATION	TIME MINUTES	OBJECTIVES	LABS, INVESTIGATIONS, AND DEMONSTRATIONS
Chapter Opener pp. 34–35	45	National Standards: SAI 1, SPSP 5	**Start-Up Activity,** Falling Water, p. 35
Section 1 Gravity and Motion	90	▶ Explain how gravity and air resistance affect the acceleration of falling objects. ▶ Explain why objects in orbit appear to be weightless. ▶ Describe how an orbit is formed. ▶ Describe projectile motion. UCP 3, ST 1, HNS 1; Labs: SAI 1	**QuickLab,** Penny Projectile Motion, p. 42 **Interactive Explorations CD-ROM,** Extreme Skiing A ***Worksheet*** is also available in the ***Interactive Explorations Teacher's Edition.*** **Discovery Lab,** A Marshmallow Catapult, p. 188 **Datasheets for LabBook,** A Marshmallow Catapult **Calculator-Based Labs,** Falling Objects **Inquiry Labs,** On the Fast Track
Section 2 Newton's Laws of Motion	135	▶ State and apply Newton's laws of motion. ▶ Compare the momentum of different objects. ▶ State and apply the law of conservation of momentum. UCP 3, 4, SAI 1, 2, PS 2b, 2c; Labs: SAI 1, PS 2b, 2c	**Demonstration,** Egg in a Buggy, p. 43 in ATE **QuickLab,** First-Law Magic, p. 45 **Making Models,** Blast Off! p. 189 **Datasheets for LabBook,** Blast Off! **Skill Builder,** Inertia-Rama! p. 52 **Datasheets for LabBook,** Inertia-Rama! **Skill Builder,** Quite a Reaction, p. 190 **Datasheets for LabBook,** Quite a Reaction **Whiz-Bang Demonstrations,** Newton's Eggciting Experiment **Whiz-Bang Demonstrations,** Inertia Can Hurt Ya **Whiz-Bang Demonstrations,** Fountain of Knowledge **Long-Term Projects & Research Ideas,** Any Color You Want, so Long as It's Black

*See page **T23** for a complete correlation of this book with the*

NATIONAL SCIENCE EDUCATION STANDARDS.

TECHNOLOGY RESOURCES

 Guided Reading Audio CD
English or Spanish, Chapter 2

 Science Discovery Videodiscs
Science Sleuths: A Day at the Races

 CNN. Scientists in Action, Force in the Circus, Segment 8

 Interactive Explorations CD-ROM
CD 2, Exploration 5, Extreme Skiing

 One-Stop Planner CD-ROM with Test Generator

CLASSROOM WORKSHEETS, TRANSPARENCIES, AND RESOURCES	SCIENCE INTEGRATION AND CONNECTIONS	REVIEW AND ASSESSMENT
Directed Reading Worksheet **Science Puzzlers, Twisters, & Teasers**		
Directed Reading Worksheet, Section 1 **Math Skills for Science Worksheet,** Arithmetic with Decimals **Transparency 222,** Falling Objects Accelerate at a Constant Rate **Transparency 162,** Profile of the Earth's Atmosphere **Transparency 223,** Two Motions Combine to Form Projectile Motion **Reinforcement Worksheet,** Falling Fast	**MathBreak,** Velocity of Falling Objects, p. 37 **Math and More,** p. 37 in ATE **Cross-Disciplinary Focus,** p. 38 in ATE **Connect to Earth Science,** p. 38 in ATE **Multicultural Connection,** p. 40 in ATE **Connect to Life Science,** p. 41 in ATE **Eureka!** A Bat with Dimples, p. 58 **Careers:** Roller Coaster Designer– Steve Okamoto, p. 59	**Self-Check,** p. 38 **Quiz,** p. 41 in ATE **Section Review,** p. 42 **Alternative Assessment,** p. 42 in ATE
Directed Reading Worksheet, Section 2 **Math Skills for Science Worksheet,** Newton: Force and Motion **Transparency 224,** Newton's Second Law and Acceleration Due to Gravity **Critical Thinking Worksheet,** Forces to Reckon With **Math Skills for Science Worksheet,** Momentum	**Cross-Disciplinary Focus,** p. 43 in ATE **Apply,** p. 44 **Real-World Connection,** p. 44 in ATE **Environment Connection,** p. 46 **MathBreak,** Second-Law Problems, p. 47 **Math and More,** p. 47 in ATE **Connect to Life Science,** p. 48 in ATE **Real-World Connection,** p. 49 in ATE **Multicultural Connection,** p. 49 in ATE	**Self-Check,** p. 45 **Section Review,** p. 47 **Homework,** pp. 49, 50 in ATE **Section Review,** p. 51 **Quiz,** p. 51 in ATE **Alternative Assessment,** p. 51 in ATE

internet connect

go.hrw.com
Holt, Rinehart and Winston On-line Resources
go.hrw.com

For worksheets and other teaching aids related to this chapter, visit the HRW Web site and type in the keyword: **HSTFOR**

SCILINKS
NSTA
National Science Teachers Association
www.scilinks.org

Encourage students to use the *sci*LINKS numbers listed in the internet connect boxes to access information and resources on the **NSTA** Web site.

END-OF-CHAPTER REVIEW AND ASSESSMENT

Chapter Review in Study Guide
Vocabulary and Notes in Study Guide
Chapter Tests with Performance-Based Assessment, Chapter 2 Test
Chapter Tests with Performance-Based Assessment, Performance-Based Assessment 2
Concept Mapping Transparency 6

Chapter Resources & Worksheets

Visual Resources

TEACHING TRANSPARENCIES

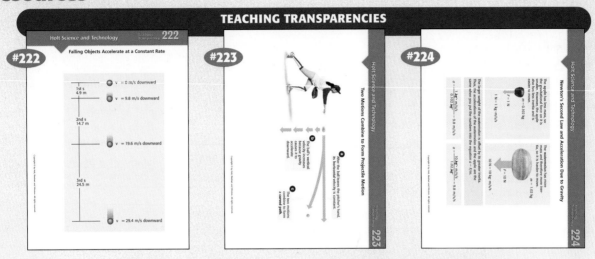

#222
Holt Science and Technology · Teaching Transparency 222
Falling Objects Accelerate at a Constant Rate

#223
Holt Science and Technology
Two Motions Combine to Form Projectile Motion

#224
Holt Science and Technology
Newton's Second Law and Acceleration Due to Gravity

TEACHING TRANSPARENCIES

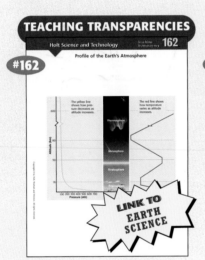

#162
Holt Science and Technology · Teaching Transparency 162
Profile of the Earth's Atmosphere

LINK TO EARTH SCIENCE

CONCEPT MAPPING TRANSPARENCY

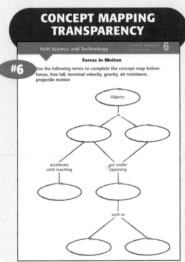

#6
Holt Science and Technology · Concept Mapping Transparency 6
Forces in Motion

Use the following terms to complete the concept map below:
forces, free fall, terminal velocity, gravity, air resistance, projectile motion

Meeting Individual Needs

DIRECTED READING

#2
DIRECTED READING WORKSHEET
Forces in Motion

Chapter Introduction

As you begin this chapter, answer the following.

1. Read the title of the chapter. List three things that you already know about this subject.

2. Write two questions about this subject that you would like answered by the time you finish this chapter.

3. How does the title of the Start-Up Activity relate to the subject of the chapter?

Section 1: Gravity and Motion (p. 36)

4. Do you agree with what Aristotle might say, that the baseball would land first, then the marble? Explain.

REINFORCEMENT & VOCABULARY REVIEW

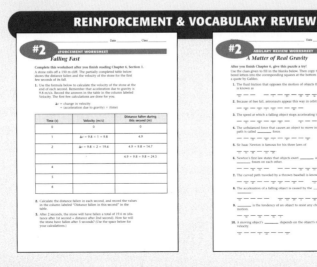

#2
REINFORCEMENT WORKSHEET
Falling Fast

Complete this worksheet after you finish reading Chapter 6, Section 1.

A stone rolls off a 150 m cliff. The partially completed table below shows the distance fallen and the velocity of the stone for the first few seconds of its fall.

1. Use the formula below to calculate the velocity of the stone at the end of each second. Remember that acceleration due to gravity is 9.8 m/s. Record the answers in the table in the column labeled Velocity. The first few calculations are done for you.

Δv = change in velocity
= (acceleration due to gravity) × (time)

Time (s)	Velocity (m/s)	Distance fallen during this second (m)
0	0	0
1	$\Delta v = 9.8 \times 1 = 9.8$	4.9
2	$\Delta v = 9.8 \times 2 = 19.6$	$4.9 + 9.8 = 14.7$
		$4.9 + 9.8 + 9.8 = 24.5$
4		
5		
6		

2. Calculate the distance fallen in each second, and record the values in the column labeled "Distance fallen in this second" in the table.

3. After 2 seconds, the stone will have fallen a total of 19.6 m (distance after 1st second + distance after 2nd second). How far will the stone have fallen after 3 seconds? (Use the space below for your calculations.)

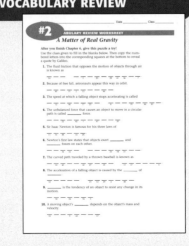

#2
VOCABULARY REVIEW WORKSHEET
A Matter of Real Gravity

After you finish Chapter 6, give this puzzle a try!

Use the clues given to fill in the blanks below. Then copy the numbered letters into the corresponding squares at the bottom to reveal a quote by Galileo.

1. The fluid friction that opposes the motion of objects through air is known as

2. Because of free fall, astronauts appear this way in orbit.

3. The speed at which a falling object stops accelerating is called

4. The unbalanced force that causes an object to move in a circular path is called _____ force.

5. Sir Isaac Newton is famous for his three laws of

6. Newton's first law states that objects exert _____ and _____ forces on each other.

7. The curved path traveled by a thrown baseball is known as

8. The acceleration of a falling object is caused by the _____ of

9. _____ is the tendency of an object to resist any change in its motion.

10. A moving object's _____ depends on the object's mass and velocity.

SCIENCE PUZZLERS, TWISTERS & TEASERS

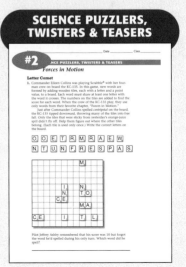

#2
SCIENCE PUZZLERS, TWISTERS & TEASERS
Forces in Motion

Letter Comet

1. Commander Eileen Collins was playing Scrabble® with her four-man crew on board the KC-135. In this game, new words are formed by adding wooden tiles, each with a letter and a point value, to a board. Each word must share at least one letter with the word it crosses. The numbers on the tiles are added to find the score for each word. When the crew of the KC-135 play, they use only words from their favorite chapter, "Forces in Motion."

   Just after Commander Collins spelled *centripetal* on the board, the KC-135 tipped downward, throwing many of the tiles into free fall. Only the tiles that were sticky from yesterday's orange-juice spill didn't fly off. Help them figure out where the other tiles belong. (Each tile is used only once.) Write the correct letters on the board.

   O O E T R M R A E W
   N T U N F R E S P A S

Pilot Jeffrey Ashby remembered that his score was 10 but forgot the word he'd spelled during his only turn. Which word did he spell?

Chapter 2 • Forces in Motion

Review & Assessment

STUDY GUIDE

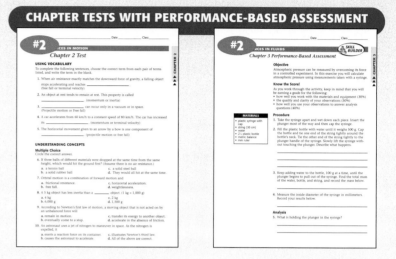

CHAPTER TESTS WITH PERFORMANCE-BASED ASSESSMENT

Lab Worksheets

INQUIRY LABS

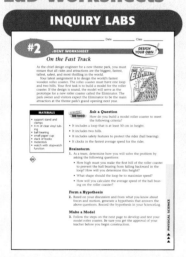

WHIZ-BANG DEMONSTRATIONS

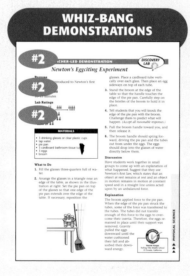

LONG-TERM PROJECTS & RESEARCH IDEAS

DATASHEETS FOR LABBOOK

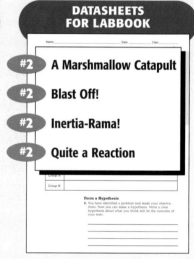

#2 A Marshmallow Catapult

#2 Blast Off!

#2 Inertia-Rama!

#2 Quite a Reaction

Applications & Extensions

CRITICAL THINKING & PROBLEM SOLVING

SCIENTISTS IN ACTION

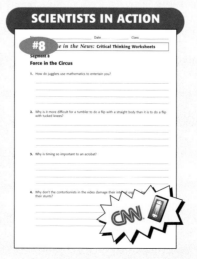

INTERACTIVE EXPLORATIONS

Chapter Background

SECTION 1

Gravity and Motion

▶ **Space Shuttles and Sky Divers**
What does the space shuttle have in common with a sky diver? What does a jumping frog have in common with a 42 m/s fastball? They are all affected by gravity, and their flights are governed by certain laws of motion. Although some observers in ancient China theorized about objects in motion and objects at rest, Sir Isaac Newton is usually given credit for stating and testing the three basic laws that describe and predict motion.

▶ **The Apple and the Moon**
Galileo's theory that all objects fall with the same acceleration in a vacuum has been verified on Earth many times. It wasn't the same old proof, though, on July 30, 1971, when astronaut David Randolph Scott stood on the surface of the moon and dropped a feather and a hammer simultaneously. Just as Galileo had predicted, in the absence of air resistance, the feather hit the ground at the same time as the hammer.

- Sir Isaac Newton is said to have realized the importance of gravitational force in 1666, when he watched an apple fall from a tree in his garden. One of Newton's contemporaries said, "It came into his thought that the power of gravity (which brought the apple from the tree to the ground) was not limited to a certain distance from the Earth, but that this power must extend much further than is usually thought. Why not as high as the moon, he said to himself, and if so that must influence her motion. Whereupon he fell a-calculating what would be the effect."

- Newton calculated the acceleration of the moon in a circular orbit around Earth and compared this with an apple's downward acceleration. He found that the accelerations were the same. He concluded that the orbital motion of the moon and the fall of the apple were the results of the same force.

▶ **Parachutes**
Older parachutes without holes trapped air in the canopy as they fell. These parachutes were difficult to control. As the air escaped, the parachute rocked back and forth, and many parachutists would get airsick. Modern parachutes are shaped like a wing and have holes or slits that the jumper can open and close. Today, a parachutist can steer a parachute to within a few meters of a desired spot and, by controlling the rate of descent, can land as gently as walking down stairs.

IS THAT A FACT!

- ➤ Galileo timed the motion of balls rolling down an inclined plane to prove that all objects fall at the same rate.

Newton's Laws of Motion

▶ Sir Isaac Newton (1642–1727)

In 1661, Isaac Newton went to study at Cambridge University. But Newton made many of his most important discoveries while spending time at the family home, Woolsthorpe Manor, near Grantham, in Lincolnshire, England, in 1665 and 1666.

▶ *Principia*

Newton's *Principia*, published in 1687, explains the three basic laws that govern the way objects move and Newton's theory of gravity. Newton explained how the force of gravity keeps the planets moving around the sun. Interestingly, Newton used his laws to predict that Earth must be a slightly flattened sphere and that comets orbit the sun in elongated elliptical paths. These predictions were later shown to be true.

▶ Friction

You may want to refer students back to Chapter 1 for a review of friction.

- How is simple friction different from air resistance? Simple friction depends only on the nature of the surfaces that are interacting with each other. Air resistance depends on both that kind of friction and on the amount of air that must be moved out of the way each second.

- How do parachutes work to increase air resistance? The parachute provides a larger surface area to pull through the air. This in turn requires that a much larger amount of air be moved out of the way each second as the parachute falls toward the Earth.

IS THAT A FACT!

➥ When a heavy steel wrecking ball is swung on a cable, it has a very large momentum. When the ball collides with a brick wall, the momentum of the ball is transferred to the wall. The wall starts to move and the cement between the bricks is torn apart. Because the individual bricks have relatively small masses, they are knocked away.

▶ Terminal Velocity

Air resistance, a type of friction, limits the velocity of an object as it falls to the Earth. As long as a falling object is somewhat streamlined and has not accelerated to high velocity, its acceleration due to gravity is a constant 9.8 m/s^2 until it reaches the Earth.

- But as the falling object speeds up, fluid friction increases as a result of turbulent flow. More and more air must be pushed out of the way each second. Eventually, the force of the air pushing upward on the falling object is equal to Earth's gravitational force pulling downward on the falling object.

- When the upward and downward forces are equal, the net force on the falling object is zero. With a zero net force, the object falls at constant velocity.

For background information about teaching strategies and issues, refer to the *Professional Reference for Teachers*.

Pre-Reading Questions

Students may not know the answers to these questions before reading the chapter, so accept any reasonable response.

Suggested Answers

1. The force of gravity causes all objects to fall toward the ground with the same acceleration, 9.8 m/s/s.

2. Projectile motion is the curved path an object follows when it is thrown or propelled near the surface of the Earth. Good examples are a leaping frog or a pass in a football game.

3. Newton's three laws of motion are physical laws that explain the relationship between forces and the motion of objects. For complete statements of Newton's laws, refer to the explanations on pages 43, 46, and 48.

4. Momentum is a property of a moving object that is related to the object's mass and velocity. The more momentum an object has, the harder it is to stop the object or change its direction.

Sections

Pre-Reading Questions

1. How does the force of gravity affect falling objects?
2. What is projectile motion?
3. What are Newton's laws of motion?
4. What is momentum?

34

VOMIT COMET

Have you ever wondered what it would be like to move around without gravity? To help train astronauts for space flight, scientists have designed a special airplane called the KC-135 that simulates what it feels like to move with reduced gravity. The KC-135 first flies upward at a steep angle. When the airplane flies downward at a 45° angle, the effect of reduced gravity is produced inside. Then, the astronaut trainees in the plane can "float." Because the floating often makes passengers queasy, the KC-135 has earned a nickname—the Vomit Comet. In this chapter, you will learn how gravity affects the motion of objects and how the laws of motion apply to your life.

---

internet connect

HRW On-line Resources

go.hrw.com

For worksheets and other teaching aids, visit the HRW Web site and type in the keyword: **HSTFOR**

SCI LINKS
NSTA

www.scilinks.com

Use the *sci*LINKS numbers at the end of each chapter for additional resources on the **NSTA** Web site.

Smithsonian Institution

www.si.edu/hrw

Visit the Smithsonian Institution Web site for related on-line resources.

CNNfyi.com

www.cnnfyi.com

Visit the CNN Web site for current events coverage and classroom resources.

FALLING WATER

Gravity is one of the most important forces in your life. In this activity, you will observe the effect of gravity on a falling object.

Procedure

1. Place a **wide plastic tub** on the floor. Punch a small hole in the side of a **paper cup,** near the bottom.

2. Hold your finger over the hole, and fill the cup with **water.** Keeping your finger over the hole, hold the cup about waist high above the tub.

3. Uncover the hole. Describe your observations in your ScienceLog.

4. Next, predict what will happen to the water if you drop the cup at the same time you uncover the hole. Write your prediction in your ScienceLog.

5. Cover the hole with your finger again, and refill the cup.

6. Uncover the hole, and drop the cup at the same time. Record your observations.

7. Clean up any spilled water with **paper towels.**

Analysis

8. What differences did you observe in the behavior of the water during the two trials?

9. In the second trial, how fast did the cup fall compared with the water?

35

START-UP
Activity

FALLING WATER

MATERIALS

FOR EACH GROUP:
- wide plastic tub
- paper cup
- water
- paper towels

Teacher's Notes

Food coloring may be added to the water so that students will see the water better. Furthermore, the activity can be done outdoors to minimize cleanup.

To reduce the mess, have students fill the cups only half full. Spread plenty of newspapers on the floor.

Answers to START-UP Activity

8. In the first trial, students should see the water coming out of the hole and falling to the ground. In the second trial, they should not see any water coming out of the hole as the cup falls.

9. The cup and the water fall at the same rate. Students may not know that both are accelerating, and students may say that both fell at the same velocity, or speed. This answer is acceptable at this point.

Focus

Gravity and Motion

In this section students explore how gravity and air resistance affect falling objects. Students learn how an orbit is formed and why objects in orbit appear to be weightless. Finally, they explore the relationship between gravity and projectile motion.

🔊 Bellringer

Warner Brothers cartoon character Wile E. Coyote often finds himself falling off a cliff. Then a giant boulder lands on top of him after he hits the ground. Before students read the first section, have them answer the following question:

If Wile E. Coyote and a boulder fall off a cliff at the same time, which do you think will hit the ground first?

Write your predictions in your ScienceLog.

1 Motivate

ACTIVITY

You will need a 12 in. softball, a women's size shot, a sturdy table to stand on, and a board or pad to protect the floor. First, show students the softball and the shot. Discuss their similar size but different masses. Then stand on top of the table. Tell students that you will drop both objects from the same height. As you hold both objects at arm's length, have them predict which will hit first. Discuss and question their predictions. Now drop both objects *at the same time*. Ask students for their observations; repeat as necessary.

Terms to Learn

terminal velocity
free fall
projectile motion

What You'll Do

◆ Explain how gravity and air resistance affect the acceleration of falling objects.
◆ Explain why objects in orbit appear to be weightless.
◆ Describe how an orbit is formed.
◆ Describe projectile motion.

Force — a push or a pull
force has size & direction

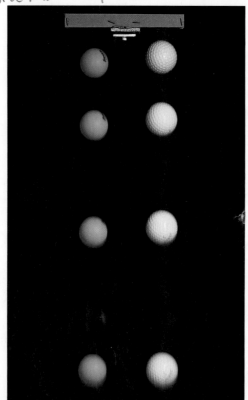

Figure 1 *A table tennis ball and a golf ball fall with the same acceleration even though they have different masses.*

Gravity and Motion

Suppose you drop a baseball and a marble at the same time from the same height. Which do you think would land first? In ancient Greece around 400 B.C., an important philosopher named Aristotle (ER is TAWT uhl) believed that the rate at which an object falls depends on the object's mass. Imagine that you could ask Aristotle which object would land first. He would predict that the baseball would land first.

All Objects Fall with the Same Acceleration

In the late 1500s, a young Italian scientist named Galileo questioned Aristotle's idea about falling objects. Galileo proved that the mass of an object does not affect the rate at which it falls. According to one story, Galileo did this by dropping two cannonballs of different masses from the top of the Leaning Tower of Pisa. The crowd watching from the ground was amazed to see the two cannonballs land at the same time. Whether or not this story is true, Galileo's idea changed people's understanding of gravity and falling objects.

Acceleration Due to Gravity Objects fall to the ground at the same rate because the acceleration due to gravity is the same for all objects. Does that seem odd? The force of gravity is greater between Earth and an object with a large mass than between Earth and a less massive object, so you may think that the acceleration due to gravity should be greater too. But a greater force must be applied to a large mass than to a small mass to produce the same acceleration. Thus, the difference in force is canceled by the difference in mass. **Figure 1** shows objects with different masses falling with the same acceleration.

SCIENTISTS AT ODDS

When Galileo attended the University of Pisa in the 1500s, scholars generally accepted Aristotle's theory that bodies fall to Earth at different velocities depending on their mass. Galileo questioned Aristotle's teachings after observing different-sized hailstones hitting the ground at the same time.

 **SCIENCE**

If a penny fell from the top of the Empire State Building (about 385 m), it would be traveling with enough velocity to dent almost anything it struck at ground level.

Accelerating at a Constant Rate All objects accelerate toward Earth at a rate of 9.8 meters per second per second, which is expressed as 9.8 m/s/s. This means that for every second that an object falls, the object's downward velocity increases by 9.8 m/s, as shown in **Figure 2**. Remember, this acceleration is the same for all objects regardless of their mass. Do the MathBreak at right to learn how to calculate the velocity of a falling object.

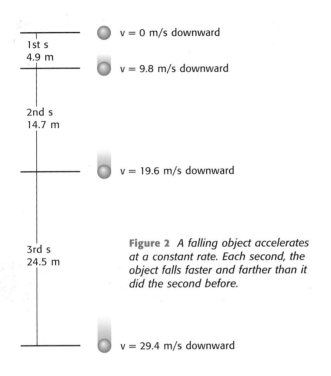

1st s
4.9 m
— v = 0 m/s downward

— v = 9.8 m/s downward

2nd s
14.7 m

— v = 19.6 m/s downward

3rd s
24.5 m

Figure 2 *A falling object accelerates at a constant rate. Each second, the object falls faster and farther than it did the second before.*

— v = 29.4 m/s downward

÷ 5 ÷ Ω ∞ +Ω √ 9 ∞≤ Σ 2
+ ÷ ≤

MATH **BREAK**

Velocity of Falling Objects

To find the change in velocity (Δv) of a falling object, multiply the acceleration due to gravity (g) by the time it takes for the object to fall in seconds (t):

$$\Delta v = g \times t$$

For example, a stone at rest is dropped from a cliff, and it takes 3 seconds to hit the ground. Its downward velocity when it hits the ground is as follows:

$$\Delta v = 9.8 \; \frac{m/s}{\cancel{s}} \times 3 \; \cancel{s}$$
$$= 29.4 \; m/s$$

Now It's Your Turn

A penny at rest is dropped from the top of a tall stairwell.

1. What is the penny's velocity after it has fallen for 2 seconds?

2. The penny hits the ground in 4.5 seconds. What is its final velocity?

Air Resistance Slows Down Acceleration

Try this simple experiment. Drop two sheets of paper—one crumpled in a tight ball and the other kept flat. Did your results contradict what you just learned about falling objects? The flat paper fell more slowly because of fluid friction that opposes the motion of objects through air. This fluid friction is also known as *air resistance*. Air resistance occurs between the surface of the falling object and the air that surrounds it.

Gravity helps make roller coasters thrilling to ride. Read about a roller coaster designer on page 59.

37

IS THAT A FACT!

Air resistance is a result of the fluid friction between the falling object and the air and also the inertia of the particles of the air. The air particles have to "move out of the way" of the falling object. Because the particles have mass, they also have inertia that resists movement.

 Teaching Transparency 222 "Falling Objects Accelerate at a Constant Rate"

 Directed Reading Worksheet Section 1

2 Teach

USING THE FIGURE

Draw students' attention to **Figures 1** and **2**. Be sure students understand that objects falling vertically do not fall at a constant speed but constantly accelerate. Have students note how the distance between the position of each ball increases with time as the ball falls. Point out that although the strobe images were photographed at equal intervals, each of the balls moves faster and travels a greater distance during each interval.

Answers to MATHBREAK

1. $9.8 \; \frac{m/s}{\cancel{s}} \times 2 \; \cancel{s} = 19.6 \; m/s$

2. $9.8 \; \frac{m/s}{\cancel{s}} \times 4.5 \; \cancel{s} = 44.1 \; m/s$

MATH and **MORE**

Have students do the following problems for additional practice:

1. A boy standing on a high cliff dives into the ocean below and strikes the water after 3 seconds. What is the boy's velocity when he hits the water? (29.4 m/s)

2. A rocks falls from a high cliff and hits the ground in 6.5 seconds. What is its final velocity? (63.7 m/s)

3. A brick falls from the top of a building and strikes the ground with a velocity of 19.6 m/s. How long does the brick fall? (2 seconds)

 Math Skills Worksheet "Arithmetic with Decimals"

Prediction Guide Before students read pages 38 and 39, ask them to explain whether a school bus or a racing car would be affected less by air resistance. (a racing car, because a racing car is built low to the ground, with smooth lines to reduce air resistance)

Answer to Self-Check

A leaf is more affected by air resistance.

CROSS-DISCIPLINARY FOCUS

History The first recorded parachute jump was completed by André-Jacques Garnerin near Paris, France, in 1797. Garnerin, a hot-air balloon pilot, was demonstrating his balloon as part of a traveling show. The balloon rose to about 700 m when it burst. As the gondola fell, many of the people in the crowd turned their heads so they would not see Garnerin fall to his death. Much to their surprise, Garnerin did not fall because he was in the balloon gondola, which floated safely to the ground under his makeshift parachute.

CONNECT TO
EARTH SCIENCE

Use the Teaching Transparency "Profile of the Earth's Atmosphere" to discuss how air resistance changes as one goes higher in the atmosphere.

Teaching Transparency 162 "Profile of the Earth's Atmosphere" LINK TO EARTH SCIENCE

✔ Self-Check

Which is more affected by air resistance—a leaf or an acorn? (See page 232 to check your answer.)

Figure 3 *The force of gravity pulls the object downward as the force of air resistance pushes it upward.*

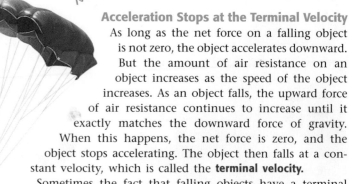

NO

This arrow represents **the force of air resistance** pushing up on the object. This force is subtracted from the force of gravity to produce the net force.

This arrow represents **the net force** on the object. Because the net force is not zero, the object still accelerates downward, but not as fast as it would without air resistance.

This arrow represents **the force of gravity** on the object. If this were the only force acting on the object, it would accelerate at a rate of 9.8 m/s/s.

NO

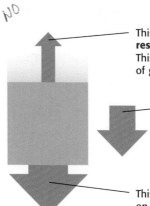

Figure 4
The parachute increases the air resistance of this sky diver, slowing him to a safe terminal velocity.

Air Resistance Affects Some Objects More than Others

The amount of air resistance acting on an object depends on the size and shape of the object. Air resistance affects the flat sheet of paper more than the crumpled one, causing the flat sheet to fall more slowly than the crumpled one. Because air is all around you, any falling object you see is affected by air resistance. **Figure 3** shows the effect of air resistance on the downward acceleration of a falling object.

Acceleration Stops at the Terminal Velocity

As long as the net force on a falling object is not zero, the object accelerates downward. But the amount of air resistance on an object increases as the speed of the object increases. As an object falls, the upward force of air resistance continues to increase until it exactly matches the downward force of gravity. When this happens, the net force is zero, and the object stops accelerating. The object then falls at a constant velocity, which is called the **terminal velocity.**

Sometimes the fact that falling objects have a terminal velocity is a good thing. The terminal velocity of hailstones is between 5 and 40 m/s, depending on the size of the stones. Every year cars, buildings, and vegetation are all severely damaged in hail storms. Imagine how much more destructive hail would be if there were no air resistance—hailstones would hit the Earth at velocities near 350 m/s! **Figure 4** shows another situation in which terminal velocity is helpful.

Skydiving DISCOVERY Force & motion Part 2 3 min

🤓 SCIENCE HUMOR

When asked why he wasn't interested in being a paratrooper, an Army pilot said, "I will never understand why anyone would want to jump out of a perfectly good airplane." Ask students if they share the pilot's opinion or if they might enjoy sky diving.

Free Fall Occurs When There Is No Air Resistance Sky divers are often described as being in free fall before they open their parachutes. However, that is an incorrect description, because air resistance is always acting on the sky diver.

An object is in **free fall** only if gravity is pulling it down and no other forces are acting on it. Because air resistance is a force (fluid friction), free fall can occur only where there is no air—in a vacuum (a place in which there is no matter) or in space. **Figure 5** shows objects falling in a vacuum. Because there is no air resistance, the two objects are in free fall.

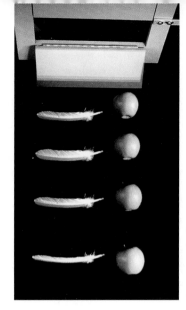

Same as pic in room

Figure 5 *Air resistance normally causes a feather to fall more slowly than an apple. But in a vacuum, the feather and the apple fall with the same acceleration because both are in free fall.*

Orbiting Objects Are in Free Fall

Read this

Show Newton in Space

Look at the astronaut in **Figure 6.** Why is the astronaut floating inside the space shuttle? It might be tempting to say it is because she is "weightless" in space. In fact, you may have read or heard that objects are weightless in space. However, it is impossible to be weightless anywhere in the universe.

Weight is a measure of gravitational force. The size of the force depends on the masses of objects and the distances between them. If you traveled in space far away from all the stars and planets, the gravitational force acting on you would be almost undetectable because the distance between you and other objects would be great. But you would still have mass, and so would all the other objects in the universe. Therefore, gravity would still attract you to other objects—even if just slightly— so you would still have weight.

False #14 DIR. READ.

Astronauts "float" in orbiting spaceships because of free fall. To understand this better, you need to understand what *orbiting* means and then consider the astronauts inside the ship.

Figure 6 *Astronauts appear to be weightless while floating inside the space shuttle—but they're not!*

39

internet connect

SCILINKS
NSTA

TOPIC: The Force of Gravity
GO TO: www.scilinks.org
sciLINKS NUMBER: HSTP130

DISCUSSION

Concept Mapping Ask students what problems they might encounter if they tried to sky dive on the moon. (The absence of an atmosphere would mean no air resistance to slow a parachute. But they would still fall because the moon does have gravity.)

Have students create a concept map showing the difference between sky diving on Earth and sky diving on the moon.

✷ USING THE FIGURE

The strobe photo in **Figure 5** shows a feather and an apple falling in a vacuum. Students may notice that the feather appears to be falling slower. In the top image, the feather is lined up with the bottom of the apple. In the bottom image, the feather is lined up with the top of the apple. Explain that it is very difficult to create a total vacuum—especially one that is large enough to allow a feather and apple to fall side by side. Although the feather and the apple are not in a total vacuum, the photo shows that their accelerations in a partial vacuum are nearly equal. Sheltered English

MEETING INDIVIDUAL NEEDS

Learners Having Difficulty
Review with students what a vacuum is (a space with no matter). Point out that the partial vacuum in which the feather and apple were placed has almost no air left in it. Therefore, the feather cannot be affected very much by air resistance and will fall with almost the same acceleration as the apple. Sheltered English

The shuttle in **Figure 7** is shown in orbit facing forward and oriented right side up (called "airplane mode"). In orbit, the shuttle spends most of the time upside down and backward. It also orbits upside down and sideways (wing first), but it rarely orbits in airplane mode. It is only in airplane mode for landings.

USING THE FIGURE

Draw students' attention to **Figure 7.** Ask students why the shuttle does not fall to Earth if gravity is pulling downward on it. (The forward motion of the shuttle occurs together with free fall to produce a path that follows the curve of Earth's surface.)

Ask what would happen if the shuttle started moving much faster or much slower. (If the shuttle moved fast enough, it would escape Earth's gravitational force and move forward, off into space. If the shuttle moved more slowly, it would begin to fall toward Earth. This is exactly what it does on reentry.)

Multicultural CONNECTION

On September 12, 1992, Dr. Mae Jemison became the first African-American woman to orbit Earth on the space shuttle *Endeavor.* Dr. Jemison, who has degrees in chemical engineering and medicine, was in charge of many of the experiments conducted during the mission.

Two Motions Combine to Cause Orbiting An object is said to be orbiting when it is traveling in a circular or nearly circular path around another object. When a spaceship orbits Earth, it is moving forward, but it is also in free fall toward Earth. **Figure 7** shows how these two motions occur together to cause orbiting.

Figure 7 How an Orbit Is Formed

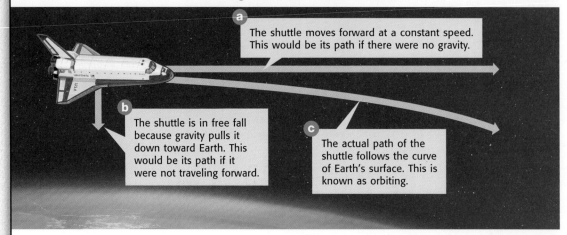

a The shuttle moves forward at a constant speed. This would be its path if there were no gravity.

b The shuttle is in free fall because gravity pulls it down toward Earth. This would be its path if it were not traveling forward.

c The actual path of the shuttle follows the curve of Earth's surface. This is known as orbiting.

As you can see in the illustration above, the space shuttle is always falling while it is in orbit. So why don't astronauts hit their heads on the ceiling of the falling shuttle? Because they are also in free fall—they are always falling, too. Because the astronaut in Figure 6 is in free fall, she appears to be floating.

The Role of Gravity in Orbiting Besides spaceships and satellites, many other objects in the universe are in orbit. The moon orbits the Earth, Earth and the other planets orbit the sun, and many stars orbit large masses in the center of galaxies. All of these objects are traveling in a circular or nearly circular path. Remember, any object in circular motion is constantly changing direction. Because an unbalanced force is necessary to change the motion of any object, there must be an unbalanced force working on any object in circular motion.

The unbalanced force that causes objects to move in a circular path is called a *centripetal force.* Gravity provides the centripetal force that keeps objects in orbit. The word *centripetal* means "toward the center." As you can see in **Figure 8,** the centripetal force on the moon points toward the center of the circle traced by the moon's orbit.

Path of moon

Centripetal force on the moon

Figure 8 *The moon stays in orbit around the Earth because Earth's gravitational force provides a centripetal force on the moon.*

40

internet**connect**

SCiLINKS NSTA

TOPIC: Gravity and Orbiting Objects
GO TO: www.scilinks.org
*sci*LINKS NUMBER: HSTP135

IS THAT A FACT!

In the text, the definition of an orbit is somewhat simplified. All orbits are ellipses. However, some orbits are ellipses that are *not* nearly circular. The orbits of comets around the sun are very eccentric (very oblong), but they are still elliptical.

Projectile Motion and Gravity

The orbit of the space shuttle around the Earth is an example of projectile (proh JEK tuhl) motion. **Projectile motion** is the curved path an object follows when thrown or propelled near the surface of the Earth. The motions of leaping dancers, thrown balls, hopping grasshoppers, and arrows shot from a bow are all examples of projectile motion. Projectile motion has two components—horizontal and vertical. The two components are independent; that is, they have no effect on each other. When the two motions are combined, they form a curved path, as shown in **Figure 9.**

define projectile: an object ....

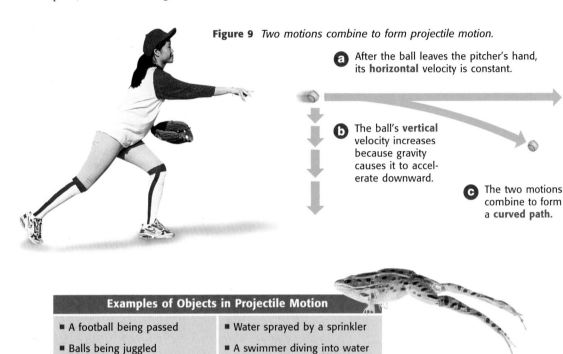

Figure 9 *Two motions combine to form projectile motion.*

a After the ball leaves the pitcher's hand, its **horizontal** velocity is constant.

b The ball's **vertical** velocity increases because gravity causes it to accelerate downward.

c The two motions combine to form a **curved path.**

Examples of Objects in Projectile Motion	
■ A football being passed	■ Water sprayed by a sprinkler
■ Balls being juggled	■ A swimmer diving into water
■ An athlete doing a high jump	■ A leaping frog

Horizontal Motion   When you throw a ball, your hand exerts a force on the ball that makes the ball move forward. This force gives the ball its horizontal motion. Horizontal motion is motion that is parallel to the ground.

After you let go of the ball, there are no horizontal forces acting on the ball (if you ignore air resistance). Therefore, there are no forces to change the ball's horizontal motion. Thus, the horizontal velocity of the ball is constant after the ball leaves your hand, as shown in Figure 9.

41

3 Extend

RESEARCH

PORTFOLIO   Have students research the effects that prolonged time in microgravity has on the bodies of astronauts and what doctors recommend the astronauts do to counteract these effects. Ask students to make a poster showing the results of their research.

4 Close

Quiz

1. Explain why a ball moves in a straight line as it rolls across a table but follows a curved path once it rolls off the edge of the table. (A ball rolling across the table has only horizontal motion; once the ball rolls off the edge, gravity pulls it downward, giving it both vertical and horizontal motion, which causes a curved path.)

2. Explain why results differ on the moon and on Earth when a hammer and a feather are dropped from the same height at exactly the same time. (On the moon, both will hit the ground at the same time because there is no atmosphere and no air resistance; on Earth, the hammer will hit the ground first because the feather will be slowed much more by air resistance.)

Teaching Transparency 223 "Two Motions Combine to Form Projectile Motion"

4) Close, continued

ALTERNATIVE ASSESSMENT

Making Models Give each group some small, thin plastic trash bags; some string; tape; metal washers; a pair of scissors; and a stopwatch. Have each group design one or more parachutes. Have students use the parachutes to lower a washer slowly from a high point in the room. Challenge the groups to make the parachute that descends the slowest. How does the size and design of a parachute affect its rate of fall?

QuickLab

Make sure students have plenty of room. The penny in projectile motion may travel 1–2 m from its starting point. If the QuickLab is done in a room without a carpet, students can listen for the sound of the pennies hitting the floor.

Answer to QuickLab

3. The penny that was knocked off the table with the ruler was in projectile motion. The pennies should land at the same time because gravity gives both pennies the same acceleration downward. The horizontal motion does not affect the vertical motion.

A Marshmallow Catapult **PG 188**

Reinforcement Worksheet "Falling Fast"

Interactive Explorations CD-ROM "Extreme Skiing"

Penny Projectile Motion

1. Position a **flat ruler** and **two pennies** on a desk or table as shown below.

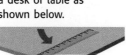

2. Hold the ruler by the end that is on the desk. Move the ruler quickly in the direction shown so that the ruler knocks the penny off the table and so that the other penny also drops. Repeat several times.

3. Which penny travels with projectile motion? In what order do the pennies hit the ground? Record and explain your answers in your ScienceLog.

internetconnect

SC*i*LINKS.
NSTA

TOPIC: The Force of Gravity, Projectile Motion
GO TO: www.scilinks.org
*sci*LINKS **NUMBER:** HSTP130, HSTP140

Vertical Motion After you throw a ball, gravity pulls it downward, giving the ball vertical motion. Vertical motion is motion that is perpendicular to the ground. Because objects in projectile motion accelerate downward, you always have to aim above a target if you want to hit it with a thrown or propelled object. That's why when you aim an arrow directly at a bull's-eye, your arrow strikes the bottom of the target rather than the middle.

Gravity pulls objects in projectile motion down with an acceleration of 9.8 m/s/s (if air resistance is ignored), just as it does all falling objects. **Figure 10** shows that the downward acceleration of a thrown object and a falling object are the same.

Figure 10 Projectile Motion and Acceleration Due to Gravity

The red ball was dropped without a horizontal push.

The yellow ball was given a horizontal push off the ledge and follows projectile motion.

The balls have the same acceleration due to gravity. The horizontal motion of the yellow ball does not affect its vertical motion.

SECTION REVIEW

1. How does air resistance affect the acceleration of falling objects?

2. Explain why an astronaut in an orbiting spaceship floats.

3. How is an orbit formed?

4. **Applying Concepts** Think about a sport you play that involves a ball. Identify at least four different instances in which an object is in projectile motion.

▼ **Answers to Section Review**

1. Air resistance slows or stops acceleration of falling objects.

2. An astronaut on an orbiting spaceship floats because both the astronaut and the spaceship are in free fall. Since both fall at the same rate, the astronaut floats inside. The astronaut has no sensation of falling.

3. An orbit is formed by combining two motions: a forward motion and free fall toward Earth. The path that results is a curve that matches the curve of Earth's surface.

4. Accept all reasonable answers. A basketball example: a player jumping to dunk the ball; a ball passed from one player to another; a ball shot toward the basket; a ball bounced on the floor.

Terms to Learn

inertia   momentum

What You'll Do

◆ State and apply Newton's laws of motion.
◆ Compare the momentum of different objects.
◆ State and apply the law of conservation of momentum.

Newton's Laws of Motion

In 1686, Sir Isaac Newton published his book *Principia*. In it, he described three laws that relate forces to the motion of objects. Although he did not discover all three of the laws, he explained them in a way that helped many people understand them. Thus, the three laws are commonly known as Newton's laws of motion. In this section, you will learn about these laws and how they influence the motion of objects.

Newton's First Law of Motion

An object at rest remains at rest and an object in motion remains in motion at constant speed and in a straight line unless acted on by an unbalanced force.

Newton's first law of motion describes the motion of an object that has a net force of zero acting on it. This law may seem complicated when you first read it, but it's easy to understand when you consider its two parts separately.

Part 1: Objects at Rest What does it mean for an object to be at rest? Objects don't get tired! An object that is not moving is said to be at rest. Objects are at rest all around you. A plane parked on a runway, a chair on the floor, and a golf ball balanced on a tee are all examples of objects at rest.

Newton's first law says that objects at rest will remain at rest unless they are acted on by an unbalanced force. That means that objects will not start moving until a push or a pull is exerted on them. A plane won't soar in the air unless it is pushed by the exhaust from its jet engines, a chair won't slide across the room unless you push it, and a golf ball won't move off the tee unless struck by a golf club, as shown in **Figure 11**.

Figure 11 *A golf ball will remain at rest on a tee until it is acted on by the unbalanced force of a moving club.*

Unbalanced force

Object at rest

Object in motion

43

CROSS-DISCIPLINARY FOCUS

History Long before Newton, others had observed relationships between forces and motion, rest, and acceleration. When Newton extended their work with his three laws of motion, he said,

"If I have seen further, it is by standing on the shoulders of Giants." Newton's genius was that he combined previous discoveries plus his own observations into a unified picture of how the universe worked.

Focus

Newton's Laws of Motion

This section introduces students to Newton's laws of motion. It also presents the concept of momentum and describes applications of the law of conservation of momentum.

Bellringer

Have students respond to the following question:

If you are sitting still in your seat on a bus that is traveling 100 km/h on a highway, is your body at rest or in motion?

Explain your answer. Use a diagram if it will help make your answer clear.

1 Motivate

DEMONSTRATION

Egg in a Buggy Place a hard-boiled egg in a small, wheeled cart. Apply a strong force to the cart so that it strikes a wall. Ask students to draw a series of pictures that shows what happens to the egg as the cart moves across the floor and strikes the wall. Then ask them to draw a picture of how the egg could be protected in the cart. Challenge students to explain what happened to the egg.

Directed Reading Worksheet Section 2

REAL-WORLD CONNECTION

A tractor trailer will often jack-knife on an icy road when the driver suddenly applies the brakes. The brakes are applied to the tractor wheels and the front part of the rig (the tractor) stops. However, the back half (the trailer) skids and continues moving in accordance with Newton's first law, causing the rig to jackknife. Ask students to speculate on how jackknife accidents might be prevented.

GUIDED PRACTICE

Have students prepare one list of situations in which people would want to avoid friction and another list of situations in which friction is helpful. (List 1: opening windows, attaining high speeds, and so on; List 2: walking, braking a car or bicycle, and so on)

Answer to APPLY

Students should notice that the dummy's head hit the steering wheel even when it was wearing a seat belt. Newton's first law says that an object in motion tends to stay in motion unless it is acted on by an unbalanced force. Thus, when the car is stopped in the collision, the dummy's body continues in motion until it is stopped by the seat belt. But the dummy's head *still* stays in motion because there is no unbalanced force—such as that from an air bag—to stop its motion.

(a) An unbalanced force from another car acts on your car, changing its motion.

(b) The collision changes your car's motion, but not yours. Your motion continues with the same velocity.

(c) Another unbalanced force, from your seat belt, changes your motion.

Figure 12 *Bumper cars let you have fun with Newton's first law.*

Friction - a force that opposes motion between to objects that are touching

Part 2: Objects in Motion
Think about riding in a bumper car at an amusement park. Your ride is pleasant as long as you are driving in an open space. But the name of the game is bumper cars, so sooner or later you are likely to run into another car, as shown in **Figure 12**.

The second part of Newton's first law explains that an object moving at a certain velocity will continue to move *forever* at the same speed and in the same direction unless some unbalanced force acts on it. Thus, your bumper car stops, but you continue to move forward until your seat belt stops you.

Friction and Newton's First Law Because an object in motion will stay in motion forever unless it is acted on by an unbalanced force, you should be able to give your desk a small push and send it sailing across the floor. If you try it, you will find that the desk quickly comes to a stop. What does this tell you?

There must be an unbalanced force that acts on the desk to stop its motion. That unbalanced force is friction. The friction between the desk and the floor works against the motion of the desk. Because of friction, it is often difficult to observe the effects of Newton's first law on the motion of everyday objects. For example, friction will cause a ball rolling on grass to slow down and stop. Friction will also make a car decelerate on a flat surface if the driver lets up on the gas pedal. Because of friction, the motion of these objects changes.

APPLY

Stopping Motion

The dummy in this crash test is wearing a seat belt, but the car does not have an air bag. Explain why Newton's first law of motion could lead to serious injuries in accidents involving cars without air bags.

44

LabBook **PG 189**
Blast Off!

IS THAT A FACT!

Antilock braking systems (ABS) controlled by a computer prevent skidding by sensing when the wheels are about to lock. They release and reapply the brakes up to 25 times a second. Instead of skidding out of control, the car slows down and stops safely.

Inertia Is Related to Mass Newton's first law of motion is sometimes called the law of inertia. **Inertia** (in UHR shuh) is the tendency of all objects to resist any change in motion. Due to inertia, an object at rest will remain at rest until something makes it move. Likewise, inertia is why a moving object stays in motion with the same velocity unless a force acts on it to change its speed or direction. Inertia causes you to slide toward the side of a car when the driver makes a sharp turn. Inertia is also why it is impossible for a plane, car, or bicycle to stop instantaneously.

Mass Is a Measure of Inertia An object with a small mass has less inertia than an object with a large mass. Therefore, it is easier to start and to change the motion of an object with a small mass. For example, a softball has less mass and therefore less inertia than a bowling ball. Because the softball has a small amount of inertia, it is easy to pitch a softball and to change its motion by hitting it with a bat. Imagine how difficult it would be to play softball with a bowling ball! **Figure 13** further illustrates the relationship between mass and inertia. Try the QuickLab at right to test the relationship yourself.

Figure 13 *Inertia makes it harder to push a car than to push a bicycle. Inertia also makes it easier to stop a moving bicycle than a car moving at the same speed.*

Self-Check

When you stand while riding a bus, why do you tend to fall backward when the bus starts moving?
(See page 232 to check your answer.)

(See page 232 to check your answer.)

QuickLab

First-Law Magic

1. On a table or desk, place a **large, empty plastic cup** on top of a **paper towel.**

2. Without touching the cup or tipping it over, remove the paper towel from under the cup. What did you do to accomplish this?

3. Repeat the first two steps a few times until you are comfortable with the procedure.

4. Fill the cup half full with **water,** and place the cup on the paper towel.

5. Once again, remove the paper towel from under the cup. Was it easier or harder to do this? Explain your answer in terms of mass and inertia.

QuickLab

MATERIALS

FOR EACH STUDENT:
- empty plastic cup
- paper towel or paper
- water

- Cups should be large—12 oz or more. 500 mL plastic beakers will also work.

- Make sure students don't fill the cups more than half full of water. This will reduce spills, but it still makes the cup noticeably more massive. Instruct students to keep the outer surfaces of the cups dry. A wet paper towel may break when pulled. Caution students to wear an apron when doing this activity.

Answers to QuickLab

2. Students will quickly learn that they have to jerk the paper towel out from under the cup as in a magic trick.

5. It should be easier for students to do the trick with water in the cup because the cup has more mass and therefore more inertia. When the cup has more inertia, it is harder to move. It is therefore easier to move the paper towel out from under it.

Answer to Self-Check

This can be answered in terms of either Newton's first law or inertia.

Newton's first law: When the bus is still, both you and the bus are at rest. The bus started moving, but no unbalanced force acted on your body, so your body stayed at rest.

Inertia: You have inertia, and that makes you difficult to move. As a result, when the bus started to move, you didn't move with it.

READING STRATEGY

Prediction Guide Before students read pages 46 and 47, have them read Newton's second law of motion. Without reading further in the section, have them try to explain the second law in their own words. They might suggest activities or draw diagrams to demonstrate how the second law works. Accept all responses. After reading the section, discuss with the class some of their activities and diagrams.

RETEACHING

When you introduce the equation for Newton's second law, point out to students that acceleration and force are directly proportional (i.e., as force increases, acceleration increases) and that acceleration and mass are inversely proportional (i.e., as mass increases, acceleration decreases). These relationships are explained qualitatively, but students may not see the connection on their own.

- 1 newton = 1 kilogram-meter per second per second
   OR
   1 N = 1 kg•m/s/s

This is important for helping students through the unit cancellation in the MathBreak and in **Figure 16.** Sheltered English

Environment
CONNECTION

Modern cars pollute the air less than older cars. One reason for this is that modern cars are less massive than older models and have considerably smaller engines. According to Newton's second law, a less massive object requires less force to achieve the same acceleration as a more massive object. This is why a smaller car can have a smaller engine and still have acceptable acceleration. And because smaller engines use less fuel, they pollute less.

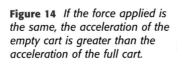

Figure 15 *Acceleration will increase when a larger force is exerted.*

46

Newton's Second Law of Motion

The acceleration of an object depends on the mass of the object and the amount of force applied.

Newton's second law describes the motion of an object when an unbalanced force is acting on it. As with Newton's first law, it is easier to consider the parts of this law separately.

Part 1: Acceleration Depends on Mass Suppose you are pushing a shopping cart at the grocery store. At the beginning of your shopping trip, you have to exert only a small force on the cart to accelerate it. But when the cart is full, the same amount of force will not accelerate the cart as much as before, as shown in **Figure 14.** This example illustrates that for the same force, an object's acceleration *decreases* as its mass *increases* and its acceleration *increases* as its mass *decreases*.

Figure 14 *If the force applied is the same, the acceleration of the empty cart is greater than the acceleration of the full cart.*

Part 2: Acceleration Depends on Force Now suppose you give the shopping cart a hard push, as shown in **Figure 15.** The cart will start moving faster than if you only gave it a soft push. This illustrates that an object's acceleration *increases* as the force on it *increases*. Conversely, an object's acceleration *decreases* as the force on it *decreases*.

The acceleration of an object is always in the same direction as the force applied. The shopping cart moved forward because the push was in the forward direction. To change the direction of an object, you must exert a force in the direction you want the object to go.

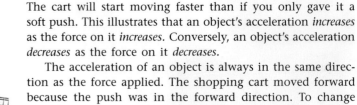

SCIENCE HUMOR

There once was a trucker from Nome,
Whose rig was loaded with foam.
Its very small mass
Made him able to pass
The other trucks all the way home.

Expressing Newton's Second Law Mathematically The relationship of acceleration (*a*) to mass (*m*) and force (*F*) can be expressed mathematically with the following equation:

$$a = \frac{F}{m}$$

This equation is often rearranged to the following form:

$$F = m \times a$$

Both forms of the equation can be used to solve problems. Try the MathBreak at right to practice using the equations. Newton's second law explains why objects fall to Earth with the same acceleration. In **Figure 16,** you can see how the larger weight of the watermelon is offset by its greater inertia. Thus, the accelerations of the watermelon and the apple are the same when you put the numbers into the equation for acceleration.

Figure 16 Newton's Second Law and Acceleration Due to Gravity

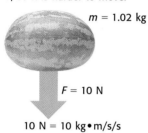

The **apple** has less mass, so the gravitational force on it is smaller. However, the apple also has less inertia and is easier to move.

m = 0.102 kg

F = 1 N

1 N = 1 kg•m/s/s

The **watermelon** has more mass and therefore more inertia, so it is harder to move.

m = 1.02 kg

F = 10 N

10 N = 10 kg•m/s/s

$$a = \frac{1 \text{ kg} \cdot \text{m/s/s}}{0.102 \text{ kg}} = 9.8 \text{ m/s/s} \qquad a = \frac{10 \text{ kg} \cdot \text{m/s/s}}{1.02 \text{ kg}} = 9.8 \text{ m/s/s}$$

÷ 5 ÷ Ω ≤ ∞ +Ω √ 9 ∞ ≤ Σ 2

MATH BREAK

Second-Law Problems

You can rearrange the equation $F = m \times a$ to find acceleration and mass as shown below.

$$a = \frac{F}{m} \qquad m = \frac{F}{a}$$

1. What is the acceleration of a 7 kg mass if a force of 68.6 N is used to move it toward Earth? (Hint: 1 N is equal to 1 kg•m/s/s.)

2. What force is necessary to accelerate a 1,250 kg car at a rate of 40 m/s/s?

3. What is the mass of an object if a force of 34 N produces an acceleration of 4 m/s/s?

SECTION REVIEW

1. How is inertia related to Newton's first law of motion?

2. Name two ways to increase the acceleration of an object.

3. **Making Predictions** If the acceleration due to gravity were somehow doubled to 19.6 m/s/s, what would happen to your weight?

internet connect

SC*i*LINKS
NSTA

TOPIC: Newton's Laws of Motion
GO TO: www.scilinks.org
*sci*LINKS NUMBER: HSTP145

47

DISCUSSION

Discuss with students how the equation $F = m \times a$ can be used to find the mass of an object. Have them imagine they hit an object of unknown mass with a force of 15 N and that the object accelerates at 5 m/s/s. What is the mass of the object? (3 kg)

Remind students that mass is a measure of an object's inertia.

Answers to MATHBREAK

1. $a = F / m = 68.6$ N / 7 kg = 9.8 m/s/s (This is acceleration due to gravity.)

2. $F = m \times a = 1,250$ kg × 40 m/s/s = 50,000 N

3. $m = F / a = 34$ N / 4 m/s/s = 8.5 kg

MATH and MORE

Have students use Newton's second law to do the following problems:

• Calculate the force of gravity acting on your 6 kg backpack. (This is the weight of your backpack.) (F = 6 kg × 9.8 m/s/s = 58.8 N)

• A 50 kg skater pushes off from a wall with a force of 200 N. What is the skater's acceleration? (4 m/s/s)

 Math Skills Worksheet "Newton: Force and Motion"

▼ **Answers to Section Review**

1. Newton's first law says that matter resists any change in motion. Inertia is the *tendency* of objects (matter) to resist changes in motion. Newton's first law is also known as the law of inertia.

2. You can increase the acceleration of an object by increasing the force causing the acceleration or by reducing the object's mass.

3. If the acceleration due to gravity were doubled, your weight would double. This is because of Newton's second law: $F = ma$. Weight is the force due to the acceleration on mass. If acceleration is doubled and mass remains the same, the force (weight) is doubled, too.

 Teaching Transparency 224 "Newton's Second Law and Acceleration Due to Gravity"

DISCUSSION

Underwater training to simulate spacewalking is a major part of astronaut training. Discuss with students what would happen to astronauts in microgravity who forget Newton's third law of motion as they tried to work on a spacecraft. (The spacecraft would seem to repel the astronauts everytime they touched it. The astronauts would probably become very tired and frustrated.) Discuss with students why underwater training would be useful for the astronauts.

CONNECT TO
LIFE SCIENCE

Ask students to find out how a squid propels itself through the water and to explain the squid's movement using Newton's third law. Have students make a poster or do a presentation to demonstrate what they have learned about squid propulsion.

Answers to Activity

Accept all reasonable answers. Things to look for: How inertia helps/harms the object of the game; how increasing or decreasing the force on an object affects its acceleration and why this is beneficial for the game; identification of action and reaction forces at work in the game.

Newton's Third Law of Motion

Whenever one object exerts a force on a second object, the second object exerts an equal and opposite force on the first.

Newton's third law can be simply stated as follows: All forces act in pairs. If a force is exerted, another force occurs that is equal in size and opposite in direction. The law itself addresses only forces. But the way that force pairs interact affects the motion of objects.

What is meant by "forces act in pairs"? Study **Figure 17** to learn how one force pair helps propel a swimmer through water.

Figure 17 *The action force and reaction force are a pair. The two forces are equal in size but opposite in direction.*

The **action force** is the swimmer's hands and feet pushing on the water.

The **reaction force** is the water pushing on the hands and feet. The reaction force moves the swimmer forward.

Action and reaction force pairs occur even when there is no motion. For example, you exert a force on a chair when you sit on it. Your weight pushing down on the chair is the action force. The reaction force is the force exerted by the chair that pushes up on your body and is equal to your weight.

Force Pairs Do Not Act on the Same Object You know that a force is always exerted by one object on another object. This is true for all forces, including action and reaction forces. However, it is important to remember that action and reaction forces in a pair do not act on the same object. If they did, the net force would always be zero and nothing would ever move! To understand this better, look back at Figure 17. In this example, the action force was exerted on the water by the swimmer's hands and feet. But the reaction force was exerted on the swimmer's hands and feet by the water. The forces did not act on the same object.

Activity

Choose a sport that you enjoy playing or watching. In your ScienceLog, list five ways that Newton's laws of motion are involved in the game you selected.

TRY at HOME

48

IS THAT A FACT!

Water emerges from a fire hose with great force. As the water rushes forward, a reaction force pushes backward on the hose. If firefighters don't have a tight grip on the hose and their feet are not firmly planted on the ground, the reaction force can topple them over backward.

The Effect of a Reaction Can Be Difficult to See Another example of a force pair is shown in **Figure 18.** Remember, gravity is a force of attraction between objects that is due to their masses. If you drop a ball off a ledge, the force of gravity pulls the ball toward Earth. This is the action force exerted by Earth on the ball. But the force of gravity also pulls Earth toward the ball. That is the reaction force exerted by the ball on Earth.

It's easy to see the effect of the action force—the ball falls to Earth. Why don't you notice the effect of the reaction force—Earth being pulled upward? To find the answer to this question, think back to Newton's second law. It states that the acceleration of an object depends on the force applied to it and on the mass of the object. The force on Earth is equal to the force on the ball, but the mass of Earth is much *larger* than the mass of the ball. Therefore, the acceleration of Earth is much *smaller* than the acceleration of the ball. The acceleration is so small that you can't even see it or feel it. Thus, it is difficult to observe the effect of Newton's third law on falling objects.

More Examples of Action and Reaction Force Pairs The examples below illustrate a variety of action and reaction force pairs. In each example, notice which object exerts the action force and which object exerts the reaction force.

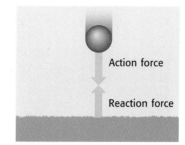

Action force

Reaction force

Figure 18 *The force of gravity between Earth and a falling object is a force pair.*

The rabbit's legs exert a force on Earth. Earth exerts an equal force on the rabbit's legs, causing the rabbit to accelerate upward.

The bat exerts a force on the ball, sending the ball into the outfield. The ball exerts an equal force on the bat, but the bat does not fly toward the catcher because the batter is exerting another force on the bat.

The shuttle's thrusters push the exhaust gases downward as the gases push the shuttle upward with an equal force.

When you hit a table with your hand, your hand will hurt. This is because the table meets your hand with a force equal in size to the force you exerted.

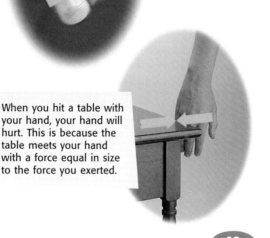

49

Multicultural CONNECTION

The Chinese invented gunpowder in the tenth century and used it in rockets for fireworks used for celebrations. These rockets were later adapted to warfare. In the thirteenth century Chinese armies launched rockets over enemy troops. In the twentieth century, rockets took humans into space and robots to other planets.

③ Extend

GOING FURTHER

The momentum (*p*) of an object can be found by multiplying its mass (*m*) times its velocity (*v*), as in the following equation:

$$p = m \times v$$

The units of momentum are kilogram meters per second. Have students find the momentum of an 80 kg basketball player driving to the basket with a constant velocity of 8 m/s. (640 kg•m/s to the basket)

Ask students to predict what will happen if the player collides with another player whose mass is 100 kg but whose velocity is 0 m/s.

USING THE FIGURE

Teacher Notes: The momentum arrows, or vectors, in **Figures 19** and **20** do not represent forces. Momentum, like force, is a vector quantity and can therefore be shown with arrows.

Critical Thinking Worksheet
"Forces to Reckon With"

Math Skills Worksheet
"Momentum"

BRAIN FOOD

Jumping beans appear to leap into the air with no forces acting on them. However, inside each bean is a small insect larva. When the larva moves suddenly, it applies a force to the shell of the bean. The momentum of the larva is transferred to the bean, and the bean "jumps."

Momentum Is a Property of Moving Objects

If a compact car and a large truck are traveling with the same velocity, it takes longer for the truck to stop than it does for the car if the same braking force is applied. Likewise, it takes longer for a fast moving car to stop than it does for a slow moving car with the same mass. The truck and the fast moving car have more momentum than the compact car and the slow moving car.

Momentum is a property of a moving object that depends on the object's mass and velocity. The more momentum an object has, the harder it is to stop the object or change its direction. Although the compact car and the truck are traveling with the same velocity, the truck has more mass and therefore more momentum, so it is harder to stop than the car. Similarly, the fast moving car has a greater velocity and thus more momentum than the slow moving car.

Momentum Is Conserved When a moving object hits another object, some or all of the momentum of the first object is transferred to the other object. If only some of the momentum is transferred, the rest of the momentum stays with the first object.

Imagine you hit a billiard ball with a cue ball so that the billiard ball starts moving and the cue ball stops, as shown in **Figure 19.** The cue ball had a certain amount of momentum before the collision. During the collision, all of the cue ball's momentum was transferred to the billiard ball. After the collision, the billiard ball moved away with the same amount of momentum the cue ball had. This example illustrates the *law of conservation of momentum.* Any time two or more objects interact, they may exchange momentum, but the total amount of momentum stays the same.

Figure 19 *The momentum before a collision is equal to the momentum after the collision.*

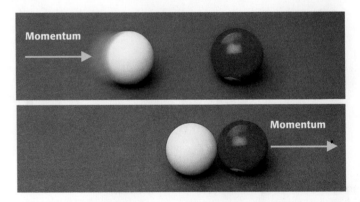

Homework

Concept Mapping Ask students to create a concept map using Newton's three laws and momentum to explain how seat belts and air bags protect passengers.

IS THAT A FACT!

Edmond Halley used Newton's ideas to predict that a comet seen in 1531, 1607, and 1682, would return in 1758. When the comet returned as predicted, it became known as Halley's comet. It last appeared in 1986. When will the comet appear again? (2061)

Bowling is another example of how conservation of momentum is used in a game. The bowling ball rolls down the lane with a certain amount of momentum. When the ball hits the pins, some of the ball's momentum is transferred to the pins and the pins move off in different directions. Furthermore, some of the pins that were hit by the ball go on to hit other pins, transferring the momentum again.

Conservation of Momentum and Newton's Third Law
Conservation of momentum can be explained by Newton's third law. In the example with the billiard ball, the cue ball hit the billiard ball with a certain amount of force. This was the action force. The reaction force was the equal but opposite force exerted by the billiard ball on the cue ball. The action force made the billiard ball start moving, and the reaction force made the cue ball stop moving, as shown in **Figure 20**. Because the action and reaction forces are equal and opposite, momentum is conserved.

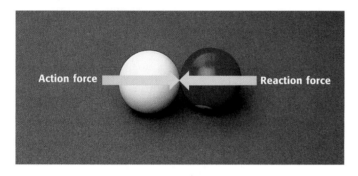

Action force   Reaction force

Figure 20 *The action force makes the billiard ball begin moving, and the reaction force stops the cue ball's motion.*

SECTION REVIEW

1. Name three action and reaction force pairs involved in doing your homework. Name what object is exerting and what object is receiving the forces.

2. Which has more momentum, a mouse running at 1 m/s north or an elephant walking at 3 m/s east? Explain your answer.

3. **Applying Concepts** When a truck pulls a trailer, the trailer and truck accelerate forward even though the action and reaction forces are the same size but in opposite directions. Why don't these forces balance each other out?

Catapult forward! Or is it backward? Find out on page 188 of the LabBook.

Quiz

1. How does Newton's second law explain why it is easier to push a bicycle than to push a car with the same acceleration? (The bicycle has a smaller mass, so a smaller force is required to give it the same acceleration as the car.)

2. What are two ways that you can increase the acceleration of a loaded grocery cart? (You can increase the force applied to the cart, or you can decrease the mass of the cart by removing some of the objects from it.)

3. How does Newton's third law explain how a rocket takes off? (The hot gases expelled from the back of the rocket produce a reaction force on the rocket that lifts and accelerates the rocket.)

ALTERNATIVE ASSESSMENT

Writing Have students imagine the following: An astronaut is sent with her pack of tools out of a spacecraft to fix a satellite. She does not have a tether connecting her to the spacecraft. Just as she completes the job, her backpack rocket fails.

Ask students to write a story about the astronaut and how she manages to return to the spacecraft. (According to Newton's third law, she could move toward the spacecraft by throwing one of her tools away from the spacecraft.)

 PG 190
Quite a Reaction

▼ Answers to Section Review

1. Accept all reasonable answers. Sample answers include using a pencil or pen (action: hand pushing on pencil; reaction: pencil pushing back on hand OR action: pencil pushing on paper; reaction: paper pushing on pencil).

2. The elephant—it has both a greater mass and greater velocity.

3. The action and reaction forces do not balance each other because the forces are acting on two different objects. Because they act on two different objects, you cannot combine them to determine a net force.

Inertia-Rama!
Teacher's Notes

Time Required

One or two 45-minute class periods

Lab Ratings

TEACHER PREP ▲▲
STUDENT SET-UP ▲
CONCEPT LEVEL ▲▲
CLEAN UP ▲

MATERIALS

Station 1
Be sure to have a few extra raw and hard-boiled eggs on hand in case of breakage. Having students spin their eggs in a box may reduce the chance that an egg will break.

Station 2
Use a relatively large coin, such as a quarter or 50-cent piece. Or you may have students try the Station 2 procedure with coins of different sizes and compare the results.

Station 3
The mass used at Station 3 should be at least 1 kg. A larger mass will give better results. The string used in Station 3 should be long and sturdy enough to suspend the mass.

Safety Caution

Remind students to review all safety cautions and icons before beginning this lab activity.

Preparation Notes

This lab may be done in one class period if enough supplies are available to avoid changing stations.

Inertia-Rama!

Inertia is a property of all matter, from small particles of dust to enormous planets and stars. In this lab, you will investigate the inertia of various shapes and types of matter. Keep in mind that each investigation requires you to either overcome or use the object's inertia.

MATERIALS

Be sure to wear safety goggles while doing this lab and to handle sharp objects with care.

Station 1
- hard-boiled egg
- raw egg

Station 2
- coin
- index card
- cup

Station 3
- spool of thread
- suspended mass
- scissors
- meterstick

Station 1: Magic Eggs
Procedure

1. There are two eggs at this station—one is hard-boiled (solid all the way through) and the other is raw (liquid inside). The masses of the two eggs are about the same. The eggs are not marked. You should not be able to tell them apart by their appearance. Without breaking them open, how can you tell which egg is which?

2. Before you do anything to either egg, make some predictions. Will there be any difference in the way the two eggs spin? Which egg will be easier to stop?

3. First, spin one egg. Then gently place your finger on it to make it stop spinning. Record your observations in your ScienceLog.

4. Repeat step 3 with the second egg.

5. Compare your predictions with your observations. (Repeat steps 3 and 4 if necessary.)

6. Identify which egg is hard-boiled and which one is raw. Explain your choices.

Analysis

7. Explain why the eggs behave differently when you spin them even though they should have the same inertia. (Hint: Think about what happens to the liquid inside the raw egg.)

8. In terms of inertia, explain why the eggs react differently when you try to stop them.

Answers

2. Accept all reasonable answers.

6. Students should identify the hard-boiled egg as the egg that spins smoothly and the raw egg as the egg that wobbles as it spins.

7. The liquid inside the raw egg sloshes; it doesn't spin smoothly like the hard-boiled egg.

8. When you stop the eggs, the hard-boiled egg stops as a whole, while the shell of the raw egg can be stopped and the liquid inside keeps spinning

Datasheets for LabBook

Station 2: Coin in a Cup Procedure

9 At this station, you will find a coin, an index card, and a cup. Place the card over the cup. Then place the coin on the card over the center of the cup, as shown below.

10 In your ScienceLog, write a method for getting the coin into the cup without touching the coin and without lifting the card.

11 Try your method. If it doesn't work, try again until you find a method that does work. When you are done, place the card and coin on the table for the next group.

Analysis

12 Use Newton's first law of motion to explain why the coin falls into the cup if you remove the card quickly.

13 Explain why pulling on the card slowly will not work even though the coin has inertia. (Hint: Friction is a force.)

Station 3: The Magic Thread Procedure

14 At this station, you will find a spool of thread and a mass hanging from a strong string. Cut a piece of thread about 40 cm long. Tie the thread around the bottom of the mass, as shown at right.

15 Pull gently on the end of the thread. Observe what happens, and record your observations in your ScienceLog.

16 Stop the mass from moving. Now hold the end of the thread so that there is a lot of slack between your fingers and the mass.

17 Give the thread a quick, hard pull. You should observe a very different event. Record your observations in your ScienceLog. Throw away the thread.

Analysis

18 Use Newton's first law of motion to explain why the results of a gentle pull are so different from the results of a hard pull.

Draw Conclusions

19 Remember that both moving and nonmoving objects have inertia. Explain why throwing a bowling ball and catching a thrown bowling ball are hard.

20 Why is it harder to run with a backpack full of books than to run with an empty backpack?

Answers

12. The coin tends to remain at rest, so when the card is removed quickly, there is not enough friction to move the coin.

13. When you pull slowly, there is enough time for the friction between the card and the coin to move the coin.

18. The mass tends to stay at rest. A gentle pull exerts a small force over a longer time and moves the mass, but a hard pull breaks the thread before the mass moves.

19. It is just as hard to catch the bowling ball as it is to throw it because the bowling ball has the same inertia in both cases.

20. Accept all reasonable answers that take into account the added inertia of the objects in the backpack. Sample answer: Starting and stopping will be harder because the extra mass increases your inertia. In addition, the books in the backpack act like the liquid inside a raw egg. As you bounce up, they resist your upward movement. As you bounce down, they are still moving upward.

53

Vicky Farland
Crane Junior High
Yuma, Arizona

Chapter Highlights

SECTION 1

terminal velocity the constant velocity of a falling object when the size of the upward force of air resistance matches the size of the downward force of gravity

free fall the condition an object is in when gravity is the only force acting on it

projectile motion the curved path an object follows when thrown or propelled near the surface of Earth

---

Chapter Highlights

SECTION 1

Vocabulary

terminal velocity (p. 38)

free fall (p. 39)

projectile motion (p. 41)

Section Notes

- All objects accelerate toward Earth at 9.8 m/s/s.

- Air resistance slows the acceleration of falling objects.

- An object is in free fall if gravity is the only force acting on it.

- An orbit is formed by combining forward motion and free fall.

- Objects in orbit appear to be weightless because they are in free fall.

- A centripetal force is needed to keep objects in circular motion. Gravity acts as a centripetal force to keep objects in orbit.

- Projectile motion is the curved path an object follows when thrown or propelled near the surface of Earth.

- Projectile motion has two components—horizontal and vertical. Gravity affects only the vertical motion of projectile motion.

Labs

A Marshmallow Catapult (p. 188)

☑ Skills Check

Math Concepts

NEWTON'S SECOND LAW The equation $a = F/m$ on page 47 summarizes Newton's second law of motion. The equation shows the relationship between the acceleration of an object, the force causing the acceleration, and the object's mass. For example, if you apply a force of 18 N to a 6 kg object, the object's acceleration is

$$a = \frac{F}{m} = \frac{18\,\text{N}}{6\,\text{kg}} = \frac{18\,\text{kg} \cdot \text{m/s/s}}{6\,\text{kg}} = 3\,\text{m/s/s}$$

Visual Understanding

HOW AN ORBIT IS FORMED An orbit is a combination of two motions—forward motion and free fall. Figure 7 on page 40 shows how the two motions combine to form an orbit.

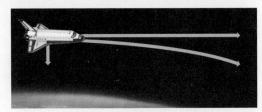

Lab and Activity Highlights

Inertia-Rama! `PG 52`

A Marshmallow Catapult `PG 188`

Blast Off! `PG 189`

Quite a Reaction `PG 190`

Datasheets for LabBook (blackline masters for these labs)

SECTION 2

Vocabulary

inertia *(p. 45)*

momentum *(p. 50)*

Section Notes

- Newton's first law of motion states that the motion of an object will not change if no unbalanced forces act on it.

- Inertia is the tendency of matter to resist a change in motion. Mass is a measure of inertia.

- Newton's second law of motion states that the acceleration of an object depends on its mass and on the force exerted on it.

- Newton's third law of motion states that whenever one object exerts a force on a second object, the second object exerts an equal and opposite force on the first.

- Momentum is the property of a moving object that depends on its mass and velocity.

- When two or more objects interact, momentum may be exchanged, but the total amount of momentum does not change. This is the law of conservation of momentum.

Labs

Blast Off! *(p. 189)*

Quite a Reaction *(p. 190)*

 Vocabulary Review Worksheet

Blackline masters of these Chapter Highlights can be found in the **Study Guide.**

---

internetconnect

 GO TO: go.hrw.com

Visit the **HRW** Web site for a variety of learning tools related to this chapter. Just type in the keyword:

KEYWORD: HSTFOR

SCILINKS **NSTA**

GO TO: www.scilinks.org

Visit the **National Science Teachers Association** on-line Web site for Internet resources related to this chapter. Just type in the *sci*LINKS number for more information about the topic:

TOPIC: The Force of Gravity	***sci*LINKS NUMBER:** HSTP130
TOPIC: Gravity and Orbiting Objects	***sci*LINKS NUMBER:** HSTP135
TOPIC: Projectile Motion	***sci*LINKS NUMBER:** HSTP140
TOPIC: Newton's Laws of Motion	***sci*LINKS NUMBER:** HSTP145

55

Lab and Activity Highlights

LabBank

 Inquiry Labs, On the Fast Track

 Long-Term Projects & Research Ideas, "Any Color You Want, so Long as It's Black"

Whiz-Bang Demonstrations,
- Newton's Eggciting Experiment
- Inertia Can Hurt Ya
- Fountain of Knowledge

Calculator-Based Labs, Falling Objects

Interactive Explorations CD-ROM

 CD 2, Exploration 5, "Extreme Skiing"

Chapter Review
Answers

USING VOCABULARY

1. inertia
2. terminal velocity
3. Projectile motion
4. momentum
5. Free fall

UNDERSTANDING CONCEPTS

Multiple Choice

6. c
7. b
8. d
9. d
10. d
11. b

Short Answer

12. An orbit is formed by combining the forward motion of the orbiting object with free fall toward Earth. The path that results is a curve that follows the curve of Earth.

13. Gravity and air resistance combine to give a net force of zero on a falling object. When this happens, the object stops accelerating downward and has reached its terminal velocity.

14. Friction is a force that opposes the motion of objects. Friction is what slows the motion of moving objects so you don't see objects moving forever in a straight line.

Concept Mapping

15. An answer to this exercise can be found at the front of this book.

Concept Mapping Transparency 6

Chapter Review

USING VOCABULARY

To complete the following sentences, choose the correct term from each pair of terms listed below:

1. An object in motion tends to stay in motion because it has ___?___. *(inertia or terminal velocity)*

2. Falling objects stop accelerating at ___?___. *(free fall or terminal velocity)*

3. ___?___ is the path that a thrown object follows. *(Free fall or Projectile motion)*

4. A property of moving objects that depends on mass and velocity is ___?___. *(inertia or momentum)*

5. ___?___ only occurs when there is no air resistance. *(Momentum or Free fall)*

UNDERSTANDING CONCEPTS

Multiple Choice

6. A feather and a rock dropped at the same time from the same height would land at the same time when dropped by
   a. Galileo in Italy.
   b. Newton in England.
   c. an astronaut on the moon.
   d. an astronaut on the space shuttle.

7. When a soccer ball is kicked, the action and reaction forces do not cancel each other out because
   a. the force of the foot on the ball is bigger than the force of the ball on the foot.
   b. the forces act on two different objects.
   c. the forces act at different times.
   d. All of the above

8. An object is in projectile motion if
   a. it is thrown with a horizontal push.
   b. it is accelerated downward by gravity.
   c. it does not accelerate horizontally.
   d. All of the above

9. Newton's first law of motion applies
   a. to moving objects.
   b. to objects that are not moving.
   c. to objects that are accelerating.
   d. Both (a) and (b)

10. Acceleration of an object
    a. decreases as the mass of the object increases.
    b. increases as the force on the object increases.
    c. is in the same direction as the force on the object.
    d. All of the above

11. A golf ball and a bowling ball are moving at the same velocity. Which has more momentum?
    a. the golf ball, because it has less mass
    b. the bowling ball, because it has more mass
    c. They both have the same momentum because they have the same velocity.
    d. There is no way to know without additional information.

Short Answer

12. Explain how an orbit is formed.

13. Describe how gravity and air resistance combine when an object reaches terminal velocity.

14. Explain why friction can make observing Newton's first law of motion difficult.

Concept Mapping

15. Use the following terms to create a concept map: gravity, free fall, terminal velocity, projectile motion, air resistance.

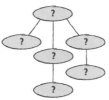

CRITICAL THINKING AND PROBLEM SOLVING

16. During a shuttle launch, about 830,000 kg of fuel is burned in 8 minutes. The fuel provides the shuttle with a constant thrust, or push off the ground. How does Newton's second law of motion explain why the shuttle's acceleration increases during takeoff?

17. When using a hammer to drive a nail into wood, you have to swing the hammer through the air with a certain velocity. Because the hammer has both mass and velocity, it has momentum. Describe what happens to the hammer's momentum after the hammer hits the nail.

18. Suppose you are standing on a skateboard or on in-line skates and you toss a backpack full of heavy books toward your friend. What do you think will happen to you and why? Explain your answer in terms of Newton's third law of motion.

MATH IN SCIENCE

19. A 12 kg rock falls from rest off a cliff and hits the ground in 1.5 seconds.

   a. Ignoring air resistance, what is the rock's velocity just before it hits the ground?

   b. What is the rock's weight after it hits the ground? (Hint: Weight is a measure of the gravitational force on an object.)

INTERPRETING GRAPHICS

20. The picture below shows a common desk toy. If you pull one ball up and release it, it hits the balls at the bottom and comes to a stop. In the same instant, the ball on the other side swings up and repeats the cycle. How does conservation of momentum explain how this toy works?

Reading Check-up

Take a minute to review your answers to the Pre-Reading Questions found at the bottom of page 34. Have your answers changed? If necessary, revise your answers based on what you have learned since you began this chapter.

57

CRITICAL THINKING AND PROBLEM SOLVING

16. Newton's second law: $a = F/m$. During takeoff, the shuttle burns fuel and therefore loses mass. However, the upward force on the shuttle remains the same. So the shuttle's acceleration increases because its mass constantly gets smaller during takeoff.

17. When the hammer hits the nail, the hammer stops. Its momentum is transferred to the nail, driving it into the wood. Momentum is also transferred from the nail to the wood and to the work bench or table top.

18. You will move away from your friend (in the direction opposite from where you throw the backpack). The action force is you pushing the backpack toward your friend. The reaction force is the backpack pushing you away from your friend.

MATH IN SCIENCE

19. a. $\Delta v = g \times t = 9.8$ m/s/s $\times$ 1.5 s = 14.7 m/s

   b. $F = m \times a = 12$ kg $\times$ 9.8 m/s/s = 117.6 N

20. The law of conservation of momentum: when two or more objects interact, the total amount of momentum must stay the same. The ball moving in the air has a certain amount of momentum, and the balls at rest have no momentum. When the moving ball hits the balls at rest, all of its momentum is transferred to them, and it comes to a stop. The momentum is transferred from ball to ball until it reaches the ball on the other end. The ball on the other end keeps all the momentum, and it moves away from the other balls.

Blackline masters of this Chapter Review can be found in the **Study Guide.**

Background

The effect that dimples have on an object in motion depends on several things, including the size of the object, the size of the dimples, and the medium through which the object is moving. A golf ball moving through air, for instance, will behave differently from a golf ball moving through water.

Dimples were first used on golf balls when golfers discovered that old balls with nicks and cuts sometimes flew farther than new, smooth balls. The same principle is applied in many different ways. For example, the cylindrical struts of an airplane's landing gear often have a rough surface in order to minimize the amount of turbulence generated.

Eureka!

A Bat with Dimples

Wouldn't it be nice to hit a home run every time? Jeff DiTullio, a teacher at MIT, in Cambridge, Massachusetts, has found a way for you to get more bang from your bat. Would you believe *dimples?*

Building a Better Bat

If you look closely at the surface of a golf ball, you'll see dozens of tiny craterlike dimples. When air flows past these dimples, it gets stirred up. By keeping air moving near the surface of the ball, the dimples help the golf ball move faster and farther through the air.

DiTullio decided to apply this same idea to a baseball bat. His hypothesis was that dimples would allow a bat to move more easily through the air. This would help batters swing the bat faster and hit the ball harder. To test his hypothesis, DiTullio pressed hundreds of little dimples about 1 mm deep and 2 mm across into the surface of a bat.

When DiTullio tested his dimpled bat in a wind tunnel, he found that it could be swung 3 to 5 percent faster. That may not sound like much, but it could add about 5 m to a fly ball!

Safe . . . or Out?

As you might imagine, many baseball players would love to have a bat that could turn a long fly ball into a home run. But are dimpled baseball bats legal?

The size and shape of every piece of equipment used in Major League Baseball games are regulated. A baseball bat, for instance, must be no more than 107 cm long and no more than 7 cm across at its widest point. When DiTullio

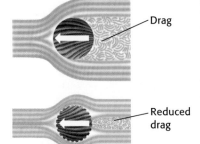
Drag

Reduced drag

▲ *By reducing the amount of drag behind the bat, dimples help the bat move faster through the air.*

designed his dimpled bat, there was no rule stating that bats had to be smooth. But when Major League Baseball found out about the new bat, they changed the rules! Today official rules require that all bats be smooth, and they prohibit any type of "experimental" bat. Someday the rules may be revised to allow DiTullio's dimpled bat. When that happens, fans of the dimpled baseball bat will all shout, "Play ball!"

Dimple Madness

▶ Now that you know how dimples can improve baseball bats, think of other uses for dimples. How might dimples improve the way other objects move through the air? Draw a sketch of a dimpled object, and describe how the dimples improve the design.

▶ *Jeff DiTullio, pictured with his dimpled baseball bat, is an aeronautical engineer— someone who studies both the way air moves and the way things move through air.*

58

Answer to Dimple Madness

Accept all reasonable answers.

CAREERS

ROLLER COASTER DESIGNER

Roller coasters have fascinated **Steve Okamoto** ever since his first ride on one. "I remember going to Disneyland as a kid. My mother was always upset with me because I kept looking over the sides of the rides, trying to figure out how they worked," he laughs. To satisfy his curiosity, Okamoto became a mechanical engineer. Today he uses his scientific knowledge to design and build machines, systems, and buildings. But his specialty is roller coasters.

His West Coaster, which sits on the Santa Monica pier in Santa Monica, California, towers five stories above the Pacific Ocean. The cars on the Steel Force, at Dorney Park, in Pennsylvania, reach speeds of over 120 km/h and drop more than 60 m to disappear into a 37 m long tunnel. The Mamba, at Worlds of Fun, in Missouri, sends cars flying along as high and as fast as the Steel Force does, but it also has two giant back-to-back hills, a fast spiral, and five "camelback" humps. The camelbacks are designed to pull riders' seats out from under them, giving the riders "air time."

Coaster Motion

Roller-coaster cars really do coast along the track. A motor pulls the cars up a high hill to start the ride. After that, the cars are powered by gravity alone. As the cars roll downhill, they pick up enough speed to whiz through the rest of the curves, loops, twists, and bumps in the track.

Designing a successful coaster is no simple task. Steve Okamoto has to calculate the cars' speed and acceleration on each part of the track. "The coaster has to go fast enough to make it up the next hill," he explains. Okamoto uses his knowledge of geometry and physics to create safe but scary curves, loops, humps, and dips. Okamoto must also keep in mind that the ride's towers and structures need to be strong enough to support both the track and the speeding cars full of people. The cars themselves need special wheels to keep them locked onto the track and seat belts or bars to keep passengers safely inside. "It's like putting together a puzzle, except the pieces haven't been cut out yet," says Okamoto.

▲ *The Wild Thing, in Shakopee, Minnesota, was designed by Steve Okamoto.*

Take the Challenge

▶ Step outside for a moment. Gather some rope and a medium-sized plastic bucket half-full of water. Can you get the bucket over your head and upside down without any water escaping? How does this relate to roller coasters?

59

Sample Answer to Take the Challenge

The water is falling down to Earth due to gravity. But if the bucket (and thus the water in it) is moving fast enough, the water's forward motion will combine with its downward motion to produce a path similar to an orbit. By the time the water falls down far enough to hit the ground, the bucket is already underneath it. The loop-the-loop in a roller coaster relies on a similar principle.

CAREERS

Roller Coaster Designer—Steve Okamoto

Background

Steve Okamoto has a degree in product design. He studied not only mechanical engineering but also studio art. Product designers consider an object's form as well as its function and take into account the interests and abilities of the product's consumer.

Two of Okamoto's first coasters were the Ninjas at Six Flags Over Mid-America, in St. Louis, Missouri, and Six Flags Magic Mountain, in Los Angeles, California.

When designing a ride, Okamoto studies site maps of the location, then goes to the amusement park to look at the actual site. Since most rides he designs are for older parks, fitting a coaster around, above, and between existing rides and buildings is one of his biggest challenges. Most rides and parks also have some kind of theme, so marketing goals and concerns figure into his designs as well. (As an example, the *Mamba* is named for one of the fastest snakes in Africa and is designed around this theme.)

Chapter Organizer

CHAPTER ORGANIZATION	TIME MINUTES	OBJECTIVES	LABS, INVESTIGATIONS, AND DEMONSTRATIONS
Chapter Opener pp. 60–61	45	National Standards: SAI 1, 2, ST 2	**Start-Up Activity,** Taking Flight, p. 61
Section 1 Fluids and Pressure	90	▶ Describe how fluids exert pressure. ▶ Analyze how fluid depth affects pressure. ▶ Give examples of fluids flowing from high to low pressure. ▶ State and apply Pascal's principle. SAI 1, 2, ST 2	**Demonstration,** p. 63 in ATE **QuickLab,** Blown Away, p. 66 **Whiz-Bang Demonstrations,** The Rise and Fall of Raisins **Whiz-Bang Demonstrations,** Going Against the Flow
Section 2 Buoyant Force	90	▶ Explain the relationship between fluid pressure and buoyant force. ▶ Predict whether an object will float or sink in a fluid. ▶ Analyze the role of density in an object's ability to float. UCP 4, ST 2; Labs SAI 1	**Demonstration,** p. 68 in ATE **QuickLab,** Ship-Shape, p. 71 **Interactive Explorations CD-ROM,** Sea the Light *A **Worksheet** is also available in the **Interactive Explorations Teacher's Edition.*** **Skill Builder,** Fluids, Force, and Floating, p. 78 **Datasheets for LabBook,** Fluids, Force, and Floating **Discovery Lab,** Density Diver, p. 192 **Datasheets for LabBook,** Density Diver
Section 3 Bernoulli's Principle	135	▶ Describe the relationship between pressure and fluid speed. ▶ Analyze the roles of lift, thrust, and drag in flight. ▶ Give examples of Bernoulli's principle in real-life situations. UCP 2, 5, SAI 1, ST 2; Labs UCP 5, SAI 1	**QuickLab,** Breathing Bernoulli-Style, p. 73 **Demonstration,** p. 73 in ATE **Demonstration,** p. 74 in ATE **Making Models,** Out the Spouts, p. 193 **Datasheets for LabBook,** Out the Spouts **EcoLabs & Field Activities,** What's the Flap All About? **Long-Term Projects & Research Ideas,** Scuba Dive

*See page **T23** for a complete correlation of this book with the*

NATIONAL SCIENCE EDUCATION STANDARDS.

TECHNOLOGY RESOURCES

 Guided Reading Audio CD
English or Spanish, Chapter 3

 Interactive Explorations CD-ROM
CD 3, Exploration 2, Sea the Light

 One-Stop Planner CD-ROM
with Test Generator

 CNN Science, Technology & Society, Pressure Paint, Segment 11

High-Tech Hang Gliders, Segment 12

Scientists in Action, Deep Flight, Segment 17

Chapter 3 • Forces in Fluids

CLASSROOM WORKSHEETS, TRANSPARENCIES, AND RESOURCES	SCIENCE INTEGRATION AND CONNECTIONS	REVIEW AND ASSESSMENT
Directed Reading Worksheet **Science Puzzlers, Twisters & Teasers,** Worksheet		
Directed Reading Worksheet, Section 1 **Math Skills for Science Worksheet,** The Pressure Is On! **Transparency 8,** Surface-to-Volume Ratio **Math Skills for Science Worksheet,** Density **Transparency 225,** Air Pressure and Breathing	**MathBreak,** Pressure, Force, and Area, p. 62 **Connect to Life Science,** p. 63 in ATE **Cross-Disciplinary Focus,** p. 63 in ATE **Connect to Earth Science,** p. 64 in ATE **Real-World Connection,** p. 65 in ATE **Multicultural Connection,** p. 65 in ATE **Real-World Connection,** p. 66 in ATE	**Section Review,** p. 64 **Section Review,** p. 67 **Quiz,** p. 67 in ATE **Alternative Assessment,** p. 67 in ATE
Directed Reading Worksheet, Section 2 **Transparency 226,** Why Does a Steel Ship Float?	**Math and More,** p. 69 in ATE **MathBreak,** How to Calculate Density, p. 70 **Connect to Life Science,** p. 71 in ATE **Geology Connection,** p. 72	**Homework,** pp. 69, 70 in ATE **Section Review,** p. 72 **Quiz,** p. 72 in ATE **Alternative Assessment,** p. 72 in ATE
Directed Reading Worksheet, Section 3 **Transparency 227,** Wing Shape Creates Differences in Air Speed **Critical Thinking Worksheet,** Build a Better Submarine **Transparency 228,** Pitching a Curve Ball **Reinforcement Worksheet,** Building Up Pressure	**Multicultural Connection,** p. 75 in ATE **Apply,** p. 76 **Cross-Disciplinary Focus,** p. 76 in ATE **Connect to Earth Science,** p. 77 in ATE **Eureka!** Stayin' Aloft–The Story of the Frisbee®, p. 84 **Holt Anthology of Science Fiction,** *Wet Behind the Ears*	**Self-Check,** p. 75 **Section Review,** p. 77 **Quiz,** p. 77 in ATE **Alternative Assessment,** p. 77 in ATE

internet connect

go.hrw.com

Holt, Rinehart and Winston On-line Resources

go.hrw.com

For worksheets and other teaching aids related to this chapter, visit the HRW Web site and type in the keyword: **HSTFLU**

National Science Teachers Association

www.scilinks.org

Encourage students to use the *sci*LINKS numbers listed in the internet connect boxes to access information and resources on the **NSTA** Web site.

END-OF-CHAPTER REVIEW AND ASSESSMENT

Chapter Review in Study Guide

Vocabulary and Notes in Study Guide

Chapter Tests with Performance-Based Assessment, Chapter 3 Test

Chapter Tests with Performance-Based Assessment, Performance-Based Assessment 3

Concept Mapping Transparency 7

Chapter Resources & Worksheets

Visual Resources

TEACHING TRANSPARENCIES

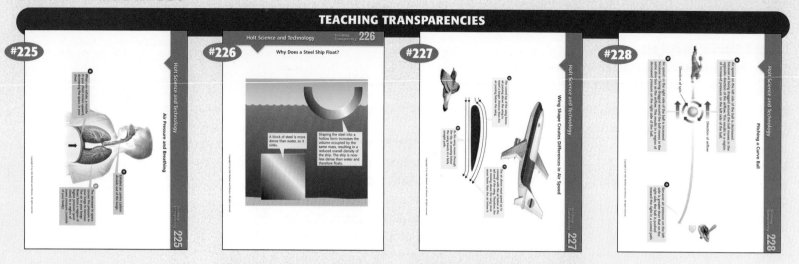

#225 — Holt Science and Technology — Air Pressure and Breathing — 225

#226 — Holt Science and Technology — Teaching Transparency 226 — Why Does a Steel Ship Float?

A block of steel is more dense than water, so it sinks.

Shaping the steel into a hollow form increases the volume occupied by the same mass, resulting in a reduced overall density of the ship. The ship is now less dense than water and therefore floats.

#227 — Holt Science and Technology — Wing Shape Creates Differences in Air Speed — 227

#228 — Holt Science and Technology — Pitching a Curve Ball — 228

TEACHING TRANSPARENCIES

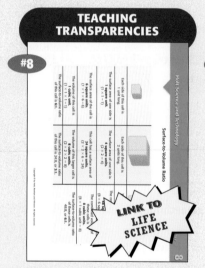

#8 — Holt Science and Technology — Surface-to-Volume Ratio — 8

LINK TO LIFE SCIENCE

CONCEPT MAPPING TRANSPARENCY

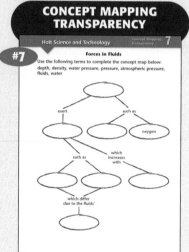

#7 — Holt Science and Technology — Concept Mapping Transparency 7 — Forces in Fluids

Use the following terms to complete the concept map below: depth, density, water pressure, pressure, atmospheric pressure, fluids, water

Meeting Individual Needs

DIRECTED READING

#3 — DIRECTED READING WORKSHEET — Forces in Fluids

Chapter Introduction
As you begin this chapter, answer the following.
1. Read the title of the chapter. List three things that you already know about this subject.

2. Write two questions about this subject that you would like answered by the time you finish this chapter.

3. How does the title of the Start-Up Activity relate to the subject of the chapter?

Section 1: Fluids and Pressure (p. 60)
4. How are dogs, flies, dolphins, and humans connected by fluids?

5. What else can a fluid do besides flow?

REINFORCEMENT & VOCABULARY REVIEW

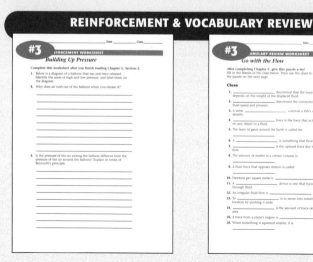

#3 — REINFORCEMENT WORKSHEET — Building Up Pressure

Complete this worksheet after you finish reading Chapter X, Section 2.
1. Below is a diagram of a balloon that has just been released. Identify the areas of high and low pressure, and label them on the diagram.

2. Why does air rush out of the balloon when you release it?

3. Is the pressure of the air exiting the balloon different from the pressure of the air around the balloon? Explain in terms of Bernoulli's principle.

#3 — VOCABULARY REVIEW WORKSHEET — Go with the Flow

After completing Chapter X, give this puzzle a try! Fill in the blanks in the clues below. Then use the clues to complete the puzzle on the next page.

Clues
1. _____ discovered that the buoyant force depends on the weight of the displaced fluid.
2. _____ discovered the connection between fluid speed and pressure.
3. A swim _____ controls a fish's overall density.
4. _____ force is force that acts upward on any object in a fluid.
5. The layer of gases around the Earth is called the _____
6. A _____ is something that flows.
7. _____ is the upward force due to fluid flow.
8. The amount of matter in a certain volume is _____
9. A fluid force that opposes motion is called _____
10. Newtons per square meter is _____
11. A _____ device is one that transfers force through fluid.
12. An irregular fluid flow is _____
13. To _____ is to move into something else's location by pushing it aside.
14. _____ is the amount of force on a given area.
15. A force from a plane's engine is _____
16. When something is squeezed smaller, it is _____

SCIENCE PUZZLERS, TWISTERS & TEASERS

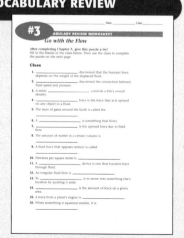

#3 — SCIENCE PUZZLERS, TWISTERS & TEASERS — Forces in Fluids

Under Pressure
2. Becky Beaker has a very adventurous robot. To keep track of her roaming robot, she has attached a device that will measure atmospheric pressure. The table at the bottom of this page indicates the approximate pressure of air at various locations where her robot might be found.

Using the questions below, you can determine the atmospheric pressure where Becky's robot is currently located. Begin with the first statement and decide if it is true or false. If it is true, circle the mathematical expression under the True column, and vice-versa. Then follow the directions that you have circled. The atmospheric pressure you end up with will guide you to the robot.

	True	False
a. Liquids are fluids, but gases are not.	start with 3 kPa	start with 2 kPa
b. Liquids generally cannot be compressed as much as gases, making liquids ideal in hydraulic systems.	multiply by 12	add 6
c. Water exerts greater pressure than air.	add 3	divide by 1
d. The upward force on an airplane is called thrust.	subtract 8	multiply by 11
e. Objects that are less dense than water tend to sink when placed in water.	add 1	divide by 9

Location	Atmospheric pressure
orbiting the Earth in a space shuttle	0 kPa
flying a jet plane	20 kPa
hiking at the top of Mt. Everest	33 kPa
driving through downtown La Paz, Bolivia	51 kPa
making sand castles at the beach	101 kPa

Where is Becky's robot? _____

Review & Assessment

STUDY GUIDE

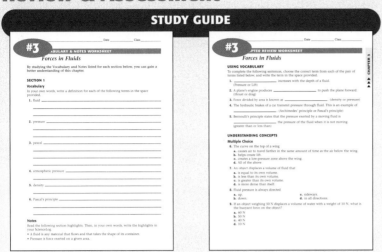

CHAPTER TESTS WITH PERFORMANCE-BASED ASSESSMENT

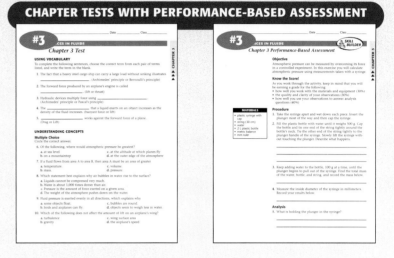

Lab Worksheets

ECOLABS & FIELD ACTIVITIES

WHIZ-BANG DEMONSTRATIONS

LONG-TERM PROJECTS & RESEARCH IDEAS

DATASHEETS FOR LABBOOK

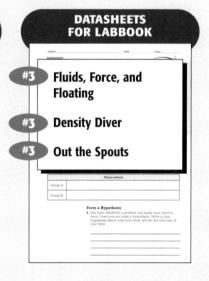

#3 Fluids, Force, and Floating

#3 Density Diver

#3 Out the Spouts

Applications & Extensions

CRITICAL THINKING & PROBLEM SOLVING

SCIENCE, TECHNOLOGY & SOCIETY

SCIENTISTS IN ACTION

INTERACTIVE EXPLORATIONS

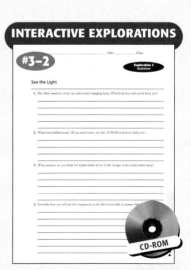

Fluids and Pressure

▶ Blaise Pascal

Blaise Pascal (1623–1662) was a famous French scientist, mathematician, philosopher, and writer of prose. He had no formal schooling but pursued his interests under his father's guidance. Pascal's father forbade him to study mathematics until he was 15 years old, but Pascal's curiosity led him to begin studying geometry in secret at the age of 12. By the time he was 14, Pascal was regularly attending sessions with the leading geometricians of his time. Pascal presented his first mathematics paper at the age of 16.

▶ Refresher on Gas Laws

Nearly all materials expand when they are heated and contract when they are cooled. Gases are not an exception. A gas expands as it gets hotter because the kinetic energy of its particles increases. When the kinetic energy increases, the particles move faster and bounce against each other harder. This causes them to move farther apart, and the gas expands. If the pressure does not change, the volume of the gas will increase as the temperature increases. This is known as Charles's law.

• The air pressure inside the tires of an automobile can be much greater than the pressure outside the tires. This is because air, like all gases, is compressible. If the temperature does not change, the pressure of a gas will increase as the volume decreases. This is known as Boyle's law.

IS THAT A FACT!

☛ The water pressure at the bottom of a small, deep pond is greater than the pressure at the bottom of a large, shallow lake because water pressure is determined by the depth of the water, not the volume of the water.

Buoyant Force

▶ Archimedes (287–212 b.c.)

Archimedes, a Greek mathematician, inventor, and physicist, lived in the ancient city of Syracuse from 287 b.c. to 212 b.c. He is famous for his work in geometry, physics, mechanics, and water and water pressure.

▶ Diving and Water Pressure

Scuba diving relies in part on the principles of buoyancy and fluid pressure. Some of the effects of water pressure can even be felt in a swimming pool. Just a few meters under water, your ears begin to hurt from the pressure of the water on your eardrums.

• As a diver descends deeper into the water with scuba gear, the diver's lungs hold more air because the air is compressed by the water pressure. As a diver rises to the surface, the air expands again. Under certain circumstances, the air in a diver's lungs could expand enough to rupture the air sacs in the diver's lungs.

▶ Neutral Buoyancy

Scuba divers use weights to compensate for the buoyancy of their body and diving gear. When a diver weighs exactly the same as an equal volume of the surrounding water, the diver can swim to any depth and remain there effortlessly. This state is called neutral buoyancy.

▶ Buoyancy and Microgravity

NASA uses large neutral-buoyancy tanks to simulate microgravity. The weight of an astronaut in a space suit can be adjusted so that the astronaut is neutrally buoyant. Astronauts practice maneuvering and working with instruments in this environment to prepare for the almost "weightless" environment of Earth orbit.

IS THAT A FACT!

☛ The tremendous force of water at the ocean's deepest depths prevent most underwater vessels from venturing there. Only a few can withstand the pressure. One revolutionary new vessel, *Deep Flight,* has an extremely strong ceramic hull, which can hold up to the pressure. *Deep Flight* may be futuristic, but humans have built underwater vessels for hundreds of years. In 1620, the Dutch inventor Cornelis van Drebbel built what is thought to be the first submarine. His vessel was not much more than a rowboat covered with greased leather. It traveled at a depth of 4 to 5 m under water in the Thames River, in London, England. King James I of England is said to have taken a short ride in this vessel.

SECTION 3

Bernoulli's Principle

▶ Daniel Bernoulli (1700–1782)

Daniel Bernoulli was born in the Netherlands in 1700. For most of his life, he lived in Basel, Switzerland.

● Bernoulli was born into a family distinguished for accomplishments in science and mathematics. His father, Johann, was famous for his work in calculus, trigonometry, and the study of geodesics. Bernoulli's uncle Jacob was integral in the development of the calculus. Bernoulli's brothers, Nicolaus and Johann II, were also noted mathematicians and physicists.

● Bernoulli's greatest work was *Hydrodynamica,* which was published in 1738. It included the concept now known as Bernoulli's principle. He also made important contributions to probability theory and studied astronomy, botany, physiology, gravity, and magnetism.

▶ Looking for Bernoulli's Principle?

Even on a calm night, air moves across the top of a chimney. This causes the pressure at the top of the chimney to be lower than the pressure in the house. According to Bernoulli's principle, the smoke in the fireplace is pushed up the chimney by the greater air pressure in the house.

● Animals that burrow must have air circulating in their burrows, or they will suffocate. The burrows always have two entrances. Usually, one is higher than the other. Wind speed usually varies with height, so the air flows at different speeds across the holes. This causes a pressure difference that forces air to circulate.

● Bernoulli's principle also explains why a soft convertible top on a car bulges when the car travels at high speeds. The air moving over the top causes an area of low pressure, and the higher pressure inside the car pushes the soft top up.

▶ The Venturi Effect

A Venturi meter is a device that uses Bernoulli's principle to determine the velocity of a fluid by measuring differences in pressure. Venturi meters are found in carburetors, flow meters, and aircraft-speed indicators. In carburetors, a Venturi meter is used to mix fuel with air.

IS THAT A FACT!

☛ Water flowing in a stream speeds up when it flows through a narrow part of the stream bed. According to Bernoulli's principle, the water pressure decreases as the speed increases.

For background information about teaching strategies and issues, refer to the *Professional Reference for Teachers.*

Forces in Fluids

 Pre-Reading Questions

Students may not know the answers to these questions before reading the chapter, so accept any reasonable response.

Suggested Answers

1. A fluid is any material that can flow and that takes the shape of its container.

2. Fluid pressure is exerted by fluid particles colliding with each other and with the walls of their container.

3. Moving fluids travel at faster speeds than nonmoving fluids and therefore exert less pressure (less force per unit area).

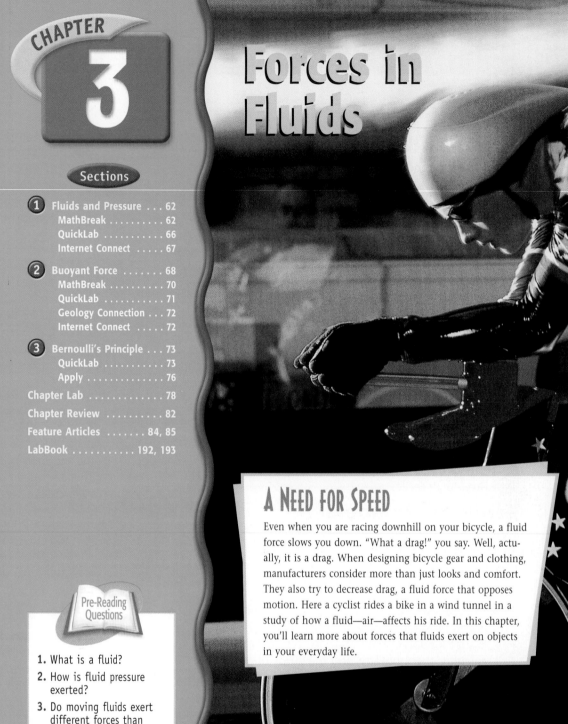

Forces in Fluids

Sections

Pre-Reading Questions

1. What is a fluid?
2. How is fluid pressure exerted?
3. Do moving fluids exert different forces than nonmoving fluids?

60

A NEED FOR SPEED

Even when you are racing downhill on your bicycle, a fluid force slows you down. "What a drag!" you say. Well, actually, it is a drag. When designing bicycle gear and clothing, manufacturers consider more than just looks and comfort. They also try to decrease drag, a fluid force that opposes motion. Here a cyclist rides a bike in a wind tunnel in a study of how a fluid—air—affects his ride. In this chapter, you'll learn more about forces that fluids exert on objects in your everyday life.

---

internet connect

 HRW On-line Resources

go.hrw.com
For worksheets and other teaching aids, visit the HRW Web site and type in the keyword: **HSTFLU**

 SC*i*LINKS NSTA

www.scilinks.com
Use the *sci*LINKS numbers at the end of each chapter for additional resources on the **NSTA** Web site.

 Smithsonian Institution

www.si.edu/hrw
Visit the Smithsonian Institution Web site for related on-line resources.

 CNNfyi.com

www.cnnfyi.com
Visit the CNN Web site for current events coverage and classroom resources.

TAKING FLIGHT

In this activity, you will build a model airplane to help you identify how wing size affects flight.

Procedure

1. Fold a **sheet of paper** in half lengthwise. Then open it. Fold the top corners toward the center crease. Then fold the entire sheet in half along the center crease.

2. With the plane on its side, fold the top front edge down so that it meets the bottom edge. Fold the top edge down again so that it meets the bottom edge.

3. Turn the plane over. Repeat step 2.

4. Raise both wings so that they are perpendicular to the body.

5. Point the plane slightly upward, and gently throw it. Repeat several times. Describe what you see.

6. Make the wings smaller by folding them one more time. Gently throw the plane. Repeat several times. Describe what you see.

7. Try to achieve the same flight path you saw when the wings were bigger. Record your technique.

Analysis

8. What happened to the plane's flight when you reduced the size of its wings? Explain.

9. What gave your plane its forward motion?

61

TAKING FLIGHT

MATERIALS
FOR EACH STUDENT: • sheet of paper

Safety Caution

Remind students to review all safety cautions and icons before beginning this lab activity.

Teacher's Notes

Standard copier paper and notebook paper work well. Avoid paper with ragged edges, such as paper from a spiral notebook. Remind students that this activity is an exception to the usual rules about flying paper planes in class. Encourage students to be precise in folding the plane. Straight, sharp creases work best. Contests for maximum distance or maximum time aloft encourage active participation. Give students enough time to make and test a couple of airplanes before beginning the competition.

Answers to START-UP Activity

8. The plane did not stay in the air as long. If I didn't throw hard, the flight was short. To get a longer flight, I had to throw much harder.

9. I gave the plane its forward motion when I threw the plane.

Focus

Fluids and Pressure

In this section students learn about the physical properties of fluids. They also learn how pressure is related to depth and density, and how fluids flow from areas of high pressure to areas of low pressure. Students learn the practical applications of Pascal's principle.

 Bellringer

Pose the following situation to your students:

One afternoon, you go outside to find your younger sister standing by her bike with a nail in her hand. The bike has a flat tire. She wants to know why the air came out of the tire when she pulled the nail out.

Have students write a few sentences to explain why air rushes out of a hole in a tire.

Answers to MATHBREAK

1. 1,500 Pa
2. 2,500 N

 Directed Reading Worksheet Section 1

 Math Skills Worksheet "The Pressure Is On!"

Terms to Learn

fluid
pressure
pascal
atmospheric pressure
density
Pascal's principle

What You'll Do

◆ Describe how fluids exert pressure.
◆ Analyze how fluid depth affects pressure.
◆ Give examples of fluids flowing from high to low pressure.
◆ State and apply Pascal's principle.

MATH BREAK

Pressure, Force, and Area

The equation on this page can be used to find pressure or rearranged to find force or area.

Force = Pressure × Area

$$\text{Area} = \frac{\text{Force}}{\text{Pressure}}$$

1. Find the pressure exerted by a 3,000 N crate with an area of 2 m².
2. Find the weight of a rock with an area of 10 m² that exerts a pressure of 250 Pa.

(Be sure to express your answers in the correct SI unit.)

Fluids and Pressure

What does a dolphin have in common with a sea gull? What does a dog have in common with a fly? What do you have in common with all these living things? The answer is that you and all these other living things spend a lifetime moving through and even breathing fluids. A **fluid** is any material that can flow and that takes the shape of its container. Fluids include liquids (such as water and oil) and gases (such as oxygen and carbon dioxide). Fluids are able to flow because the particles in fluids, unlike the particles in solids, can move easily past each other. As you will find out, the remarkable properties of fluids allow huge ships to float, divers to explore the ocean depths, and jumbo jets to soar across the skies.

All Fluids Exert Pressure

You probably have heard the terms *air pressure, water pressure,* and *blood pressure.* Air, water, and blood are all fluids, and all fluids exert pressure. So what's pressure? Well, think about this example. When you pump up a bicycle tire, you push air into the tire. And like all matter, air is made of tiny particles that are constantly moving. Inside the tire, the air particles push against each other and against the walls of the tire, as shown in **Figure 1**. The more air you pump into the tire, the more the air particles push against the inside of your tire. Together, these pushes create a force against the tire. The amount of force exerted on a given area is **pressure.** Pressure can be calculated by dividing the force that a fluid exerts by the area over which the force is exerted:

$$\text{Pressure} = \frac{\text{Force}}{\text{Area}}$$

The SI unit for pressure is the **pascal.** One pascal (1 Pa) is the force of one newton exerted over an area of one square meter (1 N/m²). Try the MathBreak at left to practice calculating pressure.

Figure 1 *The force of the air particles hitting the inner surface of the tire creates pressure, which keeps the tire inflated.*

Why Are Bubbles Round? When you blow a soap bubble, you blow in only one direction. So why doesn't the bubble get longer and longer as you blow instead of rounder and rounder? The shape of the bubble is due in part to an important property of fluids: Fluids exert pressure evenly in all directions. The air you blow into the bubble exerts pressure evenly in every direction, so the bubble expands in every direction, helping to create a sphere, as shown in **Figure 2.** This property also explains why tires inflate evenly (unless there is a weak spot in the tire).

Atmospheric Pressure

The *atmosphere* is the layer of nitrogen, oxygen, and other gases that surrounds the Earth. The atmosphere stretches about 150 km above us. If you could stack 500 Eiffel Towers on top of each other, they would come close to reaching the top of the atmosphere. However, approximately 80 percent of the gases in the atmosphere are found within 10 km of the Earth's surface. Earth's atmosphere is held in place by gravity, which pulls the gases toward Earth. The pressure caused by the weight of the atmosphere is called **atmospheric pressure.**

Atmospheric pressure is exerted on everything on Earth, including you. The atmosphere exerts a pressure of approximately 101,300 N on every square meter, or 101,300 Pa. This means that there is a weight of about 10 N (roughly the weight of a pineapple) on every square centimeter (roughly the area of the tip of your little finger) of your body. Ouch!

Why don't you feel this crushing pressure? The fluids inside your body also exert pressure, just like the air inside a balloon exerts pressure. **Figure 3** can help you understand.

Figure 2 *You can't blow a square bubble, because fluids exert pressure equally in every direction.*

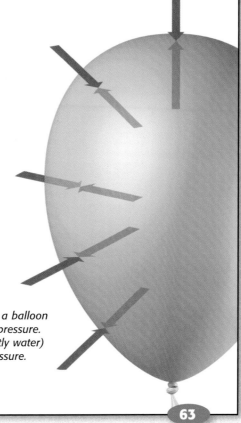

Figure 3 *The pressure exerted by the air inside a balloon keeps the balloon inflated against atmospheric pressure. Similarly, the pressure exerted by the fluid (mostly water) inside your body works against atmospheric pressure.*

63

IS THAT A FACT!

The air in a large room in your house weighs about as much as an average adult male! (about 736 N)

CROSS-DISCIPLINARY FOCUS

Language Arts Have students compose a short poem describing something about flowing fluids (examples: water, mixing liquids, air, steam, clouds, fog, or food).

Have students research the effects of atmospheric pressure on weather. Have them make a poster or concept map to display their results.

BRAIN FOOD

The extremely high altitude of Mount Everest makes even base camps on the mountain hazardous to visitors' health. Most of these base camps are more than 4,000 m above sea level. Altitude sickness affects most people who reach that elevation. Most climbers must use oxygen masks above 5,500 m because there is not enough oxygen to sustain normal body functions.

RETEACHING

Writing Have students write an essay describing how they are affected by fluid pressure on a typical day. Students should include examples such as weather, transportation, plumbing, breathing, bathing, playing outside, and so on. Encourage them to be creative.

PORTFOLIO

Figure 4 Differences in Atmospheric Pressure

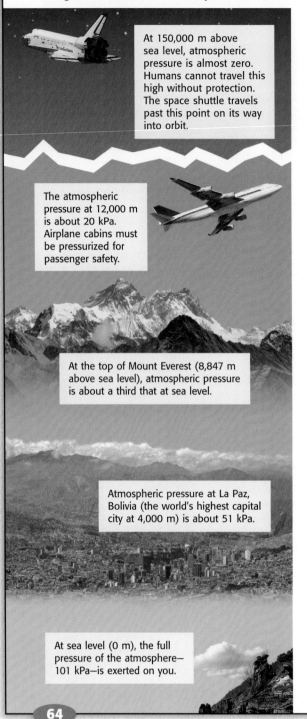

At 150,000 m above sea level, atmospheric pressure is almost zero. Humans cannot travel this high without protection. The space shuttle travels past this point on its way into orbit.

The atmospheric pressure at 12,000 m is about 20 kPa. Airplane cabins must be pressurized for passenger safety.

At the top of Mount Everest (8,847 m above sea level), atmospheric pressure is about a third that at sea level.

Atmospheric pressure at La Paz, Bolivia (the world's highest capital city at 4,000 m) is about 51 kPa.

At sea level (0 m), the full pressure of the atmosphere—101 kPa—is exerted on you.

64

Atmospheric Pressure Varies At the top of the atmosphere, pressure is almost non-existent because there is no atmosphere pressing down. At the top of Mount Everest in south-central Asia (which is the highest point on Earth), atmospheric pressure is about 33,000 Pa, or 33 kilopascals (kPa). At sea level, atmospheric pressure is about 101 kPa.

Pressure Depends on Depth As shown in **Figure 4,** pressure increases as you descend through the atmosphere. In other words, the pressure increases as the atmosphere gets "deeper." This is an important point about fluids: Pressure depends on the depth of the fluid. At lower levels of the atmosphere, there is more fluid above you being pulled by Earth's gravitational force, so there is more pressure.

If you travel to higher or lower points in the atmosphere, the fluids in your body have to adjust to maintain equal pressure. You may have experienced this if your ears have "popped" when you were in a plane taking off or a car traveling down a steep mountain road. Small pockets of air behind your eardrums contract or expand as atmospheric pressure increases or decreases. The "pop" occurs when air is released due to these pressure changes.

SECTION REVIEW

1. How do particles in a fluid exert pressure on a container?

2. Why are you not crushed by atmospheric pressure?

3. **Applying Concepts** Explain why dams on deep lakes should be thicker at the bottom than near the top.

1. The moving particles in a fluid collide against each other and against the walls of the container. This creates pressure.

2. The pressure exerted by the fluids in your body works against atmospheric pressure.

3. Water pressure increases with depth. Therefore, more pressure is exerted at the bottom of the dam than at the top. The dam must be thicker at the bottom to withstand this added pressure.

Water Pressure

Water is a fluid; therefore, it exerts pressure, just like the atmosphere does. Water pressure also increases with depth because of gravity. Take a look at **Figure 5**. The deeper a diver goes in the water, the greater the pressure becomes because more water above the diver is being pulled by Earth's gravitational force. In addition, the atmosphere presses down on the water, so the total pressure on the diver includes water pressure as well as atmospheric pressure.

But pressure does not depend on the total amount of fluid present, only on the depth of the fluid. A swimmer would feel the same pressure swimming at 5 m below the surface of a small pond as at 5 m below the surface of an ocean, even though there is more water in the ocean.

Density Makes a Difference Water is about 1,000 times more dense than air. (Remember, **density** is the amount of matter in a certain volume, or mass per unit volume.) Because water is more dense than air, a certain volume of water has more mass—and therefore weighs more—than the same volume of air. Therefore, water exerts greater pressure than air.

For example, if you climb a 10 m tree, the decrease in atmospheric pressure is too small to notice. But if you dive 10 m underwater, the pressure on you increases to 201 kPa, which is almost twice the atmospheric pressure at the surface!

Figure 5 Differences in Water Pressure

Pressure exerted on a diver 10 m below the water's surface is twice the pressure at the surface.

At 500 m below the surface, pressure is about 5,000 kPa. Divers at or below this level must wear special suits to survive the pressure.

The wreck of the *Titanic* rests 3,660 m below sea level. The water pressure at this depth is 36,600 kPa.

The viper fish lives 8,000 m below the ocean's surface. No fish are found below this level. The water pressure at this depth is 80,000 kPa.

In 1960, the *Trieste* descended to the deepest part of the ocean (11,000 m), where the pressure is 110,000 kPa.

REAL-WORLD CONNECTION

The pressure on a diver's body increases as the diver goes deeper underwater. The increased pressure on the diver's chest makes breathing more difficult. Scuba divers use a pressure regulator to solve this problem. As they go deeper, the regulator increases the pressure of the air released from the diver's air tanks. The pressure of the released air equals the pressure of the water on the diver, making breathing easier.

Multicultural CONNECTION

Have students do research on Japanese pearl divers. They should investigate the techniques these deep divers use to cope with the water pressure and the effects of pressure on the divers.

Math Skills Worksheet
"Density"

SCIENCE HUMOR

Q: What do you call a pod of whales on a deep dive?

A: grays under pressure

REAL-WORLD CONNECTION

Have students make a poster showing the airflow in their homes. Have them write a short description of the circulation of the air using the concept of fluid pressure. Students should include one or more ways they have used to track air movement accurately.

ACTIVITY

MATERIALS
FOR EACH STUDENT: • clean plastic cups • water • straws • pins

Safety Caution: Remind students to handle pins carefully and that everyone should wear safety goggles.

Tell students to sip some water through the straw. Then have them make a small hole in the straw about 5 cm from the top. Have students explain what happens when they try to drink water through the straw again. (Some liquid will rise up the straw, but air flowing through the hole will tend to push the liquid down.)

Teaching Transparency 225 "Air Pressure and Breathing"

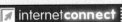

internetconnect

*SCi*LINKS. NSTA

TOPIC: Fluids and Pressure
GO TO: www.scilinks.org
*sci*LINKS NUMBER: HSTP160

Figure 6 *Atmospheric pressure helps you sip through a straw!*

Fluids Flow from High Pressure to Low Pressure

Look at **Figure 6.** When you drink through a straw, you remove some of the air in the straw. Because there is less air, the pressure in the straw is reduced. But the atmospheric pressure on the surface of the liquid remains the same. This creates a difference between the pressure inside the straw and the pressure outside the straw. The outside pressure forces the liquid up into the straw and into your mouth. So just by sipping your drink through a straw, you can observe another important property of fluids: Fluids flow from regions of high pressure to regions of low pressure.

Go with the Flow Take a deep breath—that's fluid flowing from high to low pressure! When you inhale, a muscle increases the space in your chest, giving your lungs room to expand. This expansion lowers the pressure in your lungs so that it becomes lower than the outside air pressure. Air then flows into your lungs—from higher to lower pressure. This air carries oxygen that you need to live. **Figure 7** shows how exhaling also causes fluids to flow from higher to lower pressure. You can see this same exchange when you open a carbonated beverage or squeeze toothpaste onto your toothbrush.

QuickLab

Blown Away

1. Lay an **empty plastic soda bottle** on its side.
2. Wad **a small piece of paper** (about 4 × 4 cm) into a ball.
3. Place the paper ball just inside the bottle's opening.
4. Blow straight into the opening.
5. Record your observations in your ScienceLog.
6. Explain your results in terms of high and low fluid pressures.

TRY at HOME

Figure 7 *Just as when you inhale, fluids flow from high to low pressure when you exhale.*

c Exhaled air carries carbon dioxide out of the lungs.

b The decrease in space causes the pressure in your lungs to increase. The air in your lungs flows from a region of higher pressure (your chest) to a region of lower pressure (outside of your body).

a When you exhale, a muscle in your chest moves upward, decreasing the space in your chest.

QuickLab

MATERIALS
FOR EACH STUDENT: • empty plastic soda bottle • 4 × 4 cm paper

Answers to QuickLab

5. Students should observe that the paper wad flies out of the bottle.
6. By blowing into the bottle, the air pressure inside the bottle is increased. Fluids flow from high pressure to low pressure, so the air inside flows out of the bottle, carrying the paper wad with it.

Pascal's Principle

Imagine that the water-pumping station in your town can now increase the water pressure by 20 Pa. Will the water pressure be increased more at a supermarket two blocks away or at a home 2 km away?

Believe it or not, the increase in water pressure will be transmitted through all of the water and will be the same—20 Pa—at both locations. This is explained by Pascal's principle, named for Blaise Pascal, the seventeenth-century French scientist who discovered it. **Pascal's principle** states that a change in pressure at any point in an enclosed fluid will be transmitted equally to all parts of that fluid.

Putting Pascal's Principle to Work

Devices that use liquids to transmit pressure from one point to another are called *hydraulic* (hie DRAW lik) devices. Hydraulic devices use liquids because they cannot be compressed, or squeezed, into a smaller space very much. This property allows liquids to transmit pressure more efficiently than gases, which can be compressed a great deal.

Hydraulic devices can multiply forces. The brakes of a typical car are a good example. In **Figure 8,** a driver's foot exerts pressure on a cylinder of liquid. Pascal's principle tells you that this pressure is transmitted equally to all parts of the liquid-filled brake system. This liquid presses a brake pad against each wheel, and friction brings the car to a stop. The force is multiplied because the pistons that push the brake pads on each wheel are much larger than the piston that is pushed by the brake pedal.

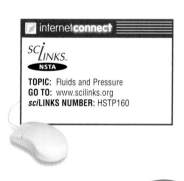

Figure 8 *Thanks to Pascal's principle, the touch of a foot can stop tons of moving metal.*

SECTION REVIEW

1. Explain how atmospheric pressure helps you drink through a straw.

2. What does Pascal's principle state?

3. **Making Predictions** When you squeeze a balloon, where is the pressure inside the balloon increased the most? Explain your answer in terms of Pascal's principle.

internet**connect**

SCI*LINKS*
NSTA

TOPIC: Fluids and Pressure
GO TO: www.scilinks.org
*sci*LINKS **NUMBER:** HSTP160

67

Focus

Buoyant Force

This section describes how differences in fluid pressure create buoyant force. Students are introduced to Archimedes' principle and learn how to calculate the buoyant force exerted on an object. Finally, students learn the factors that determine whether an object floats or sinks in a fluid.

🔊 Bellringer

Pose the following question to your students:

Which of the following objects will float in water?

a rock, an orange, a screw, a quarter, a candle, a plastic-foam "peanut," a chalkboard eraser

Ask them to write a hypothesis about why an aircraft carrier, which has a mass of thousands of tons, does not sink.

1 Motivate

DEMONSTRATION

Add 20 mL each of molasses, cooking oil, and water to a 100 mL graduated cylinder. Either before students enter the classroom or while they observe, insert several different objects that will float on different layers. You might also try adding droplets of alcohol. Use the results of the demonstration to launch a discussion about buoyant force.

Directed Reading Worksheet Section 2

Terms to Learn

buoyant force
Archimedes' principle

What You'll Do

◆ Explain the relationship between fluid pressure and buoyant force.
◆ Predict whether an object will float or sink in a fluid.
◆ Analyze the role of density in an object's ability to float.

Buoyant Force

Why does a rubber duck float on water? Why doesn't it sink to the bottom of your bath-tub? Even if you pushed the rubber duck to the bottom, it would pop back to the surface when you released it. Some force pushes the rubber duck to the top of the water. That force is **buoyant force,** the upward force that fluids exert on all matter.

Air is a fluid, so it exerts a buoyant force. But why don't you ever see rubber ducks floating in air? Read on to find out!

Buoyant Force Is Caused by Differences in Fluid Pressure

Look at **Figure 9.** Water exerts fluid pressure on all sides of an object. The pressure exerted horizontally on one side of the object is equal to the pressure exerted horizontally on the opposite side. These equal pressures cancel one another. Thus, the only fluid pressures affecting the object are at the top and at the bottom. Because pressure increases with depth, the pressure on the bottom of the object is greater than the pressure at the top, as shown by the width of the arrows. Therefore, the water exerts a net upward force on the object. This upward force is buoyant force.

Determining Buoyant Force Archimedes (ahr kuh MEE deez), a Greek mathematician who lived in the third century B.C., discovered how to determine buoyant force. **Archimedes' principle** states that the buoyant force on an object in a fluid is an upward force equal to the weight of the volume of fluid that the object displaces. (*Displace* means "to take the place of.") For example, suppose the object in Figure 9 displaces 250 mL of water. The weight of that volume of displaced water is about 2.5 N. Therefore, the buoyant force on the object is 2.5 N. Notice that the weight of the object has nothing to do with the buoyant force. Only the weight of the displaced fluid determines the buoyant force on an object.

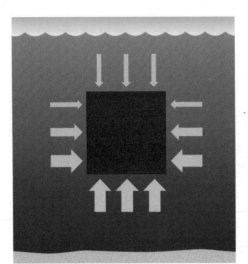
Figure 9 *There is more fluid pressure on the bottom of an object because pressure increases with depth. This results in an upward force on the object—buoyant force.*

SCIENCE HUMOR

Q: Why did the banker jump into the swimming pool?

A: He needed to float a loan.

Weight Vs. Buoyant Force

An object in a fluid will sink if it has a weight greater than the weight of the fluid that is displaced. In other words, an object will sink if its weight is greater than the buoyant force acting on it. An object floats only when it displaces a volume of fluid that has a weight equal to the object's weight—that is, if the buoyant force on the object is equal to the object's weight.

Sinking The lake scene in **Figure 10** looks quite peaceful, but there are forces being exerted! The rock weighs 75 N. It displaces 5 L of water. According to Archimedes' principle, the buoyant force is equal to the weight of the displaced water—about 50 N. Because the rock's weight is greater than the buoyant force, the rock sinks.

Floating The fish weighs 12 N. It displaces a volume of water that has a weight of 12 N. Because the fish's weight is equal to the buoyant force, the fish floats in the water. Now look at the duck. The duck weighs 9 N. The duck does not sink. What does that tell you? The buoyant force on the duck must be equal to the duck's weight. But the duck isn't even all the way underwater! Only the duck's feet, legs, and stomach have to be underwater in order to displace enough water to equal 9 N. Thus, the duck floats.

Buoying Up If the duck dove underwater, it would then displace more water, and the buoyant force would therefore be greater. When the buoyant force on an object is greater than the object's weight, the object is *buoyed up* (pushed up) out of the water until what's left underwater displaces an amount of water that equals the object's entire weight. That's why a rubber duck pops to the surface when it is pushed to the bottom of a filled bathtub.

Activity

Find five things that float in water and five things that sink in water. What do the floating objects have in common? What do the sinking objects have in common?

TRY at HOME

READING 📖 STRATEGY

Prediction Guide Before students read the next three pages, ask them whether the following statements are true or false:

1. The shape of an object helps determine whether it will float. (true)
2. Something made of steel cannot float in water. (false)
3. The force of gravity is less in water than on dry land. (false)

Have students evaluate their answers after they read the next three pages.

MATH and MORE

Ask students to solve the following problem:

A force of 15 N is required to lift an object that is underwater. The object displaces 2 L of water (1 L of water weighs 10 N). What is the weight of the object out of water? (force required to lift object in water = weight of object out of water − buoyant force

15 N = weight of object out of water − 20 N

weight of object out of water = 20 N + 15 N = 35 N)

Figure 10 *Will an object sink or float? It depends on whether the buoyant force is less than or equal to the object's weight.*

Weight = 12 N
Buoyant force = 12 N
Fish floats in the water

Weight = 9 N
Buoyant force = 9 N
Duck floats on the surface

Weight = 75 N
Buoyant force = 50 N
Rock sinks

Homework

Concept Mapping Have students create a buoyant force concept map and discuss objects that float on the surface, objects that float between the surface and the bottom, and objects that sink to the bottom.

Answer to Activity

Accept all reasonable answers. Students may answer that floating objects are light and sinking objects are heavy. Drop a penny in a glass of water, and ask students if the penny weighs more than an aircraft carrier. Review and discuss the concept of density. If necessary, reread with them the "Weight Vs. Buoyant Force" section to help clarify this difficult concept.

BRAIN FOOD

Can a helium balloon keep rising forever? Helium is less dense than air, so a balloon filled with helium weighs less than the same volume of air. Air exerts a buoyant force on the balloon and pushes it up. The balloon will continue to rise as long as the weight of the displaced air is greater than the weight of the balloon. Eventually, the weight of the balloon will equal the weight of the displaced air, and the balloon will stop rising.

ACTIVITY

Making Models Students will make a model of a hot-air balloon. Before they begin, discuss how heating the air inside the balloon changes the balloon's overall density and therefore changes its buoyancy. Provide students with tissue paper, tape, glue, string, and other materials to make a model balloon. Hold each completed model in place and fill it with hot air from a hair dryer. Release the model to see if it flies. Have students evaluate their balloon's performance.

LabBook **PG 192**
Density Diver

÷ 5 ÷ Ω ≤ ∞ +Ω ∨ 9 ∞≤ Σ 2
+

MATH BREAK

How to Calculate Density

The volume of any sample of matter, no matter what state or shape, can be calculated using this equation:

$$\text{Density} = \frac{\text{Mass}}{\text{Volume}}$$

1. What is the density of a 20 cm³ sample of liquid with a mass of 25 g?

2. A 546 g fish displaces 420 cm³ of water. What is the density of the fish?

An Object Will Float or Sink Based on Its Density

Think again about the rock at the bottom of the lake. The rock displaces 5 L of water, which means that the volume of the rock is 5,000 cm³. (Remember that liters are used only for fluid volumes.) But 5,000 cm³ of rock weighs more than an equal volume of water. This is why the rock sinks. Because mass is proportional to weight on Earth, you can say that the rock has more mass per volume than water. Remember, mass per unit volume is *density*. The rock sinks because it is more dense than water. The duck floats because it is less dense than water. In Figure 10, the density of the fish is exactly equal to the density of the water.

More Dense Than Air Think back to the question about the rubber duck: "Why does it float on water but not in air?" The rubber duck floats because it is less dense than water. However, most substances are *more* dense than air. Therefore, there are few substances that float in air. The plastic that makes up the rubber duck is more dense than air, so the rubber duck doesn't float in air.

Less Dense Than Air One substance that is less dense than air is helium, a gas. In fact, helium is over 70 times less dense than air. A volume of helium displaces a volume of air that is much heavier than itself, so helium floats. That's why helium is used in airships and parade balloons, like the one shown in **Figure 11.**

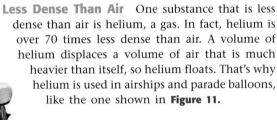
Figure 11 *Helium in a balloon floats in air for the same reason a duck floats in water—it is less dense than the surrounding fluid.*

70

Homework

Concept Mapping Have students create a concept map showing how an airship is similar to an aircraft carrier or a cruise ship.

IS THAT A FACT!

Before plastics can be recycled, they must first be separated by type. Most containers display a number that identifies the type of plastic used. Containers that do not display number codes can be separated by density by floating them in liquids of different densities.

The Mystery of Floating Steel

Steel is almost eight times more dense than water. And yet huge steel ships cruise the oceans with ease, even while carrying enormous loads. But hold on! Didn't you just learn that substances that are more dense than water will sink in water? You bet! So how does a steel ship float?

The secret is in the shape of the ship. What if a ship were just a big block of steel, as shown in **Figure 12**? If you put that steel block into water, the block would sink because it is more dense than water. For this reason, ships are built with a hollow shape, as shown below. The amount of steel in the ship is the same as in the block, but the hollow shape increases the volume of the ship. Because density is mass per volume, an increase in the ship's volume leads to a decrease in its density. Therefore, ships made of steel float because their *overall density* is less than the density of water. This is true of boats of any size, made of any material. Most ships are actually built to displace even more water than is necessary for the ship to float so that the ship won't sink when people and cargo are loaded onboard.

BRAIN FOOD

The *Seawise Giant* is the largest ship in the world. It is so large that crew members often use bicycles to travel around the ship.

Figure 12 A Ship's Shape Makes the Difference

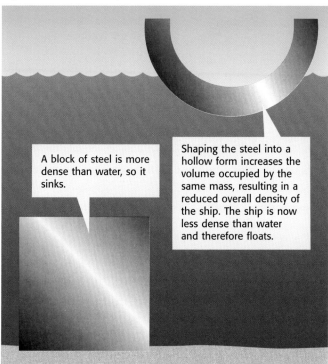

A block of steel is more dense than water, so it sinks.

Shaping the steel into a hollow form increases the volume occupied by the same mass, resulting in a reduced overall density of the ship. The ship is now less dense than water and therefore floats.

QuickLab

Ship-Shape

1. Roll a **piece of clay** into a ball the size of a golf ball, and drop it into a **container of water**. Record your observations in your ScienceLog.

2. With your hands, flatten the ball of clay until it is a bit thinner than your little finger, and press it into the shape of a bowl or canoe.

3. Place the clay boat gently in the water. How does the change of shape affect the buoyant force on the clay? How is that change related to the average density of the clay boat? Record your answers in your ScienceLog.

71

QuickLab

MATERIALS

FOR EACH STUDENT:
• clay
• medium-sized bowl or pail for every two or three students
• water

Safety Caution: Caution students to wear an apron when doing this lab.

Answer to QuickLab

3. Forming the clay into a boat shape causes it to displace more water, which increases the buoyant force. The change in shape causes the average density of the clay boat to decrease so that the clay boat is less dense than the water. Therefore, the clay boat floats.

4 Close

Quiz

1. How can you determine the buoyant force acting on an object? (Determine the weight of the volume of fluid displaced by the object.)

2. What factors determine how heavy an object can be and still float? (density and shape)

3. What happens when you place an object that has exactly the same density as water in water? (It neither sinks nor floats; it remains where you place it.)

4. How can a scuba diver keep from floating back to the surface of the water? (The diver can add weights.)

ALTERNATIVE ASSESSMENT

Ask students to use what they have learned to explain how a life jacket might help someone who falls out of a boat. (Most life jackets are made from porous material filled with air.) (A life jacket would help keep the person from sinking because the air inside the life jacket would increase the person's volume but not his or her weight. The person's overall density would decrease, allowing the person to float to the surface of the water.)

Interactive Explorations CD-ROM "Sea the Light"

The rock that makes up the Earth's continents is about 15 percent less dense than the molten (melted) mantle rock below it. Because of this difference in densities, the continents are "floating" on the mantle.

Density on the Move A submarine is a special kind of ship that can travel on the surface of the water and underwater. Submarines have special tanks that can be opened to allow sea water to flow in. This water adds mass, thus increasing the submarine's overall density so it can descend into the ocean. Crew members can control the amount of water taken in, thereby controlling the submarine's change in density and thus its depth in the ocean. Compressed air is used to blow the water out of the tanks so the submarine can rise through the water. Most submarines are built of high-strength metals that withstand water pressure. Still, most submarines can go no deeper than 400 m below the surface of the ocean.

How Is a Fish Like a Submarine? No, this is not a trick question! Like a submarine, some fish adjust their overall density in order to stay at a certain depth in the water. Most bony fish have an organ called a *swim bladder*, shown in **Figure 13**. This swim bladder is filled with gases produced in the fish's blood. The inflated swim bladder increases the fish's volume, thereby decreasing the fish's overall density and keeping it from sinking in the water. The fish's nervous system controls the amount of gas in the bladder according to the fish's depth in the water. Some fish, such as sharks, do not have a swim bladder. These fish must swim constantly to keep from sinking to the bottom of the water.

Figure 13 *Most bony fish have an organ called a swim bladder that allows the fish to adjust its overall density.*

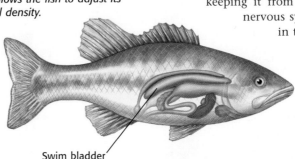

Swim bladder

SECTION REVIEW

1. Explain how differences in fluid pressure create buoyant force on an object.

2. An object weighs 20 N. It displaces a volume of water that weighs 15 N.
   a. What is the buoyant force on the object?
   b. Will this object float or sink? Explain your answer.

3. Iron has a density of 7.9 g/cm^3. Mercury has a density of 13.6 g/cm^3. Will iron float or sink in mercury? Explain your answer.

4. **Applying Concepts** Why is it inaccurate to say that all heavy objects will sink in water?

▼ *Answers to Section Review*

1. Water pressure is exerted on all sides of an object. The pressures exerted horizontally on both sides cancel each other out. The pressure exerted at the bottom is greater than that exerted at the top because pressure increases with depth. This creates an overall upward force on the object—the buoyant force.

2. a. 15 N

b. It will sink because its weight is greater than the buoyant force acting on it.

3. It will float because it is less dense than mercury.

4. Whether an object sinks or floats depends on density, not weight. A heavy object can have an overall density that is less than that of water and can therefore float.

Terms to Learn

Bernoulli's principle
lift
thrust
drag

What You'll Do

- Describe the relationship between pressure and fluid speed.
- Analyze the roles of lift, thrust, and drag in flight.
- Give examples of Bernoulli's principle in real-life situations.

Bernoulli's Principle

Has this ever happened to you? You've just turned on the shower. Upon stepping into the water stream, you decide that the water pressure is not strong enough. You turn the faucet to provide more water, and all of a sudden the bottom edge of the shower curtain starts swirling around your legs. What's going on? It might surprise you that the explanation for this unusual occurrence also explains how wings help birds and planes fly and how pitchers throw curve balls.

Fluid Pressure Decreases as Speed Increases

The strange reaction of the shower curtain is caused by a property of moving fluids that was first described in the eighteenth century by Daniel Bernoulli (buhr NOO lee), a Swiss mathematician. **Bernoulli's principle** states that as the speed of a moving fluid increases, its pressure decreases. In the case of the shower curtain, the faster the water moves, the less pressure it exerts. This creates an imbalance between the pressure inside the shower curtain and the pressure outside it. Because the pressure outside is now greater than the pressure inside, the shower curtain is pushed toward the water stream.

Science in a Sink You can see Bernoulli's principle at work in **Figure 14.** A table-tennis ball is attached to a string and swung gently into a moving stream of water. Instead of being pushed back out, the ball is actually held in the moving water when the string is given a tug. Why does the ball do that? The water is moving, so it has a lower pressure than the surrounding air. The higher air pressure then pushes the ball into the area of lower pressure—the water stream. Try this at home to see for yourself!

Figure 14 *This ball is pushed by the higher pressure of the air into an area of reduced pressure—the water stream.*

73

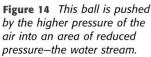

Breathing Bernoulli-Style

1. Hold **two pieces of paper** by their top edges, one in each hand, so that they hang next to one another about 5 cm apart.
2. Blow a steady stream of air between the two sheets of paper.
3. Record your observations in your ScienceLog. Explain the results according to Bernoulli's principle. *TRY at HOME*

QuickLab

MATERIALS

FOR EACH STUDENT:
- two pieces of paper

Answer to QuickLab

3. Blowing a steady stream of air between the pieces of paper causes them to move toward each other—an example of Bernoulli's principle. The fast-moving air between the pieces of paper has a lower pressure than the air outside the pieces of paper. The higher pressure outside pushes the pieces of paper together.

MEETING INDIVIDUAL NEEDS

Learners Having Difficulty
Before you discuss Bernoulli's principle, it may help some students to imagine the pressure of a fluid as the combined pressure of many particles striking a surface. Have students imagine a swarm of bees trapped in a short section of a long piece of pipe. As the bees fly around inside the pipe, they bounce off each other and off the walls of the pipe, creating pressure. Now imagine the bees are suddenly able to fly the entire length of the pipe. Because they now have more room, they bounce against the walls of the pipe much less frequently, creating less pressure inside the pipe.

MEETING INDIVIDUAL NEEDS

Advanced Learners Ask students to examine the wing shapes shown in **Figure 15.** Have students use their knowledge of Bernoulli's principle to hypothesize about what type of wings might work in flight. Does the wing have to be curved? How does each of Newton's laws apply to both curved and flat wings? Is flight possible without wings?

DEMONSTRATION

Point the airflow of a portable hair dryer straight up, and suspend a table-tennis ball in the airstream. Change the direction of the airflow slightly to maneuver the ball. Have students speculate on the forces that are at work in this demonstration.

It's a Bird! It's a Plane! It's Bernoulli's Principle!

The most common commercial airplane in the skies today is the Boeing 737 jet. A 737 jet is almost 37 m long and has a wingspan of 30 m. Even without passengers, the plane weighs 350,000 N. That's more than 35 times heavier than an average car! How can something so big and heavy get off the ground, much less fly 10,000 m into the sky? Wing shape plays a role in helping these big planes—as well as smaller planes and even birds—achieve flight, as shown in **Figure 15.**

According to Bernoulli's principle, the faster-moving air above the wing exerts less pressure than the slower-moving air below the wing. The increased pressure that results below the wing exerts an upward force. This upward force, known as **lift,** pushes the wings (and the rest of the airplane or bird) upward against the downward pull of gravity.

BRAIN FOOD

The first successful flight of an engine-driven heavier-than-air machine occurred in Kitty Hawk, North Carolina, in 1903. Orville Wright was the pilot. The plane flew only 37 m (about the length of a 737 jet) before landing, and the entire flight lasted only 12 seconds.

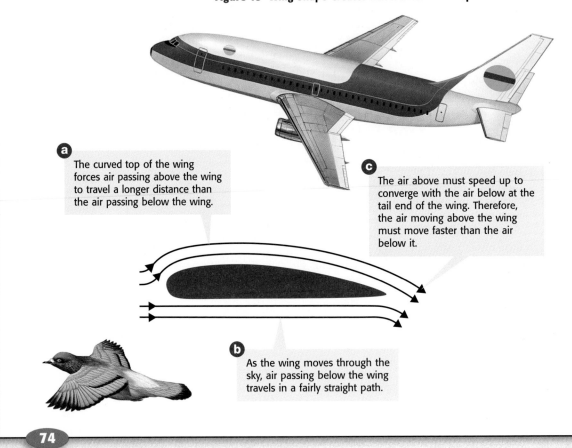

Figure 15 Wing Shape Creates Differences in Air Speed

a The curved top of the wing forces air passing above the wing to travel a longer distance than the air passing below the wing.

c The air above must speed up to converge with the air below at the tail end of the wing. Therefore, the air moving above the wing must move faster than the air below it.

b As the wing moves through the sky, air passing below the wing travels in a fairly straight path.

MISCONCEPTION ///ALERT\\\

In teaching about airplane flight, emphasize that there is more to understanding lift than can be explained by Bernoulli's principle alone. Newton's third law also plays a part—a tilted wing deflects horizontal airflow downward (the action force exerted by the wing on the air). In reaction, the air exerts an upward force on the wing. This effect also contributes to lift.

Thrust and Wing Size Determine Lift

The amount of lift created by a plane's wing is determined in part by the size of the wing and the speed at which air travels around the wing. The speed of an airplane is in large part determined by its **thrust**—the forward force produced by the plane's engine. In general, a plane with a greater amount of thrust moves faster than a plane with less thrust. This faster speed means air travels around the wing at a greater speed, which increases lift.

You can understand the relationship between wing size, thrust, and speed by thinking about a jet plane, like the one in **Figure 16.** This plane is able to fly with a relatively small wing size because its engine creates an enormous amount of thrust. This thrust pushes the plane through the sky at tremendous speeds. Therefore, the jet generates sufficient lift with small wings by moving very quickly through the air. Smaller wings keep a plane's weight low, which also contributes to speed.

Compared with the jet, a glider, like the one in **Figure 17,** has a large wing area. A glider is an engineless plane that rides rising air currents to stay in flight. Without engines, gliders produce no thrust and move more slowly than many other kinds of planes. Thus, a glider must have large wings to create the lift necessary to keep it in the air.

Figure 16 *The engine of this jet creates a great deal of thrust, so the wings don't have to be very big.*

Figure 17 *The wings of this glider are very large in order to maximize the amount of lift achieved.*

✔ Self-Check

Does air travel faster or slower over the top of a wing? *(See page 232 to check your answer.)*

Bernoulli's Principle Is for the Birds Birds don't have engines, of course, so they must flap their wings to push themselves through the air. The hawk shown at left uses its large wing size to fly with a minimum of effort. By extending its large wings to their full length and gliding on wind currents, a hawk can achieve enough lift to stay in the air while flapping only occasionally. Smaller birds must flap their wings more often to stay in the air.

75

🌐 Multicultural CONNECTION

More than 8,000 years ago, Australian aborigines discovered the aerodynamic qualities of a type of hunting stick called a boomerang. Have students research boomerangs and compare a boomerang's flight to airplane flight.

 Teaching Transparency 227 "Wing Shape Creates Differences in Air Speed"

 Critical Thinking Worksheet "Build a Better Submarine"

GROUP ACTIVITY

Safety Caution: Caution students to wear goggles, gloves, and aprons while doing this activity.

Prepare a solution consisting of 250 mL of dishwashing liquid, 50–60 drops of glycerin, and 4.5 L of water. Give small groups of students containers of the solution and straws or other bubble-blowing tools. You may also want to provide them with index cards or fans to help create a breeze.

Ask the groups to devise ways to keep the bubbles from hitting the floor. Have them describe methods that increase the pressure under the bubble or decrease the pressure over it.

LabBook PG 193
Out the Spouts

MEETING INDIVIDUAL NEEDS

Advanced Learners Have students research how engineers use wind tunnels to test the design of airplane wings. Then have students use what they have learned to build their own wings and wind tunnel, and show the class how to test the wing designs.

Answer to Self-Check

Air travels faster over the top of a wing.

internet**connect**

SCiLINKS
NSTA

TOPIC: Bernoulli's Principle
GO TO: www.scilinks.org
*sci*LINKS NUMBER: HSTP170

Answer to APPLY

The upside-down wing shape causes air to travel faster under the spoiler, reducing the air pressure. The higher air pressure above the spoiler "pushes" the car down, reducing the chances that the rear wheels will lose contact with the ground.

CROSS-DISCIPLINARY FOCUS

Language Arts Have students imagine being a hawk or an albatross. (They may need to do a little research.) Have students write a report or make a poster or concept map describing how the principles of flight apply to them as they travel through the sky.

3 Extend

GOING FURTHER

Have students work together in groups to research and select a design for a paper airplane they think would have the longest flight time. When all groups have made their plane, take the class outside to fly the planes. Each group should select a member to throw their plane gently from the same location. Have students record the results for five flights, then average the times and write the data on the board. Discuss the differences in the planes that may account for the observed results.

Teaching Transparency 228
"Pitching a Curve Ball"

Lift and Spoilers

At high speeds, air moving around the body of this race car could lift the car just as it lifts a plane's wing. This could cause the wheels to lose contact with the ground, sending the car out of control. To prevent this situation, an upside-down wing, or spoiler, is mounted on the rear of the car. How do spoilers help reduce the danger of accidents?

Drag Opposes Motion in Fluids

Have you ever walked into a strong wind and noticed that the wind seemed to slow you down? Fluids exert a force that opposes motion. The force that opposes or restricts motion in a fluid is called **drag.** In a strong wind, air "drags" on your clothes and body, making it difficult for you to move forward. Drag forces in flight work against the forward motion of a plane or bird and are usually caused by an irregular flow of air around the wings. An irregular or unpredictable flow of fluids is known as *turbulence.*

Lift is often reduced when turbulence causes drag. At faster speeds, drag can become a serious problem, so airplanes are equipped with ways to reduce turbulence as much as possible when in flight. For example, flaps like those shown in **Figure 18** can be used to change the shape or area of a wing, thereby reducing drag and increasing lift. Similarly, birds can adjust their wing feathers in response to turbulence to achieve greater lift.

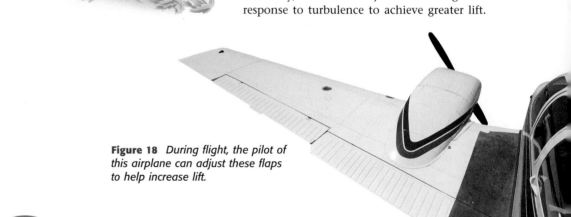

Figure 18 *During flight, the pilot of this airplane can adjust these flaps to help increase lift.*

SCIENTISTS AT ODDS

In the 1940s, pilots of high-speed airplanes reported that as they approached the speed of sound (343 m/s at 20°C), their planes began to shake and the controls did not function properly. At these speeds, shock waves formed a cone of turbulence around the plane, interrupting the airflow over the wings. Some scientists believed that an airplane could not go faster than the speed of sound because the turbulence from shock waves would tear the wings apart. Others believed that with better designs, planes could pass this speed. Jet planes with swept-back wings and stronger frames eventually surpassed the speed of sound.

Wings Are Not Always Required

You don't have to look up at a bird or a plane flying through the sky to see Bernoulli's principle in your world. In fact, you've already learned how Bernoulli's principle can affect such things as shower curtains and race cars. Any time fluids are moving, Bernoulli's principle is at work. In **Figure 19,** you can see how Bernoulli's principle can mean the difference between a home run and a strike during a baseball game.

Bernoulli's principle at play—read how Frisbees® were invented on page 84.

Figure 19 *A pitcher can take advantage of Bernoulli's principle to produce a confusing curveball that is difficult for the batter to hit.*

a Air speed on the left side of the ball is decreased because air being dragged around the ball moves in the opposite direction of the airflow. This results in a region of increased pressure on the left side of the ball.

Direction of airflow

Direction of spin

b Air speed on the right side of the ball is increased because air being dragged around the ball moves in the same direction as the airflow. This results in a region of decreased pressure on the right side of the ball.

c Because air pressure on the left side is greater than that on the right side, the ball is pushed toward the right in a curved path.

SECTION REVIEW

1. Does fluid pressure increase or decrease as fluid speed increases?

2. Explain how wing shape can contribute to lift during flight.

3. What force opposes motion through a fluid?

4. **Interpreting Graphics** When the space through which a fluid flows becomes narrow, fluid speed increases. Explain how this could lead to a collision for the two boats shown at right.

Answers to Section Review

1. Fluid pressure decreases.

2. Many wings are shaped so that air passing over the wing travels a longer distance than air traveling under the wing. The air above the wing must speed up to converge with the air below. This faster-moving air reduces the pressure above the wing, and higher pressure below the wing results in lift (upward force on the wing).

3. drag

4. As the fluid speed between the boats increases, the fluid pressure decreases. The pressure on the outer sides of the boats then becomes greater than the pressure between them. This increased pressure from the outside can push the boats together, causing them to collide.

A hurricane is a large, circular storm system that usually occurs in late summer or early fall. In a powerful hurricane, winds can reach speeds of 150 km/h. This fast-moving wind may reduce outside air pressure so much that the higher air pressure inside a house causes windows to break and the roof to fly off.

4 Close

Quiz

1. What forces act on an aircraft? (lift, thrust, drag, and gravity)

2. When an airplane is flying, how does the air pressure above a wing compare with that below the wing? (Air pressure above the wing is lower.)

3. Why do shower curtains often have weights or magnets at the bottom? (to prevent them from being pushed toward the water stream)

ALTERNATIVE ASSESSMENT

Display two or three photographs or models of different types of aircraft, such as a glider, a jet, a biplane, or even an airship. Ask students to select two of the aircraft to compare and contrast them in terms of lift, drag, thrust, and gravity. What are the characteristics of each aircraft that allow it to fly?

Reinforcement Worksheet
"Building Up Pressure"

Section 3 • Bernoulli's Principle   **77**

Skill Builder Lab

Fluids, Force, and Floating
Teacher's Notes

Time Required

One or two 45-minute class periods

Lab Ratings

EASY			HARD

TEACHER PREP ♦
STUDENT SET-UP ♦♦
CONCEPT LEVEL ♦♦♦
CLEAN UP ♦

MATERIALS

The supplies listed are for one group of 3–4 students. The tank or tub should have vertical sides. A small or medium-sized tub works best so that changes in volume can be observed easily. Masses should be added near the center of the baking pan. A fish tank or aquarium works well for this activity.

Preparation Notes

Before you begin this lab, review the concept of buoyant force with students. Make sure students wear an apron when doing this lab activity.

If you use a tub or pan without vertical sides, the buoyant force and the weight of the pans and masses will not be equal. In most cases the buoyant force will be greater than the weight.

Have students measure the side of the baking pan and mark the one-quarter, one-half, and three-quarter levels.

Fluids, Force, and Floating

Why do some objects sink in fluids but others float? In this lab, you'll get a sinking feeling as you determine that an object floats when its weight is less than the buoyant force exerted by the surrounding fluid.

MATERIALS

- large rectangular tank or plastic tub
- water
- metric ruler
- small rectangular baking pan
- labeled masses
- metric balance
- paper towels

Procedure

1. Copy the table on the next page into your ScienceLog.

2. Fill the tank or tub half full with water. Measure (in centimeters) the length, width, and initial height of the water. Record your measurements in the table.

3. Using the equation given in the table, determine the initial volume of water in the tank. Record your results in the table.

4. Place the pan in the water, and place masses in the pan, as shown on the next page. Keep adding masses until the pan sinks to about three-quarters of its height. Record the new height of the water in the table. Then use this value to determine and record the new volume of water.

5. Determine the volume of the water that was displaced by the pan and masses, and record this value in the table. The displaced volume is equal to the new volume minus the initial volume.

6. Determine the mass of the displaced water by multiplying the displaced volume by its density (1 g/cm³). Record the mass in the table.

7. Divide the mass by 100. The value you get is the weight of the displaced water in newtons (N). This weight is equal to the buoyant force. Record the weight of the displaced water in the table.

8. Remove the pan and masses, and determine their total mass (in grams), using the balance. Convert the mass to weight (N), as you did in step 7. Record the weight of the masses and pan in the table.

78

 Datasheets for LabBook

Sharon L. Woolf
Langston Hughes Middle School
Reston, Virginia

Measurement	Trial 1	Trial 2
Length (l), cm		
Width (w), cm		
Initial height (h_1), cm		
Initial volume (V_1), cm³ $V_1 = l \times w \times h_1$		
New height (h_2), cm		
New volume (V_2), cm³ $V_2 = l \times w \times h_2$		
Displaced volume (ΔV), cm³ $\Delta V = V_2 - V_1$		
Mass of displaced water, g $m = \Delta V \times 1 \text{ g/cm}^3$		
Weight of displaced water, N (buoyant force)		
Weight of pan and masses, N		

DO NOT WRITE IN BOOK

9 Place the empty pan back in the tank. Perform a second trial by repeating steps 4–8. This time, add masses until the pan is just about to sink.

Analysis

10 In your ScienceLog, compare the buoyant force (the weight of the displaced water) with the weight of the pan and masses for both trials.

11 How did the buoyant force differ between the two trials? Explain.

12 Based on your observations, what would happen if you were to add even more mass to the pan than you did in the second trial? Explain your answer in terms of

the buoyant force, balanced forces, and unbalanced forces.

13 What would happen if you put the masses in the water without the pan? What difference does the pan's shape make?

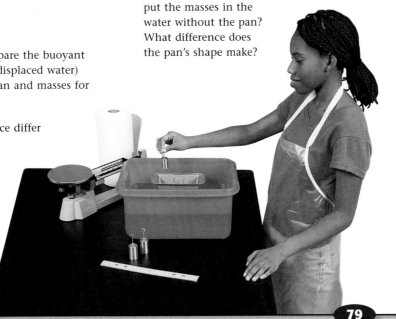

Answers

10. In each trial, the buoyant force and the weight should be the same.

11. The buoyant force is larger in the second trial because more water is displaced.

12. The pan would sink because the forces would not be balanced. The pan's weight would increase, but the buoyant force (the weight of the water displaced) would stay about the same. So, the weight would be greater than the buoyant force.

13. The masses would sink because the shape of the pan would allow the masses to displace more water than the masses alone displace.

Lab Notes

Volumes of liquids are usually expressed in milliliters (mL). Here the volume measurements for the water displaced are based on a rectangular container (the tank or tub), so cubic centimeters (cm³) are used.

Math Skills Worksheet "Subtraction Review"

Chapter Highlights

Chapter Highlights

SECTION 1

fluid any material that can flow and that takes the shape of its container

pressure the amount of force exerted on a given area

pascal the SI unit for pressure; equal to the force of one newton exerted over an area of one square meter

atmospheric pressure the pressure caused by the weight of the atmosphere

density the amount of matter in a given space; mass per unit volume

Pascal's principle the principle that states that a change in pressure at any point in an enclosed fluid is transmitted equally to all parts of that fluid

SECTION 2

buoyant force the upward force that fluids exert on all matter; buoyant force opposes gravitational force

Archimedes' principle the principle that states that the buoyant force on an object in a fluid is an upward force equal to the weight of the volume of fluid that the object displaces

SECTION 1

Vocabulary
- **fluid** (p. 62)
- **pressure** (p. 62)
- **pascal** (p. 62)
- **atmospheric pressure** (p. 63)
- **density** (p. 65)
- **Pascal's principle** (p. 67)

Section Notes

- A fluid is any material that flows and that takes the shape of its container.
- Pressure is force exerted on a given area.
- Moving particles of matter create pressure by colliding with one another and with the walls of their container.
- Fluids exert pressure equally in all directions.
- The pressure caused by the weight of Earth's atmosphere is called atmospheric pressure.
- Fluid pressure increases as depth increases.
- Fluids flow from areas of high pressure to areas of low pressure.
- Pascal's principle states that a change in pressure at any point in an enclosed fluid will be transmitted equally to all parts of the fluid.
- Hydraulic devices transmit changes of pressure through liquids.

SECTION 2

Vocabulary
- **buoyant force** (p. 68)
- **Archimedes' principle** (p. 68)

Section Notes

- All fluids exert an upward force called buoyant force.
- Buoyant force is caused by differences in fluid pressure.
- Archimedes' principle states that the buoyant force on an object is equal to the weight of the fluid displaced by the object.

☑ Skills Check

Math Concepts

PRESSURE If an object exerts a force of 10 N over an area of 2 m², the pressure exerted can be calculated as follows:

$$\text{Pressure} = \frac{\text{Force}}{\text{Area}}$$
$$= \frac{10 \text{ N}}{2 \text{ m}^2}$$
$$= \frac{5 \text{ N}}{1 \text{ m}^2}, \text{ or } 5 \text{ Pa}$$

Visual Understanding

ATMOSPHERIC PRESSURE Why aren't you crushed by atmospheric pressure? Figure 3 on page 63 can help you understand.

BUOYANT FORCE To understand how differences in fluid pressure cause buoyant force, review Figure 9 on page 68.

BERNOULLI'S PRINCIPLE AND WING SHAPE Turn to page 74 to review how a wing is often shaped to take advantage of Bernoulli's principle in creating lift.

Lab and Activity Highlights

Fluids, Force, and Floating **PG 78**

Density Diver **PG 192**

Out the Spouts **PG 193**

Datasheets for LabBook (blackline masters for these labs)

SECTION 2

- Any object that is more dense than the surrounding fluid will sink; any object that is less dense than the surrounding fluid will float.

Labs

Density Diver (p. 192)

SECTION 3

Vocabulary

Bernoulli's principle (p. 73)

lift (p. 74)

thrust (p. 75)

drag (p. 76)

Section Notes

- Bernoulli's principle states that fluid pressure decreases as the speed of a moving fluid increases.

- Wings are often shaped to allow airplanes to take advantage of decreased pressure in moving air in order to achieve flight.

- Lift is an upward force that acts against gravity.

- Lift on an airplane is determined by wing size and thrust (the forward force produced by the engine).

- Drag opposes motion through fluids.

VOCABULARY DEFINITIONS, *continued*

SECTION 3

Bernoulli's principle the principle that states that as the speed of a moving fluid increases, its pressure decreases

lift an upward force on an object (such as a wing) caused by differences in pressure above and below the object; lift opposes the downward pull of gravity

thrust the forward force produced by an airplane's engines; thrust opposes drag

drag the force that opposes or restricts motion in a fluid; drag opposes thrust

 Vocabulary Review Worksheet

 Blackline masters of these Chapter Highlights can be found in the **Study Guide.**

---

internet**connect**

 GO TO: go.hrw.com

Visit the **HRW** Web site for a variety of learning tools related to this chapter. Just type in the keyword:

KEYWORD: HSTFLU

 NSTA

GO TO: www.scilinks.org

Visit the **National Science Teachers Association** on-line Web site for Internet resources related to this chapter. Just type in the *sci*LINKS number for more information about the topic:

TOPIC: Submarines and Undersea Technology	*sci*LINKS NUMBER: HSTP155
TOPIC: Fluids and Pressure	*sci*LINKS NUMBER: HSTP160
TOPIC: The Buoyant Force	*sci*LINKS NUMBER: HSTP165
TOPIC: Bernoulli's Principle	*sci*LINKS NUMBER: HSTP170

81

Lab and Activity Highlights

LabBank

 Whiz-Bang Demonstrations
- The Rise and Fall of Raisins
- Going Against the Flow

EcoLabs & Field Activities, What's the Flap All About?

 Long-Term Projects & Research Ideas, Scuba Dive

Interactive Explorations CD-ROM

 CD 3, Exploration 2, "Sea the Light"

Chapter Review
Answers

USING VOCABULARY

1. Pressure
2. thrust
3. pressure
4. Pascal's principle
5. less than

UNDERSTANDING CONCEPTS

Multiple Choice

6. d
7. a
8. d
9. d
10. b
11. c

Short Answer

12. Thrust and wing size determine the amount of lift achieved by an airplane.
13. Water pressure is greater at a depth of 2 m in a small pond. Pressure increases with depth, regardless of the amount of fluid present.
14. Yes; the object displaces fluid. The buoyant force on the object equals the weight of the water displaced. In this case, however, the weight of the object was larger than the buoyant force, so the object sank.
15. Liquids are used in hydraulic brakes because liquids cannot be compressed easily. Gases are compressible.

Concept Mapping

16. 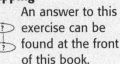 An answer to this exercise can be found at the front of this book.

**Concept Mapping
Transparency 7**

Chapter Review

USING VOCABULARY

To complete the following sentences, choose the correct term from each of the pair of terms listed below:

1. ___?___ increases with the depth of a fluid. *(Pressure* or *Lift)*

2. A plane's engine produces ___?___ to push the plane forward. *(thrust* or *drag)*

3. Force divided by area is known as ___?___. *(density* or *pressure)*

4. The hydraulic brakes of a car transmit pressure through fluid. This is an example of ___?___. *(Archimedes' principle* or *Pascal's principle)*

5. Bernoulli's principle states that the pressure exerted by a moving fluid is ___?___ *(greater than* or *less than)* the pressure of the fluid when it is not moving.

UNDERSTANDING CONCEPTS

Multiple Choice

6. The curve on the top of a wing
   a. causes air to travel farther in the same amount of time as the air below the wing.
   b. helps create lift.
   c. creates a low-pressure zone above the wing.
   d. All of the above

7. An object displaces a volume of fluid that
   a. is equal to its own volume.
   b. is less than its own volume.
   c. is greater than its own volume.
   d. is more dense than itself.

8. Fluid pressure is always directed
   a. up.   c. sideways.
   b. down.   d. in all directions.

9. If an object weighing 50 N displaces a volume of water with a weight of 10 N, what is the buoyant force on the object?
   a. 60 N
   b. 50 N
   c. 40 N
   d. 10 N

10. A helium-filled balloon will float in air because
    a. there is more air than helium.
    b. helium is less dense than air.
    c. helium is as dense as air.
    d. helium is more dense than air.

11. Materials that can flow to fit their containers include
    a. gases.
    b. liquids.
    c. both gases and liquids.
    d. neither gases nor liquids.

Short Answer

12. What two factors determine the amount of lift achieved by an airplane?

13. Where is water pressure greater, at a depth of 1 m in a large lake or at a depth of 2 m in a small pond? Explain.

14. Is there buoyant force on an object at the bottom of an ocean? Explain your reasoning.

15. Why are liquids used in hydraulic brakes instead of gases?

82

Concept Mapping

16. Use the following terms to create a concept map: fluid, pressure, depth, buoyant force, density.

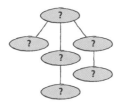

CRITICAL THINKING AND PROBLEM SOLVING

17. Compared with an empty ship, will a ship loaded with plastic-foam balls float higher or lower in the water? Explain your reasoning.

18. Inside all vacuum cleaners is a high-speed fan. Explain how this fan causes dirt to be picked up by the vacuum cleaner.

19. A 600 N clown on stilts says to two 600 N clowns sitting on the ground, "I am exerting twice as much pressure as the two of you together!" Could this statement be true? Explain your reasoning.

MATH IN SCIENCE

20. Calculate the area of a 1,500 N object that exerts a pressure of 500 Pa (N/m²). Then calculate the pressure exerted by the same object over twice that area. Be sure to express your answers in the correct SI unit.

INTERPRETING GRAPHICS

Examine the illustration of an iceberg below, and answer the questions that follow.

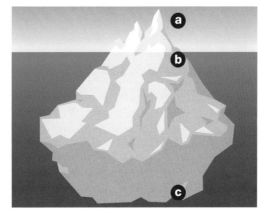

21. At what point (*a*, *b*, or *c*) is water pressure greatest on the iceberg?

22. How much of the iceberg has a weight equal to the buoyant force?
 a. all of it
 b. the section from *a* to *b*
 c. the section from *b* to *c*

23. How does the density of ice compare with the density of water?

24. Why do you think icebergs are so dangerous to passing ships?

Reading Check-up
Take a minute to review your answers to the Pre-Reading Questions found at the bottom of page 60. Have your answers changed? If necessary, revise your answers based on what you have learned since you began this chapter.

83

CRITICAL THINKING AND PROBLEM SOLVING

17. The ship will float lower in the water because the plastic-foam balls will add to the total mass of the ship but will not increase the volume. Therefore, the overall density of the ship will increase, causing the ship to sink a little.

18. The fan causes the air inside the vacuum cleaner to move faster, which decreases pressure. The higher air pressure outside of the vacuum then pushes dirt into the vacuum cleaner.

19. Yes, the statement could be true. Pressure is equal to force over area, that is, an amount of force applied over a certain area. The clown on stilts is exerting force over a much smaller area than the two clowns on the ground are. Therefore, it is possible that the clown on stilts is exerting twice as much force as the other two clowns are.

MATH IN SCIENCE
20. 3 m²; 250 Pa

INTERPRETING GRAPHICS
21. *c*
22. *a*
23. Ice is less dense than water.
24. Only a small portion of an iceberg floats above water, as shown in the image. A ship may actually be closer to running into a massive block of ice underwater than it would appear on the surface. If the ship is not turned or stopped in time, it could collide with or scrape the iceberg.

Blackline masters of this Chapter Review can be found in the **Study Guide.**

Background

In 1947, some people believed that an alien spacecraft had crashed in a desert in New Mexico. Based on that story and claimed sightings of UFOs in the Pacific Northwest, newspapers around the country began reporting the appearance of "flying saucers." Morrison and Franscioni recognized a good opportunity and decided to call their toy the "Flying Saucer." Morrison tried selling the "Flying Saucer" in stores and at county fairs. People were amazed as the saucer spun through the air, seeming to defy gravity. Some thought it must travel along an invisible wire because it stayed in the air so long. Seeing a sales opportunity, Morrison gave away the saucer for free but charged customers $1 for the invisible wire!

Teaching Strategy

Go to an open area with your students. Have students throw the Frisbees with different amounts of thrust, or have them vary the angle of attack when they throw their disk. Discuss Bernoulli's principle and other aspects of lift. Have students attempt to throw a Frisbee without any spin (eliminating the angular momentum that gives the disk stability in flight). Compare a spinning Frisbee with a spinning top or a moving bicycle.

Eureka!

Stayin' Aloft—The Story of the Frisbee®

Whoa! Nice catch! Your friend 30 m away just sent a disk spinning toward you. As you reached for it, a gust of wind floated it up over your head. With a quick jump, you snagged it. A snap of your wrist sends the disk soaring back. You are "Frisbee-ing," a game more than 100 years old. But back then, there were no plastic disks, only pie plates.

From Pie Plate...

In the late 1800s, ready-made pies baked in tin plates began to appear in stores and restaurants. A bakery near Yale University, in New Haven, Connecticut, embossed its name, Frisbie's Pies, on its pie plates. When a few fun-loving college students tossed empty pie plates, they found that the metal plates had a marvelous ability to stay in the air. Soon the students began alerting their companions of an incoming pie plate by shouting "Frisbie!" So tossing pie plates became known as Frisbie-ing. By the late 1940s, the game was played across the country.

...to Plastic

In 1947, California businessmen Fred Morrison and Warren Franscioni needed to make a little extra money. They were familiar with pie-plate tossing, and they knew the plates often cracked when they landed and developed sharp edges that caused injuries.

At the time, plastic was becoming widely available. Plastic is more durable and flexible than metal, and it isn't as likely to injure fingers. Why not make a "pie plate" out of plastic, thought Morrison and Franscioni? They did, and their idea was a huge success.

Years later, a toy company bought the rights to make the toy. One day the president of the company heard someone yelling "Frisbie!" while tossing a disk and decided to use that name, changing the spelling to "Frisbee."

Saucer Science

It looks simple, but Frisbee flight is quite complicated. It involves *thrust,* the force you give the disk to move it through the air; *angle of attack,* the slight upward tilt you give the disk when you throw it; and *lift,* the upward forces (explained by Bernoulli's principle) acting on the Frisbee to counteract gravity. But perhaps the most important aspect of Frisbee physics is *spin,* which gives the Frisbee stability as it flies. The faster a Frisbee spins, the more stable it is and the farther it can fly.

What Do You Think?

▶ From what you've learned in class, why do you think the Frisbee has a curved lip? Would a completely flat Frisbee fly as well? Why or why not? Find out more about the interesting aerodynamics of Frisbee flight. Fly a Frisbee for the class, and explain what you've learned.

Answer to What Do You Think?

A Frisbee has a curved lip in order to create lift. The air passing over the top of the Frisbee moves faster than the air traveling underneath. According to Bernoulli's principle, the pressure of air traveling over the top of the Frisbee is lower than that of the air traveling underneath. The increased pressure below the Frisbee exerts an upward force called lift. A flat Frisbee would not fly as well because its shape would create almost no lift.

Science Fiction

"Wet Behind the Ears"

by Jack C. Haldeman II

Willie Joe Thomas is a college student who lied to get into college and cheated to get a swimming scholarship. Now he is faced with a major swim meet, and his coach has told him that he has to swim or be kicked off the team. Willie Joe could lose his scholarship. What's worse, he would have to get a *job.*

"Wet Behind the Ears" is Willie Joe's story. It's the story of someone who has always taken the easy way (even if it takes more work), of someone who lies and cheats as easily as he breathes. Willie Joe could probably do things the right way, but it never even occurred to him to try it!

So when Willie Joe's roommate, Frank Emerson, announces that he has made an amazing discovery in the chemistry lab, Willie Joe doesn't much care. Frank works too hard. Frank follows the rules. Willie Joe isn't impressed.

But when he is running late for the all-important swim meet, Willie Joe remembers what Frank's new compound does. Frank said it was a "sliding compound." Willie Joe may not know chemistry, but "slippery" he understands. And Frank also said something about selling the stuff to the Navy to make its ships go faster. Hey, if it works for ships . . .

See what happens when Willie Joe tries to save his scholarship. Go to the *Holt Anthology of Science Fiction,* and read "Wet Behind the Ears," by Jack C. Haldeman II.

85

Further Reading Try some of Haldeman's other sports-related science fiction stories, such as the following:

"Louisville Slugger," *Isaac Asimov's Science Fiction Magazine,* Summer 1977.

"Thrill of Victory," *Isaac Asimov's Science Fiction Magazine,* Summer 1978.

"Dirt Track Demon," *Aladdin: Master of the Lamp,* Resnick & Greenberg, eds. New York: D.A.W. Books, 1992.

"South of Eden, Somewhere Near Salinas," *By Any Other Fame,* Mike Resnick, ed. New York: D.A.W. Books, 1994.

SCIENCE FICTION

"Wet Behind the Ears"
by Jack C. Haldeman II

Genuine effort can be less work than cheating, but Willie Joe just isn't the kind of person who exerts himself—even in a sink-or-swim situation.

Teaching Strategy

Reading Level This is a relatively short story that should not be difficult for the average student to read and comprehend.

Background

About the Author Sports and science fiction may seem like an unlikely combination, but Jack C. Haldeman enjoys both. He has written science fiction stories, sports stories, and stories such as "Wet Behind the Ears," which is a bit of both! Before becoming a writer, Haldeman received a college degree in life science and worked as a research assistant, a medical technician, a statistician, a photographer, and an apprentice in a print shop.

Many of Haldeman's stories are funny. For instance, "What Weighs 8,000 Pounds and Wears Red Sneakers?" describes a family that discovers their front yard is an elephant graveyard. Haldeman has also written several science fiction novels that explore issues in biology and in weapons development.

Chapter Organizer

CHAPTER ORGANIZATION	TIME MINUTES	OBJECTIVES	LABS, INVESTIGATIONS, AND DEMONSTRATIONS
Chapter Opener pp. 86–87	45	National Standards: SAI 1, ST 2, HNS 3	**Start-Up Activity,** C'mon, Lever a Little! p. 87
Section 1 Work and Power	90	▶ Determine when work is being done on an object. ▶ Calculate the amount of work done on an object. ▶ Explain the difference between work and power. UCP 3, SAI 1; Labs SAI 1	**QuickLab,** More Power to You, p. 91 **Discovery Lab,** A Powerful Workout, p. 106 **Datasheets for LabBook,** A Powerful Workout **Calculator-Based Labs,** Power of the Sun **Inquiry Labs,** Get an Arm and an Egg Up
Section 2 What Is a Machine?	90	▶ Explain how a machine makes work easier. ▶ Describe and give examples of the force-distance trade-off that occurs when a machine is used. ▶ Calculate mechanical advantage. ▶ Explain why machines are not 100 percent efficient. UCP 3, ST 2, SPSP 5, HNS 1	**Whiz-Bang Demonstrations,** Pull-Ease, Please! **Whiz-Bang Demonstrations,** A Clever Lever
Section 3 Types of Machines	90	▶ Identify and give examples of the six types of simple machines. ▶ Analyze the mechanical advantage provided by each simple machine. ▶ Identify the simple machines that make up a compound machine. UCP 5, ST 2, SPSP 5; Labs UCP 3, SAI 1, ST 1	**Skill Builder,** Inclined to Move, p. 194 **Datasheets for LabBook,** Inclined to Move **Skill Builder,** Wheeling and Dealing, p. 196 **Datasheets for LabBook,** Wheeling and Dealing **Design Your Own,** Building Machines, p. 195 **Datasheets for LabBook,** Building Machines **Long-Term Projects & Research Ideas,** To Complicate Things

---

See page **T23** for a complete correlation of this book with the

NATIONAL SCIENCE EDUCATION STANDARDS.

TECHNOLOGY RESOURCES

 Guided Reading Audio CD
English or Spanish, Chapter 4

 Science Discovery Videodiscs
Image and Activity Bank with Lesson Plans:
Mechanical Advantage
Science Sleuths: The Moving Monument

 CNN. Multicultural Connections, Who Built the Egyptian Pyramids? Segment 7
Science, Technology & Society, Snake Robots, Segment 13

 One-Stop Planner CD-ROM with Test Generator

Chapter 4 • Work and Machines

CLASSROOM WORKSHEETS, TRANSPARENCIES, AND RESOURCES	SCIENCE INTEGRATION AND CONNECTIONS	REVIEW AND ASSESSMENT
Directed Reading Worksheet **Science Puzzlers, Twisters & Teasers**		
Transparency 229, Work or Not Work? **Directed Reading Worksheet,** Section 1 **Transparency 230,** Work Depends on Force and Distance **Math Skills for Science Worksheet,** Work and Power	**MathBreak,** Working It Out, p. 90 **Math and More,** p. 90 in ATE	**Self-Check,** p. 89 **Section Review,** p. 91 **Quiz,** p. 91 in ATE **Alternative Assessment,** p. 91 in ATE
Directed Reading Worksheet, Section 2 **Transparency 230,** Input Force and Distance **Transparency 231,** Machines Change the Size or Direction (or Both) of a Force **Math Skills for Science Worksheet,** Mechanical Advantage	**Cross-Disciplinary Focus,** p. 92 in ATE **Holt Anthology of Science Fiction,** *Clean Up Your Room* **Cross-Disciplinary Focus,** p. 94 in ATE **Connect to Life Science,** p. 95 in ATE **MathBreak,** Finding the Advantage, p. 96 **Math and More,** p. 96 in ATE **Apply,** p. 97 **Eureka!** Wheelchair Innovators, p. 113	**Homework,** pp. 94, 95 in ATE **Section Review,** p. 97 **Quiz,** p. 97 in ATE **Alternative Assessment,** p. 97 in ATE
Directed Reading Worksheet, Section 3 **Critical Thinking Worksheet,** Building Works of Art **Reinforcement Worksheet,** Finding Machines in Everyday Life **Reinforcement Worksheet,** Mechanical Advantage and Efficiency	**Math and More,** p. 102 in ATE **Real-World Connection,** p. 103 in ATE **Science, Technology, and Society:** Micromachines, p. 112	**Section Review,** p. 102 **Section Review,** p. 105 **Quiz,** p. 105 in ATE **Alternative Assessment,** p. 105 in ATE

  internet connect

 go.hrw.com **Holt, Rinehart and Winston On-line Resources**
go.hrw.com

For worksheets and other teaching aids related to this chapter, visit the HRW Web site and type in the keyword: **HSTWRK**

 National Science Teachers Association
www.scilinks.org

Encourage students to use the *sci*LINKS numbers listed in the internet connect boxes to access information and resources on the **NSTA** Web site.

END-OF-CHAPTER REVIEW AND ASSESSMENT

Chapter Review in Study Guide
Vocabulary and Notes in Study Guide
Chapter Tests with Performance-Based Assessment, Chapter 4 Test
Chapter Tests with Performance-Based Assessment, Performance-Based Assessment 4
Concept Mapping Transparency 8

Chapter Resources & Worksheets

Visual Resources

TEACHING TRANSPARENCIES

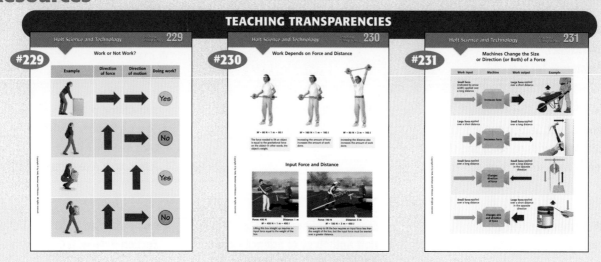

CONCEPT MAPPING TRANSPARENCY

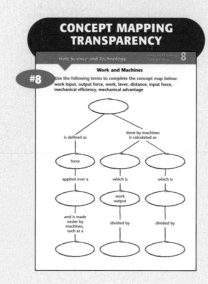

Meeting Individual Needs

DIRECTED READING

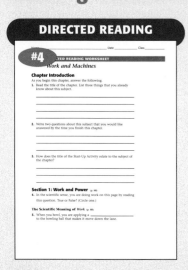

REINFORCEMENT & VOCABULARY REVIEW

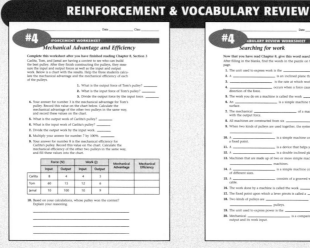

SCIENCE PUZZLERS, TWISTERS & TEASERS

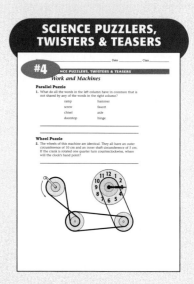

Chapter 4 • Work and Machines

Review & Assessment

STUDY GUIDE

#4 VOCABULARY & NOTES WORKSHEET

Work and Machines

By studying the Vocabulary and Notes listed for each section below, you can gain a better understanding of this chapter.

SECTION 1

Vocabulary

In your own words, write a definition for each of the following terms in the space provided.

1. work

2. joule

3. power

4. watt

Notes

Read the following section highlights. Then, in your own words, write the highlights in your ScienceLog.

• Work occurs when a force causes an object to move in the direction of the force. The unit for work is the joule (J).
• Work is done on an object only when a force makes an object move and only while that force is applied.
• For work to be done on an object, the direction of the object's motion must be in the same direction as the force applied.
• Work can be calculated by multiplying force by distance.
• Power is the rate at which work is done. The unit for power is the watt (W).
• Power can be calculated by dividing the amount of work by the time taken to do that work.

#4 CHAPTER REVIEW WORKSHEET

Work and Machines

USING VOCABULARY

For each pair of terms, explain the difference in their meanings.

1. joule/watt

2. work output/work input

3. mechanical efficiency/mechanical advantage

4. screw/inclined plane

5. simple machine/compound machine

CHAPTER TESTS WITH PERFORMANCE-BASED ASSESSMENT

#4 WORK AND MACHINES

Chapter 4 Test

USING VOCABULARY

To complete the following sentences, choose the correct term from each pair of terms listed, and write the term in the blank.

1. A _____ is the SI unit equivalent to 1 N·m. (watt or joule)

2. The work you do on a machine, such as turning a screwdriver, is called _____. (work input or work output)

3. Because of friction, the _____ of a machine is always less than 100 percent. (mechanical advantage or mechanical efficiency)

4. A _____ is a bar that pivots on a fulcrum. (lever or wedge)

5. A block and tackle is an example of a _____. (wheel and axle or compound machine)

UNDERSTANDING CONCEPTS

Multiple Choice

Circle the correct answer.

6. In which situation is a person doing work on an object?
  a. A school crossing guard raises a stop sign that weighs 10 N.
  b. A student walks 1 m/s while wearing a backpack that weighs 15 N.
  c. A man exerts a 330 N force on a rope attached to a house.
  d. A worker holds a box 1 m off the floor.

7. Juan and Anita each lift an identical stack of books the same distance onto a table, but Anita does the job twice as fast. Therefore, her actions involve twice as much
  a. work output.
  b. work input.
  c. power.
  d. efficiency.

8. Which of the following machines always has a mechanical advantage of less than 1?
  a. wheel and axle
  b. third class lever
  c. a long, thin wedge
  d. a poorly lubricated, movable pulley

9. What does a fixed pulley change?
  a. both the size and direction of a force
  b. the size of a force
  c. the direction of a force
  d. neither the direction nor the size of a force

10. When a machine increases the size of the force exerted, the distance through which the force is exerted
  a. must increase.
  b. must decrease.
  c. must stay the same.
  d. must double.

#4 WORK AND MACHINES — DESIGN YOUR OWN

Chapter 4 Performance-Based Assessment

Objective

You have learned about work, machines, and the force-distance relationship. In this lab you will test that knowledge by building a pulley-based machine. You will be reviewing the concept of work throughout this activity.

Know the Score!

As you work through the activity, keep in mind that you will be earning a grade for the following:
• how well you work with the materials and choose the correct scenario (20%)
• how well you explain your observations (30%)
• whether you construct an operational model (50%)

MATERIALS
• broomstick or wooden dowel
• 2 rulers
• 3 pulleys
• 3 m rope
• 3 rope pieces (3)
• 5 N weights (3)
• 1 N weights (3)

Procedure

1. You will be given a choice of two scenarios. One will be workable and the other will be unworkable. Choose the scenario that is workable.

2. Design a pulley system. You will use this system to show that the scenario you have chosen is workable.

3. Using the materials supplied to you, build the pulley system you have designed.

4. Does your pulley system show that this is a workable scenario? Explain.

5. If you have constructed a workable system, go to step 6. If not, return to step 1 and begin work on the other scenario.

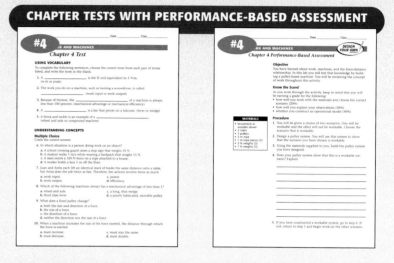

Lab Worksheets

INQUIRY LABS

#4 STUDENT WORKSHEET — DESIGN YOUR OWN

#4

Get an Arm and an Egg Up

The Happy Farm Egg Company has grown from a 20-chicken henhouse to a 1,500-chicken corporation in only three years. The increased business is great, but the factory equipment, acquired from an old canning plant, was not built to handle the fragile eggs. Each day, more than 200 eggs are broken as they are moved to different parts of the factory for cleaning, sorting, grading, and packaging. Losing 1 egg is no big deal, but losing 200 eggs every day creates a high cost for this new company. The costs are mounting.

The owner of Happy Farms, Shelly Khaj, has decided to invest in a new type of hydraulic technology. This system consists of a series of hydraulic arms that lift eggs from the gatherers to the pickup window, across to the sorting and grading section, and down to the packaging area.

As a hydraulics designer, you have been asked to provide Happy Farms with a working model. However, you are competing against several other hydraulic designers. The designer with the most effective model will be awarded the contract to build the full-scale hydraulic system. You have one week to turn Happy Farms' scrambled system into an over-easy operation. Good luck!

MATERIALS FOR THE ACTUATOR
• 90 cm of flexible plastic tubing
• metric ruler
• scissors
• 2 small, round balloons
• 2 empty tennis-ball cans (no lids)
• masking tape
• 2 metal bolt ties
• 12 oz aluminum cans (4)

USEFUL TERMS
hydraulic operated by the pressure created when fluid is forced through a tube
actuator a device that uses the pressure of a fluid to move or control an object

Ask a Question
How do you build a hydraulic system for moving an egg upward, to the left, and then down?

Conduct an Experiment

Join with 2 or 3 other students to discuss how you might solve the problem. Hydraulic arms are moved by actuators, devices that use the pressure of a liquid to move or control an object.

1. Cut a 2.5 cm length of plastic tubing. Carefully thread the stem of the balloon through the plastic tubing.

2. From inside the tennis-ball can, carefully thread the tubing and balloon stem out through the hole of the can, as shown below. Secure the tubing in place with tape.

3. Repeat steps 1–2 with the second tennis-ball can.

4. Inflate both balloons to about half their capacity. For each balloon, hold the balloon closed while inserting one end of the rest of the tubing into the balloon. Seal each connection with a twist tie. For a tight seal, wrap the tie at least twice around the balloon stem. You have constructed an actuator.

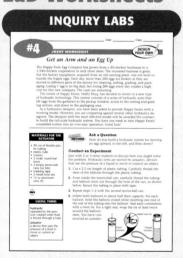

WHIZ-BANG DEMONSTRATIONS

#4 TEACHER-LED DEMONSTRATION — DISCOVERY LAB

#4

Pull-ease, Please!

Purpose
_____ how a simple machine _____ easier.

Time
_____ minutes

Lab Ratings

To Do

1. Ask two students to hold the brooms horizontally about 50 cm apart.

2. Tie the rope or cord to one broom, and wrap it around the handles as shown.

MATERIALS
• 2 identical brooms
• rope or strong cord, about 3 m long
• metric ruler or measuring tape

3. Invite a third student to hold the free end of the rope. Ask the class: Do you think the third student can pull the brooms together while the other two are holding them apart? Why or why not? *(Expected answer: No; two students should be able to exert more force than one.)*

4. Tell the student holding the rope to pull on it. The two brooms will move together even while the other two students try to keep them apart.

Explanation

The brooms and rope act together to form a pulley system. A pulley is a simple machine that can be used to increase a force. The force of the student pulling the rope was multiplied by the number of points where the rope pulled on the broom. Therefore, the third student exerted a force that was five times that of each of the other students.

LONG-TERM PROJECTS & RESEARCH IDEAS

#4 STUDENT WORKSHEET — DESIGN YOUR OWN

#4

To Complicate Things

Rube Goldberg was a cartoonist famous for drawing elaborate, complicated machines that accomplished simple tasks. His work was so unique and well liked that his name is used to describe all machines that are similar to the ones he drew. There are even contests to see who can design and build the most elaborate Rube Goldberg machine. A good Rube Goldberg machine uses many complex steps to complete a task that would normally take only one or two steps. For instance, a machine designed to turn on a light switch might involve rolling bowling balls, burning candles, jumping frogs, popping rubber bands, and spilling water. The more complicated Rube Goldberg machines are, the better.

Don't Keep It Simple

1. Build your own Rube Goldberg machine that lifts a shoe at least 30 cm, waters a plant, turns off an alarm clock, or performs another simple action. Be creative in your choice of materials, but be sure they are not flammable or hazardous. The machine should perform at least five steps to accomplish its task. Try to keep your machine compact—it shouldn't be bigger than 1 m³. Use as many simple machines as you can in your Rube Goldberg machine. Compete with your classmates to see who can be the most creative and use the most steps.

Another Long-Term Project Idea

2. Wind power is one of the most promising sources of pollution-free energy for the future. Research windmill designs that have been used throughout history in different parts of the world. Build models of different windmills, and find out which designs work best for certain tasks. Consider the following questions: How have windmill designs changed? Where and how are windmills being used today? Write this information on note cards, and attach them to your model.

Research Idea

3. Did you know that some bicycles built in the 1800s had wooden wheels and iron tires? These bikes were so uncomfortable to ride that they were called "bone-shakers." Research the history of the bicycle. What were the early bicycle designs? When was the first "modern" bicycle built? What variations have there been on the modern bicycle? How could current bicycle designs be improved? Draw a series of diagrams of bicycles, from the earliest models through today's models. Include your design for the "bike of the future."

PHYSICAL SCIENCE

DATASHEETS FOR LABBOOK

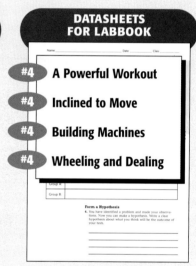

#4 A Powerful Workout

#4 Inclined to Move

#4 Building Machines

#4 Wheeling and Dealing

Group A:

Group B:

Form a Hypothesis

4. You have identified a problem and made your observations. Now you can make a hypothesis. Write a clear hypothesis about what you think will be the outcome of your tests.

Applications & Extensions

CRITICAL THINKING & PROBLEM SOLVING

#4 CRITICAL THINKING WORKSHEET

Building Works of Art

Dear Jamal,

The class trip to the science convention was incredible! We stayed at the Wonders of the World Hotel, which is identical to a famous Egyptian pyramid. Here is an advertisement I found in the lobby:

WONDERS OF THE WORLD HOTEL

Welcome! Our fine hotel was built to look like a famous Egyptian pyramid. We paid attention to every detail even down to the type of stone. The Wonders of the World Hotel was built in less than a year—that's 1/50 of the time it took to build an Egyptian pyramid! Wonders of the World Construction Company uses only the most modern equipment and machines to bring you the comfort and quality you deserve. Please use our other sites in the future. Works in progress include:
• a sports arena that is a replica of the Colosseum in Rome
• an office complex that looks just like the Statue of Liberty

I wrote to the Wonders of the World Construction Company for information on their other projects. Maybe my class could visit another one next year!

Carmen

USEFUL TERMS
replica an accurate copy of a work of art

Comprehending Ideas

1. The Wonders of the World Hotel was built in less than a year. Does this mean that less work was required to build this hotel than was required to build the original Egyptian pyramid? Explain.

2. During hotel construction, workers discovered they could carry a load of bricks more easily up a ramp than up a ladder. Why is it easier to use a ramp?

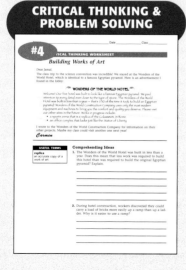

MULTICULTURAL CONNECTIONS

#7 Science in the News: Critical Thinking Worksheets

Who Built the Egyptian Pyramids?

1. Why were some people unwilling to believe that ancient Egyptians built the pyramids?

2. Why do you think the Egyptians used a spiraling ramp instead of a straight ramp to move the stone blocks? *Hint:* Think about the ramp as a simple machine.

3. What function does scientific experimentation serve in this pyramid investigation?

4. Besides the written records, how do you think scientists learned about the ancient Egyptians from their tombs?

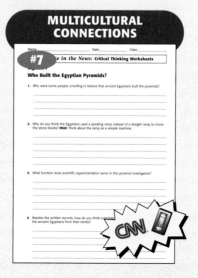

CNN

SCIENCE TECHNOLOGY

#13 Science in the News: Critical Thinking Worksheets

Snake Robots

1. Why do you think scientists would want to model a robot after a snake's body?

2. Identify two ways scientists believe their flexible robots will one day be used.

3. Identify an animal other than a snake that could be a useful model for a flexible robot.

4. Why do you think there is much enthusiasm about robots?

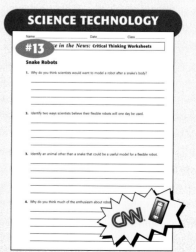

CNN

Chapter Background

SECTION 1

Work and Power

▶ James Prescott Joule (1818–1889)

James Joule was an English physicist who established that mechanical energy, electrical energy, and thermal energy are basically the same and that one type of energy can be converted into another. This principle is the basis of the first law of thermodynamics, the conservation of energy. It states that the total energy in any closed system remains the same, even when the energy is converted from one type to another.

- Joule developed mathematical equations that described the thermal energy of current in electrical wire and the amount of work needed to produce a unit of thermal energy. The standard unit of work is called the *joule,* named in his honor.

▶ Converting Energy

In physics, energy is the ability to do work. Energy can exist in different forms, such as thermal, electrical, nuclear, potential, kinetic, and chemical. All forms of energy have to do with motion or position. Energy can be converted from one form to another. The electrical energy used to drive all sorts of devices is generated by engines that create thermal energy, batteries, or fuel cells. Energy and energy resources are covered in Chapter 5.

IS THAT A FACT!

- ▶ The term *horsepower* was coined in the late eighteenth century by Scottish engineer James Watt, who used horses as a measure of power in his experiments. In the English system, one horsepower is 33,000 ft-lb of work per minute, or the force necessary to lift 33,000 lb 1 ft in 1 minute. This unit was based on the dray horse, a horse adapted for drawing heavy loads.

SECTION 2

What Is a Machine?

▶ Leonardo da Vinci (1452–1519)

Leonardo da Vinci was an Italian painter, sculptor, and inventor. The motivating interest behind all of his work was the appearance of everyday things and how they operated. He studied the flight of birds, the movement of water, the growth of plants, and the anatomy of the human body.

- One of da Vinci's interests was the mechanical advantage that could be obtained with gears. Da Vinci made drawings of complex machines that were centuries ahead of their time. Among his drawings were plans for tanks, a helicopter, and other aircraft. He was especially concerned with the problems of friction and resistance. He described and drew screws, gears, hydraulic jacks, transmission gears, and swiveling devices.

- Da Vinci felt that the basic laws of mechanics operated the same way in all aspects of the world and were the keys to understanding the world and reproducing it through art.

IS THAT A FACT!

☞ Many industrial towns in early America were located where water flow could be assured all year. Water and wind were the primary sources of mechanical energy until the end of the eighteenth century, when steam power was developed. Steam-powered mechanical devices launched the Industrial Revolution.

▶ Perpetual Motion

Inventors for centuries have tried to build a perpetual-motion machine—a device that would run forever once it is set in motion. Unfortunately, no such machines can ever work because they would violate the laws of thermodynamics.

• A perpetual-motion machine would work by delivering as much or more energy than is put into it. The first law of thermodynamics states that the total energy of a closed system is constant. The second law states that some energy is always lost as thermal energy from a closed system when energy is used to do work. The practical effect of these two laws is that the output energy from any machine will never be as great as the energy put into it.

• Friction—in which kinetic energy is converted to waste thermal energy—can be reduced but never eliminated. While some machines can be made to run very efficiently, they will always need a source of energy to operate, and they will never be able to produce more energy than is put into them.

Types of Machines

▶ The Invention of Machines

The first machines were tools used by prehistoric people to help them hunt and gather food. A wedge shaped out of stone made an excellent cutting tool. Early axes were wedges made of stone. Levers were used in hoes, oars, and slings. Because simple machines multiply force or distance, they provided our early ancestors with a tremendous survival advantage.

▶ The Plow

The plow was one of the first agricultural machines to be invented, and it is still one of the most important. Evidence shows that plows first appeared more than 6,000 years ago. The first plow was not much more than a digging stick drawn by a person or an animal. As primitive as it was, the plow allowed people to dig deeper to turn over and loosen the soil. Plants could put down deeper, stronger roots in plowed soil, increasing crop yields. This simple machine magnified the effort of a single person enough to produce food for many people. The plow freed some people from having to grow food so they could begin to build, sew, or trade.

IS THAT A FACT!

☞ Tiny machines are being built with gears and levers so small they can only be seen under a powerful microscope. Scientists are learning how to make even tinier machines out of molecules. Tiny gears have been shaped out of strands of DNA molecules, and hydrogen molecules may one day control microscopic computers. For more information, see "Micromachines," on page 112.

For background information about teaching strategies and issues, refer to the *Professional Reference for Teachers.*

Work and Machines

Pre-Reading Questions

Students may not know the answers to these questions before reading the chapter, so accept any reasonable response.

Suggested Answers

1. Doing work means making an object move in the direction of the force applied to it.

2. Machines make doing work easier by changing the size or direction (or both) of a force. Machines increase force at the expense of distance or increase distance at the expense of force.

3. Simple machines include levers (a hammer pulling a nail), inclined planes (a ramp), wedges (a knife), screws (a jar lid), wheel and axle (a doorknob), and pulleys (the cord mechanism on horizontal blinds).

Work and Machines

Sections

Pre-Reading Questions

1. What does it mean to do work?
2. How are machines helpful when doing work?
3. What are some examples of simple machines?

"ONE, TWO, STROKE!"...

...shouts the coach as the team races to the finish line. This paddling team is competing in Hong Kong's annual Dragon Boat Races. The Dragon Boat Festival is a 2,000-year-old Chinese tradition that commemorates the death of the national hero, Qu Yuan. The paddlers you see here are using the paddles to move the boat forward. Even though they are celebrating by racing their dragon boat, in scientific terms this team is doing *work*. How is this possible? Read on to find out!

86

---

internet connect

HRW On-line Resources

go.hrw.com

For worksheets and other teaching aids, visit the HRW Web site and type in the keyword: **HSTWRK**

www.scilinks.com

Use the *sci*LINKS numbers at the end of each chapter for additional resources on the **NSTA** Web site.

Smithsonian Institution®

www.si.edu/hrw

Visit the Smithsonian Institution Web site for related on-line resources.

CNNfyi.com

www.cnnfyi.com

Visit the CNN Web site for current events coverage and classroom resources.

C'MON, LEVER A LITTLE!

In this activity, you will use a simple machine, a lever, to make your task a little easier.

Procedure

1. Gather a few **books** and stack them on a table, one on top of the other.

2. Slide your index finger underneath the edge of the bottom book. Using only the force of your finger, try to lift one side of the books 2 or 3 cm off the table. Is it difficult? Write your observations in your ScienceLog.

3. Slide the end of a **wooden ruler** underneath the edge of the bottom book. Then slip a **large pencil eraser** under the ruler.

4. Again using only your index finger, push down on the edge of the ruler and try to lift the books. Record your observations.

   Caution: Push down slowly to keep the ruler and eraser from flipping.

Analysis

5. Which was easier, lifting the books with your finger or with the ruler? Explain.

6. What was different about the direction of the force your finger applied on the books compared with the direction of the force you applied on the ruler?

87

C'MON, LEVER A LITTLE!

MATERIALS
FOR EACH GROUP:
• a couple of books
• string
• wooden ruler
• large pencil eraser

Safety Caution

The rulers should be fairly stiff and sturdy. Use lightweight books if necessary. If the books are not too heavy and the activity is done carefully, the rulers should not get broken. Caution students to wear safety goggles during this activity.

Teacher's Notes

The word *lever* comes from the Latin word *levare*, meaning "to lift." The lever was one of the first simple machines to be developed. It is thought that tree limbs may have been used by early humans as pry bars to move heavy rocks.

Answers to START-UP Activity

5. Students should find that lifting the books with the ruler was easier because it required less effort (force).

6. The direction of the force applied by students' fingers on the books was up, and the direction of the force applied on the ruler was down. Using the ruler changed the direction of the force.

Focus

Work and Power

This section introduces the scientific definitions of work and power. Students learn how to calculate work and power.

🔔 Bellringer

On the board, give students the following task:

Select the activities below that require the least amount of work. Write your answers in your ScienceLog.

- carrying heavy books home
- reading a 300-page novel
- skiing for 1 hour
- lifting a 45 kg mass
- holding a steel beam in place for 3 hours
- jacking up a car

Remind students to explain what work is being done in each of their selections.

1) Motivate

DISCUSSION

After reading the section on work and power, discuss with students the use of the words *work* and *power* in everyday language. Identify usages that do not match the scientific definition of work, and discuss why they are different. Remind them that in this section work is discussed in terms of physically moving objects rather than in terms of energy expenditure.

Terms to Learn

work	power
joule	watt

What You'll Do

- ◆ Determine when work is being done on an object.
- ◆ Calculate the amount of work done on an object.
- ◆ Explain the difference between work and power.

Work and Power

Suppose your science teacher has just given you a homework assignment. You have to read an entire chapter by tomorrow! Wow, that's a lot of work, isn't it? Actually, in the scientific sense, you won't be doing any work at all! How can that be?

The Scientific Meaning of *Work*

In science, **work** occurs when a force causes an object to move in the direction of the force. In the example above, you may put a lot of mental effort into doing your homework, but you won't be using a force to move an object. Therefore, in the scientific sense, you will not be doing work.

Now think about the example shown in **Figure 1.** This student is having a lot of fun, isn't she? But she is doing work, even though she is having fun. That's because she's applying a force to the bowling ball to make it move through a distance. However, it's important to understand that she is doing work on the ball only as long as she is touching it. The ball will continue to move away from her after she releases it, but she will no longer be doing work on the ball because she will no longer be applying a force to it.

Figure 1 *You might be surprised to find out that bowling is doing work!*

Working Hard or Hardly Working? You should understand that applying a force doesn't always result in work being done. Suppose your neighbor asks you to help push his stalled car. You push and push, but the car doesn't budge. Even though you may be exhausted and sweaty, you haven't done any work on the car. Why? Because the car hasn't moved. Remember, work is done on an object only when a force makes that object move. In this case, your pushing doesn't make the car move. You only do work on the car if it starts to move.

88

MISCONCEPTION //// ALERT \\\\

In the second paragraph, the text states that the girl does work on the bowling ball only when she is touching it. The ball continues to move when she lets go of it, but she's no longer applying a force to it. Review the Forces in Motion chapter and Newton's first law. It takes a little force to get the ball moving because the resistance of mass to changes in motion must be overcome. Disregarding friction, once the ball is moving, no additional force is needed to keep it moving at constant speed because no other force impedes its horizontal motion.

Force and Motion in the Same Direction Suppose you're in the airport and you're late for a flight. You have to run through the airport carrying a heavy suitcase. Because you're making the suitcase move, you're doing work on it, right? Wrong! For work to be done, the object must move in the same direction as the force. In this case, the motion is in a different direction than the force, as shown in **Figure 2.** So no work is done on the suitcase. However, work *is* done on the suitcase when you lift it off the ground.

You'll know that work is done on an object if two things occur: (1) the object moves as a force is applied and (2) the direction of the object's motion is the same as the direction of the force applied. The pictures and the arrows in the chart below will help you understand how to determine when work is being done on an object.

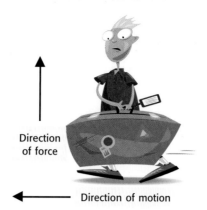

Direction of force

← Direction of motion

Figure 2 *You exert an upward force on the suitcase. But the motion of the suitcase is forward. Therefore, you are not doing work on the suitcase.*

Work or Not Work?

Example	Direction of force	Direction of motion	Doing work?
(person pushing box)	→	→	Yes
(person walking with backpack)	↑	→	No
(person lifting groceries)	↑	↑	Yes
(person carrying groceries walking)	↑	→	No

✓ **Self-Check**

If you pulled a wheeled suitcase instead of carrying it, would you be doing work on the suitcase? Why or why not? *(See page 232 to check your answer.)*

SCIENCE HUMOR

Q: Did you hear about the criminals who never had to do any work?

A: They were joule thieves.

2 Teach

USING THE FIGURE

Have students develop their own chart similar to the one on this page using activities from their everyday lives, including sports and games. When their charts are completed, have students exchange charts and look for misconceptions about work. Discuss these in class.

Throughout this chapter, the *width* of the force arrows represents the magnitude of the force, and the *length* of the arrow represents the distance over which it is exerted.

READING ✍ STRATEGY

Prediction Guide Before students read this section, ask them whether they agree with the following statements:

1. Any time a force is applied to an object, work is being done.
2. Power, work, and force are the same.
3. More power means doing work faster.

Answer to Self-Check

Pulling a wheeled suitcase is doing work because the force applied and the motion of the suitcase are in the same direction.

Teaching Transparency 229 "Work or Not Work?"

Directed Reading Worksheet Section 1

MATH and MORE

Have students, in groups of three or four, select a sport, and discuss the different ways work is done in that sport. Have them estimate how much work is done in an average game.

ACTIVITY

MATERIALS

FOR EACH PAIR:
• meterstick and string
• spring scale
• objects to lift

Have each pair attach each object in turn to the spring scale and slowly lift or pull it, then record how much force was used. Next have them measure the distance the object moved and record it in meters. Have them calculate how much work was done.

Teaching Transparency 230 "Work Depends on Force and Distance"

MATH BREAK

Working It Out

Use the equation for work shown on this page to solve the following problems:

1. A man applies a force of 500 N to push a truck 100 m down the street. How much work does he do?

2. In which situation do you do more work?
   a. You lift a 75 N bowling ball 2 m off the floor.
   b. You lift two 50 N bowling balls 1 m off the floor.

Calculating Work

Do you do more work when you lift an 80 N barbell or a 160 N barbell? It would be tempting to say that you do more work when you lift the 160 N barbell because it weighs more. But actually, you can't answer this question with the information given. You also need to know how high each barbell is being lifted. Remember, work is a force applied through a distance. The greater the distance through which you exert a given force, the more work you do. Similarly, the greater the force you exert through a given distance, the more work you do.

The amount of work (W) done in moving an object can be calculated by multiplying the force (F) applied to the object by the distance (d) through which the force is applied, as shown in the following equation:

$$W = F \times d$$

Recall that force is expressed in newtons, and the meter is the basic SI unit for length or distance. Therefore, the unit used to express work is the newton-meter (N•m), which is more simply called the **joule (J)**. Look at **Figure 3** to learn more about calculating work. You can also practice calculating work yourself by doing the MathBreak on this page.

Figure 3 Work Depends on Force and Distance

$W = 80 \text{ N} \times 1 \text{ m} = 80 \text{ J}$

The force needed to lift an object is equal to the gravitational force on the object—in other words, the object's weight.

$W = 160 \text{ N} \times 1 \text{ m} = 160 \text{ J}$

Increasing the amount of force increases the amount of work done.

$W = 80 \text{ N} \times 2 \text{ m} = 160 \text{ J}$

Increasing the distance also increases the amount of work done.

internet connect

SCI LINKS **NSTA**

TOPIC: Work and Power
GO TO: www.scilinks.org
*sci*LINKS **NUMBER:** HSTP180

SCIENCE HUMOR

Q: What is the unit of power?

A: Watt.

Q: I said, What is the unit of power?

A: Watt!

Q: I SAID . . .

Power—How Fast Work Is Done

Like *work,* the term *power* is used a lot in everyday language but has a very specific meaning in science. **Power** is the rate at which work is done. To calculate power (*P*), you divide the amount of work done (*W*) by the time (*t*) it takes to do that work, as shown in the following equation:

$$P = \frac{W}{t}$$

You just learned that the unit for work is the joule, and the basic unit for time is the second. Therefore, the unit used to express power is joules per second (J/s), which is more simply called the **watt (W).** So if you do 50 J of work in 5 seconds, your power is 10 J/s, or 10 W. You can calculate your own power in the QuickLab at right.

Increasing Power Power is how fast work happens. Power is increased when more work is done in a given amount of time. Power is also increased when the time it takes to do a certain amount of work is decreased, as shown in **Figure 4.**

Figure 4 *No matter how fast you can sand with sandpaper, an electric sander can do the same amount of work faster. Therefore, the electric sander has more power.*

QuickLab

More Power to You

1. Use a loop of **string** to attach a **spring scale** to a **book.**

2. Slowly pull the book across a table by the spring scale. Use a **stopwatch** to determine the time this takes. In your ScienceLog, record the amount of time it took and the force used as the book reached the edge of the table.

3. With a **metric ruler,** measure the distance you pulled the book.

4. Now quickly pull the book across the same distance. Again record the time and force.

5. Calculate work and power for both trials.

6. How were the amounts of work and power affected by your pulling the book faster? Record your answers in your ScienceLog.

SECTION REVIEW

1. Work is done on a ball when a pitcher throws it. Is the pitcher still doing work on the ball as it flies through the air? Explain.

2. Explain the difference between work and power.

3. **Doing Calculations** You lift a chair that weighs 50 N to a height of 0.5 m and carry it 10 m across the room. How much work do you do on the chair?

internetconnect

SC*i*LINKS.
NSTA

TOPIC: Work and Power
GO TO: www.scilinks.org
sciLINKS NUMBER: HSTP180

91

Answers to Section Review

1. The pitcher is no longer doing work on the ball as it flies through the air because he is no longer exerting a force on it. (However, work is being done on the ball by the Earth, which exerts a force on the ball and pulls it back toward the ground.)

2. Work occurs when a force causes an object to move in the direction of the force, and power is the rate at which work is done. The more work you do in a given amount of time, or the less time it takes you to do a given amount of work, the greater your power.

3. Work is done on the chair only when it is picked up, not when it is carried across the room. Therefore, *W* = 50 N × 0.5 m = 25 J.

Focus

What Is a Machine?

This section explains how machines make work easier. Students learn to calculate and compare the mechanical advantage of machines and their mechanical efficiency.

Bellringer

Pose the following question to your students, and have them write a one-paragraph answer in their ScienceLog:

Why do we use machines?

1 Motivate

DISCUSSION

Show students a selection of pictures of familiar objects that represent simple machines either alone or in combination. Discuss with students how each of the objects can be used to make work easier. Save the pictures for Section 3 of this chapter, when you can use them to have students identify the simple machines in each picture.

Directed Reading Worksheet Section 2

Terms to Learn

machine
work input
work output
mechanical advantage
mechanical efficiency

What You'll Do

◆ Explain how a machine makes work easier.
◆ Describe and give examples of the force-distance trade-off that occurs when a machine is used.
◆ Calculate mechanical advantage.
◆ Explain why machines are not 100 percent efficient.

What Is a Machine?

Imagine you're in the car with your mom on the way to a party when suddenly—*KABLOOM hisssss*—a tire blows out. "Now I'm going to be late!" you think as your mom pulls over to the side of the road. You watch as she opens the trunk and gets out a jack and a tire iron. Using the tire iron, she pries the hubcap off and begins to unscrew the lug nuts from the wheel. She then puts the jack under the car and turns the handle several times until the flat tire no longer touches the ground. After exchanging the flat tire with the spare, she lowers the jack and puts the lug nuts and hubcap back on the wheel. "Wow!" you think, "That wasn't as hard as I thought it would be." As your mom drops you off at the party, you think how lucky it was that she had the right equipment to change the tire.

Figure 5 *You might be surprised to find out that all of these common objects are machines.*

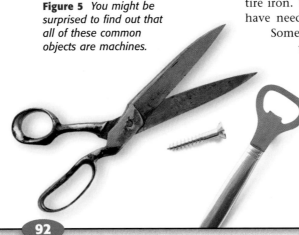

Machines—Making Work Easier

Now imagine changing a tire without the jack and the tire iron. Would it have been so easy? No, you would have needed several people just to hold up the car! Sometimes you need a little help to do work. That's where machines come in. A **machine** is a device that helps make work easier by changing the size or direction of a force.

When you think of machines, you might think of things like cars, big construction equipment, or even computers. But not all machines are complicated or even have moving parts. In fact, the tire iron, jack, and lug nut shown above are all machines. Even the items shown in **Figure 5** are machines.

CROSS-DISCIPLINARY FOCUS

Home Economics Show students some common kitchen utensils, such as knives, forks, can and bottle openers, nutcrackers, and manual egg beaters. Allow students to examine the utensils and discuss their uses. Then have students speculate about how each machine makes work easier.

Work In, Work Out Suppose you need to get the lid off a can of paint. What do you do? Well, one way to pry the lid off is to use the flat end of a common machine known as a screwdriver, as shown in **Figure 6.** You place the tip of the screwdriver under the edge of the lid and then push down on the handle. The other end of the screwdriver lifts the lid as you push down. In other words, you do work on the screwdriver, and the screwdriver does work on the lid. This example illustrates that two kinds of work are always involved when a machine is used— the work done on the machine and the work the machine does on another object.

Output force

Input force

Figure 6 *When you use a machine, you do work on the machine, and the machine does work on something else.*

The width of the arrows representing **input force** and **output force** indicates the relative size of the forces. The length of the arrows indicates the distance through which they are exerted.

Remember that work is a force applied through a distance. Look again at Figure 6. The work you do on a machine is called **work input.** You apply a force, called the *input force,* to the machine and move it through a distance. The work done by the machine is called **work output.** The machine applies a force, called the *output force,* through a distance. The output force opposes the forces you and the machine are working against—in this case, the weight of the lid and the friction between the can and the lid.

How Machines Help You might think that machines help you because they increase the amount of work done. But that's not true. If you multiplied the forces by the distances through which they are applied in Figure 6 (remember, $W = F \times d$), you would find that the screwdriver does *not* do more work on the lid than you do on the screwdriver. Work output can *never* be greater than work input.

READING 📖 STRATEGY

Concept Mapping Have students begin constructing a concept map of this section and continue it as they progress through the section. They should illustrate at least half the bubbles with their own drawings or photographs from magazines. The illustrations should elaborate on or relate to the ideas included in the map. Sheltered English

DISCUSSION

Encourage a student debate about the benefits and drawbacks of machines since the Industrial Revolution. Students should understand that although machines have many benefits, they may bring problems (pollution, workplace injury).

USING SCIENCE FICTION

Have students read the story "Clean Up Your Room!" by Laura Anne Gilman in the *Holt Anthology of Science Fiction.* As you discuss the story, ask students to compare the positive and negative aspects of technology in our lives.

Advanced Learners Have students think of a problem that has no apparent solution. The problem may also be something that students think may become a problem in the future. Challenge them to invent a machine that solves that problem. Have them describe it as carefully as possible and illustrate it with their own artwork.

CROSS-DISCIPLINARY FOCUS

History Have students research prehistoric uses of machines, especially the earliest occurrences of machines that change the size or direction of force in the same ways as the examples in the chart on page 95.

ACTIVITY

Graphing A certain task takes 480 J of work. Remind students that many combinations of $F \times d$ result in 480 J of work (480 N × 1 m; or 64 N × 7.5 m). Help students find combinations of forces and distances whose products are 480 J. Have them use these number pairs to plot and connect points on a graph (with F on the x-axis and d on the y-axis). Discuss the graphs and what they show about the relationship between force and distance. (F and d are inversely related.) (Students can start with any two of the quantities, calculate the third, then do the graph.)

Teaching Transparency 230 "Input Force and Distance"

Machines Do Not Save Work Machines make work easier because they change the size or direction of the input force. And using a screwdriver to open a paint can changes *both* the size and direction of the input force. Just remember that using a machine does not mean that you do less work. As you can see in **Figure 7**, the same amount of work is involved with or without the ramp. The ramp decreases the amount of input force necessary to do the work of lifting the box. But the distance over which the force is exerted increases. In other words, the machine allows a smaller force to be applied over a longer distance.

Figure 7 *A simple plank of wood acts as a machine when it is used to help raise a load.*

Force: 450 N   Distance: 1 m

$W = 450 \text{ N} \times 1 \text{ m} = 450 \text{ J}$

Lifting this box straight up requires an input force equal to the weight of the box.

Force: 150 N   Distance: 3 m

$W = 150 \text{ N} \times 3 \text{ m} = 450 \text{ J}$

Using a ramp to lift the box requires an input force less than the weight of the box, but the input force must be exerted over a greater distance.

The Force-Distance Trade-off When a machine changes the size of the force, the distance through which the force is exerted must also change. Force or distance can increase, but not together. When one increases, the other must decrease. This is because the work output is never greater than the work input.

The diagram on the next page will help you better understand this force-distance trade-off. It also shows that some machines affect only the direction of the force, not the size of the force or the distance through which it is exerted.

94

Homework

Have students keep a "machine diary" for a week. Each day, they should describe the machines they used or came in contact with over the course of the day. Have them expand their ideas of what a machine is by examining ordinary actions like writing or playing and deciding whether a machine is involved.

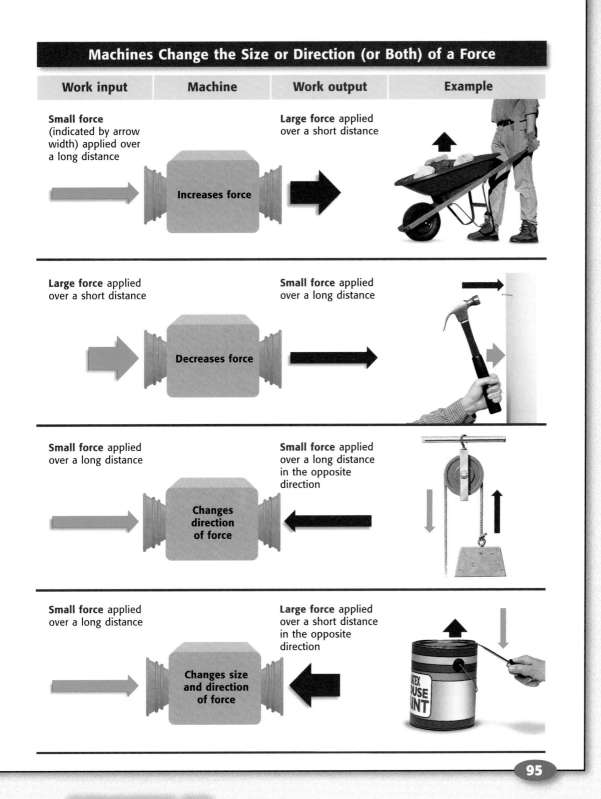

Machines Change the Size or Direction (or Both) of a Force

Work input	Machine	Work output	Example
Small force (indicated by arrow width) applied over a long distance	**Increases force**	**Large force** applied over a short distance	
Large force applied over a short distance	**Decreases force**	**Small force** applied over a long distance	
Small force applied over a long distance	**Changes direction of force**	**Small force** applied over a long distance in the opposite direction	
Small force applied over a long distance	**Changes size and direction of force**	**Large force** applied over a short distance in the opposite direction	

95

GUIDED PRACTICE

Concept Mapping Give students examples of several different types of machines, such as those used in construction or industry. Have them analyze whether each machine changes the size or direction (or both) of a force. When they have finished their analysis, have students make a concept map showing their results.
Sheltered English

RETEACHING

For each of the examples of machines on page 95, have students design a different machine that would accomplish the same job. The machine can be as simple or as elaborate as desired. Does the new machine change force in the same way as the original?

Homework

Writing Have students go through their homes and select five machines that they find there. Encourage them to find unusual examples, things they might not use everyday. Have them write one-paragraph descriptions of these machines in terms of the mechanical advantage they offer.

 Teaching Transparency 231 "Machines Change the Size or Direction (or Both) of a Force"

CONNECT TO LIFE SCIENCE

Humans aren't the only animals that use tools. Chimpanzees fashion specialized twigs to snare termites from inside their mounds, and some otters use carefully selected rocks to crack open shellfish.

There are examples of other species using tools—a distinct evolutionary advantage. Have students find information about such tool use and make some creative presentations to the class.

3 **Extend**

Answers to MATHBREAK

1. $MA = \frac{2000\ N}{200\ N} = 10$

2. 1; it could be useful for tasks in which it is necessary to change the direction of a force.

3. Both a and b make work easier than doing work without a machine. A task would be easier with b because it has a larger mechanical advantage.

MATH and MORE

Teacher Notes: When the output force is greater than the input force, the mechanical advantage is greater than 1. When the output force is less than the input force, the mechanical advantage is less than 1.

Have students determine which of the following machines has a greater mechanical advantage:

- a machine to which you apply a force of 50 N and the machine applies a force of 150 N (*MA* = 3)

- a machine to which you apply a force of 60 N and the machine applies a force of 200 N (*MA* = 3.3)

Math Skills Worksheet
"Mechanical Advantage"

GOING FURTHER

Show students one of Rube Goldberg's cartoons. Ask them to decipher what is happening in the cartoon. Focus students' attention on the action in each step and the results of the action. Challenge students to design and draw their own machine that uses multiple steps to perform a simple task.

MATH BREAK

Finding the Advantage

1. You apply 200 N to a machine, and the machine applies 2,000 N to an object. What is the mechanical advantage?

2. You apply 10 N to a machine, and the machine applies 10 N to another object. What is the mechanical advantage? Can such a machine be useful? Why or why not?

3. Which of the following makes work easier to do?
   a. a machine with a mechanical advantage of 15
   b. a machine to which you apply 15 N and that exerts 255 N

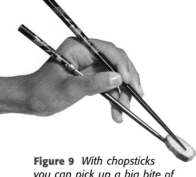

Figure 9 *With chopsticks you can pick up a big bite of food with just a little wiggle of your fingers.*

internet**connect**

SCILINKS
NSTA
TOPIC: Mechanical Efficiency
GO TO: www.scilinks.org
*sci*LINKS NUMBER: HSTP185

Mechanical Advantage

Do some machines make work easier than others? Yes, because some machines can increase force more than others. A machine's **mechanical advantage** tells you how many times the machine multiplies force. In other words, it compares the input force with the output force. You can find mechanical advantage by using the following equation:

$$\text{Mechanical advantage } (MA) = \frac{\text{output force}}{\text{input force}}$$

Take a look at **Figure 8.** In this example, the output force is greater than the input force. Using the equation above, you can find the mechanical advantage of the handcart:

$$MA = \frac{500\ N}{50\ N} = 10$$

Input force = 50 N

Output force = 500 N

Figure 8 *A machine that has a large mechanical advantage can make lifting a heavy load a whole lot easier.*

Because the mechanical advantage of the handcart is 10, the output force is 10 times bigger than the input force. The larger the mechanical advantage, the easier a machine makes your work. But as mechanical advantage increases, the distance that the output force moves the object decreases.

Remember that some machines only change the direction of the force. In such cases, the output force is equal to the input force, and the mechanical advantage is 1. Other machines have a mechanical advantage that is less than 1. That means that the input force is greater than the output force. Although such a machine actually decreases your force, it does allow you to exert the force over a longer distance, as shown in **Figure 9**.

Mechanical Efficiency

As mentioned earlier, the work output of a machine can never be greater than the work input. In fact, the work output of a machine is always *less* than the work input. Why? Because some of the work done by the machine is used to overcome the friction created by the use of the machine. But keep in mind that no work is *lost*. The work output plus the work done to overcome friction equals the work input.

The less work a machine has to do to overcome friction, the more *efficient* it is. **Mechanical efficiency** (e FISH uhn see) is a comparison of a machine's work output with the work input. A machine's mechanical efficiency is calculated using the following equation:

$$\text{Mechanical efficiency} = \frac{\text{work output}}{\text{work input}} \times 100$$

The 100 in this equation means that mechanical efficiency is expressed as a percentage. Mechanical efficiency tells you what percentage of the work input gets converted into work output. No machine is 100 percent efficient, but reducing the amount of friction in a machine is a way to increase its mechanical efficiency. Inventors have tried for many years to create a machine that has no friction to overcome, but so far they have been unsuccessful. If a machine could be made that had 100 percent mechanical efficiency, it would be called an *ideal machine*.

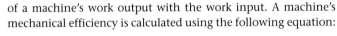

APPLY

Oil Improves Efficiency

Car manufacturers recommend regular oil changes. That's because over time, motor oil in a car's engine starts to get dark and thick and doesn't flow as well as fresh motor oil. Why do you think a car engine needs motor oil? How does getting regular oil changes improve the mechanical efficiency of a car's engine?

SECTION REVIEW

1. Explain how using a ramp makes work easier.

2. Why can't a machine be 100 percent efficient?

3. Suppose you exert 15 N on a machine, and the machine exerts 300 N on another object. What is the machine's mechanical advantage?

4. **Comparing Concepts** For the machine described in question 3, how does the distance through which the output force is exerted differ from the distance through which the input force is exerted?

internetconnect

SciLINKS
NSTA

TOPIC: Mechanical Efficiency
GO TO: www.scilinks.org
***sci*LINKS NUMBER:** HSTP185

Types of Machines

This section describes the six simple machines and explains how to determine the mechanical advantage of each. Students learn about compound machines (combinations of simple machines) they commonly encounter, and they learn how combining simple machines affects efficiency.

 **Bellringer**

Pose the following question:

What type of machine can be found on at least half the students in this room right now? (zipper)

1 Motivate

ACTIVITY

MATERIALS
FOR EACH GROUP:
• string
• meterstick
• ring stand with ring
• scissors
• 5 large metal washers tied together

Divide the class into small groups. Tell each group to use the string to hang the meterstick from the ring so the meterstick is balanced (hangs level). Then tell them to tie the washers to the meterstick at the 2-cm mark. Challenge them to find a way to again balance the meterstick without adding any weights to the opposite end. Discuss the students' solutions to the problem.

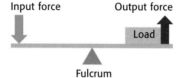

Terms to Learn

lever   wheel and axle
inclined plane pulley
wedge   compound
screw   machine

What You'll Do

◆ Identify and give examples of the six types of simple machines.
◆ Analyze the mechanical advantage provided by each simple machine.
◆ Identify the simple machines that make up a compound machine.

Figure 10 A First Class Lever

Input force   Output force

Load

Fulcrum

Types of Machines

All machines are constructed from these six simple machines: *lever, inclined plane, wedge, screw, wheel and axle,* and *pulley.* You've seen a couple of these machines already—a screwdriver can be used as a lever, and a ramp is an inclined plane. In the next few pages, each of the six simple machines will be discussed separately. Then you'll learn how compound machines are formed from combining simple machines.

Levers

Have you ever used the claw end of a hammer to remove a nail from a piece of wood? If so, you were using the hammer as a lever. A **lever** is a simple machine consisting of a bar that pivots at a fixed point, called a *fulcrum.* Levers are used to apply a force to a load. There are three classes of levers, based on the locations of the fulcrum, the load, and the input force.

First Class Levers With a first class lever, the fulcrum is between the input force and the load, as shown in **Figure 10.** First class levers always change the direction of the input force. And depending on the location of the fulcrum, first class levers can be used to increase force or to increase distance. Some examples of first class levers are shown below.

Examples of First Class Levers

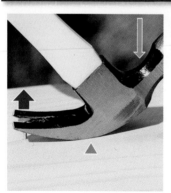

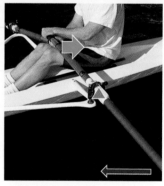

When the fulcrum is closer to the load than to the input force, a **mechanical advantage of greater than 1 results.** The output force is increased because it is exerted over a shorter distance.

When the fulcrum is exactly in the middle, a **mechanical advantage of 1 results.** The output force is not increased because the input force's distance is not increased.

When the fulcrum is closer to the input force than to the load, a **mechanical advantage of less than 1 results.** Although the output force is less than the input force, a gain in distance occurs.

98

Besides their obvious uses in bottle openers and nail pullers, levers are also used in devices such as fishing rods, cranes, typewriters, pianos, parking meters, and scales.

Second Class Levers With a second class lever, the load is between the fulcrum and the input force, as shown in **Figure 11.** Second class levers do not change the direction of the input force, but they allow you to apply less force than the force exerted by the load. Because the output force is greater than the input force, you must exert the input force over a greater distance. Some examples of second class levers are shown at right.

Figure 11 A Second Class Lever

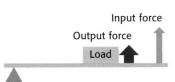

Third Class Levers With a third class lever, the input force is between the fulcrum and the load, as shown in **Figure 12.** Third class levers do not change the direction of the input force. In addition, they do *not* increase the input force. Therefore, the output force is always less than the input force. Some examples of third class levers are shown at right.

Figure 12 A Third Class Lever

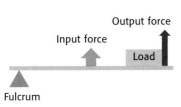

Examples of Second Class Levers

Using a second class lever results in a **mechanical advantage of greater than 1.** The closer the load is to the fulcrum, the more the force is increased and the greater the mechanical advantage.

Examples of Third Class Levers

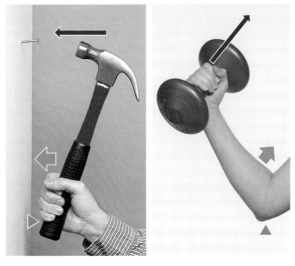

Using a third class lever results in a **mechanical advantage of less than 1** because force is decreased. But third class levers are helpful because they increase the distance through which the output force is exerted.

99

IS THAT A FACT!

The human body uses simple machines. Muscles and bones form first class and third class levers. When you look up, the skull pivots on the neck vertebrae, forming a first class lever. When you kick a soccer ball, the contracting muscle pulls your leg upward, acting like a third class lever.

ACTIVITY

FOR EACH GROUP:
• paper fastener
• rubber band
• ruler
• thick cardboard (16 × 5 cm)
• string
• model car or truck

Have students form groups of 2–3. Have each group use a paper fastener to attach a rubber band near one end of a piece of thick cardboard. Have them tie a piece of string to the other end of the rubber band and tie it to a model car or truck. Have them use a ruler to make a scale on the cardboard to measure the length of the rubber band as it stretches.

Ask students to make charts recording the changes in forces on inclined planes of varying heights.

USING THE FIGURE

Use **Figure 13** and the diagram below it to explain how you can determine mechanical advantage of an inclined plane using distances. Explain it as follows:

Work input = work output
$$F \text{ (input)} \times d \text{ (input)} =$$
$$F \text{ (output)} \times d \text{ (output)}$$

This equation can be rearranged into ratios to show

$$\frac{F \text{ (input)}}{F \text{ (output)}} = \frac{d \text{ (output)}}{d \text{ (input)}}$$

The force ratio can be used to determine mechanical advantage. But because the distance ratio is equivalent to the force ratio, it can also be used to determine mechanical advantage.

Inclined Planes

To build the Great Pyramid, located in Giza, Egypt, the Egyptians moved more than 2 million stone blocks, most averaging 2,000 kg. One of the machines they used was the *inclined plane*. An **inclined plane** is a simple machine that is a straight, slanted surface. A ramp is an example of an inclined plane.

Inclined planes can make work easier. Look at **Figure 13.** Using an inclined plane to load an upright piano into the back of a truck is easier than just lifting it into the truck. Rolling the piano into the truck along an inclined plane requires a smaller input force than is required to lift the piano into the truck. But remember that machines do not save work—therefore, the input force must be exerted over a longer distance.

Figure 13 *The work you do on the piano to roll it up the ramp is the same as the work you would do to lift it straight up. An inclined plane simply allows you to apply a smaller force over a greater distance.*

Compare work done with and without an inclined plane on page 194 of the LabBook.

Mechanical Advantage of Inclined Planes   The longer the inclined plane is compared with its height, the greater the mechanical advantage. The mechanical advantage (*MA*) of an inclined plane can be calculated by dividing the *length* of the inclined plane by the *height* to which the load is lifted, as shown below:

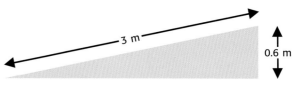

$$MA = \frac{3 \text{ m}}{0.6 \text{ m}} = 5$$

LabBook **PG 194**
Inclined to Move

SCIENCE HUMOR

Q: Why didn't the ramp help out when the piano was being loaded onto the truck?

A: It didn't have the inclination.

Wedges

Imagine trying to cut a watermelon in half with a spoon. It wouldn't be easy, would it? A knife is a much more useful utensil for cutting because it's a *wedge*. A **wedge** is a double inclined plane that moves. When you move a wedge through a distance, it applies a force on an object. A wedge applies an output force that is greater than your input force, but you apply the input force over a greater distance. The greater the distance you move the wedge, the greater the force it applies on the object. For example, the deeper you move a knife into a watermelon, as shown in **Figure 14,** the more force the knife applies to the two halves. Eventually, it pushes them apart. Other useful wedges include doorstops, plows, axe heads, and chisels.

Figure 14 *Wedges, which are often used to cut materials, allow you to exert your force over an increased distance.*

Mechanical Advantage of Wedges The longer and thinner the wedge is, the greater the mechanical advantage. That's why axes and knives cut better when you sharpen them—you are making the wedge thinner. Therefore, less input force is required. The mechanical advantage of a wedge can be determined by dividing the *length* of the wedge by its greatest *thickness,* as shown below.

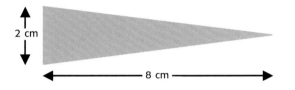

$$MA = \frac{8 \text{ cm}}{2 \text{ cm}} = 4$$

2 cm

8 cm

Screws

A **screw** is an inclined plane that is wrapped in a spiral. When a screw is rotated, a small force is applied over the long distance along the inclined plane of the screw. Meanwhile, the screw applies a large force through the short distance it is pushed. In other words, you apply a small input force over a large distance, while the screw exerts a large output force over a small distance. Screws are used most commonly as fasteners. Some examples of screws are shown in **Figure 15.**

Figure 15 *When you turn a screw, you exert a small input force over a large turning distance, but the screw itself doesn't move very far.*

IS THAT A FACT!

Both a jar lid and the top of a jar are screws. The ridges on the jar and on the lid act as screws, holding the jar and the lid together.

101

MATH and MORE

Provide three or four screws for each student. Have students calculate and compare the mechanical advantage for each screw by dividing the length of the inclined plane by the height. To measure the length of the screw threads, have students wrap a piece of string around five turns of the screw, then unwind and measure the string. By counting the total number of screw threads over the entire length of the screw, they can estimate the total length. This total length should be used for the length of the inclined plane. To determine the height, students should measure the screw from the top screw thread to the bottom.

MEETING INDIVIDUAL NEEDS

Learners Having Difficulty

Brainstorm with students to generate a list of everyday objects that contain wheels and axles. Write the list on the board, then ask students to point out the wheel and the axle in each one. Sheltered English

Lab**B**ook **PG 196**
Wheeling and Dealing

Figure 16 *The threads on the top screw are closer together and wrap more times around, so that screw has a greater mechanical advantage than the one below it.*

Mechanical Advantage of Screws If you could "unwind" the inclined plane of a screw, you would see that it is very long and has a gentle slope. Recall that the longer an inclined plane is compared with its height, the greater its mechanical advantage. Similarly, the longer the spiral on a screw is and the closer together the threads, the greater the screw's mechanical advantage, as shown in **Figure 16.**

SECTION REVIEW

1. Give an example of each of the following simple machines: first class lever, second class lever, third class lever, inclined plane, wedge, and screw.

2. A third class lever has a mechanical advantage of less than 1. Explain why it is useful for some tasks.

3. **Interpreting Graphics** Look back at Figures 6, 7, and 8 in Section 2. Identify the type of simple machine shown in each case. (If a lever is shown, identify its class.)

Figure 17
How a Wheel and Axle Works

a When a small input force is applied to the wheel, it rotates through a circular distance.

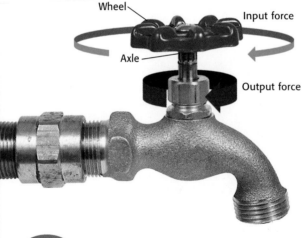

Wheel
Input force
Axle
Output force

Wheel and Axle

Did you know that when you turn a doorknob you are using a machine? A doorknob is an example of a **wheel and axle,** a simple machine consisting of two circular objects of different sizes. A wheel can be a crank, such as the handle on a fishing reel, or it can be a knob, such as a volume knob on a radio. The axle is the smaller of the two circular objects. Doorknobs, wrenches, ferris wheels, screwdrivers, and steering wheels all use a wheel and axle. **Figure 17** shows how a wheel and axle works.

b As the wheel turns, so does the axle. But because the axle is smaller than the wheel, it rotates through a smaller distance, which makes the output force larger than the input force.

Answers to Section Review

1. Sample answers: first class lever: a screwdriver used to pry the lid off a paint can; second class lever: a wheelbarrow; third class lever: your leg as you kick a soccer ball (your knee is the fulcrum); inclined plane: a ramp on the back of a moving truck; wedge: a knife; screw: a jar lid

2. A third class lever helps because it increases the distance through which the output force is exerted. For example, when you move the handle of a fishing pole just slightly, the other end of the pole moves a great distance.

3. Figure 6: The screwdriver is a first class lever; Figure 7: The ramp is an inclined plane; Figure 8: The handcart is a first class lever.

Mechanical Advantage of a Wheel and Axle The mechanical advantage of a wheel and axle can be determined by dividing the *radius* (the distance from the center to the edge) of the wheel by the radius of the axle, as shown at right. Turning the wheel results in a mechanical advantage of greater than 1 because the radius of the wheel is larger than the radius of the axle.

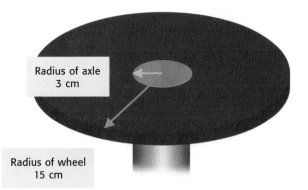

Radius of axle
3 cm

Radius of wheel
15 cm

$$MA = \frac{15 \text{ cm}}{3 \text{ cm}} = 5$$

Pulleys

When you open window blinds by pulling on a cord, you're using a pulley. A **pulley** is a simple machine consisting of a grooved wheel that holds a rope or a cable. A load is attached to one end of the rope, and an input force is applied to the other end. There are two kinds of pulleys—*fixed* and *movable*. Fixed and movable pulleys can be combined to form a *block and tackle*.

Fixed Pulleys Some pulleys only change the direction of a force. This kind of pulley is called a fixed pulley. Fixed pulleys do not increase force. A fixed pulley is attached to something that does not move. By using a fixed pulley, you can pull down on the rope in order to lift the load up. This is usually easier than trying to lift the load straight up. Elevators make use of fixed pulleys.

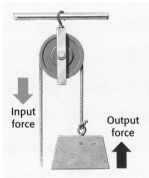

Input force

Output force

A **fixed pulley** only spins. So the distance through which the input force and the output force are exerted—and thus the forces themselves—are the same. Therefore, a fixed pulley provides a mechanical advantage of 1.

Movable Pulleys Unlike fixed pulleys, movable pulleys are attached to the object being moved. A movable pulley does not change a force's direction. Movable pulleys do increase force, but you must exert the input force over a greater distance than the load is moved. This is because you must make *both* sides of the rope move in order to lift the load.

Input force

Output force

A **movable pulley** moves up with the load as it is lifted. Force is multiplied because the combined input force is exerted over twice the distance of the output force. The mechanical advantage of a movable pulley is the number of rope segments that support the load. In this example, the mechanical advantage is 2.

103

internet**connect**

*sci*LINKS
NSTA

TOPIC: Simple Machines
GO TO: www.scilinks.org
*sci*LINKS NUMBER: HSTP190

③ Extend

GOING FURTHER

Obtain discarded machines, such as turntables, door locks and keys, table fans, mechanical clocks, or other compound machines. Make several of them available in areas where students can disassemble them. Over a period of a few days, have each student make a chart comparing pieces of the devices with the set of simple machines. Which devices are the most complex?

GROUP ACTIVITY

Divide the classroom into groups. Assign a simple machine to each group. Each group will be responsible for developing a tabletop display that describes its simple machine. The display should make use of models, objects, photographs and drawings, text labels, and other ways of presenting information on the topic. Encourage students to have fun and to be creative in their presentations.

LabBook PG 195
Building Machines

Critical Thinking Worksheet "Building Works of Art"

Reinforcement Worksheet "Finding Machines in Everyday Life"

internetconnect

SCiLINKS **TOPIC:** Compound Machines
GO TO: www.scilinks.org
sciLINKS NUMBER: HSTP195

Figure 18 *The combination of pulleys used by this crane allows it to lift heavy pieces of scrap metal.*

Block and Tackles When a fixed pulley and a movable pulley are used together, the pulley system is called a *block and tackle*. A block and tackle can have a large mechanical advantage if several pulleys are used. A block and tackle used within a larger pulley system is shown in **Figure 18.**

Input force

Output force

The mechanical advantage of this **block and tackle** is 4 because there are four rope segments that support the load. This block and tackle multiplies your input force four times, but you have to pull the rope 4 m just to lift the load 1 m.

Compound Machines

You are surrounded by machines. As you saw earlier, you even have machines in your body! But most of the machines in your world are **compound machines,** machines that are made of two or more simple machines. You've already seen one example of a compound machine: a block and tackle. A block and tackle consists of two or more pulleys. On this page and the next, you'll see some other examples of compound machines.

Activity

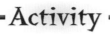

List five machines that you have encountered today and indicate what type of machine each is. Try to include at least one compound machine and one machine that is part of your body.

TRY at HOME

Can Opener

The axle has gear teeth on it that grip the can and act as tiny levers to push the can along when the axle turns.

Wheel and axle

Wedge

Second class lever

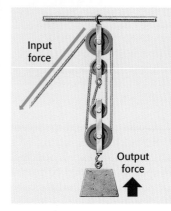

104

Answer to Activity

Student responses will vary. Some machines students might name include: a doorknob (wheel and axle), a wheelchair ramp (inclined plane), a cap on a shampoo bottle (screw), a garage door (by pulling down on a rope that runs through a pulley), and a fingernail (when used as a wedge to turn pages in a book).

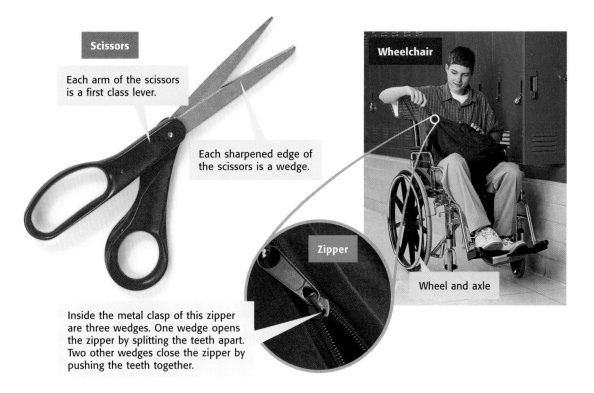

Scissors

Each arm of the scissors is a first class lever.

Each sharpened edge of the scissors is a wedge.

Wheelchair

Wheel and axle

Zipper

Inside the metal clasp of this zipper are three wedges. One wedge opens the zipper by splitting the teeth apart. Two other wedges close the zipper by pushing the teeth together.

Mechanical Efficiency of Compound Machines In general, the more moving parts a machine has, the lower its mechanical efficiency. Thus the mechanical efficiency of compound machines is often quite low. For compound machines that involve many simple machines, such as automobiles and airplanes, it is very important that friction be reduced as much as possible through the use of lubrication and other techniques. Too much friction could cause heating and damage the simple machines involved, which could create safety problems and could be expensive to repair.

SECTION REVIEW

1. Give an example of a wheel and axle.

2. Identify the simple machines that make up tweezers and nail clippers.

3. **Doing Calculations** The radius of the wheel of a wheel and axle is four times greater than the radius of the axle. What is the mechanical advantage of this machine?

internetconnect

*sci*LINKS
NSTA

TOPIC: Simple Machines, Compound Machines
GO TO: www.scilinks.org
*sci*LINKS **NUMBER:** HSTP190, HSTP195

105

▼ Answers to Section Review

1. Examples include the crank on a can opener, the reel on a fishing rod, a screwdriver, a doorknob, the crank on an ice cream maker, and the film-advance mechanism on an old camera.

2. Each side of the tweezers is a third class lever. The sharpened edges of nail clippers are wedges, and the arm that activates the clipper is a second class lever.

3. The mechanical advantage of a wheel and axle is determined by the ratio of the wheel radius to the axle radius. So this machine would have a mechanical advantage of 4.

Quiz

1. Why are simple machines so useful? (They make work easier.)

2. Identify types of simple machines you might find on a playground. Describe how each of them modifies work. (seesaw: lever changes direction of input force; merry-go-round: wheel and axle makes the input force on the axle cause the wheel to move in a circle)

3. How does reducing friction increase the mechanical efficiency of a compound machine? (Less work input is used to overcome friction, so work output is higher and mechanical efficiency is higher.)

ALTERNATIVE ASSESSMENT

Have each student write a story that incorporates six simple or compound machines. The machines must operate in some way appropriate to the story line. Suggest that students illustrate their stories.

Examples of Compound Machines:

• tweezers
• bicycle
• automobile
• jack
• airplane
• nail clippers
• typewriter
• pencil sharpener
• tire iron

Reinforcement Worksheet "Mechanical Advantage and Efficiency"

Discovery Lab

A Powerful Workout

A Powerful Workout Teacher's Notes

Time Required

One or two 45-minute class periods

Lab Ratings

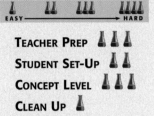

EASY —————————→ HARD

TEACHER PREP 🍾🍾🍾
STUDENT SET-UP 🍾🍾
CONCEPT LEVEL 🍾🍾🍾
CLEAN UP 🍾

MATERIALS

The materials listed for this lab are for the entire class or for smaller groups. Students in wheelchairs can use a ramp instead of a flight of stairs.

Safety Caution

Make sure that students use caution when climbing the stairs. Students with asthma or any other respiratory problems should not do this lab. Any student who becomes winded should sit down and take deep breaths. Caution students that this is not a race to see who can get the fastest time.

Answer

2. Answers will vary. Accept all reasonable hypotheses.

 Datasheets for LabBook

Discovery Lab
USING SCIENTIFIC METHODS

A Powerful Workout *TRY at HOME*

Does the amount of work you do depend on how fast you do it? No! But doing work in a shorter amount of time does affect your power—the rate at which work is done. In this lab, you'll calculate your work and power when climbing a flight of stairs at different speeds. Then you'll compare your power with that of an ordinary household object—a 100 W light bulb.

MATERIALS

- flight of stairs
- metric ruler
- stopwatch

Ask a Question

1. How does your power when climbing a flight of stairs compare with the power of a 100 W light bulb?

Form a Hypothesis

2. In your ScienceLog, write a hypothesis that answers the question in step 1. Explain your reasoning.

3. Copy Table 1 into your ScienceLog, or use a computer to construct a similar one.

Test the Hypothesis

4. Measure the height of one stair step. Record the measurement in Table 1.

5. Count the number of stairs, including the top step, and record this number in Table 1.

6. Calculate the height (in meters) of the stairs by multiplying the number of steps by the height of one step. Record your answer. (You will need to convert from centimeters to meters.)

Table 1 Data Collection				
Height of step (cm)	Number of steps	Height of stairs (m)	Time for slow walk (s)	Time for quick walk (s)
		DO NOT WRITE IN BOOK		

Table 2 Work and Power Calculations			
Weight (N)	Work (J)	Power for slow walk (W)	Power for quick walk (W)

DO NOT WRITE IN BOOK

7 Using a stopwatch, measure how many seconds you take to walk slowly up the flight of stairs. Record your measurement in Table 1.

8 Now measure how many seconds you take to walk quickly up the flight of stairs. Be careful not to overexert yourself.

Analyze the Results

9 Copy Table 2 into your ScienceLog, or use a computer to construct a similar one.

10 Determine your weight in newtons by multiplying your weight in pounds (lb) by 4.45 N/lb. Record your weight in Table 2.

11 Using the following equation, calculate and record your work done to climb the stairs:

$$work = force \times distance$$

Remember that 1 N•m is 1 J. (Hint: Remember that force is expressed in newtons.)

12 Calculate and record your power for each trial (the slow walk and the quick walk), using the following equation:

$$power = \frac{work}{time}$$

Remember that the unit for power is the watt (1 W = 1 J/s).

Draw Conclusions

13 In step 11 you calculated your work done in climbing the stairs. Why didn't you calculate your work for each trial?

14 Look at your hypothesis in step 2. Was your hypothesis supported? In your ScienceLog, communicate a valid conclusion that describes how your power in each trial compares with the power of a 100 W light bulb.

15 The work done to move one electron in a light bulb is very small. Make two inferences about why the power is large. (Hint: How many electrons are in the filament of a light bulb? Why was more power used in your second trial?)

Communicate Results

16 Write your average power in a class data table. Calculate the average power for the class. How many students would be needed to equal the power of a 100 W bulb?

Where is work done in a light bulb?
Electrons in the filament move back and forth very quickly. These moving electrons do work by heating up the filament and making it glow.

107

Answers

10. Answers will vary. For reference, 100 lb = 445 N.

11. Answers will vary, based on the weight calculation from step 10. For reference, 445 N × 4 m = 1,780 J.

12. Answers will vary. For reference, $\frac{1,780 \text{ J}}{10 \text{ s}} = 178$ W; $\frac{1,780 \text{ J}}{5 \text{ s}} = 356$ W

13. The work is the same, no matter how long it takes.

14. Answers will vary, based on original hypotheses. The statement should reflect a comparison between the student's power calculations and the power of a 100 W light bulb.

15. The power of a light bulb is large because there are millions of electrons moving in the filament and the electrons are moving very quickly.

16. Answers will vary, depending on the average power calculated by the class. Sample answer: The average power for the class was 250 W, so it would take two and a half 100 W bulbs to equal the power of one student.

Lab Notes

To help calculate averages, set up a class data table on the board. The table should have four columns: Student; Power S (for Power, Slow Walk); Power Q (for Power, Quick Walk); and Average (each student's average power). Remind students how to calculate their average power and the average power for the whole class. To find their individual average power, they add the power for their slow walk plus the power for their quick walk and divide by two. To calculate the class average power, they add all the individual averages together and divide by the number of students in the class.

Terry Rakes
Elmwood Junior High
Rogers, Arkansas

Chapter Highlights

Chapter Highlights

VOCABULARY DEFINITIONS

SECTION 1

work the action that results when a force causes an object to move in the direction of the force; $W = F \times d$

joule the unit used to express work and energy; equivalent to the newton-meter (N•m)

power the rate at which work is done; $P = W/t$

watt the unit used to express power; equivalent to joules per second (J/s)

SECTION 2

machine a device that helps make work easier by changing the size or direction (or both) of a force

work input the work done on a machine; the product of the input force and the distance through which it is exerted

work output the work done by a machine; the product of the output force and the distance through which it is exerted

mechanical advantage a number that tells how many times a machine multiplies force; can be calculated by dividing the output force by the input force

mechanical efficiency a comparison expressed as a percentage of a machine's work output with the work input; can be calculated by dividing work output by work input and then multiplying by 100

SECTION 1

Vocabulary

work (p. 88)

joule (p. 90)

power (p. 91)

watt (p. 91)

Section Notes

- Work occurs when a force causes an object to move in the direction of the force. The unit for work is the joule (J).

- Work is done on an object only when a force makes an object move and only while that force is applied.

- For work to be done on an object, the direction of the object's motion must be in the same direction as the force applied.

- Work can be calculated by multiplying force by distance.

- Power is the rate at which work is done. The unit for power is the watt (W).

- Power can be calculated by dividing the amount of work by the time taken to do that work.

SECTION 2

Vocabulary

machine (p. 92)

work input (p. 93)

work output (p. 93)

mechanical advantage (p. 96)

mechanical efficiency (p. 97)

Section Notes

- A machine makes work easier by changing the size or direction (or both) of a force.

- When a machine changes the size of a force, the distance through which the force is exerted must also change. Force or distance can increase, but not together.

☑ Skills Check

Math Concepts

WORK AND POWER Suppose a woman raises a 65 N object 1.6 m in 4 s. The work done and her power can be calculated as follows:

$$W = F \times d \qquad P = \frac{W}{t}$$

$$= 65 \text{ N} \times 1.6 \text{ m} \qquad = \frac{104 \text{ J}}{4 \text{ s}}$$

$$= 104 \text{ J} \qquad = 26 \text{ W}$$

Visual Understanding

MACHINES MAKE WORK EASIER A machine can change the size or direction (or both) of a force. Review the table on page 95 to learn more about how machines make work easier.

COMPOUND MACHINES A compound machine is made of two or more simple machines. Review the examples on pages 104 and 105.

Lab and Activity Highlights

A Powerful Workout `PG 106`

Inclined to Move `PG 194`

Building Machines `PG 195`

Wheeling and Dealing `PG 196`

Datasheets for LabBook (blackline masters for these labs)

SECTION 2

- Mechanical advantage tells how many times a machine multiplies force. It can be calculated by dividing the output force by the input force.

- Mechanical efficiency is a comparison of a machine's work output with work input. Mechanical efficiency is calculated by dividing work output by work input and is expressed as a percentage.

- Machines are not 100 percent efficient because some of the work done by a machine is used to overcome friction. So work output is always less than work input.

SECTION 3

Vocabulary

lever (p. 98)
inclined plane (p. 100)
wedge (p. 101)
screw (p. 101)
wheel and axle (p. 102)
pulley (p. 103)
compound machine (p. 104)

Section Notes

- All machines are constructed from these six simple machines: lever, inclined plane, wedge, screw, wheel and axle, and pulley.

- Compound machines consist of two or more simple machines.

- Compound machines have low mechanical efficiencies because they have more moving parts and thus more friction to overcome.

Labs

Inclined to Move (p. 194)
Building Machines (p. 195)
Wheeling and Dealing (p. 196)

internetconnect

GO TO: go.hrw.com

Visit the **HRW** Web site for a variety of learning tools related to this chapter. Just type in the keyword:

KEYWORD: HSTWRK

SC*LINKS*
N S T A

GO TO: www.scilinks.org

Visit the **National Science Teachers Association** on-line Web site for Internet resources related to this chapter. Just type in the *sci*LINKS number for more information about the topic:

TOPIC: Work and Power	*sci*LINKS NUMBER: HSTP180
TOPIC: Mechanical Efficiency	*sci*LINKS NUMBER: HSTP185
TOPIC: Simple Machines	*sci*LINKS NUMBER: HSTP190
TOPIC: Compound Machines	*sci*LINKS NUMBER: HSTP195

SECTION 3

lever a simple machine consisting of a bar that pivots at a fixed point, called a fulcrum; there are three classes of levers, based on where the input force, output force, and fulcrum are placed in relation to the load: first class levers, second class levers, and third class levers

inclined plane a simple machine that is a straight, slanted surface; a ramp

wedge a simple machine that is a double inclined plane that moves; a wedge is often used for cutting

screw a simple machine that is an inclined plane wrapped in a spiral

wheel and axle a simple machine consisting of two circular objects of different sizes; the wheel is the larger of the two circular objects

pulley a simple machine consisting of a grooved wheel that holds a rope or a cable; there are two kinds of pulleys—fixed and movable

compound machine machine that is made of two or more simple machines

Vocabulary Review Worksheet

Blackline masters of these Chapter Highlights can be found in the **Study Guide.**

Lab and Activity Highlights

LabBank

Inquiry Labs, Get an Arm and an Egg Up

Whiz-Bang Demonstrations
- Pull-Ease, Please!
- A Clever Lever

Calculator-Based Labs,
Power of the Sun

Long-Term Projects & Research Ideas,
To Complicate Things

Chapter Review
Answers

USING VOCABULARY

1. joule—unit used to express work; watt—unit used to express power.
2. work output—work done by a machine; work input—work you do on a machine (Work output is always less than work input.)
3. Mechanical efficiency and mechanical advantage both compare characteristics of a machine. Mechanical efficiency is a percentage that compares a machine's work output with its work input. Mechanical advantage compares a machine's output force with its input force.
4. An inclined plane and a screw are both simple machines. An inclined plane is a straight, slanted surface, such as a ramp. A screw is an inclined plane wrapped in a spiral.
5. A simple machine is one of the following: inclined plane, wedge, screw, wheel and axle, pulley, or lever. A compound machine consists of one or more simple machines.

UNDERSTANDING CONCEPTS

Multiple Choice

6. c	**10.** d
7. b	**11.** c
8. a	**12.** d
9. c	

Short Answer

13. A pair of scissors consists of two first class levers (arms) and two wedges (blades).
14. Sample answer: Some machines allow you to apply a small force over a large distance in order to get a larger output force. That larger output force, however, is exerted over a smaller distance. Sometimes, it is preferable for a machine to increase distance, as when using chopsticks as third class levers. Chopsticks allow you to move your fingers

Chapter Review

USING VOCABULARY

For each pair of terms, explain the difference in their meanings.

1. joule/watt
2. work output/work input
3. mechanical efficiency/mechanical advantage
4. screw/inclined plane
5. simple machine/compound machine

UNDERSTANDING CONCEPTS

Multiple Choice

6. Work is being done when
   a. you apply a force to an object.
   b. an object is moving after you apply a force to it.
   c. you exert a force that moves an object in the direction of the force.
   d. you do something that is difficult.

7. The work output for a machine is always less than the work input because
   a. all machines have a mechanical advantage.
   b. some of the work done is used to overcome friction.
   c. some of the work done is used to overcome distance.
   d. power is the rate at which work is done.

8. The unit for work is the
   a. joule.   c. newton.
   b. joule per second.   d. watt.

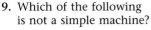

9. Which of the following is not a simple machine?
   a. a faucet handle
   b. a jar lid
   c. a can opener
   d. a seesaw

10. Power is
    a. how strong someone or something is.
    b. how much force is being used.
    c. how much work is being done.
    d. how fast work is being done.

11. The unit for power is the
    a. newton.   c. watt.
    b. kilogram.   d. joule.

12. A machine can increase
    a. distance at the expense of force.
    b. force at the expense of distance.
    c. neither distance nor force.
    d. Both (a) and (b)

Short Answer

13. Identify the simple machines that make up a pair of scissors.

14. In two or three sentences, explain the force-distance trade-off that occurs when a machine is used to make work easier.

15. Explain why you do work on a bag of groceries when you pick it up but not when you are carrying it.

a little distance to move the ends of the chopsticks a larger distance.

15. Sample answer: Work is done when motion due to a force occurs in the same direction as the force. When you pick up a bag of groceries, you exert a force up, and the bag moves up, so you are doing work. When you carry a bag of groceries, you exert an upward force but you are moving the bag forward, so you are not doing work.

Concept Mapping

16. An answer to this exercise can be found at the front of this book.

Concept Mapping

16. Create a concept map using the following terms: work, force, distance, machine, mechanical advantage.

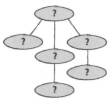

CRITICAL THINKING AND PROBLEM SOLVING

17. Why do you think levers usually have a greater mechanical efficiency than other simple machines do?

18. The winding road shown below is actually a series of inclined planes. Describe how a winding road makes it easier for vehicles to travel up a hill.

19. Why do you think you would not want to reduce the friction involved in using a winding road?

MATH IN SCIENCE

20. You and a friend together apply a force of 1,000 N to a 3,000 N automobile to make it roll 10 m in 1 minute and 40 seconds.
    a. How much work did you and your friend do together?
    b. What was your combined power?

INTERPRETING GRAPHICS

For each of the images below, identify the class of lever used and calculate the mechanical advantage.

21.

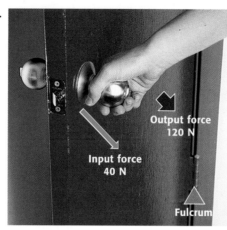

Output force 120 N

Input force 40 N

Fulcrum

22.

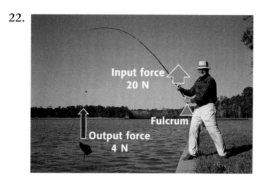

Input force 20 N

Fulcrum

Output force 4 N

Reading Check-up

Take a minute to review your answers to the Pre-Reading Questions found at the bottom of page 86. Have your answers changed? If necessary, revise your answers based on what you have learned since you began this chapter.

111

CRITICAL THINKING AND PROBLEM SOLVING

17. Sample answer: Because some work input is used to overcome friction, work output is always less than work input. Levers do not have a lot of moving parts, so they don't generate as much friction as other machines. Less work input is used to overcome friction. As a result, the mechanical efficiency of a lever is usually greater than that of other simple machines.

18. Sample answer: A winding road makes climbing a hill easier because the length of the winding road is longer than the length of a road straight up the hill. Because the mechanical advantage of an inclined plane is determined by dividing the length of the inclined plane by its height, the more the road winds, the easier it is for a car to get up the hill.

19. Sample answer: Friction between the road and car tires is necessary for a car to travel along a road. Although friction reduces mechanical efficiency, reducing the friction between tires and the roadway would prevent cars from traveling safely along a winding road.

MATH IN SCIENCE

20. a. Work = 1,000 N × 10 m = 10,000 J

    b. Power = $\frac{10,000 \text{ J}}{100 \text{ s}}$ = 100 W

INTERPRETING GRAPHICS

21. second class lever,
    $MA = \frac{120 \text{ N}}{40 \text{ N}} = 3$

22. third class lever,
    $MA = \frac{4 \text{ N}}{20 \text{ N}} = 0.20$

Concept Mapping Transparency 8

Blackline masters of this Chapter Review can be found in the **Study Guide.**

Science, Technology, and Society

Micromachines

Background

Advances in microtechnology have allowed scientists to achieve impressive results in many fields. For example, medical researchers are working on special pills equipped with sensors, tiny pumps, and drug reservoirs.

Other technological advances include microscopic filters and air turbines for controlling the temperature of microchip arrays. One team of scientists has created a molecular "on-off switch" that could be used to store information in computers.

A scanning tunneling microscope (STM) can be used to study the surfaces of materials that can carry electric current. As the probe of the STM approaches a material, a current called a tunneling current is created between the material and the probe. The strength of the current at different locations allows the STM to create an image of the material's surface. The inventors of the STM won the Nobel Prize in physics in 1986.

The technology of making things smaller and smaller keeps growing and growing. Powerful computers can now be held in the palm of your hand. But what about motors smaller than a grain of pepper? Or gnat-sized robots that can swim through the bloodstream? These are just a couple of the possibilities for micromachines.

▲ *The earliest working micromachine had a turning central rotor.*

Microscopic Motors

Researchers have already built gears, motors, and other devices so small that you could accidentally inhale one! For example, one engineer devised a motor so small that five of the motors would fit on the period at the end of this sentence. This micromotor is powered by static electricity instead of electric current, and the motor spins at 15,000 revolutions per minute. This is about twice as fast as most automobile engines running at top speed.

Small Sensors

So far micromachines have been most useful as sensing devices. Micromechanical sensors can be used in places too small for ordinary instruments. For example, blood-pressure sensors can fit inside blood vessels and can detect minute changes in a person's blood pressure. Each sensor has a patch so thin that it bends when the pressure changes.

Cell-Sized Robots

Some scientists are investigating the possibility of creating cell-sized machines called nanobots. These tiny robots may have many uses in medicine. For instance, if nanobots could be injected into a person's bloodstream, they might be used to destroy disease-causing organisms such as viruses and bacteria. Nanobots might also be used to count blood cells or to deliver medicine.

The ultimate in micromachines would be machines created from individual atoms and molecules. Although these machines do not currently exist, scientists are already able to manipulate single atoms and molecules. For example, the "molecular man" shown below is made of individual molecules. These molecules are moved by using a scanning tunneling microscope.

A Nanobot's "Life"

► Imagine that you are a nanobot traveling through a person's body. What types of things do you think you would see? What type of work could you do? Write a story that describes what your experiences as a nanobot might be like.

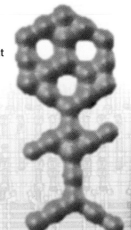

► *"Molecular man" is composed of 28 carbon monoxide molecules.*

Answer to A Nanobot's "Life"

Encourage creativity and scientific accuracy by providing students with a body atlas or similar reference work. Tell them that they are all specialized nanobots who can travel through only certain systems of the body (such as the circulatory, endocrine, or nervous system) and certain organs or types of tissue. Ask them to describe their environment. What common problems might occur in their environment, and what could they do to help? (For example, a nanobot inside a lung would see bronchial tubes, alveoli, and capillaries. It could break down contaminants in the air sacs, help fight off infections, or remove fluids in patients who have pneumonia.)

Eureka!
Wheelchair Innovators

Two recent inventions have dramatically improved the technology of wheelchairs. With these new inventions, some wheelchair riders can now control their chairs with voice commands and others can take a cruise over a sandy beach.

Voice-Command Wheelchair

At age 27, Martine Kemph invented a voice-recognition system that enables people without arms or legs to use spoken commands to operate their motorized wheelchairs. Here's how it works: The voice-recognition computer translates spoken words into digital commands, which are then directed to electric motors. These commands completely control the operating speed and direction of the motors, giving the operator total control over the chair's movement.

Kemph's system can execute spoken commands almost instantly. In addition, the system is easy to program, so each user can tailor the computer's list of commands to his or her needs.

Kemph named the computer Katalvox, using the root words *katal,* which is Greek for "to understand," and *vox,* which is Latin for "voice."

The Surf Chair

Mike Hensler was a lifeguard at Daytona Beach, Florida, when he realized that it was next to impossible for someone in a wheelchair to come onto the beach. Although he had never invented a machine before, Hensler decided to build a wheelchair that could be maneuvered across sand without getting stuck. He began spending many evenings in his driveway with a pile of lawn-chair parts, designing the chair by trial and error.

The result of Hensler's efforts looks very different from a conventional wheelchair. With huge rubber wheels and a thick frame of white PVC pipe, the Surf Chair not only moves easily over sandy terrain but also is weather resistant and easy to clean. The newest models of the Surf Chair come with optional attachments, such as a variety of umbrellas, detachable armrests and footrests, and even places to attach fishing rods.

▲ *Mike Hensler tries out his Surf Chair.*

Design One Yourself

▶ Can you think of any other ways to improve wheelchairs? Think about it, and put your ideas down on paper. To inspire creative thinking, consider how a wheelchair could be made lighter, faster, safer, or easier to maneuver.

113

Answer to Design One Yourself

Accept all reasonable designs. Make sure students have properly considered safety features and usefulness in their designs.

Background

Martine Kemph's Katalvox-driven wheelchair is already being used in medical institutions in Moscow and Paris, at Stanford University Hospital, and at the Mayo Clinic. Also, NASA is testing Katalvox for its ability to control cameras mounted on robotic arms. As an inventor intent on helping people, Kemph has had a very good role model: her father is a polio survivor who invented a car that could be driven without the use of legs.

In designing the Surf Chair, Hensler purposefully avoided materials that would make the chair look cumbersome or clinical. Since the beach is a place to relax and have fun, Hensler designed his chair to blend easily into such an environment. This fun and practical wheelchair is now available at many public beaches. Daytona Beach, for example, provides free use of the Surf Chair for people who need wheelchairs.

Teaching Strategies

Have students design a device to help mobility-impaired people in the home. You might want to give them a specific goal, such as designing a device to retrieve something from the refrigerator.

Chapter Organizer

CHAPTER ORGANIZATION	TIME MINUTES	OBJECTIVES	LABS, INVESTIGATIONS, AND DEMONSTRATIONS
Chapter Opener pp. 114–115	45	National Standards: SAI 1, PS 3a	**Start-Up Activity**, Energy Swings, p. 115
Section 1 **What Is Energy?**	90	▶ Explain the relationship between energy and work. ▶ Compare kinetic and potential energy. ▶ Summarize the different forms of energy. UCP 3, PS 3a, 3d–3f	**Demonstration**, p. 116 in ATE **Demonstration**, All Wound Up! p. 117 in ATE **QuickLab**, Hear That Energy! p. 122 **Whiz-Bang Demonstrations**, Wrong-Way Roller?
Section 2 **Energy Conversions**	90	▶ Describe an energy conversion. ▶ Give examples of energy conversions among the different forms of energy. ▶ Explain the role of machines in energy conversions. ▶ Explain how energy conversions make energy useful. ST 2, SPSP 5, PS 3a, 3f; Labs SAI 1, PS 3a	**Discovery Lab**, Finding Energy, p. 140 **Datasheets for LabBook**, Finding Energy **Skill Builder**, Energy of a Pendulum, p. 198 **Datasheets for LabBook**, Energy of a Pendulum **Whiz-Bang Demonstrations**, Pendulum Peril
Section 3 **Conservation of Energy**	90	▶ Explain how energy is conserved within a closed system. ▶ Explain the law of conservation of energy. ▶ Give examples of how thermal energy is always a result of energy conversion. ▶ Explain why perpetual motion is impossible. UCP 1, 3, ST 2; Labs ST 1	**Demonstration**, p. 131 in ATE **Design Your Own**, Eggstremely Fragile, p. 199 **Datasheets for LabBook**, Eggstremely Fragile **Labs You Can Eat**, Power-Packed Peanuts **Calculator-Based Labs**, A Hot Hand
Section 4 **Energy Resources**	90	▶ Name several energy resources. ▶ Explain how the sun is the source of most energy on Earth. ▶ Evaluate the advantages and disadvantages of using various energy resources. ST 2, SPSP 4, HNS 1, PS 3e, 3f	**Interactive Explorations CD-ROM**, The Generation Gap *A **Worksheet** is also available in the **Interactive Explorations Teacher's Edition**.* **Labs You Can Eat**, Now You're Cooking! **Long-Term Projects & Research Ideas**, Great Balls of Fire

*See page **T23** for a complete correlation of this book with the*

NATIONAL SCIENCE EDUCATION STANDARDS.

TECHNOLOGY RESOURCES

 Guided Reading Audio CD English or Spanish, Chapter 5

 Interactive Explorations CD-ROM CD 1, Exploration 6, The Generation Gap

 One-Stop Planner CD-ROM with Test Generator

 CNN. **Science, Technology & Society,** Segments 6 and 14

Multicultural Connections, Segment 8

Scientists in Action, Segment 7

CLASSROOM WORKSHEETS, TRANSPARENCIES, AND RESOURCES	SCIENCE INTEGRATION AND CONNECTIONS	REVIEW AND ASSESSMENT
Directed Reading Worksheet **Science Puzzlers, Twisters & Teasers**		
Transparency 232, Energy and Work **Directed Reading Worksheet,** Section 1 **Transparency 233,** Thermal Energy	**Multicultural Connection,** p. 118 in ATE **MathBreak,** Calculating Energy, p. 119 **Math and More,** p. 119 in ATE **Cross-Disciplinary Focus,** p. 121, 122 in ATE **Real-World Connection,** p. 122 in ATE	**Section Review,** p. 119 **Section Review,** p. 123 **Quiz,** p. 123 in ATE **Alternative Assessment,** p. 123 in ATE
Transparency 234, Energy Conversion on a Trampoline **Directed Reading Worksheet,** Section 2 **Transparency 235,** Photosynthesis **Transparency 236,** Energy Transfer in a Bicycle **Transparency 237,** Energy Conversions in a Car Engine **Math Skills for Science Worksheet,** A Bicycle Trip **Reinforcement Worksheet,** See What I Saw, Energetic Cooking	**Apply,** p. 126 **Connect to Environmental Science,** p. 126 in ATE **Multicultural Connection,** p. 127 in ATE **Real-World Connection,** p. 130 in ATE **Across the Sciences:** Green Buildings, p. 146	**Self-Check,** p. 125 **Section Review,** p. 127 **Homework,** p. 129 in ATE **Section Review,** p. 130 **Quiz,** p. 130 in ATE **Alternative Assessment,** p. 130 in ATE
Directed Reading Worksheet, Section 3	**Real-World Connection,** p. 132 in ATE **Biology Connection,** p. 133	**Section Review,** p. 133 **Quiz,** p. 133 in ATE **Alternative Assessment,** p. 133 in ATE
Directed Reading Worksheet, Section 4 **Science Skills Worksheet,** Grasping Graphing **Transparency 116,** Formation of Coal **Critical Thinking Worksheet,** The Armchair Enviro-Challenge	**Cross-Disciplinary Focus,** p. 135 in ATE **Connect to Earth Science,** p. 135 in ATE **Multicultural Connection,** p. 138 in ATE **Connect to Environmental Science,** p. 139 in ATE **Careers:** Power-Plant Manager—Cheryl Mele, p. 147	**Homework,** p. 136 in ATE **Section Review,** p. 139 **Quiz,** p. 139 in ATE **Alternative Assessment,** p. 139 in ATE

 internetconnect

 Holt, Rinehart and Winston On-line Resources
go.hrw.com

For worksheets and other teaching aids related to this chapter, visit the HRW Web site and type in the keyword: **HSTENG**

 National Science Teachers Association
www.scilinks.org

Encourage students to use the *sci*LINKS numbers listed in the internet connect boxes to access information and resources on the **NSTA** Web site.

END-OF-CHAPTER REVIEW AND ASSESSMENT

Chapter Review in Study Guide
Vocabulary and Notes in Study Guide
Chapter Tests with Performance-Based Assessment, Chapter 5 Test, Performance-Based Assessment 5
Concept Mapping Transparency 9

Chapter Resources & Worksheets

Visual Resources

TEACHING TRANSPARENCIES

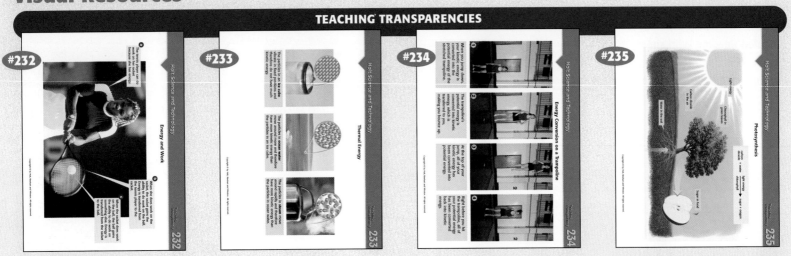

#232 — Energy and Work — *Holt Science and Technology* — 232

#233 — Thermal Energy — *Holt Science and Technology* — 233

#234 — Energy Conversion on a Trampoline — *Holt Science and Technology* — 234

#235 — Photosynthesis — *Holt Science and Technology* — 235

TEACHING TRANSPARENCIES

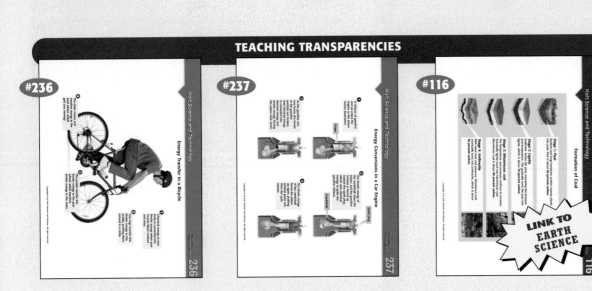

#236 — Energy Transfer in a Bicycle — *Holt Science and Technology* — 236

#237 — Energy Conversions in a Car Engine — *Holt Science and Technology* — 237

#116 — Formation of Coal — *Holt Science and Technology* — 116

LINK TO EARTH SCIENCE

CONCEPT MAPPING TRANSPARENCY

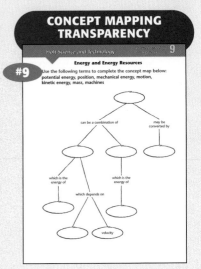

Holt Science and Technology — 9

#9

Energy and Energy Resources

Use the following terms to complete the concept map below: potential energy, position, mechanical energy, motion, kinetic energy, mass, machines

Meeting Individual Needs

DIRECTED READING

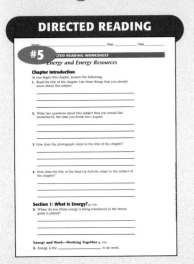

#5 RECTED READING WORKSHEET

Energy and Energy Resources

Chapter Introduction

As you begin this chapter, answer the following.

1. Read the title of the chapter. List three things that you already know about this subject.

2. Write two questions about this subject that you would like answered by the time you finish this chapter.

3. How does the photograph relate to the title of the chapter?

4. How does the title of the Start-Up Activity relate to the subject of the chapter?

Section 1: What Is Energy? (p. 116)

5. Where do you think energy is being transferred as the tennis game is played?

Energy and Work—Working Together (p. 116)

6. Energy is the _____ to do work.

REINFORCEMENT & VOCABULARY REVIEW

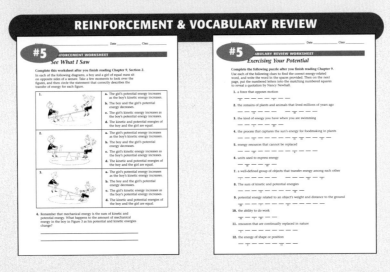

#5 NFORCEMENT WORKSHEET

See What I Saw

Complete this worksheet after you finish reading **Chapter 9, Section 2.**

In each of the following diagrams, a boy and a girl of equal mass sit on opposite sides of a seesaw. Take a few moments to look over the figures, and then circle the statement that correctly describes the transfer of energy for each figure.

1.
- **a.** The girl's potential energy increases as the boy's kinetic energy increases.
- **b.** The boy and the girl's potential energy decreases.
- **c.** The girl's kinetic energy increases as the boy's potential energy decreases.
- **d.** The kinetic and potential energies of the boy and the girl are equal.

2.
- **a.** The girl's potential energy increases as the boy's kinetic energy increases.
- **b.** The boy and the girl's potential energy decrease.
- **c.** The girl's kinetic energy increases as the boy's potential energy increases.
- **d.** The kinetic and potential energies of the boy and the girl are equal.

3.
- **a.** The girl's potential energy increases as the boy's kinetic energy increases.
- **b.** The boy and the girl's potential energy decreases.
- **c.** The girl's potential energy increases as the boy's potential energy increases.
- **d.** The kinetic and potential energies of the boy and the girl are equal.

4. Remember that mechanical energy is the sum of kinetic and potential energy. What happens to the amount of mechanical energy in the boy in Figure 3 as his potential and kinetic energies change?

#5 ABULARY REVIEW WORKSHEET

Exercising Your Potential

Complete the following puzzle after you finish reading **Chapter 9.**

Use each of the following clues to find the correct energy-related word, and write the word in the spaces provided. Then on the next page, put the numbered letters into the matching numbered squares to reveal a quotation by Nancy Newball.

1. a force that opposes motion

2. the remains of plants and animals that lived millions of years ago

3. the kind of energy you have when you are swimming

4. the process that captures the sun's energy for foodmaking in plants

5. energy resources that cannot be replaced

6. units used to express energy

7. a well-defined group of objects that transfer energy among each other

8. the sum of kinetic and potential energies

9. potential energy related to an object's weight and distance to the ground

10. the ability to do work

11. resources that are continually replaced in nature

12. the energy of shape or position

SCIENCE PUZZLERS, TWISTERS & TEASERS

#5 NCE PUZZLERS, TWISTERS & TEASERS

Energy and Energy Resources

When They Were in the 8th Grade (Tall Tales)

1. When they were in the 8th grade, some famous scientists and inventors had some strange ideas about various types of energy. From the clues, identify the types of energy and write them in the blanks.

- **a.** Sir Isaac Newton wanted to invent an air conditioner for birds. He constructed a wind tunnel and pointed it at the apple tree where his favorite birds perched themselves. As a result, the _____ energy of the apples was converted into _____ energy and they fell on Newton's head. And now we have a theory of gravity.

- **b.** Dennis Oppenheimer wanted to make water lighter so that his pack would weigh less when he went hiking. He decided to do this by splitting the hydrogen atom (of which there are two per each water molecule) in half. The result was a large explosion caused by a chain reaction. The energy produced was _____ energy.

- **c.** Albert Einstein wanted to measure the intensity of the light from Alpha Centauri, the star closest to the Earth after our sun. He knew that once the vibrations of electrically charged particles left Alpha Centauri it would take the _____ energy a year to reach his telescope. His anticipation made the year seem like a decade. From this he developed the theory of relativity.

Word Connections

2. Each of the following sentences contains a hidden word from the chapter. These words can be found by looking at part of one word somewhere in the sentence and connecting it to the beginning of the next word(s). For example, the word *undo* could be hidden between the words *run, dogs.* Circle the hidden word in each example.

- **a.** Don't ask me, Chan. I calibrated the other sphygmomanometers.

- **b.** Man, these peppers are potent! I already can't feel my tongue!

- **c.** These are sour celery drops, a fabulous candy I just invented.

Chapter 5 • Energy and Energy Resources

Review & Assessment

STUDY GUIDE

#5 VOCABULARY & NOTES WORKSHEET

Energy and Energy Resources

By studying the Vocabulary and Notes listed for each section below, you can gain a better understanding of this chapter.

SECTION 1

Vocabulary

In your own words, write a definition for each of the following terms in the space provided.

1. energy
2. kinetic energy
3. potential energy
4. mechanical energy

Notes

Read the following section highlights. Then, in your own words, write the highlights in your ScienceLog.

• Energy is the ability to do work, and work is the transfer of energy. Both energy and work are expressed in joules.
• Kinetic energy is energy of motion and depends on speed and mass.
• Potential energy is energy of position or shape. Gravitational potential energy depends on weight and height.
• Mechanical energy is the sum of kinetic energy and potential energy.
• Thermal energy, sound energy, electrical energy, and light energy can all be forms of kinetic energy.
• Chemical energy, electrical energy, sound energy, and nuclear energy can all be forms of potential energy.

#5 CHAPTER REVIEW WORKSHEET

Energy and Energy Resources

USING VOCABULARY

For each pair of terms, explain the difference in their meanings.

1. potential energy/kinetic energy
2. friction/energy conversion
3. energy conversion/law of conservation of energy
4. energy resources/fossil fuels

CHAPTER TESTS WITH PERFORMANCE-BASED ASSESSMENT

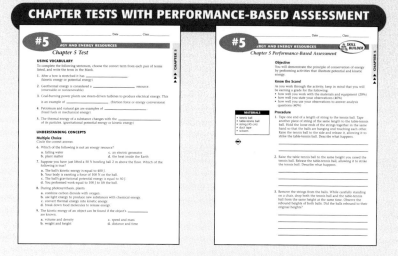

#5 ENERGY AND ENERGY RESOURCES

Chapter 5 Test

USING VOCABULARY

To complete the following sentences, choose the correct term from each pair of terms listed, and write the term in the blank.

1. After a bow is stretched it has _____ (kinetic energy or potential energy)
2. Geothermal energy is considered a _____ resource. (renewable or nonrenewable)
3. Coal-burning power plants use steam-driven turbines to produce electrical energy. This is an example of _____ (friction force or energy conversions)
4. Petroleum and natural gas are examples of _____ (fossil fuels or mechanical energy)
5. The thermal energy of a substance changes with the _____ of its particles. (gravitational potential energy or kinetic energy)

UNDERSTANDING CONCEPTS

Multiple Choice
Circle the correct answer.

6. Which of the following is not an energy resource?
   a. falling water   c. an electric generator
   b. plant matter   d. the heat inside the Earth
7. Suppose you have just lifted a 50 N bowling ball 2 m above the floor. Which of the following is true?
   a. The ball's kinetic energy is equal to 400 J.
   b. Your body is exerting a force of 100 N on the ball.
   c. The ball's gravitational potential energy is equal to 50 J.
   d. You performed work equal to 100 J to lift the ball.
8. During photosynthesis, plants
   a. combine carbon dioxide with oxygen.
   b. use light energy to produce new substances with chemical energy.
   c. convert thermal energy into kinetic energy.
   d. break down food molecules to release energy.
9. The kinetic energy of an object can be found if the object's _____ are known.
   a. volume and density   c. speed and mass
   b. weight and height   d. distance and time

#5 ENERGY AND ENERGY RESOURCES | SKILL BUILDER

Chapter 5 Performance-Based Assessment

Objective
You will demonstrate the principle of conservation of energy by performing activities that illustrate potential and kinetic energy.

Know the Score!
As you work through the activity, keep in mind that you will be earning a grade for the following:
• how well you work with the materials and equipment (20%)
• how well you state your observations (40%)
• how well you use your observations to answer analysis questions (40%)

MATERIALS
• tennis ball
• table-tennis ball
• string (45 cm)
• duct tape
• scissors

Procedure

1. Tape one end of a length of string to the tennis ball. Tape another piece of string of the same length to the table-tennis ball. Hold the loose ends of the strings together in the same hand so that the balls are hanging and touching each other. Raise the tennis ball to the side and release it, allowing it to strike the table-tennis ball. Describe what happens.

2. Raise the table tennis ball to the same height you raised the tennis ball. Release the table-tennis ball, allowing it to strike the tennis ball. Describe what happens.

3. Remove the strings from the balls. While carefully standing on a chair, drop both the tennis ball and the table-tennis ball from the same height at the same time. Observe the rebound heights of both balls. Did the balls rebound to their original heights?

Lab Worksheets

LABS YOU CAN EAT

#5 STUDENT WORKSHEET | DISCOVERY LAB

Power-Packed Peanuts

The world runs on many different kinds of fuel—cars run on gasoline and our homes are often heated by oil. But did you know you can burn a peanut to heat water? A peanut may surprise you with this amazing underground bite that can pack a powerful punch! Let's take a look at just how much energy we can find in a peanut.

MATERIALS
• alcohol thermometer
• support stand with ring clamp
• wire gauze
• clean, empty can
• shelled peanut
• paper clip
• cork covered in aluminum foil
• metric ruler
• 125 mL graduated cylinder
• water
• matches

SCIENTIFIC METHOD
Ask a Question
How do you measure the amount of energy in a peanut?

Conduct an Experiment
1. Set up the apparatus as shown below. Be sure to place the thermometer so that the tip is in the can but does not touch the bottom of the can. The can should be 2.5–5 cm from the top of the peanut.
2. Pour 100 mL of water into the can, and record the water temperature in the Temperature Chart on page 97.
3. Light a match, and set fire to the peanut. **Caution:** Be careful not to burn yourself.
4. When the flame goes out, monitor the water temperature until it no longer changes. Record your measurements in the Temperature Chart on page 97, and then calculate the increase in temperature.

WHIZ-BANG DEMONSTRATIONS

#5 TEACHER-LED DEMONSTRATION | DISCOVERY LAB

Pendulum Peril

Purpose: Students observe the movement of a pendulum to understand conversions between potential and kinetic energy.

Time Required
10–15 minutes

Lab Ratings
TEACHER PREP
CONCEPT LEVEL
CLEAN UP

MATERIALS
• tap water
• balloon
• nylon string about 3 m long

What to Do
1. Attach the string to the ceiling. Fill the balloon with water and attach it securely to the free end of the string.
2. Adjust the length of the string so that the balloon just reaches your nose when you stand with your back against a wall. Securely tighten all of the knots.
3. Stand against the wall and hold the water balloon a few centimeters from your face. Ask students what they expect to happen when you release the balloon. (Expected answer: It will swing forward and then swing back and hit you in the face. You will get soaked!)

4. Now, with feigned anxiety, release the balloon and wait for it to swing back. Do not push the balloon or move your head!

Explanation
When the balloon is held in place, there is gravitational potential energy associated with its position. When the balloon is released, some of this potential energy is gradually converted into kinetic energy. At the midpoint of the swing, the kinetic energy is at a maximum, so the balloon is swinging at its fastest. After the midpoint of the swing, the kinetic energy is gradually converted back into potential energy. In the absence of friction, this cycle would continue indefinitely, and the balloon

continued...

LONG-TERM PROJECTS & RESEARCH IDEAS

#5 STUDENT WORKSHEET | DESIGN YOUR OWN

Great Balls of Fire

While sitting on her front porch during a thunderstorm in 1985, a Massachusetts woman saw a "whole ball of fire" rolling up her street. It was sparking and crackling and sending out small fingers of lightning to the cars and telephone poles it passed. The ball, about a meter in diameter, split into three pieces, then into six, then joined back to three, and then back to its original size before disappearing. The power in the neighborhood went out for 2.5 hours.

Seem strange? Most people have witnessed lightning bolts in thunderstorms, but few have ever seen ball lightning. Although rare, it has been noted by individuals all the way back to the ancient Greeks. Ball lightning has been reported to enter airplanes and even to "chase" a flight attendant around the cabin! The nature of ball lightning is not well understood, ranking it among the more interesting scientific mysteries of the day.

INTERNET KEYWORD
ball lightning

A Striking Idea
1. Using the library and the Internet, find out more about ball lightning. How often is it reported? What are some theories to explain it? Are there any myths about ball lightning? Write a report in the form of a scientific magazine article. If possible, include quotes from firsthand reports of its sightings.

Another Research Idea
2. Where will the energy our children use come from? Though we rely on fossil fuels for the majority of our energy today, their limited supply and environmental impact force us to keep seeking new ways to generate energy. What are the most promising alternative energy sources being explored today? Choose one technology and create a Web page or report about it. Include its advantages and disadvantages, its potential for large-scale use, and a brief history of its development.

Long-Term Project Idea
3. Is your refrigerator taking money from you? Is your dishwasher sapping precious energy? Some appliances use more energy than others to do the same amount of work. Visit an appliance store, choose one type of appliance, and record the information shown on the yellow Energy Guide tag (the estimated cost of using that appliance for one year) for each model of that appliance. Make a chart listing several appliances in one category from highest to lowest Energy Guide rating. What features might lower the Energy Guide rating for the appliance you chose? Prepare a report with your findings.

DATASHEETS FOR LABBOOK

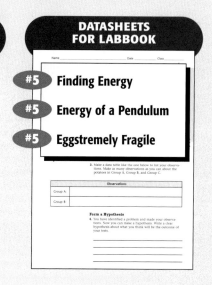

#5 Finding Energy

#5 Energy of a Pendulum

#5 Eggstremely Fragile

3. Make a data table like the one below to list your observations. Make as many observations as you can about the potatoes in Group A, Group B, and Group C.

Observations	
Group A:	
Group B:	

Form a Hypothesis
4. You have identified a problem and made your observations. Now you can make a hypothesis. Write a clear hypothesis about what you think will be the outcome of your tests.

Applications & Extensions

CRITICAL THINKING & PROBLEM SOLVING

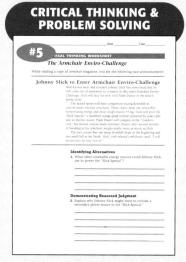

#5 CRITICAL THINKING WORKSHEET

The Armchair Enviro-Challenge

While reading a copy of *Armchair* magazine, you see the following race announcement:

Johnny Slick to Enter Armchair Enviro-Challenge

Well-known racer and inventor Johnny Slick has announced that he will come out of retirement to compete in this year's Armchair Enviro-Challenge. Slick will race his inch tred *Flash Dance* in the seated sprint event.

The seated sprint with last competitors racing downhill in custom-made wheeled armchairs. These chairs must use renewable, nonpolluting energy and must weigh exactly 45 kg. Slick will pilot the "Slick Special," a modified orange-plaid recliner powered by solar cells and an electric motor. Flash Dance will compete in the "Comfort-One." his newest custom-made armchair. Dunner, after several months of breaking in his armchair, weighs nearly twice as much as Slick.

The race course has one steep downhill slope at the beginning and one small hill at the finish. Slick, with relaxed confidence, said, "I will pilot this into an easy victory!"

Identifying Alternatives
1. What other renewable energy sources could Johnny Slick use to power the "Slick Special"?

Demonstrating Reasoned Judgment
2. Explain why Johnny Slick might want to include a secondary power source in his "Slick Special."

MULTICULTURAL CONNECTIONS

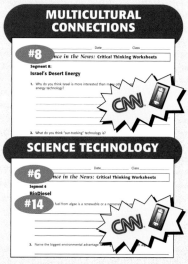

#8 Science in the News: Critical Thinking Worksheets

Segment 8:
Israel's Desert Energy

1. Why do you think Israel is more interested than many other energy technology?

2. What do you think "sun-tracking" technology is?

SCIENCE TECHNOLOGY

#6 Science in the News: Critical Thinking Worksheets

Segment 6
BioDiesel

#14 fuel from algae is a renewable or a nonrenewable

2. Name the biggest environmental advantage

SCIENTISTS IN ACTION

#7 Science in the News: Critical Thinking Worksheets

Forming the Future of Energy Efficiency

1. Do you think that efficiency is key to solving the global warming problem? Explain.

2. What incentives could home owners and businesses be offered to become more energy efficient?

3. Why haven't all businesses or homes become energy-efficient despite recent advances in energy-efficient technology?

4. Give two examples of energy-efficient devices described in the video in your home.

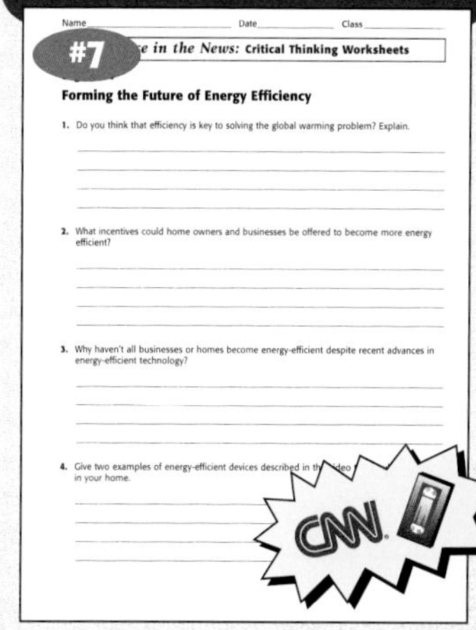

INTERACTIVE EXPLORATIONS

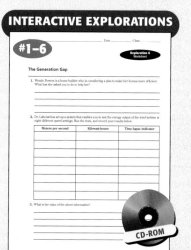

#1–6 Exploration 6 Worksheet

The Generation Gap

1. Wendy Powers is a home builder who is considering a plan to make her homes more efficient. What has she asked you to do to help her?

2. Dr. Labcoat has set up a system that enables you to test the energy output of the wind turbine at eight different speed settings. Run the tests, and record your results below.

Meters per second	Kilowatt-hours	Time-lapse indicator

3. What is the value of the above information?

Chapter Background

SECTION 1

What Is Energy?

▶ Energy

Energy is the ability to do work. *Work* occurs when a force causes an object to move in the direction of the force. Both energy and work are expressed in units called *joules* (J), named for James Prescott Joule. One joule is the amount of work done when a force of 1 N acts through a distance of 1 m ($1 J = 1 N \times 1 m$).

▶ James Prescott Joule

The English scientist James Prescott Joule (1818–1889) was the son of a wealthy brewery owner. Joule used his financial resources to conduct research in a variety of areas.

- Joule worked to improve the efficiency of electric motors so they could be used to replace steam engines. His research was some of the first to show the connection between thermal energy and other forms of energy.

IS THAT A FACT!

- ▶ The countries of North America consume about 30 percent of the total world energy output. The countries of the former Soviet Union consume about 11 to 15 percent.

SECTION 2

Energy Conversions

▶ Kinetic and Potential Energy

The conversion of potential energy to kinetic energy and vice versa is classically demonstrated by lifting and dropping an object.

- A moving object has kinetic energy. The amount of kinetic energy depends on the mass of the object and the speed at which it is moving.

▶ Gravitational Potential Energy

An object that has been lifted from its position on the Earth has gravitational potential energy. If you drop the object and nothing is in its way, the gravitational potential energy will immediately begin to change into kinetic energy as the object accelerates toward the Earth.

▶ Conversion of Light Energy to Chemical Energy

Plants use photosynthesis to make molecules with high chemical energy, such as sugars, from water and carbon dioxide, which have low chemical energy. To increase the amount of chemical energy, light energy is converted to chemical energy, and ATP is formed. In a separate series of reactions, plants convert sugars to starches.

- When you eat plants, your digestive system transforms the high-energy sugars and starches into smaller, lower-energy molecules. The chemical energy in the sugars and starches fuels all your body functions and movements and provides the thermal energy that keeps your body temperature constant.

▶ Conversion of Chemical Energy to Electrical Energy

Batteries consist of cells. A cell converts chemical energy into electrical energy. Any cell has two electrodes and an electrolyte. Between the electrodes are positive and negative ions. Positively charged ions have fewer electrons than protons, and negatively charged ions have more electrons than protons. When a circuit is completed, the electrodes react with the electrolyte, causing electrons to leave one of the electrodes and build up on the other. Work is done in separating the charges, and that work is stored in the battery as electrical potential energy.

- Whenever the electrodes of the battery are connected with a wire, work is done on the electrons in the wire as electrical energy flows from the negative electrode of the battery to the positive electrode.

SECTION 3

Conservation of Energy

▶ The Law of Conservation of Energy

In the presence of friction, mechanical energy *(KE + PE)* is *not* conserved. But mechanical energy does not take into account the other objects and conversions within a closed system. Total energy is always conserved, even if mechanical energy is not.

IS THAT A FACT!

- ☛ The British Patent Office does not accept applications for perpetual motion machines. Such a machine would violate the laws of physics and is therefore considered impossible.

- ☛ The United States Patent Office receives (and accepts) about 100 applications yearly for perpetual motion machines.

SECTION 4

Energy Resources

▶ Fossil Fuels

Fossil fuels require hundreds of thousands, or even millions, of years to form.

- Coal is formed from plant material that is compressed in swamps.

- Petroleum and natural gas both form from decayed organisms.

▶ Energy Alternatives

Nature can supply energy in a variety of ways. Wind energy, tidal energy, hydroelectric energy, and solar energy are all alternatives to the nonrenewable fossil fuels used today.

- Although the sun is technically a limited energy source, it still has approximately 5 billion years left in its life span. For the time being, it is considered a limitless source of energy.

> **For background information about teaching strategies and issues, refer to the *Professional Reference for Teachers.***

Energy and Energy Resources

Pre-Reading Questions

Students may not know the answers to these questions before reading the chapter, so accept any reasonable response.

Suggested Answers

1. Energy is the ability to do work.

2. Energy is converted from one form to another when you do work.

3. An energy resource is a natural resource, such as coal or oil, that can be converted into useful forms of energy.

CHAPTER 5

Energy and Energy Resources

Pre-Reading
Questions

1. What is energy?

2. How is energy converted from one form to another?

3. What is an energy resource?

114

THE RACE IS ON!

Imagine that you're a driver in this race. Your car will need a lot of energy to finish, so you should make sure your car is fueled up and ready. You'll probably need a lot of gasoline, right? Nope, just a lot of sunshine! The car in this photo is solar powered—energy from the sun makes it go. In this chapter, you'll learn about different types of energy. You'll also learn where the energy that runs our cars and our appliances comes from.

---

internet connect

 HRW On-line Resources

go.hrw.com

For worksheets and other teaching aids, visit the HRW Web site and type in the keyword: **HSTENG**

www.scilinks.com

Use the *sci*LINKS numbers at the end of each chapter for additional resources on the **NSTA** Web site.

 Smithsonian Institution

www.si.edu/hrw

Visit the Smithsonian Institution Web site for related on-line resources.

 CNN fyi.com

www.cnnfyi.com

Visit the CNN Web site for current events coverage and classroom resources.

ENERGY SWINGS!

All matter has energy. But what is energy? In this activity, you'll observe a moving pendulum to learn about energy.

Procedure

1. Make a pendulum by tying a **15 cm long string** around the hook of the **100 g hooked mass.**

2. Hold the string with one hand. Pull the mass slightly to the side, and let go of the mass without pushing it. Watch at least 10 swings of the pendulum.

3. In your ScienceLog, record your observations. Be sure to note how fast and how high the pendulum swings.

4. Repeat step 2, but pull the mass farther to the side.

5. Record your observations, noting how fast and how high the pendulum swings.

Analysis

6. Do you think the pendulum has energy? Explain your answer.

7. What causes the pendulum to move?

8. Do you think the pendulum has energy before you let go of the mass? Explain your answer.

115

ENERGY SWINGS!

MATERIALS
FOR EACH GROUP:
• 15 cm string
• 100 g hooked mass

Safety Caution

Remind students to review all safety cautions and icons before beginning this activity. Goggles must be worn for this activity.

Answers to START-UP Activity

6. Accept all reasonable responses. Sample answer: The pendulum has energy because it moves.

7. Accept all reasonable responses. Sample answer: Gravity causes the pendulum to move.

8. Accept all reasonable responses. Sample answer: The pendulum has energy. It is storing the energy that I used to move it. That energy is released when I let go of the pendulum.

Focus

What Is Energy?

This section introduces the concept of energy. Students will learn about the relationship between energy and work. They will also learn about the difference between kinetic and potential energy and how they relate to mechanical energy. This section also discusses and compares different forms of energy.

 **Bellringer**

Write the following on the board:

"Energy is the ability to ____."

Ask students to think about this phrase and to write in their ScienceLog how they think it should be completed. Lead a brief discussion to introduce the concept that energy is the ability to do work.

1 Motivate

DEMONSTRATION

At the beginning of class, do the following:

Strike a match and let it burn for a few moments. Wind up a windup toy and let it run. Turn off the lights in the classroom and turn on a flashlight. Finally, knock a tennis ball off a table so that it bounces onto the floor.

After these demonstrations, ask students to explain how energy was involved in each event. Lead students to conclude that there are many different forms of energy.

Terms to Learn

energy
kinetic energy
potential energy
mechanical energy

What You'll Do

◆ Explain the relationship between energy and work.
◆ Compare kinetic and potential energy.
◆ Summarize the different forms of energy.

What Is Energy?

It's match point. The crowd is dead silent. The tennis player steps up to serve. With a look of determination, she bounces the tennis ball several times. Next, in one fluid movement, she tosses the ball into the air and then slams it with her racket. The ball flies toward her opponent, who steps up and swings her racket at the ball. Suddenly, *THWOOSH!!* The ball goes into the net, and the net wiggles from the impact. Game, set, and match!!

Energy and Work—Working Together

Energy is around you all the time. So what is it exactly? In science, you can think of **energy** as the ability to do work. Work occurs when a force causes an object to move in the direction of the force. How are energy and work involved in playing tennis? In this example, the tennis player does work on her racket, the racket does work on the ball, and the ball does work on the net. Each time work is done, something is given by one object to another that allows it to do work. That "something" is energy. As you can see in **Figure 1,** work is a transfer of energy.

Because work and energy are so closely related, they are expressed in the same units—joules (J). When a given amount of work is done, the same amount of energy is involved.

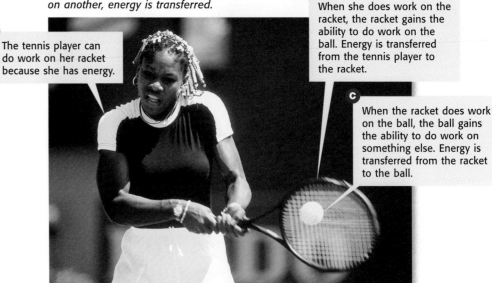

Figure 1 *When one object does work on another, energy is transferred.*

a The tennis player can do work on her racket because she has energy.

b When she does work on the racket, the racket gains the ability to do work on the ball. Energy is transferred from the tennis player to the racket.

c When the racket does work on the ball, the ball gains the ability to do work on something else. Energy is transferred from the racket to the ball.

116

 Teaching Transparency 232 "Energy and Work"

 Directed Reading Worksheet Section 1

IS THAT A FACT!

One joule is approximately the amount of energy it takes to lift an apple 1 m. In sports, some activities take a bit more energy. The average serve of a tennis ball takes 75 J of kinetic energy, a single fastball pitch takes 120 J, and a forward pass in football takes 150 J.

Kinetic Energy Is Energy of Motion

From the tennis example on the previous page, you learned that energy is transferred from the racket to the ball. As the ball flies over the net, it has **kinetic** (ki NET ik) **energy,** the energy of motion. All moving objects have kinetic energy. Does the tennis player have kinetic energy? Definitely! She has kinetic energy when she steps up to serve and when she swings the racket. When she's standing still, she doesn't have any kinetic energy. However, the parts of her body that are moving—her eyes, her heart, and her lungs—do have some kinetic energy.

Objects with kinetic energy can do work. If you've ever gone bowling, you've done work using kinetic energy. When you throw the ball down the lane, you do work on it, transferring your kinetic energy to the ball. As a result, the bowling ball can do work on the pins. Another example of doing work with kinetic energy is shown in **Figure 2.**

Figure 2 *When you swing a hammer, you give it kinetic energy, which it uses to do work on the nail.*

Kinetic Energy Depends on Speed and Mass An object's kinetic energy can be determined with the following equation:

$$\text{Kinetic energy} = \frac{mv^2}{2}$$

In this equation, *m* stands for an object's mass, and *v* stands for an object's speed. The faster something is moving, the more kinetic energy it has. In addition, the more massive a moving object is, the more kinetic energy it has. But which do you think has more of an effect on an object's kinetic energy, its mass or its speed? As you can see from the equation, speed is squared, so speed has a greater effect on kinetic energy than does mass. You can see an example of how kinetic energy depends on speed and mass in **Figure 3.**

Figure 3 *The red car has more kinetic energy than the green car because the red car is moving faster. But the truck has more kinetic energy than the red car because the truck is more massive.*

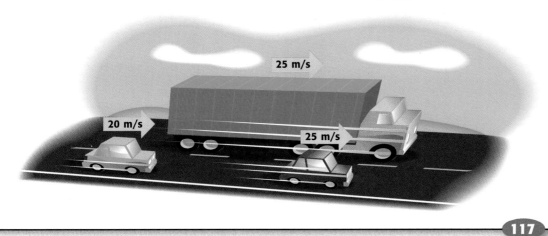

25 m/s

20 m/s

25 m/s

DEMONSTRATION

All Wound Up! Divide the class into small groups, and provide each group with a windup toy. Instruct them to wind up their toy and observe what happens. Ask students how many different types of energy are involved in this activity. At this point, students may identify only the kinetic energy of the toy as it moves. Explain that there are at least three other forms of energy here. (Chemical energy from food that enables the student to wind up the toy; potential energy in the wound-up spring of the toy; a small amount of thermal energy as the spring unwinds.)

Teacher Notes: The equation to determine kinetic energy is

$$\text{Kinetic energy} = \frac{mv^2}{2}$$

Speed has a greater impact on kinetic energy than does mass because speed is squared. When mass doubles, kinetic energy doubles. But when speed doubles, kinetic energy quadruples. The term "speed" is used here because, for this lesson, the object's direction does not matter.

117

Students Having Difficulty
Use a pendulum to show the difference between potential energy and kinetic energy. As you pull the pendulum to the side, explain that you are giving it energy. Hold the pendulum to the side. Write the term *potential energy* on the board. Draw a picture of the pendulum's position next to the term. Allow the pendulum to swing down, and write the term *kinetic energy* on the board. Draw a picture of the pendulum moving away from its potential-energy position. Discuss with students the difference between kinetic energy and potential energy.
Sheltered English

Multicultural CONNECTION

Bungee jumping began as a ritual ceremony, called land diving, of the people of Pentecost Island, in the Pacific archipelago of Vanuatu. Every year, the men of the community build a tower about 25 m tall. They then dive from platforms on the tower with vines attached to their ankles. After seeing a film of the land divers, the members of the Dangerous Sport Club, at Oxford University, in England, held the first bungee jump off of a bridge in 1979. (You may want to inform students that the potential energy of a stretched bow or a stretched rubber band is called *elastic potential energy*.)

internet**connect**

*sci*LINKS
NSTA

TOPIC: What Is Energy?
GO TO: www.scilinks.org
*sci*LINKS **NUMBER:** HSTP205

Figure 4 *The stored potential energy of the bow and string allows them to do work on the arrow when the string is released.*

Potential Energy Is Energy of Position

Not all energy involves motion. **Potential energy** is the energy an object has because of its position or shape. For example, the stretched bow shown in **Figure 4** has potential energy. The bow is not moving, but it has energy because work has been done to change its shape. A similar example of potential energy is in a stretched rubber band.

Gravitational Potential Energy Depends on Weight and Height When you lift an object, you do work on it by using a force that opposes gravitational force. As a result, you give that object *gravitational potential energy*. Books on a bookshelf have gravitational potential energy, as does your backpack after you lift it onto your back. As you can see in **Figure 5,** the amount of gravitational potential energy an object has depends on its weight and its distance above Earth's surface.

Figure 5 Weight and Height Affect Gravitational Potential Energy

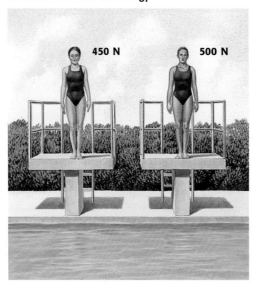

ⓐ The diver on the left weighs less and therefore has less gravitational potential energy than the diver on the right. The diver on the left did less work to climb up the platform.

ⓑ The diver on the higher platform has more gravitational potential energy than the diver on the lower platform. The diver on the higher platform did more work to climb up to the platform.

118

Calculating Gravitational Potential Energy   You can calculate gravitational potential energy by using the following equation:

Gravitational potential energy = weight × height

Because weight is expressed in newtons and height is expressed in meters, gravitational potential energy is expressed in newton-meters (N•m), or joules (J). So a 25 N object at a height of 3 m has 25 N × 3 m = 75 J of gravitational potential energy.

Recall that work = force × distance. Weight is the amount of force you must exert on an object in order to lift it, and height is a distance. So calculating an object's gravitational potential energy is done by calculating the amount of work done on the object to lift it to a given height. You can practice calculating gravitational potential energy as well as kinetic energy in the MathBreak at right.

Mechanical Energy Sums It All Up

How would you describe the energy of the juggler's pins in **Figure 6**? Well, to describe their total energy, you would describe their mechanical energy. **Mechanical energy** is the total energy of motion and position of an object. Mechanical energy can be all potential energy, all kinetic energy, or some of both. The following equation defines mechanical energy as the sum of kinetic and potential energy:

Mechanical energy = potential energy + kinetic energy

When potential energy increases (or decreases), kinetic energy has to decrease (or increase) in order for mechanical energy to remain constant. So the amount of an object's kinetic or potential energy may change, but its mechanical energy remains the same. You'll learn more about these changes in the next section.

MATH **BREAK**

Calculating Energy

1. What is the kinetic energy of a 4,000 kg elephant running at 3 m/s? at 4 m/s?

2. If you lift a 50 N watermelon to the top of a 2 m refrigerator, how much gravitational potential energy do you give the watermelon?

Figure 6   *As a pin is juggled, its mechanical energy is the sum of its potential energy and its kinetic energy at any point.*

MATH and **MORE**

Objects on the moon weigh one-sixth what they do on Earth. Suppose the elephant in problem 1 of the MathBreak has a mass of 4,000 kg and goes to the moon to participate in the Elephant Olympics. What would the elephant's gravitational potential energy be if it climbed up onto the 3 m diving board and waited for its turn to dive? (Hint: 1 kg = approx. 10 N on Earth, so 4,000 kg × 10 = 40,000 N. The elephant on the diving board on the moon would have gravitational potential energy of approximately 20,000 J = 40,000 N × 1/6 × 3 m)

Answers to MATHBREAK

1. 18,000 J; 32,000 J

2. 100 J

BRAIN FOOD

Before a music box will play music, it must be wound up. When you wind a music box, you do work on the gears inside. The energy required to do this work gets stored as potential energy. The music box then has the ability to do the work of playing music. A similar example is a windup watch.

SECTION REVIEW

1. How are energy and work related?

2. What is the difference between kinetic and potential energy?

3. **Applying Concepts**   Explain why a high-speed collision might cause more damage to vehicles than a low-speed collision.

⓫⓫⓿ **119**

▼ ***Answers to Section Review***

1. Energy is the ability to do work; work is a transfer of energy.

2. Kinetic energy is the energy of motion, and potential energy is an object's energy due to its position or shape.

3. A high-speed collision would cause more damage to vehicles because the vehicles would have more kinetic energy due to their high speed ($KE = \frac{mv^2}{2}$). The vehicles would do more work on one another, resulting in large amounts of damage.

Students may confuse heat with thermal energy. In this textbook, heat is a transfer of energy from a higher temperature object to a lower temperature object. The energy that is transferred is thermal energy.

MEETING INDIVIDUAL NEEDS

Advanced Learners The thermal energy of Earth's oceans has a profound effect on climate and weather. An example of this is the phenomenon known as El Niño, and its counterpart, La Niña. Have students research these two phenomena and in a report or on a poster, describe how thermal energy is responsible for them.

USING THE FIGURE

Use **Figure 7** to help students understand that the thermal energy of a substance is related to the substance's temperature as well as its state. Point out the difference in the appearance of the particles of ocean water and the particles of steam. Explain that equal masses of liquid water and steam at the same temperature (100°C) have different amounts of thermal energy. The reason is that work must be done to force particles of liquid water apart when water changes to steam. The energy used to do this work is stored by the particles of steam as potential energy. The particles of liquid water and the particles of steam may have the same average kinetic energy, but the particles of steam have more potential energy. As a result, the steam has more thermal energy than the liquid water. Students will learn more about this process in the chapter titled "Heat and Heat Technology."

Forms of Energy

All energy involves either motion or position. But energy takes different forms. These forms of energy include thermal, chemical, electrical, sound, light, and nuclear energy. In the next few pages, you will learn how the different forms of energy relate to kinetic and potential energy.

Thermal Energy All matter is made of particles that are constantly in motion. Because the particles are in motion, they have kinetic energy. The particles also have energy because of how they are arranged. *Thermal energy* is the total energy of the particles that make up an object. At higher temperatures, particles move faster. The faster the particles move, the more kinetic energy they have and the greater the object's thermal energy is. In addition, particles of a substance that are farther apart have more energy than particles of the same substance that are closer together. Look at **Figure 7.** Thermal energy also depends on the number of particles in a substance.

Figure 7 *The particles in the steam have the most energy, but the ocean has the most thermal energy because it contains the most particles.*

The particles in an **ice cube** vibrate in fixed positions and therefore do not have a lot of energy.

The particles in **ocean water** are not in fixed positions and can move around. They have more energy than the particles in an ice cube.

The particles in **steam** are far apart. They move rapidly and have more energy than the particles in ocean water.

Chemical Energy What is the source of the energy in food? Food consists of chemical compounds. When compounds, such as the sugar in some foods, are formed, work is done to join, or bond, the different atoms together to form molecules. *Chemical energy* is the energy of a compound that changes as its atoms are rearranged to form new compounds. Chemical energy is a form of potential energy. Some molecules that have many atoms bonded together, such as gasoline, have a lot of chemical energy. In **Figure 8** on the next page, you can see an example of chemical energy.

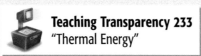

Teaching Transparency 233
"Thermal Energy"

IS THAT A FACT!

The chemical energy of glucose (sugar) is released slowly by the cells in your body. You cannot perceive this reaction taking place. Energy is released more rapidly when wood burns. You feel this energy as thermal energy. A very rapid release of energy is called an explosion.

Figure 8 Examples of Chemical Energy

When wood is burned, the chemical energy stored in the wood is used to toast your marshmallows.

Chemical energy is stored in the marshmallow's sugar molecules.

When you eat a marshmallow, chemical energy stored in the sugar becomes available for you to use.

Electrical Energy The electrical outlets in your home allow you to use electrical energy. *Electrical energy* is the energy of moving electrons. Electrons are the negatively charged particles of atoms. An atom is the smallest particle into which an element can be divided.

Suppose you plug an electrical device, such as the portable stereo shown in **Figure 9,** into an outlet and turn it on. The electrons in the wires will move back and forth, changing directions 120 times per second. As they do, energy is transferred to different parts within the stereo. The electrical energy created by moving electrons is used to do work. The work of a stereo is to produce sound.

The electrical energy available to your home is produced at power plants. Huge generators rotate magnets within coils of wire to produce electrical energy. Because the electrical energy results from the changing position of the magnet, electrical energy can be considered a form of potential energy. As soon as a device is plugged into an outlet and turned on, electrons move back and forth within the wires of the cord and within parts of the device. So electrical energy can also be considered a form of kinetic energy.

Figure 9 *The movement of electrons produces the electrical energy that a stereo uses to produce sound.*

121

CROSS-DISCIPLINARY FOCUS

History Today we take electrical energy for granted. It is always there at the flick of a switch. However, as late as 1930, only one out of 10 rural homes in the United States had electric service. Running lines many miles out to homes in the countryside was costly, and many power companies did not spend the money to do so. In 1935 and 1936, the Rural Electrification Administration (REA) was established to provide electrical energy to rural homes and farms. The REA made loans to nonprofit cooperatives to build electric systems in rural areas. Because of the REA, more than 99 percent of rural homes and farms in the United States now have electric service.

MEETING INDIVIDUAL NEEDS

Advanced Learners Have students find out how dry cells and batteries work. How do dry cells and batteries supply electrical energy? Why do they "run out"? How does a rechargeable battery work? Why are there so many different kinds of dry cells and batteries? Students can present their results on a poster or in a short report.

BRAIN FOOD

The plant with the ability to generate the most electric power from solar energy is the Harper Lake Site, in the Mojave Desert, California. It has the capability to produce about 160 MW. The largest wind-powered generator is on Oahu, Hawaii, which can produce about 7,300 kW when the wind reaches 32 mph.

QuickLab

MATERIALS

FOR EACH STUDENT:
- empty coffee can
- wax paper
- rubber band
- pencil with an eraser

Answers to QuickLab

2. Sample answer: a sound something like a drum.

3. Sample answer: The sound was louder when I tapped harder. The paper has a larger vibration when it is hit harder, so it causes the air particles near it to vibrate harder. More energy is transmitted by the air particles, so the sound is louder.

4. Sample answer: The paper was not able to vibrate as much when it was held still, so the sound was more muffled. Sound energy is a form of mechanical energy because vibration involves a change of position (potential energy) and changes in back-and-forth motion (kinetic energy).

REAL-WORLD CONNECTION

Lasers are a special kind of light energy. Lasers are used to read discs in CD and DVD players. Most supermarkets and retail stores have price scanners that use lasers to read bar codes on packages, and many stores use a portable laser to take inventory. Lasers are also used in several types of surgery, especially in skin and eye surgery. A variety of industries use lasers to measure, weld, cut, and drill metal objects.

Figure 10 *As the guitar strings vibrate, they cause particles in the air to vibrate. These vibrations transmit energy.*

Hear That Energy!

1. Make a simple drum by covering the open end of an **empty coffee can** with **wax paper.** Secure the wax paper with a **rubber band.**

2. Using the eraser end of a **pencil,** tap lightly on the wax paper. In your ScienceLog, describe how the paper responds. What do you hear?

3. Repeat step 2, but tap the paper a bit harder. In your ScienceLog, compare your results with those of step 2.

4. Cover half of the wax paper with one hand. Now tap the paper. What happened? How can you describe sound energy as a form of mechanical energy?

TRY at HOME

122

internetconnect

*SCI*LINKS
NSTA

TOPIC: Forms of Energy
GO TO: www.scilinks.org
*sci*LINKS NUMBER: HSTP210

Sound Energy You probably know that your vocal cords determine the sound of your voice. When you speak, air passes through your vocal cords, making them vibrate, or move back and forth. *Sound energy* is caused by an object's vibrations. **Figure 10** describes how a vibrating object transmits energy through the air around it.

Sound energy is a form of potential and kinetic energy. To make an object vibrate, work must be done to change its position. For example, when you pluck a guitar string, you stretch it and release it. The stretching changes the string's position. As a result, the string stores potential energy. In the release, the string uses its potential energy to move back to its original position. The moving guitar string has kinetic energy, which the string uses to do work on the air particles around it. The air particles vibrate and transmit this kinetic energy from particle to particle. When the vibrating air particles cause your eardrum to vibrate, you hear the sound of the guitar.

Light Energy Light allows us to see, but did you know that not all light can be seen? **Figure 11** shows a type of light that we use but can't see. *Light energy* is produced by the vibrations of electrically charged particles. Like sound vibrations, light vibrations cause energy to be transmitted. But unlike sound, the vibrations that transmit light energy don't cause other particles to vibrate. In fact, light energy can be transmitted through a vacuum (the absence of matter).

Figure 11 *The energy used to cook food in a microwave is a form of light energy.*

CROSS-DISCIPLINARY FOCUS

Music Look at different musical instruments to illustrate the many ways sound energy is produced. Discuss the sources of the work that produces musical sounds; for example, a harpist's fingers pluck the strings of a harp, whereas a trombone player's lips vibrate a column of air.

Nuclear Energy What form of energy can come from a tiny amount of matter, can be used to generate electrical energy, and gives the sun its energy? It's *nuclear* (NOO klee uhr) *energy,* the energy associated with changes in the nucleus (NOO klee uhs) of an atom. Nuclear energy is produced in two ways—when two or more nuclei (NOO klee IE) join together or when the nucleus of an atom splits apart.

In the sun, shown in **Figure 12,** hydrogen nuclei join together to make a larger helium nucleus. This reaction releases a huge amount of energy, which allows the sun to light and heat the Earth.

The nuclei of some atoms, such as uranium, store a lot of potential energy. When work is done to split these nuclei apart, that energy is released. This type of nuclear energy is used to generate electrical energy at nuclear power plants, such as the one shown in **Figure 13.**

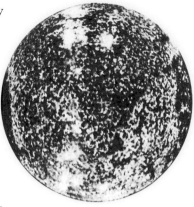

Figure 12 *Without the nuclear energy from the sun, life on Earth would not be possible.*

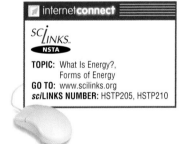

Figure 13 *In a nuclear power plant, small amounts of matter can produce large amounts of nuclear energy.*

SECTION REVIEW

1. What determines an object's thermal energy?

2. Describe why chemical energy is a form of potential energy.

3. Explain how sound energy is produced when you beat a drum.

4. **Analyzing Relationships** When you hit a nail into a board using a hammer, the head of the nail gets warm. In terms of kinetic and thermal energy, describe why you think this happens.

internet**connect**

SCi*LINKS*
NSTA

TOPIC: What Is Energy?, Forms of Energy
GO TO: www.scilinks.org
*sci***LINKS NUMBER:** HSTP205, HSTP210

123

▼ *Answers to Section Review*

1. An object's thermal energy depends on its temperature, the arrangement of its particles, and the number of particles in the object.

2. Sample answer: When a substance forms, work is done to bond particles of matter together. The energy that creates the new bonds is stored in the substance as potential energy.

3. Sample answer: When you beat a drum, you give it mechanical energy by moving the drumskin back and forth (vibrating). The vibrations cause air particles to vibrate, transmitting energy that results in sound.

4. Sample answer: The kinetic energy of the moving hammer is transferred to the head of the nail, causing particles in the nail to move faster. The faster the particles move, the greater their thermal energy.

Focus

Energy Conversions

This lesson discusses energy conversions. Students will be given examples of ways that energy is converted from one form to another. This section also explains the role of machines in energy conversions.

Bellringer

Display a plant, a Bunsen burner or small propane camping stove, and a pendulum. Ask students what they think these objects have in common. (They are all capable of converting energy from one form to another.)

1 Motivate

DISCUSSION

Have a windup alarm clock set up for students to see. Display a label next to the clock that reads "Potential Energy." The clock should be wound and set to go off when students are seated and attentive. When the clock alarm sounds, turn the label around so that it reads "Kinetic Energy." Ask students to try to define *kinetic energy* and *potential energy* based on the demonstration. Guide the discussion so that it addresses energy conversions. Encourage students to explain how the clock converted energy.

Terms to Learn

energy conversion

What You'll Do

- ◆ Describe an energy conversion.
- ◆ Give examples of energy conversions among the different forms of energy.
- ◆ Explain the role of machines in energy conversions.
- ◆ Explain how energy conversions make energy useful.

Figure 14 *Kinetic and potential energy are converted back and forth as you jump up and down on a trampoline.*

Energy Conversions

When you use a hammer to pound a nail into a board, you transfer your kinetic energy to the hammer, and the hammer transfers that kinetic energy to the nail. But energy is involved in other ways too. For example, sound energy is produced when you hit the nail. An energy transfer often leads to an **energy conversion,** a change from one form of energy into another. Any form of energy can be converted into any other form of energy, and often one form of energy is converted into more than one other form. In this section, you'll learn how energy conversions make your daily activities possible.

From Kinetic to Potential and Back

Take a look at **Figure 14.** Have you ever jumped on a trampoline? What types of energy are involved in this bouncing activity? Because you're moving when you jump, you have kinetic energy. And each time you jump into the air, you change your position with respect to the ground, so you also have gravitational potential energy. Another kind of potential energy is involved too—that of the trampoline stretching when you jump on it.

① When you jump down, your kinetic energy is converted into the potential energy of the stretched trampoline.

② The trampoline's potential energy is converted into kinetic energy, which is transferred to you, making you bounce up.

③ At the top of your jump, all of your kinetic energy has been converted into potential energy.

④ Right before you hit the trampoline, all of your potential energy has been converted back into kinetic energy.

124

Teaching Transparency 234
"Energy Conversion on a Trampoline"

Directed Reading Worksheet Section 2

Another example of the energy conversions between kinetic and potential energy is the motion of a pendulum (PEN dyoo luhm). Shown in **Figure 15,** a pendulum is a mass hung from a fixed point so that it can swing freely. When you lift the pendulum to one side, you do work on it, and the energy used to do that work is stored by the pendulum as potential energy. As soon as you let the pendulum go, it swings because the Earth exerts a force on it. The work the Earth does converts the pendulum's potential energy into kinetic energy.

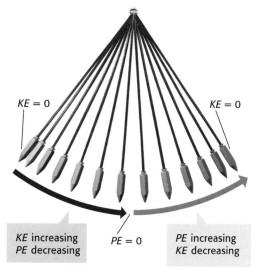

$KE = 0$ $KE = 0$

**KE increasing
PE decreasing** $PE = 0$ **PE increasing
KE decreasing**

Figure 15 *A pendulum's mechanical energy is all kinetic (KE) at the bottom of its swing and all potential (PE) at the top of its swing.*

✔ Self-Check

At what point does a roller coaster have the greatest potential energy? the greatest kinetic energy? *(See page 232 to check your answer.)*

Conversions Involving Chemical Energy

You've probably heard the expression "Breakfast is the most important meal of the day." What does this statement mean? Why does eating breakfast help you start the day? As your body digests food, chemical energy is released and is available to you, as discussed in **Figure 16.**

Figure 16 *Your body performs energy conversions.*

Chemical energy of food is converted into . . .

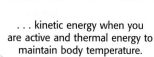
. . . kinetic energy when you are active and thermal energy to maintain body temperature.

USING THE FIGURE

Use **Figure 15** to help students understand the conversion of potential energy to kinetic energy. Then display a pendulum and use it to illustrate the energy conversions. Discuss how the pendulum displays potential energy (at the top of the swing) and kinetic energy (as it moves through the swing). When the pendulum is at the top of the swing, kinetic energy is zero. When the pendulum is at the bottom of the swing, potential energy is zero. Make sure that students understand why the value for each kind of energy at the respective positions is zero.

Answers to Self-Check

A roller coaster has the greatest potential energy at the top of the highest hill (usually the first hill), and the greatest kinetic energy at the bottom of the highest hill.

LabBook  **PG 198**
Energy of a Pendulum

WEIRD SCIENCE

If sound waves could be converted into electrical energy, 100 quadrillion mosquito buzzes could power a reading lamp.

IS THAT A FACT!

One appliance that uses a great deal of electrical energy is the water heater (4,200–4,800 kWh/year). At the other extreme, an electric toothbrush uses only about 5 kWh/year.

Would you believe that the chemical energy in the food you eat is a result of the sun's energy? It's true! When you eat fruits, vegetables, grains, or meat from animals that ate fruits, vegetables, or grains, you are taking in chemical energy that resulted from a chemical change involving the sun's energy. As shown in **Figure 17**, photosynthesis (FOHT oh SIN thuh sis) uses light energy to produce new substances with chemical energy. In this way light energy is converted into chemical energy.

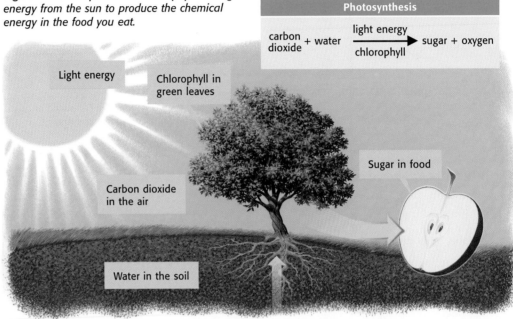

Figure 17 *Green plants use chlorophyll and light energy from the sun to produce the chemical energy in the food you eat.*

APPLY

Camping with Energy

If you go camping, you probably use a stove, such as the one shown here, to prepare meals. Describe some of the energy conversions that take place when lighting the stove, cooking the food, eating the prepared meal, and then setting out on a long hike.

Teaching Transparency 235 "Photosynthesis"

IS THAT A FACT!

Using the process of photosynthesis, plants are able to convert solar energy and water into 500 billion metric tons of carbohydrate per year. Of that 500 billion tons, 80 percent is produced in the sea.

Conversions Involving Electrical Energy

You use electrical energy all the time—when you listen to the radio, when you make toast, and when you take a picture with a camera. Electrical energy can be easily converted into other forms of energy. **Figure 18** shows how electrical energy is converted in a hair dryer.

Figure 18 Energy Conversions in a Hair Dryer

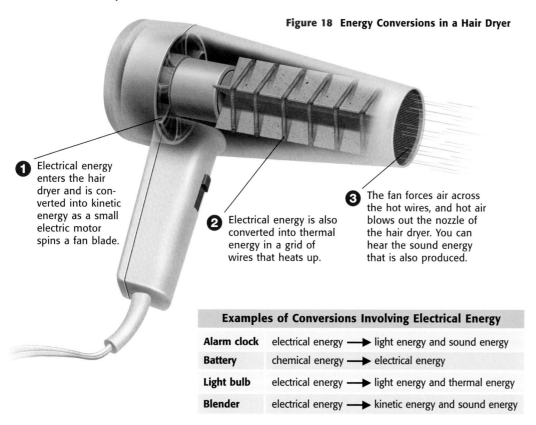

1 Electrical energy enters the hair dryer and is converted into kinetic energy as a small electric motor spins a fan blade.

2 Electrical energy is also converted into thermal energy in a grid of wires that heats up.

3 The fan forces air across the hot wires, and hot air blows out the nozzle of the hair dryer. You can hear the sound energy that is also produced.

Examples of Conversions Involving Electrical Energy

Alarm clock	electrical energy ⟶ light energy and sound energy
Battery	chemical energy ⟶ electrical energy
Light bulb	electrical energy ⟶ light energy and thermal energy
Blender	electrical energy ⟶ kinetic energy and sound energy

SECTION REVIEW

1. What is an energy conversion?

2. Describe an example in which electrical energy is converted into thermal energy.

3. Describe an energy conversion involving chemical energy.

4. **Applying Concepts** Describe the kinetic-potential energy conversions that occur when you bounce a basketball.

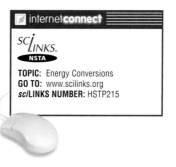

internet**connect**

*sci*LINKS. NSTA

TOPIC: Energy Conversions
GO TO: www.scilinks.org
*sci*LINKS NUMBER: HSTP215

127

USING THE FIGURE

Concept Mapping Have students refer to **Figure 18** and the chart on this page to create a concept map of different ways electrical energy is converted. The map should begin with the nature of the work done on each object and end with the type(s) of energy produced.

Multicultural CONNECTION

There are more than 33 million cyclists in the United States. While most people in the United States tend to ride bicycles for competition, recreation, or exercise, people in other parts of the world use bicycles for daily transportation. For example, people in China often use a bicycle when they need to travel short distances, such as from home to work. How would traffic problems differ in the United States if most people rode bicycles to work?

internet**connect**

SC*i*LINKS. NSTA

TOPIC: Energy Conversions
GO TO: www.scilinks.org
*sci*LINKS NUMBER: HSTP215

▼ Answers to Section Review

1. An energy conversion is a change from one form of energy to another. Any form of energy can be converted into any other form of energy.

2. Sample answer: In an iron, electrical energy is converted into thermal energy.

3. Sample answer: When you light a natural-gas stove, the chemical energy

in the natural gas is converted into thermal energy.

4. When you bounce a basketball, you give it kinetic energy. At the moment the ball hits the ground, its kinetic energy is greatest and its potential energy is zero. At that moment, the change of shape of the ball that occurs

when it hits the ground gives the ball some potential energy that is used as the ball moves back upward. When the ball bounces back up toward your hand, its kinetic energy is converted into potential energy because its position changes. At the moment the ball is at the top of its bounce, its kinetic energy is zero.

MEETING INDIVIDUAL NEEDS

Advanced Learners Ball bearings are round, smooth objects that reduce friction between two objects. The more perfectly rounded the ball bearing is, the more friction is reduced. Ball bearings produced on Earth cannot be perfectly round and smooth because of the effect of gravity on the manufacturing process. Bearings produced in space would eliminate almost all of gravity's effects and produce a perfectly smooth ball bearing. Have interested students report on the process of making ball bearings on Earth and in space.

Teaching Transparency 236 "Energy Transfer in a Bicycle"

Teaching Transparency 237 "Energy Conversions in a Car Engine"

Math Skills Worksheet "A Bicycle Trip"

Energy and Machines

You've been learning about energy, its different forms, and how it can undergo conversions. Another way to learn about energy is to look at how machines use energy. A machine can make work easier by changing the size or direction (or both) of the force required to do the work. Suppose you want to crack open a walnut. Using a nutcracker, like the one shown in **Figure 19,** would be much easier (and less painful) than using your fingers. You transfer your energy to the nutcracker, and it transfers energy to the nut. But the nutcracker will not transfer more energy to the nut than you transfer to the nutcracker. In addition, some of the energy you transfer to a machine can be converted by the machine into other forms of energy. Another example of how energy is used by a machine is shown in **Figure 20.**

CRR-UNCH!

Figure 19 *Some of the kinetic energy you transfer to a nutcracker is converted into sound energy as the nutcracker transfers energy to the nut.*

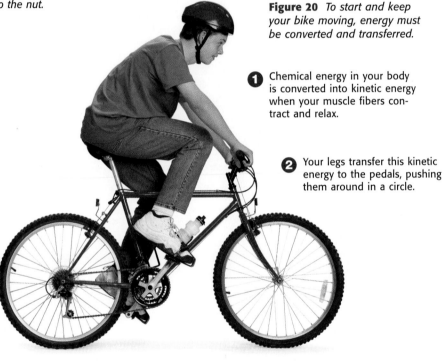

Figure 20 *To start and keep your bike moving, energy must be converted and transferred.*

1 Chemical energy in your body is converted into kinetic energy when your muscle fibers contract and relax.

2 Your legs transfer this kinetic energy to the pedals, pushing them around in a circle.

4 The chain moves and transfers energy to the back wheel, which gets you moving!

3 The pedals transfer this kinetic energy to the gear wheel, which transfers kinetic energy to the chain.

128

IS THAT A FACT!

The pedicar, introduced in 1973, was a pedal-powered, one-passenger, all-weather vehicle. It was conceived as an alternative to the gas-powered automobile and cost about $550 at the time of its introduction. The pedicar was capable of reaching speeds of 8–15 mph.

Machines Are Energy Converters As you saw in the examples on the previous page, when machines transfer energy, energy conversions can often result. For example, you can hear the sounds that your bike makes when you pedal it, change gears, or brake swiftly. That means that some of the kinetic energy being transferred gets converted into sound energy as the bike moves. Some machines are especially useful because they are energy converters. **Figure 21** shows an example of a machine specifically designed to convert energy from one form to another. In addition, the chart at right lists other machines that perform useful energy conversions.

Some Machines that Convert Energy	
■ electric motor	■ microphone
■ windmill	■ toaster
■ doorbell	■ dishwasher
■ gas heater	■ lawn mower
■ telephone	■ clock

Figure 21 *The continuous conversion of chemical energy into thermal energy and kinetic energy in a car's engine is necessary to make a car move.*

① A mixture of gasoline and air enters the engine as the piston moves downward.

Piston

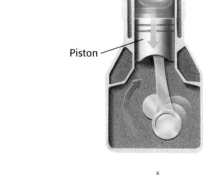

② The kinetic energy of the crankshaft raises the piston, and the gasoline mixture is forced up toward the spark plug, which uses electrical energy to ignite the gasoline mixture.

Spark plug

Crankshaft

③ As the gasoline mixture burns, chemical energy is converted into thermal energy and kinetic energy, forcing the piston back down.

④ The kinetic energy of the crankshaft forces the piston up again, pushing exhaust gases out. Then the cycle repeats.

129

Science Bloopers

The design for a nuclear-powered automobile was proposed by Ford automotive designers in the 1950s. The name of the car was to be the Ford Nucleon, and it was to be propelled by a small atomic reactor located in the rear of the car. The car was never built for several reasons.

IS THAT A FACT!

Only about 20 percent of the energy released by burning gasoline in a car engine is converted to kinetic energy to move the car forward. Most of the rest is converted to thermal energy, which is wasted.

4) Close

Quiz

1. Give an example of an energy conversion that produces a useful result. (Answers will vary, but students might mention the conversion of chemical energy in their food into the kinetic energy of their movements.)

2. Demonstrate the conversion of potential to kinetic energy using a pendulum model. (As the pendulum is lifted upward, it gains potential energy. When the pendulum is released and swings downward, that potential energy is converted to kinetic energy.)

ALTERNATIVE ASSESSMENT

Ask students to categorize their daily activities according to the forms of energy they use. Categories could include electrical energy, chemical energy, and mechanical energy. Instruct students to try to list five activities for each category.
 Sheltered English

REAL-WORLD CONNECTION

Windmills were first used in about the fifth century A.D. to pump water or to turn grindstones. Today, wind power offers a viable alternative to the energy crisis. Especially promising is the melding of computer technology with the wind turbine. In the past, windmills turned at a single speed. In the 1990s, windmills were designed to move at whatever rate the wind moves them. A computer-controlled electronic circuit allows turbines to generate current with a constant frequency, regardless of wind speed.

Figure 22 *In a wind turbine, the kinetic energy of the wind can be collected and converted into electrical energy.*

Science
CONNECTION

Turn to page 146 to find out about buildings that are energy efficient as well as environmentally friendly.

Why Energy Conversions Are Important

Everything we do is related to energy conversions. Heating our homes, obtaining energy from a meal, growing plants, and many other activities all require energy conversions.

Making Energy Useful You can think of energy conversions as a way of getting energy in the form that you need. Machines help harness existing energy and make that energy work for you. Did you know that the wind could help you cook a meal? A wind turbine, shown in **Figure 22,** can perform an energy conversion that would allow you to use an electric stove to do just that.

Making Conversions Efficient You may have heard that a car may be considered energy efficient if it gets good gas mileage, and your home may be energy efficient if it is well insulated. In terms of energy conversions, *energy efficiency* (e FISH uhn see) is a comparison of the amount of energy before a conversion with the amount of useful energy after a conversion. For example, the energy efficiency of a light bulb would be a comparison of the electrical energy going into it with the light energy coming out of it. The less electrical energy that is converted into thermal energy instead of into light energy, the more efficient the bulb.

Not all of the energy in a conversion becomes useful energy. Just as work input is always greater than work output, energy input is also always greater than energy output. But the closer the energy output is to the energy input, the more efficient the conversion is. Making energy conversions more efficient is important because greater efficiency means less waste.

SECTION REVIEW

1. What is the role of machines in energy conversions?

2. Give an example of a machine that is an energy converter, and explain how the machine converts one form of energy to another.

3. **Applying Concepts** A car that brakes suddenly comes to a screeching halt. Is the sound energy produced in this conversion a useful form of energy? Explain your answer.

130

▼ **Answers to Section Review**

1. Machines can transfer energy from one object to another as they make work easier. For example, when you use a crowbar to remove a hubcap, you transfer energy to the crowbar, and the crowbar transfers energy to the hubcap. The way the energy is transferred determines how much easier the work is to do.

2. Accept all reasonable answers. Sample answer: A wind turbine converts the kinetic energy of wind into electrical energy.

3. The sound energy of the screeching is not a useful form of energy because it cannot be used to do work.

Terms to Learn

friction
law of conservation of energy

What You'll Do

◆ Explain how energy is conserved within a closed system.
◆ Explain the law of conservation of energy.
◆ Give examples of how thermal energy is always a result of energy conversion.
◆ Explain why perpetual motion is impossible.

Conservation of Energy

Many roller coasters have a mechanism that pulls the cars up to the top of the first hill, but the cars are on their own the rest of the ride. As the cars go up and down the hills on the track, their potential energy is converted into kinetic energy and back again. But the cars never return to the same height they started from. Does that mean that energy gets *lost* somewhere along the way? Nope—it just gets converted into other forms of energy.

Where Does the Energy Go?

In order to find out where a roller coaster's original potential energy goes, you have to consider more than just the hills of the roller coaster. You have to consider friction too. **Friction** is a force that opposes motion between two surfaces that are touching. For the roller coaster to move, work must be done to overcome the friction between the cars' wheels and the coaster track and between the cars and the surrounding air. The energy used to do this work comes from the original amount of potential energy that the cars have on the top of the first hill. The need to overcome friction affects the design of a roller coaster track. In **Figure 23,** you can see that the second hill will always be shorter than the first.

When energy is used to overcome friction, some of the energy is converted into thermal energy. Some of the cars' potential energy is converted into thermal energy on the way down the first hill, and then some of their kinetic energy is converted into thermal energy on the way up the second hill. So energy isn't lost at all—it just undergoes a conversion.

Figure 23 *Due to friction, not all of the cars' potential energy (PE) is converted into kinetic energy (KE) as the cars go down the first hill. In addition, not all of the cars' kinetic energy is converted into potential energy as the cars go up the second hill.*

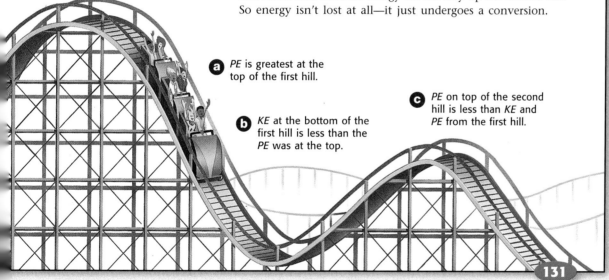

a *PE is greatest at the top of the first hill.*

b *KE at the bottom of the first hill is less than the PE was at the top.*

c *PE on top of the second hill is less than KE and PE from the first hill.*

131

MISCONCEPTION ALERT

Students may assume that all processes involving work and energy are 100 percent efficient. Remind students that all motion and all processes involving work are opposed by friction. It is because of friction that so much kinetic energy is converted to thermal energy. Let students create their own thermal energy by rapidly rubbing their palms together for 30 seconds. They will feel the thermal energy produced by the friction between their hands.

Focus

Conservation of Energy

This section introduces the law of conservation of energy. Students will learn how all energy is continuously being converted into other forms, and they will discover why the law of conservation of energy makes the concept of perpetual motion impossible.

🔊 Bellringer

Pose the following questions to students:

How does a roller coaster work? Where does the energy come from to make the car go along the track? Where does all the energy go? Explain the meaning of the sentence, "All of the energy put into a process still exists somewhere at the end of that process."

1 Motivate

DEMONSTRATION

Show students a simple, high-density rubber ball. Explain to students that this ball was designed to bounce for a long time, but that it must eventually stop according to the law of conservation of energy. Allow the ball to begin bouncing. As it bounces, ask students to observe both the height and the number of bounces. Ask them to theorize why the ball eventually stops. What happens to the kinetic energy of the ball's movement?

Directed Reading Worksheet Section 3

READING 📖 STRATEGY

Prediction Guide Ask students to interpret the sentence, "Energy can be neither created nor destroyed." Write the predictions on the board, and discuss them before students read pages 132 and 133.

LabBook **PG 199**
Eggstremely Fragile

REAL-WORLD CONNECTION

Resistance to the flow of electrical energy is a major concern to electric utility companies that transmit electrical energy through miles of wire. To reduce the amount of energy lost to resistance, power companies use very high voltages in the transmission lines that carry electrical energy from generating stations to cities. Voltage in these lines ranges from 138,000 to 765,000 V. These higher voltages minimize the amount of energy lost to resistance. Transformers reduce the voltage for distribution in cities and neighborhoods. Finally, neighborhood transformers reduce the voltage to 120 to 240 V for use in the home.

📶 internet**connect**

SC/LINKS
NSTA

TOPIC: Law of Conservation of Energy
GO TO: www.scilinks.org
*sci*LINKS NUMBER: HSTP217

Try to keep an egg from breaking while learning more about the law of conservation of energy on page 199 in the LabBook.

Energy Is Conserved Within a Closed System

A *closed system* is a well-defined group of objects that transfer energy between one another. For example, a closed system that involves a roller coaster consists of the track, the cars, and the surrounding air. On a roller coaster, some mechanical energy (the sum of kinetic and potential energy) is always converted into thermal energy because of friction. Sound energy is also a result of the energy conversions in a roller coaster. You can understand that energy is not lost on a roller coaster only when you consider all of the factors involved in a closed system. If you add together the cars' kinetic energy at the bottom of the first hill, the thermal energy due to overcoming friction, and the sound energy produced, you end up with the same total amount of energy as the original amount of potential energy. In other words, energy is conserved.

Law of Conservation of Energy No situation has been found where energy is not conserved. Because this phenomenon is always observed during energy conversions, it is described as a law. According to the **law of conservation of energy,** energy can be neither created nor destroyed. The total amount of energy in a closed system is always the same. Energy can be changed from one form to another, but all the different forms of energy in a system always add up to the same total amount of energy, no matter how many energy conversions occur.

Consider the energy conversions in a light bulb, shown in **Figure 24.** You can define the closed system to include the outlet, the wires, and the parts of the bulb. While not all of the original electrical energy is converted into light energy, no energy is lost. At any point during its use, the total amount of electrical energy entering the light bulb is equal to the total amount of light and thermal energy that leaves the bulb. Energy is conserved.

Figure 24 Energy Conservation in a Light Bulb

Some energy is converted to thermal energy, which makes the bulb feel warm.

Some electrical energy is converted into light energy.

Some electrical energy is converted into thermal energy because of friction in the wire.

132

IS THAT A FACT!

At extremely low temperatures, some materials become *superconductors,* materials that have almost no resistance to the flow of electrical energy. These materials are used to create giant electromagnets that generate strong magnetic fields with very little thermal-energy loss.

SCIENCE HUMOR

Q: What happened when the sandpaper and the wood got together to settle their differences?

A: The discussion got heated! There was just too much friction between them.

No Conversion Without Thermal Energy

Any time one form of energy is converted into another form, some of the original energy always gets converted into thermal energy. The thermal energy due to friction that results from energy conversions is not useful energy. That is, this thermal energy is not used to do work. Think about a car. You put gas into a car, but not all of the gasoline's chemical energy makes the car move. Some waste thermal energy will always result from the energy conversions. Much of this waste thermal energy exits a car engine through the radiator and the exhaust pipe.

Perpetual Motion? No Way! People have dreamed of constructing a machine that runs forever without any additional energy—a *perpetual* (puhr PECH oo uhl) *motion machine*. Such a machine would put out exactly as much energy as it takes in. But because some waste thermal energy always results from energy conversions, perpetual motion is impossible. The only way a machine can keep moving is to have a continuous supply of energy. For example, the "drinking bird" shown in **Figure 25** continually uses thermal energy from the air to evaporate the water from its head. So it is *not* a perpetual motion machine.

Biology
CONNECTION

Whenever you do work, you use chemical energy stored in your body that comes from food you've eaten. As you do work, some of that chemical energy is always converted into thermal energy. That's why your body heats up after performing a task, such as raking leaves, for several minutes.

Figure 25   The "Drinking Bird"

a When the bird "drinks," the felt covering its head gets wet.

b When the bird is upright, water evaporates from the felt, decreasing the temperature and pressure in the head. Fluid is drawn up from the tail, where pressure is higher, and the bird tips.

c After the bird "drinks," fluid returns to the tail, the bird flips upright, and the cycle repeats.

SECTION REVIEW

1. Describe the energy conversions that take place in a pendulum, and explain how energy is conserved.

2. Why is perpetual motion impossible?

3. **Analyzing Viewpoints**   Imagine that you drop a ball. It bounces a few times, but then it stops. Your friend says that the ball has lost all of its energy. Using what you know about the law of conservation of energy, respond to your friend's statement.

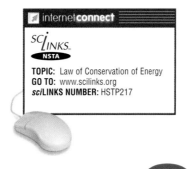

internetconnect

sci**LINKS**
NSTA

TOPIC: Law of Conservation of Energy
GO TO: www.scilinks.org
*sci***LINKS NUMBER:** HSTP217

ACTIVITY

Divide the class into three groups, and go outside as a class. This activity will explore how the body converts chemical energy to thermal energy. One group should simply stand or sit for 5 minutes. Meanwhile, the second group should walk at a comfortable pace, and the third group should engage in a running activity. After 5 minutes, have students discuss the amount of thermal energy produced by their body.

Which group of students produced the most thermal energy? Which produced the least? Why?

4) Close

Quiz

1. Think of an example other than the ones given in this section to illustrate the law of conservation of energy. (Answers will vary but should reflect an understanding of energy conservation.)

2. What condition would have to exist for perpetual motion to be possible? (no waste thermal energy produced; no friction)

ALTERNATIVE ASSESSMENT

Have students draw a diagram of a system in which energy conservation is demonstrated. The diagram should include labels indicating the kinds of energy involved.

▼ *Answers to Section Review*

1. Answers will vary, but students should include that potential energy is converted to kinetic energy, kinetic energy to potential, and both potential and kinetic to thermal energy because of friction. All energy is conserved because some energy becomes thermal energy.

2. In every system, some of the energy put in is converted to thermal energy that is waste energy. A machine cannot run forever unless energy is continually added.

3. Answers must include the fact that energy isn't lost in the entire system of the ball, the ground, and the air around the ball; it is converted into other forms.

Focus

Energy Resources

Students learn about renewable and nonrenewable energy resources and about advantages and disadvantages of energy resources.

 **Bellringer**

Write the names of several different energy resources on the board (sunlight, coal, wind). Ask students to predict which ones are nonrenewable (a finite supply) and renewable (an endless supply) resources.

1 Motivate

ACTIVITY

Give each student a large piece of paper and colored pencils. Tell them to pick an activity they do every day. Ask them to trace the energy involved in their activity back to its source. For example, if their activity is playing computer games, they would trace the light and sound energy from the computer. The light and sound were made possible by the electrical energy from the outlet in their home, so they would trace the production of the electrical energy back to its source. The power plant produced electrical energy from some fuel, such as coal or natural gas. If they can, have students trace the fuel back to its source as well.

 Directed Reading Worksheet Section 4

Terms to Learn

energy resource
nonrenewable resources
fossil fuels
renewable resources

What You'll Do

◆ Name several energy resources.
◆ Explain how the sun is the source of most energy on Earth.
◆ Evaluate the advantages and disadvantages of using various energy resources.

Energy Resources

Energy is used to light and warm our homes; to produce food, clothing, and other products; and to transport people and products from place to place. Where does all this energy come from? An **energy resource** is a natural resource that can be converted by humans into other forms of energy in order to do useful work. In this section, you will learn about several energy resources, including the resource responsible for most other energy resources—the sun.

Nonrenewable Resources

Some energy resources, called **nonrenewable resources,** cannot be replaced after they are used or can be replaced only over thousands or millions of years. Fossil fuels are the most important nonrenewable resources.

Fossil Fuels Coal, petroleum, and natural gas, shown in **Figure 26,** are the most common fossil fuels. **Fossil fuels** are energy resources that formed from the buried remains of plants and animals that lived millions of years ago. These plants stored energy from the sun by photosynthesis. Animals used and stored this energy by eating the plants or by eating animals that ate plants. So fossil fuels are concentrated forms of the sun's energy.

This piece of coal containing a fern fossil shows that coal formed from plants that lived millions of years ago.

Figure 26 Formation of Fossil Fuels

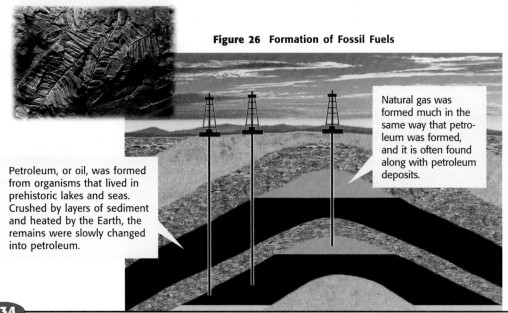

Natural gas was formed much in the same way that petroleum was formed, and it is often found along with petroleum deposits.

Petroleum, or oil, was formed from organisms that lived in prehistoric lakes and seas. Crushed by layers of sediment and heated by the Earth, the remains were slowly changed into petroleum.

134

BRAIN FOOD

It takes about 454 kg of lead-acid batteries (like the one in most cars) to store the same amount of energy that about 4 L of gasoline contains.

IS THAT A FACT!

Recycling just one aluminum can saves enough energy to run a television set for 4 hours.

Now, millions of years later, energy from the sun is released when fossil fuels are burned. Any fossil fuel contains stored energy from the sun that can be converted into other types of energy. The information below shows how important fossil fuels are to our society.

Coal

Most coal used in the United States is burned to produce steam to run electric generators.

Coal Use (U.S.)

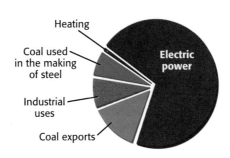

Heating
Coal used in the making of steel
Industrial uses
Coal exports
Electric power

Petroleum

Petroleum supplies us with gasoline, kerosene, and wax as well as petrochemicals, which are used to make synthetic fibers, such as rayon.

Annual Oil Production—Past & Predicted

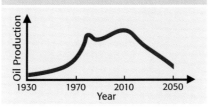

Oil Production

1930   1970   2010   2050
Year

Finding alternative energy resources will become more important in years to come.

Natural Gas

Natural gas is used in heating systems, in stoves and ovens, and in vehicles as an alternative to gasoline.

Natural gas is the cleanest burning fossil fuel.

Comparing Fossil Fuel Emissions

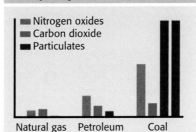

- Nitrogen oxides
- Carbon dioxide
- Particulates

Natural gas   Petroleum   Coal

135

CONNECT TO EARTH SCIENCE

Use Teaching Transparency 116 to help students understand how energy is stored in coal.

Teaching Transparency 116
"Formation of Coal"

LINK TO EARTH SCIENCE

MATH and MORE

The worldwide distribution of coal reserves in billion metric tons (1 metric ton = 1000 kg) is as follows:

- 66 in Africa
- 695 in Asia
- 404 in Europe
- 271 in North America
- 7 in South and Central America

Help students construct both a pie chart and a bar graph to display this information. Discuss the two different presentations and when each might be useful.

Science Skills Worksheet
"Grasping Graphing"

CROSS-DISCIPLINARY FOCUS

Writing **History** Ask students to write a short story about how a day in their life would be if no fossil-fuel energy (oil, gasoline, natural gas, and coal) were available. The story should include descriptions of when and how their daily activities would be performed, which things would be different, and which might stay the same.

PORTFOLIO

USING THE FIGURE

Have students study **Figure 27** on this page. Make sure students understand each step for converting fossil fuels into electrical energy by discussing each one. Ask students to create a concept map explaining each of the steps. Sheltered English

Homework

Instruct students to find out what type of power their home uses. Many homes use a combination of energy sources. Have students find out the names of the companies that supply power to their home.

REAL-WORLD CONNECTION

Here are two ways to get more kilometers to the gallon. First, decrease driving speed from 113 km/h (70 mph) to 88 km/h (55 mph); this will increase fuel economy by 21 percent. Second, keep tires properly inflated. Underinflated tires decrease fuel economy by 5 percent.

BRAIN FOOD

In 1882, Thomas Edison built the first electrical generating station designed to provide electrical energy to homes and businesses in Manhattan.

Turn to page 147 to read about a day in the life of a power-plant manager.

Electrical Energy from Fossil Fuels One way to generate electrical energy is to burn fossil fuels. In fact, fossil fuels are the primary source of electrical energy generated in the United States. Earlier in this chapter, you learned that electrical energy can result from energy conversions. Kinetic energy is converted into electrical energy by an *electric generator*. This energy conversion is part of a larger process, shown in **Figure 27**, of converting the chemical energy in fossil fuels into the electrical energy you use every day.

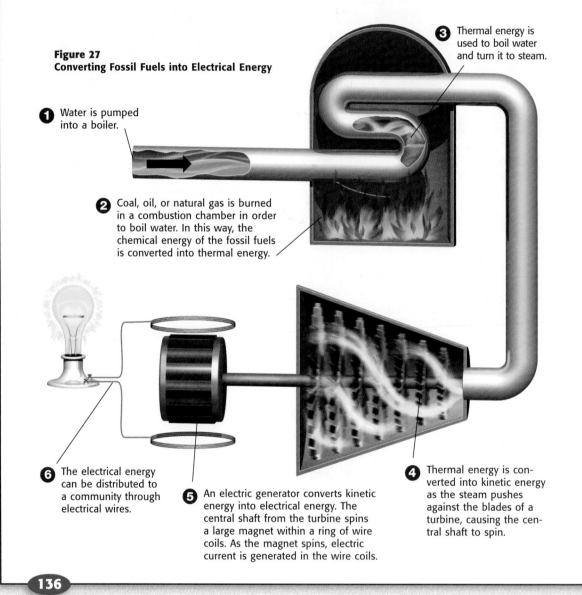

**Figure 27
Converting Fossil Fuels into Electrical Energy**

❶ Water is pumped into a boiler.

❷ Coal, oil, or natural gas is burned in a combustion chamber in order to boil water. In this way, the chemical energy of the fossil fuels is converted into thermal energy.

❸ Thermal energy is used to boil water and turn it to steam.

❹ Thermal energy is converted into kinetic energy as the steam pushes against the blades of a turbine, causing the central shaft to spin.

❺ An electric generator converts kinetic energy into electrical energy. The central shaft from the turbine spins a large magnet within a ring of wire coils. As the magnet spins, electric current is generated in the wire coils.

❻ The electrical energy can be distributed to a community through electrical wires.

IS THAT A FACT!

Of all the energy used by a standard incandescent light bulb, only one-tenth is converted to light energy. The rest is thermal energy. That's why light bulbs are so hot after they have been on for a while!

Nuclear Energy Another way to generate electrical energy is to use nuclear energy. Like fossil-fuel power plants, a nuclear power plant generates thermal energy that boils water to produce steam. The steam then turns a turbine, which rotates a generator that converts kinetic energy into electrical energy. However, the fuels used in nuclear power plants are different from fossil fuels. Nuclear energy is generated from radioactive elements, such as uranium, shown in **Figure 28**. In a process called *nuclear fission* (FISH uhn), the nucleus of a uranium atom is split into two smaller nuclei, releasing nuclear energy. Because the supply of these elements is limited, nuclear energy can be thought of as a nonrenewable resource.

Renewable Resources

Some energy resources, called **renewable resources,** can be used and replaced in nature over a relatively short period of time. Some renewable resources, such as solar energy and wind energy, are considered practically limitless.

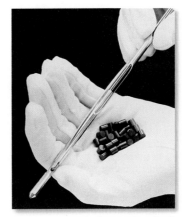

Figure 28 *A single uranium fuel pellet contains the energy equivalent of about 1 metric ton of coal.*

Solar Energy

Sunlight can be converted into electrical energy through solar cells, which can be used in devices such as calculators or installed in a home to provide electrical energy.

Some houses allow sunlight into the house through large windows. The sunlight is converted into thermal energy that heats the house naturally.

Energy from Water

The sun causes water to evaporate and fall again as rain that flows through rivers. The potential energy of water in a reservoir is converted into kinetic energy as the water flows downhill through a dam.

Falling water turns a turbine in a dam, which is connected to a generator that converts kinetic energy into electrical energy. Electrical energy produced from falling water is called *hydroelectricity.*

internet**connect**

SCi**LINKS** **TOPIC:** Energy Resources
GO TO: www.scilinks.org
NSTA *sci*LINKS NUMBER: HSTP225

MAKING MODELS

Ask students to choose one of the alternative energy sources described in this section. Have students create either a poster or a model of their choice. Models or posters should show how the resource is harnessed as well as how it produces electrical energy. Arrange for students to present their projects to other classes.
Sheltered English

DEBATE

Energy Alternatives Ask groups of students to represent different alternative energy resources. Using this section and the table on page 139 as a reference, each group should research its energy resource. Have the class debate which energy resources should be developed and which ones shouldn't. Be sure students offer full explanations for their positions. At the end of the debate, ask students to vote for the most effective alternative energy resource. This debate can also be part of the debate described on page 137.

GOING FURTHER

Invite an expert in the field of alternative energy sources to visit the classroom. If this is not possible, have students find information about such experts. Then have students prepare a short report on their findings.

Interactive Explorations CD-ROM,
"The Generation Gap"

Wind Energy

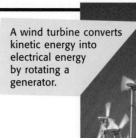

Wind is caused by the sun's uneven heating of the Earth's surface, which creates currents of air. The kinetic energy of wind can turn the blades of a windmill. Windmills are often used to pump water from the ground.

A wind turbine converts kinetic energy into electrical energy by rotating a generator.

Geothermal Energy

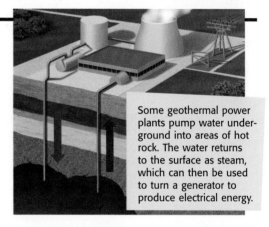

Thermal energy resulting from the heating of Earth's crust is called *geothermal energy.* Ground water that seeps into hot spots near the surface of the Earth can form geysers.

Some geothermal power plants pump water underground into areas of hot rock. The water returns to the surface as steam, which can then be used to turn a generator to produce electrical energy.

Biomass

Plants capture and store energy from the sun. Organic matter, such as plants, wood, and waste, that can be burned to release energy is called *biomass.* Nonindustrialized countries rely heavily on biomass for energy.

Certain plants can also be converted into liquid fuel. For example, corn can be used to make ethanol, which is often mixed with gasoline to make a cleaner-burning fuel for cars.

138

🌐 Multicultural CONNECTION

The island nation of Japan utilizes the surrounding ocean to produce energy. Tidal energy is an alternative energy source that uses the rise and fall of the ocean tides to run turbines that produce electrical energy. Ask students to think of other countries that might use tidal energy to produce electrical energy.

The Two Sides to Energy Resources

The table below compares several energy resources. Depending on where you live, what you need energy for, and how much you need, sometimes one energy resource is a better choice than another.

Energy resource	Advantages	Disadvantages
Fossil fuels	■ provide a large amount of thermal energy per unit of mass ■ easy to get and easy to transport ■ can be used to generate electrical energy and make products, such as plastic	■ nonrenewable ■ burning produces smog ■ burning coal releases substances that can cause acid precipitation ■ risk of oil spills
Nuclear	■ very concentrated form of energy ■ power plants do not produce smog	■ produces radioactive waste ■ radioactive elements are nonrenewable
Solar	■ almost limitless source of energy ■ does not produce pollution	■ expensive to use for large-scale energy production ■ only practical in sunny areas
Water	■ renewable ■ does not produce air pollution	■ dams disrupt a river's ecosystem ■ available only in areas that have rivers
Wind	■ renewable ■ relatively inexpensive to generate ■ does not produce air pollution	■ only practical in windy areas
Geothermal	■ almost limitless source of energy ■ power plants require little land	■ only practical in locations near hot spots ■ waste water can damage soil
Biomass	■ renewable	■ requires large areas of farmland ■ produces smoke

SECTION REVIEW

1. Compare fossil fuels and biomass.
2. Why is nuclear energy a nonrenewable resource?
3. Trace electrical energy back to the sun.
4. **Interpreting Graphics** Use the pie chart at right to explain why renewable resources will become more important in years to come.

U.S. Energy Sources

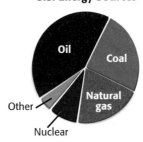

Answers to Section Review

1. Answers will vary but should include the fact that both result from living things and both can be burned to release energy. Fossil fuels are millions of years old, while biomass is organic matter obtained from living things today.

2. because the elements from which it is generated are in limited supply

3. Sample answer: The steam turning the turbine that generates electrical energy comes from water heated by the burning of a fossil fuel, such as coal. The coal is a result of organisms that lived millions of years ago that used light energy from the sun.

4. When the nonrenewable resources we rely on are used up, we will have to use renewable resources.

Discovery Lab

USING SCIENTIFIC **METHODS**

Discovery Lab

Finding Energy
Teacher's Notes

Time Required

Two 45-minute class periods

Lab Ratings

EASY ———————→ HARD

TEACHER PREP

STUDENT SET-UP

CONCEPT LEVEL

CLEAN UP

MATERIALS

The materials listed for this lab are enough for each group of 2–3 students. Rolling carts are available from suppliers of science classroom materials. The ramp should be at least 1 m long.

Procedure Notes

Use one day to set up and collect data. Use the second day for calculations, or assign the calculations as homework.

Answer

1. Accept all reasonable hypotheses.

Datasheets for LabBook

Finding Energy

When you coast down a big hill on a bike or skateboard, you may notice that you pick up speed. Because you are moving, you have kinetic energy—the energy of motion. Where does that energy come from? In this lab, you will find out.

MATERIALS

- 2 or 3 books
- wooden board
- masking tape
- meterstick
- metric balance
- rolling cart
- stopwatch

140

Form a Hypothesis

1 Where does the kinetic energy come from when you roll down a hill? Write your hypothesis in your ScienceLog.

Conduct an Experiment

2 Copy Table 1 into your ScienceLog or use a computer to construct a similar table.

3 Create a model of a bike on a hill. First, make a ramp with the books and board.

4 Use masking tape to make a starting line. Be sure the starting line is far enough from the top so the cart can be placed behind the line.

5 Place a strip of masking tape at the bottom of the ramp to mark the finish line.

6 Determine the height of the ramp by measuring the height of the starting line and subtracting the height of the finish line. Record the height of the ramp in meters in Table 1.

7 Measure the distance in meters between the starting line and the finish line. Record this distance as the length of the ramp in Table 1.

8 Use the metric balance to find the mass of the cart in grams. Convert this to kilograms by dividing by 1,000. Record the mass in kilograms in Table 1.

9 Multiply the mass by 10 to get the weight of the cart in newtons. Record the weight in Table 1.

CLASSROOM TESTED & APPROVED

Rebecca Ferguson
North Ridge Middle School
North Richland Hills, Texas

Table 1 Data Collection							
Height of ramp (m)	Length of ramp (m)	Mass of cart (kg)	Weight of cart (N)	Time of trial (s)			Average time (s)
				1	2	3	
		DO NOT WRITE IN BOOK					

Table 2 Calculations			
Average speed (m/s)	Final speed (m/s)	Kinetic energy at bottom (J)	Gravitational potential energy at top (J)
	DO NOT WRITE IN BOOK		

Collect Data

10 Set the cart behind the starting line, and release it. Use the stopwatch to time how long it takes for the cart to reach the finish line. Record the time in Table 1.

11 Repeat step 10 twice more, and average the results. Record the average time in Table 1.

Analyze the Results

12 Copy Table 2 into your ScienceLog, or use a computer to construct a similar one.

13 Using your data and the following equations, calculate and record the quantities for the cart in Table 2:

a. $average\ speed = \dfrac{length\ of\ ramp}{average\ time}$

b. $final\ speed = 2 \times average\ speed$

   (This equation works because the cart accelerates smoothly from 0 m/s.)

c. $kinetic\ energy = \dfrac{mass \times (final\ speed)^2}{2}$

   (Remember that $1\ kg \bullet m^2/s^2 = 1\ J$, the unit used to express energy.)

d. $gravitational\ potential\ energy = weight \times height$

   (Remember that $1\ N = 1\ kg \bullet m/s^2$, so $1\ N \times 1\ m = 1\ kg \bullet m^2/s^2 = 1\ J$.)

Draw Conclusions

14 How does the cart's gravitational potential energy at the top of the ramp compare with its kinetic energy at the bottom? Communicate a valid conclusion about whether or not your hypothesis was supported.

15 You probably found that the gravitational potential energy of the cart at the top of the ramp was close but not exactly equal to the kinetic energy of the cart at the bottom. Analyze this information to construct a reasonable explanation for this finding using direct evidence.

16 While riding your bike, you coast down both a small hill and a large hill. Compare your final speed at the bottom of the small hill with your final speed at the bottom of the large hill. Explain your answer.

141

Answers

Answers

14. The cart's gravitational potential energy at the top of the ramp is very close to its kinetic energy at the bottom of the ramp. Whether this finding supports the original hypothesis will depend on the original hypothesis.

15. The cart's gravitational potential energy at the top of the ramp is slightly greater than its kinetic energy at the bottom of the ramp because some of the energy is used to do work against friction. Without friction, the two energy measurements would be the same.

16. You would have a greater final speed at the bottom of the large hill than at the bottom of the small hill. The amount of gravitational potential energy depends on height. Starting from a greater height means starting with more gravitational potential energy, which is converted into kinetic energy as you coast down the hill.

Science Skills Worksheet
"Working with Hypotheses"

Chapter Highlights

Chapter Highlights

VOCABULARY DEFINITIONS

SECTION 1

energy the ability to do work

kinetic energy the energy of motion; kinetic energy depends on speed and mass

potential energy the energy of position or shape

mechanical energy the total energy of motion and position of an object

SECTION 2

energy conversion a change from one form of energy into another; any form of energy can be converted into any other form of energy

---

SECTION 1

Vocabulary

    energy (*p. 116*)

    kinetic energy (*p. 117*)

    potential energy (*p. 118*)

    mechanical energy (*p. 119*)

Section Notes

• Energy is the ability to do work, and work is the transfer of energy. Both energy and work are expressed in joules.

• Kinetic energy is energy of motion and depends on speed and mass.

• Potential energy is energy of position or shape. Gravitational potential energy depends on weight and height.

• Mechanical energy is the sum of kinetic energy and potential energy.

• Thermal energy, sound energy, electrical energy, and light energy can all be forms of kinetic energy.

• Chemical energy, electrical energy, sound energy, and nuclear energy can all be forms of potential energy.

SECTION 2

Vocabulary

    energy conversion (*p. 124*)

Section Notes

• An energy conversion is a change from one form of energy to another. Any form of energy can be converted into any other form of energy.

• Machines can transfer energy and convert energy into a more useful form.

• Energy conversions help to make energy useful by changing energy into the form you need.

Labs

    Energy of a Pendulum (*p. 198*)

☑ Skills Check

Math Concepts

GRAVITATIONAL POTENTIAL ENERGY To calculate an object's gravitational potential energy, multiply the weight of the object by its height above the Earth's surface. For example, the gravitational potential energy (*GPE*) of a box that weighs 100 N and that is sitting in a moving truck 1.5 m above the ground is calculated as follows:

$$GPE = \text{weight} \times \text{height}$$

$$GPE = 100 \text{ N} \times 1.5 \text{ m} = 150 \text{ J}$$

Visual Understanding

POTENTIAL-KINETIC ENERGY CONVERSIONS When you jump up and down on a trampoline, potential and kinetic energy are converted back and forth. Review the picture of the pendulum on page 125 for another example of potential-kinetic energy conversions.

ENERGY RESOURCES Look back at the diagram on page 136. Converting fossil fuels into electrical energy requires several energy conversions.

Lab and Activity Highlights

Finding Energy   **PG 140**

Energy of a Pendulum   **PG 198**

Eggstremely Fragile   **PG 199**

Datasheets for LabBook
(blackline masters for these labs)

SECTION 3

Vocabulary

friction *(p. 131)*
**law of conservation
of energy** *(p. 132)*

Section Notes

- Because of friction, some energy is always converted into thermal energy during an energy conversion.

- Energy is conserved within a closed system. According to the law of conservation of energy, energy can be neither created nor destroyed.

- Perpetual motion is impossible because some of the energy put into a machine will be converted into thermal energy due to friction.

Labs

Eggstremely Fragile *(p. 199)*

SECTION 4

Vocabulary

energy resource *(p. 134)*
nonrenewable resources *(p. 134)*
fossil fuels *(p. 134)*
renewable resources *(p. 137)*

Section Notes

- An energy resource is a natural resource that can be converted into other forms of energy in order to do useful work.

- Nonrenewable resources cannot be replaced after they are used or can only be replaced after long periods of time. They include fossil fuels and nuclear energy.

- Fossil fuels are nonrenewable resources formed from the remains of ancient organisms. Coal, petroleum, and natural gas are fossil fuels.

- Renewable resources can be used and replaced in nature over a relatively short period of time. They include solar energy, wind energy, energy from water, geothermal energy, and biomass.

- The sun is the source of most energy on Earth.

- Depending on where you live and what you need energy for, one energy resource can be a better choice than another.

SECTION 3

friction a force that opposes motion between two surfaces that are touching

law of conservation of energy the law that states that energy is neither created nor destroyed

SECTION 4

energy resource a natural resource that can be converted by humans into other forms of energy in order to do useful work

nonrenewable resources natural resources that cannot be replaced or that can be replaced only over thousands or millions of years

fossil fuels nonrenewable energy resources that form in the Earth's crust over millions of years from the buried remains of once-living organisms

renewable resources natural resources that can be used and replaced over a relatively short time

---

internet**connect**

GO TO: go.hrw.com

Visit the **HRW** Web site for a variety of learning tools related to this chapter. Just type in the keyword:

KEYWORD: HSTENG

GO TO: www.scilinks.org

Visit the **National Science Teachers Association** on-line Web site for Internet resources related to this chapter. Just type in the *sci*LINKS number for more information about the topic:

TOPIC: What Is Energy?	*sci*LINKS NUMBER: HSTP205
TOPIC: Forms of Energy	*sci*LINKS NUMBER: HSTP210
TOPIC: Energy Conversions	*sci*LINKS NUMBER: HSTP215
TOPIC: Law of Conservation of Energy	*sci*LINKS NUMBER: HSTP217
TOPIC: Energy Resources	*sci*LINKS NUMBER: HSTP225

143

Vocabulary Review Worksheet

Blackline masters of these Chapter Highlights can be found in the **Study Guide.**

Lab and Activity Highlights

LabBank

Whiz-Bang Demonstrations
- Wrong-Way Roller?
- Pendulum Peril

Calculator-Based Labs, A Hot Hand

Labs You Can Eat
- Power-Packed Peanuts
- Now You're Cooking!

Long-Term Projects & Research Ideas, Great Balls of Fire

CD 1, Exploration 6, "The Generation Gap"

Chapter Review
Answers

USING VOCABULARY

1. Potential energy is energy of position or shape. Kinetic energy is energy of motion.

2. Friction is a force that opposes motion between two surfaces that are touching. In an energy conversion, friction always causes some form of energy to be converted into thermal energy.

3. During an energy conversion, one form of energy is changed into another form of energy. The law of conservation of energy states that energy is neither created nor destroyed during any energy conversion.

4. Energy resources are natural resources that can be converted by humans into other forms of energy in order to do useful work. Fossil fuels are an energy resource that formed from the remains of organisms that lived millions of years ago.

5. Renewable resources are natural resources that can be used and replaced over a relatively short time. Nonrenewable resources are natural resources that cannot be replaced or that can be replaced only over thousands or millions of years.

UNDERSTANDING CONCEPTS

Multiple Choice

6. d	**10.** d
7. b	**11.** c
8. b	**12.** c
9. d	**13.** c

Short Answer

14. Sample answer: Thermal energy depends partly on the kinetic energy of the particles that make up an object. The more kinetic energy the particles have, the more thermal energy the object has. Chemical energy is a kind of potential energy because when a substance forms, work is done to bond particles of matter together. The energy required to do this work

Chapter Review

USING VOCABULARY

For each pair of terms, explain the difference in their meanings.

1. potential energy/kinetic energy

2. friction/energy conversion

3. energy conversion/law of conservation of energy

4. energy resources/fossil fuels

5. renewable resources/nonrenewable resources

UNDERSTANDING CONCEPTS

Multiple Choice

6. Kinetic energy depends on
   a. mass and volume.
   b. speed and weight.
   c. weight and height.
   d. speed and mass.

7. Gravitational potential energy depends on
   a. mass and speed.
   b. weight and height.
   c. mass and weight.
   d. height and distance.

8. Which of the following is not a renewable resource?
   a. wind energy
   b. nuclear energy
   c. solar energy
   d. geothermal energy

9. Which of the following is a conversion from chemical energy to thermal energy?
   a. Food is digested and used to regulate body temperature.
   b. Charcoal is burned in a barbecue pit.
   c. Coal is burned to boil water.
   d. all of the above

10. Machines can
    a. increase energy.
    b. transfer energy.
    c. convert energy.
    d. Both (b) and (c)

11. In every energy conversion, some energy is always converted into
    a. kinetic energy.
    b. potential energy.
    c. thermal energy.
    d. mechanical energy.

12. An object that has kinetic energy must be
    a. at rest.
    b. lifted above the Earth's surface.
    c. in motion.
    d. None of the above

13. Which of the following is *not* a fossil fuel?
    a. gasoline   c. firewood
    b. coal   d. natural gas

Short Answer

14. Name two forms of energy, and relate them to kinetic or potential energy.

15. Give three specific examples of energy conversions.

16. Explain how energy is conserved within a closed system.

17. How are fossil fuels formed?

is stored in the new compound as potential energy that can be released when the compound is broken down.

15. Sample answers: When a person jumps off a diving board, his or her potential energy is converted into kinetic energy. When steam turns the blades of a turbine, the thermal energy of the steam is converted into the kinetic energy of the moving turbine. When a hair dryer is turned on, electrical energy is converted

into kinetic energy of the turning fan and thermal energy of the hot coils inside the hair dryer.

16. A closed system is a well-defined group of objects that transfer energy among one another. Within a closed system, energy is neither created or destroyed; it just gets converted into other forms of energy.

Concept Mapping

18. Use the following terms to create a concept map: energy, machines, energy conversions, thermal energy, friction.

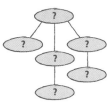

19. What happens when you blow up a balloon and release it? Describe what you would see in terms of energy.

20. After you coast down a hill on your bike, you eventually come to a complete stop unless you keep pedaling. Relate this to the reason why perpetual motion is impossible.

21. Look at the photo of the pole-vaulter below. Trace the energy conversions involved in this event, beginning with the pole-vaulter's breakfast of an orange-banana smoothie.

22. If the sun were exhausted of its nuclear energy, what would happen to our energy resources on Earth?

MATH IN SCIENCE

23. A box has 400 J of gravitational potential energy.
   a. How much work had to be done to give the box that energy?
   b. If the box weighs 100 N, how far was it lifted?

INTERPRETING GRAPHICS

24. Look at the illustration below, and answer the questions that follow.

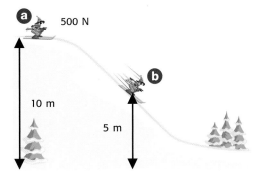

500 N

10 m

5 m

   a. What is the skier's gravitational potential energy at point *A*?
   b. What is the skier's gravitational potential energy at point *B*?
   c. What is the skier's kinetic energy at point *B*? (Hint: mechanical energy = potential energy + kinetic energy.)

Reading Check-up

Take a minute to review your answers to the Pre-Reading Questions found at the bottom of page 114. Have your answers changed? If necessary, revise your answers based on what you have learned since you began this chapter.

145

Concept Mapping Transparency 9

Blackline masters of this Chapter Review can be found in the **Study Guide.**

---

17. Fossil fuels are the remains of plants and animals that lived millions of years ago. Plants converted energy from the sun by photosynthesis. Animals got this energy by eating plants or other animals. Over millions of years, the remains of these organisms became coal, petroleum, and natural gas.

Concept Mapping

18. An answer to this exercise can be found at the front of this book.

CRITICAL THINKING AND PROBLEM SOLVING

19. Sample answer: When you blow up a balloon, you stretch it. Because you change the balloon's shape, you give it potential energy. When you release the balloon, it zooms around because the potential energy is converted into kinetic energy.

20. Sample answer: Your bike can't keep moving because kinetic energy is converted into thermal energy due to friction between the tires and the road.

21. Sample answer: The pole-vaulter's breakfast provided chemical energy that was converted into kinetic energy as he started his vault. As his pole bends, it stores potential energy. This is then converted into the kinetic energy that lifts him into the air. As he rises, his kinetic energy is converted into gravitational potential energy. This is converted to kinetic energy as he falls.

22. Sample answer: Without the sun as the source of most energy, we would eventually run out of energy resources.

MATH IN SCIENCE

23. a. 400 J
    b. 4 m

INTERPRETING GRAPHICS

24. a. 5,000 J
    b. 2,500 J
    c. 2,500 J

ACROSS THE SCIENCES

PHYSICAL SCIENCE • LIFE SCIENCE

Green Buildings

How do you make a building green without painting it? You make sure it does as little damage to the environment as possible. *Green,* in this case, does not refer to the color of pine trees or grass. Instead, *green* means "environmentally safe." And the "green movement" is growing quickly.

Green Methods and Materials

One strategy that architects employ to turn a building green is to minimize its energy consumption. They also reduce water use wherever possible. One way to do this would be to create landscapes that use only native plants that require little watering. Green builders also use recycled building materials whenever possible. For example, crushed light bulbs can be recycled into floor tiles, and recycled cotton can replace fiberglass as insulation.

Seeing Green

Although green buildings cost more than conventional buildings to construct, they save a lot of money in the long run. For example, the

Audubon Building, in Manhattan, saves $100,000 in maintenance costs every year—that is $60,000 in electricity bills alone! The building uses more than 60 percent less energy and electricity than a conventional building does. Inside, the workers enjoy natural lighting, cleaner air, and an environment that is free of unnecessary chemicals.

Some designers want to create buildings that are even more environmentally friendly than the Audubon Building. Walls can be made of straw bales or packed dirt, and landscapes can be maintained with rainwater collected from rooftops. By conserving, recycling, and reducing waste, green builders are doing a great deal to help the environment.

Design It Yourself!

► Design a building, a home, or even a dog-house that is made of only recycled materials. Be inventive! When you think you have the perfect design, create a scale model. Describe how your green structure saves resources.

◄ *The walls of this building are being made out of worn-out tires packed with soil. The walls will later be covered with stucco.*

146

Background

According to the Environmental Protection Agency, more than 240 million tires are discarded every year. However, because many landfills do not accept tires, these tires are often simply stockpiled aboveground, where they sit indefinitely. They are not only an eyesore and a fire hazard but also can be a health hazard: water-filled tires are ideal breeding grounds for insects such as mosquitoes and flies.

Old tires can be recycled for use in "green" buildings. Sturdy walls can be made by stacking old tires like bricks. The tires are filled with dirt and covered with cement or clay. This technique recycles materials and is energy efficient. Tire walls absorb thermal energy when the weather is hot and release thermal energy when the weather is cool; they act as temperature regulators without setting a single thermostat control.

Discussion

Conduct a discussion about ways students could make the classroom into a "green" room. (Examples might include installing low-wattage lights and putting insulating sheets of plastic over the windows in winter.)

Answers to Design It Yourself!

In their design, students may wish to incorporate some of the materials discussed in the text. Encourage them to be innovative by thinking about what materials are available and what use these materials might serve. For example, they could use cardboard for walls, soda straws for thatched roofs, or old clothes for curtains or tablecloths.

CAREERS

POWER-PLANT MANAGER

As a power-plant manager, **Cheryl Mele** is responsible for almost a billion watts of electric power generation at the Decker Power Plant in Austin, Texas. More than 700 MW are produced using a steam-driven turbine system with natural gas fuel and oil as a backup fuel. Another 200 MW are generated by gas turbines. The steam-driven turbine system and gas turbines together provide enough electrical energy for many homes and businesses.

According to Cheryl Mele, her job as plant manager includes "anything that needs doing." Her training as a mechanical engineer allows her to conduct routine testing and to diagnose problems successfully. A firm believer in protecting our environment, Mele operates the plant responsibly. Mele states, "It is very important to keep the plant running properly and burning as efficiently as possible." Her previous job helping to design more-efficient gas turbines helped make her a top candidate for the job of plant manager.

The Team Approach

Mele uses the team approach to maintain the power plant. She says, "We think better as a team. We all have areas of expertise and interest, and we maximize our effectiveness." Mele observes that working together makes everyone's job easier.

Advice to Young People

Mele believes that mechanical engineering and managing a power plant are interesting careers because you get to work with many exciting new technologies. These professions are excellent choices for both men and women. In these careers you interact with creative people as you try to improve mechanical equipment to make it more efficient and reduce harm to the environment. Her advice for young people is to pursue what interests you. "Be sure to connect the math you learn to the science you are doing," she says. "This will help you to understand both."

A Challenge

▶ With the help of an adult, find out how much electrical energy your home uses each month. How many homes like yours could Mele's billion-watt power plant supply energy to each month?

▶ *Cheryl Mele manages the Decker Power Plant in Austin, Texas.*

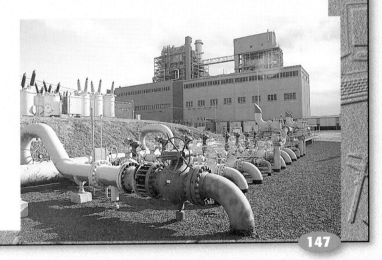

147

CAREERS

Power-Plant Manager– Cheryl Mele

Background

Cheryl Mele earned a bachelor of science degree in mechanical engineering. She worked as a programmer for General Electric, became interested in power-plant design, and joined a General Electric design group. Mele worked as a mechanical engineer for Austin Energy, where her diverse experiences made her the top choice for plant manager.

Students should be familiar with the general principles of the generation of electrical energy, including the use of different fuel sources to power a turbine (steam from coal, natural gas, or nuclear energy).

Teaching Strategy

As an extension of the investigation, students can find ways to use less electrical energy in order to minimize their impact on the environment.

Answers to A Challenge

Answers will vary depending on a variety of factors, such as the size of the student's home, the number of people in the family, and what the structure is made of. Answers to the second part of the challenge will vary, but a billion-watt power plant could provide enough electrical energy for hundreds of thousands, or even millions, of ordinary homes.

Chapter Organizer

CHAPTER ORGANIZATION	TIME MINUTES	OBJECTIVES	LABS, INVESTIGATIONS, AND DEMONSTRATIONS
Chapter Opener pp. 148–149	45	National Standards: UCP 2, 5, SAI 2, ST 1, SPSP 2, 5, HNS 1, PS 3a, 3b, 3f	**Start-Up Activity,** Some Like It Hot, p. 149
Section 1 Temperature	90	▶ Describe how temperature relates to kinetic energy. ▶ Give examples of thermal expansion. ▶ Compare temperatures on different temperature scales. UCP 1, 2, 3, SAI 2, SPSP 5, PS 3a, 3b	**Demonstration,** p. 150 in ATE **QuickLab,** Hot or Cold? p. 151 **Whiz-Bang Demonstrations,** Cool It **Calculator-Based Labs,** How Low Can You Go?
Section 2 What Is Heat?	90	▶ Define *heat* as the transfer of energy between objects at different temperatures. ▶ Compare conduction, convection, and radiation. ▶ Use specific heat capacity to calculate heat. ▶ Explain the differences between temperature, thermal energy, and heat. UCP 2, 3, SPSP 2, 5, PS 3a, 3b, 3f; Labs UCP 2, 3, SAI 1, ST 1, PS 3a, 3b	**Demonstration,** p. 156 in ATE **QuickLab,** Heat Exchange, p. 157 **Demonstration,** Convection Currents, p. 158 in ATE **Discovery Lab,** Feel the Heat, p. 174 **Datasheets for LabBook,** Feel the Heat **Design Your Own,** Save the Cube! p. 200 **Datasheets for LabBook,** Save the Cube! **Making Models,** Counting Calories, p. 201 **Calculator-Based Labs,** Counting Calories
Section 3 Matter and Heat	90	▶ Identify three states of matter. ▶ Explain how heat affects matter during a change of state. ▶ Describe how heat affects matter during a chemical change. UCP 2, 3, SPSP 5, PS 1a, 1b	**Demonstration,** p. 164 in ATE **Calculator-Based Labs,** Feel the Heat **Labs You Can Eat,** Baked Alaska
Section 4 Heat Technology	90	▶ Analyze several kinds of heating systems. ▶ Describe how a heat engine works. ▶ Explain how a refrigerator keeps food cold. ▶ Give examples of some effects of heat technology on the environment. SPSP 2, 5, PS 3a, 3b	**EcoLabs & Field Activities,** Energy-Efficient Home **Long-Term Projects & Research Ideas,** Firewalking Exposed

---

See page **T23** *for a complete correlation of this book with the*

NATIONAL SCIENCE EDUCATION STANDARDS.

TECHNOLOGY RESOURCES

 Guided Reading Audio CD
English or Spanish, Chapter 6

One-Stop Planner CD-ROM with Test Generator

 CNN. **Eye on the Environment,** Geothermal Energy, Segment 22

Chapter 6 • Heat and Heat Technology

CLASSROOM WORKSHEETS, TRANSPARENCIES, AND RESOURCES	SCIENCE INTEGRATION AND CONNECTIONS	REVIEW AND ASSESSMENT
Science Puzzlers, Twisters & Teasers **Directed Reading Worksheet**		
Directed Reading Worksheet, Section 1 **Transparency 238,** Three Temperature Scales **Math Skills for Science Worksheet,** Using Temperature Scales	**MathBreak,** Converting Temperatures, p. 153 **Math and More,** p. 153 in ATE **Science, Technology, and Society:** The Deep Freeze, p. 180	**Section Review,** p. 154 **Quiz,** p. 154 in ATE **Alternative Assessment,** p. 154 in ATE **Homework,** p. 154 in ATE
Directed Reading Worksheet, Section 2 **Transparency 239,** Reaching Thermal Equilibrium **Transparency 240,** Conduction **Transparency 165,** The Greenhouse Effect **Transparency 240,** Convection **Critical Thinking Worksheet,** Try and Try Again **Math Skills for Science Worksheet,** Knowing Nutrition **Reinforcement Worksheet,** Feel the Heat	**Apply,** p. 158 **Connect to Earth Science,** p. 158 in ATE **Connect to Astronomy,** p. 159 in ATE **Meteorology Connection,** p. 160 **Cross-Disciplinary Focus,** p. 160 in ATE **MathBreak,** Calculating Energy Transfer, p. 161 **Math and More,** p. 161 in ATE **Cross-Disciplinary Focus,** p. 161 in ATE **Cross-Disciplinary Focus,** p. 162 in ATE	**Homework,** pp. 156, 161 in ATE **Section Review,** p. 159 **Self-Check,** p. 163 **Section Review,** p. 163 **Quiz,** p. 163 in ATE **Alternative Assessment,** p. 163 in ATE
Directed Reading Worksheet, Section 3 **Transparency 241,** Models of a Solid, a Liquid, and a Gas **Transparency 242,** Changes of State for Water	**Connect to Life Science,** p. 164 in ATE **Biology Connection,** p. 166 **Across the Sciences:** Diaplex, p. 181	**Self-Check,** p. 165 **Section Review,** p. 166 **Quiz,** p. 166 in ATE **Alternative Assessment,** p. 166 in ATE
Directed Reading Worksheet, Section 4 **Transparency 243,** Solar Heating Systems **Transparency 237,** Energy Conversions in a Car Engine	**Cross-Disciplinary Focus,** pp. 167, 170, 172 in ATE **Oceanography Connection,** p. 170 **Real-World Connection,** p. 171 in ATE **Environment Connection,** p. 173	**Homework,** p. 168 in ATE **Section Review,** p. 173 **Quiz,** p. 173 in ATE **Alternative Assessment,** p. 173 in ATE

 internet**connect**

 go.hrw.com Holt, Rinehart and Winston On-line Resources
go.hrw.com

For worksheets and other teaching aids related to this chapter, visit the HRW Web site and type in the keyword: **HSTHOT**

 SCILINKS National Science Teachers Association
www.scilinks.org

Encourage students to use the *sci*LINKS numbers listed in the internet connect boxes to access information and resources on the **NSTA** Web site.

END-OF-CHAPTER REVIEW AND ASSESSMENT

Chapter Review in Study Guide
Vocabulary and Notes in Study Guide
Chapter Tests with Performance-Based Assessment, Chapter 6 Test, Performance-Based Assessment 6
Concept Mapping Transparency 10

Chapter 6 • Chapter Organizer **147B**

Chapter Resources & Worksheets

Visual Resources

TEACHING TRANSPARENCIES

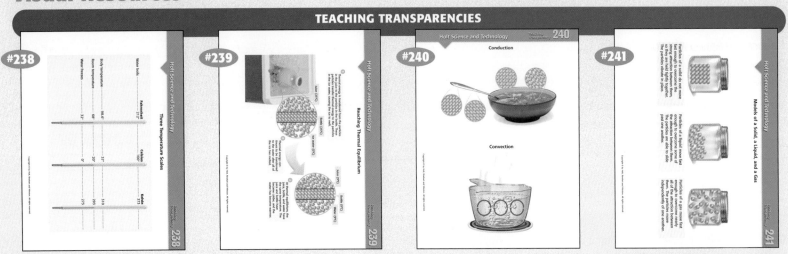

#238 Holt Science and Technology — Three Temperature Scales — Teaching Transparency 238

#239 Holt Science and Technology — Reaching Thermal Equilibrium — Teaching Transparency 239

#240 Holt Science and Technology — Conduction / Convection — Teaching Transparency 240

#241 Holt Science and Technology — Models of a Solid, a Liquid, and a Gas — Teaching Transparency 241

TEACHING TRANSPARENCIES

CONCEPT MAPPING TRANSPARENCY

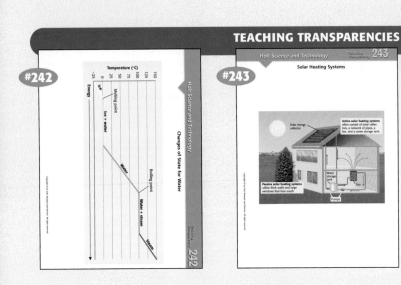
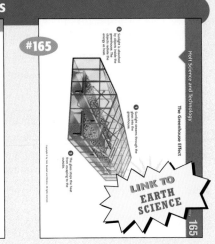
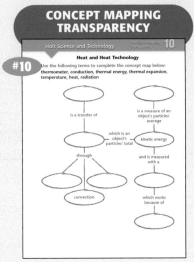

#242 Holt Science and Technology — Changes of State for Water — Teaching Transparency 242

#243 Holt Science and Technology — Solar Heating Systems — Teaching Transparency 243

#165 Holt Science and Technology — The Greenhouse Effect — Teaching Transparency 165

LINK TO EARTH SCIENCE

#10 Holt Science and Technology — Concept Mapping Transparency 10 — Heat and Heat Technology

Use the following terms to complete the concept map below:
thermometer, conduction, thermal energy, thermal expansion, temperature, heat, radiation

---

Meeting Individual Needs

DIRECTED READING

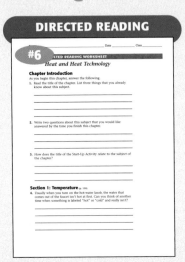

#6 DIRECTED READING WORKSHEET — Heat and Heat Technology

Chapter Introduction

As you begin this chapter, answer the following.
1. Read the title of the chapter. List three things that you already know about this subject.

2. Write two questions about this subject that you would like answered by the time you finish this chapter.

3. How does the title of the Start-Up Activity relate to the subject of the chapter?

Section 1: Temperature (p. 199)

4. Usually when you turn on the hot-water knob, the water that comes out of the faucet isn't hot at first. Can you think of another time when something is labeled "hot" or "cold" and really isn't?

REINFORCEMENT & VOCABULARY REVIEW

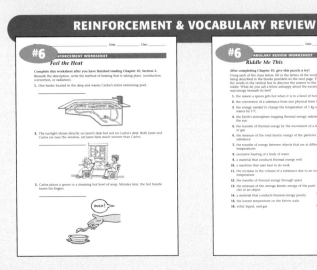

#6 REINFORCEMENT WORKSHEET — Feel the Heat

Complete this worksheet after you have finished reading Chapter 10, Section 2. Beneath the description, write the method of heating that is taking place. (conduction, convection, or radiation)

1. One heater located in the deep end warms Carlos's entire swimming pool.

2. The sunlight shines directly on Janet's desk but not on Carlos's desk. Both Janet and Carlos are near the window, yet Janet feels much warmer than Carlos.

3. Carlos places a spoon in a steaming hot bowl of soup. Minutes later, the hot handle burns his fingers.

OUCH

#6 VOCABULARY REVIEW WORKSHEET — Riddle Me This

After completing Chapter 10, give this puzzle a try!

Using each of the clues below, fill in the letters of the word or phrase being described in the blanks provided on the next page. Then read the words in the vertical box to discover the answer to the following riddle: What do you call a feline unhappy about the excessive thermal energy beneath its feet?

1. the reason a spoon gets hot when it is in a bowl of hot soup
2. the conversion of a substance from one physical form to another
3. the energy needed to change the temperature of 1 kg of a substance by 1°C
4. the Earth's atmosphere trapping thermal energy radiated by the sun
5. the transfer of thermal energy by the movement of a liquid or gas
6. the measure of the total kinetic energy of the particles in a substance
7. the transfer of energy between objects that are at different temperatures
8. excessive heating of a body of water
9. a material that conducts thermal energy well
10. a machine that uses heat to do work
11. the increase in the volume of a substance due to an increase in temperature
12. the transfer of thermal energy through space
13. the measure of the average kinetic energy of the particles of an object
14. a material that conducts thermal energy poorly
15. the lowest temperature on the Kelvin scale
16. solid, liquid, and gas

SCIENCE PUZZLERS, TWISTERS & TEASERS

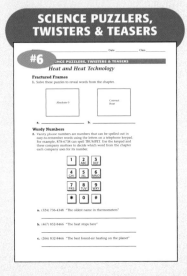

#6 SCIENCE PUZZLERS, TWISTERS & TEASERS — Heat and Heat Technology

Fractured Frames

1. Solve these puzzles to reveal words from the chapter.

Absolute 0

Convect Heat

a. _____   b. _____

Wordy Numbers

2. Vanity phone numbers are numbers that can be spelled out in easy-to-remember words using the letters on a telephone keypad. For example, 876-6738 can spell TRUMPET. Use the keypad and these company mottos to decide which words from the chapter each company uses for its number.

1	2 ABC	3 DEF
4 GHI	5 JKL	6 MNO
7 PRS	8 TUV	9 WXY
*	0	#

a. (324) 736-4348 "The oldest name in thermometers"

b. (467) 852-8466 "The heat stops here"

c. (266) 832-8466 "The best forced-air heating on the planet"

Review & Assessment

STUDY GUIDE

#6 VOCABULARY & NOTES WORKSHEET
Heat and Heat Technology

By studying the Vocabulary and Notes listed for each section below, you can gain a better understanding of this chapter.

SECTION 1
Vocabulary
In your own words, write a definition of each of the following terms in the space provided.

1. temperature

2. thermal expansion

3. absolute zero

Notes
Read the following section highlights. Then, in your own words, write the highlights in your ScienceLog.
- Temperature is a measure of the average kinetic energy of the particles of a substance. It is a specific measurement of how hot or cold a substance is.
- Thermal expansion is the increase in volume of a substance due to an increase in temperature. Temperature is measured according to the expansion of the liquid in a thermometer.
- Fahrenheit, Celsius, and Kelvin are three temperature scales.
- Absolute zero—0 K, or –273°C—is the lowest possible temperature.
- A thermostat works according to the thermal expansion of a bimetallic strip.

#6 CHAPTER REVIEW WORKSHEET
Heat and Heat Technology

USING VOCABULARY
For each pair of terms, explain the difference in their meanings.
1. temperature/thermal energy

2. heat/thermal energy

3. conductor/insulator

4. conduction/convection

5. states of matter/change of state

CHAPTER TESTS WITH PERFORMANCE-BASED ASSESSMENT

#6 HEAT AND HEAT TECHNOLOGY
Chapter 6 Test

USING VOCABULARY
To complete the following sentences, choose the correct term from each pair of terms listed, and write the term in the blank.
1. The condensation of water is a _____ (state of matter or change of state)
2. Aluminum changes temperature more slowly than lead; therefore, aluminum has a higher _____ than lead. (thermal energy or specific heat capacity)
3. When one end of an iron nail is held in a flame, thermal energy is transferred along the nail by _____ (convection or conduction)
4. Thermal energy flows between objects that differ in _____ (thermal expansion or temperature)
5. A(n) _____ uses heat to do work. (insulator coil or heat engine)

UNDERSTANDING CONCEPTS
Multiple Choice
Circle the correct answer.
6. A tile floor feels colder on your bare feet than a wooden floor because the tile floor
   a. is a better insulator.
   b. has a smoother surface than a wooden floor.
   c. is a better conductor than a wooden floor.
   d. will always have a lower temperature than a wooden floor.
7. The lowest possible temperature is
   a. 273 K.   c. 0°C.
   b. 0°F.   d. 0 K.
8. In which state does water have the lowest average kinetic energy?
   a. liquid   c. solid
   b. gas   d. each state has the same kinetic energy
9. When water vapor condenses,
   a. the surrounding air is cooled.   c. the surrounding air is warmed.
   b. the water particles speed apart.   d. a solid is formed.
10. Which of the following represents the greatest amount of energy?
   a. 1,000 cal   c. 100 kcal
   b. 500 Cal   d. 100,000 J

#6 HEAT AND HEAT TECHNOLOGY
Chapter 6 Performance-Based Assessment
SKILL BUILDER

Objective
You have studied how changing temperatures affect materials. You will use your knowledge to build a working thermometer and to find the air temperature in your classroom.

Know the Score!
As you work through the activity, keep in mind that you will be earning a grade for the following:
- how well you work with the materials (40%)
- how well you state your observations (30%)
- how well you explain those observations (30%)

MATERIALS
- capillary tube, 10 cm long, containing colored alcohol
- ruler
- 2 rubber bands
- ice-water bath
- clock or watch
- hot plate
- boiling-water bath
- tongs
- heat-resistant gloves

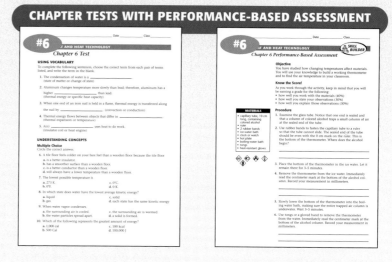

Procedure
1. Examine the glass tube. Notice that one end is sealed and that a column of colored alcohol traps a small column of air at the sealed end of the tube.
2. Use rubber bands to fasten the capillary tube to a ruler so that the tube cannot slide. The sealed end of the tube should be even with the 0 cm mark on the ruler. This is the bottom of the thermometer. Where does the alcohol begin?

3. Place the bottom of the thermometer in the ice water. Let it remain there for 3–5 minutes.
4. Remove the thermometer from the ice water. Immediately read the centimeter mark at the bottom of the alcohol column. Record your measurement in millimeters.

5. Slowly lower the bottom of the thermometer into the boiling water bath, making sure the entire trapped air column is underwater. Wait 3–5 minutes.
6. Use tongs or a gloved hand to remove the thermometer from the water. Immediately read the centimeter mark at the bottom of the alcohol column. Record your measurement in millimeters.

Lab Worksheets

LABS YOU CAN EAT

#6 STUDENT WORKSHEET
Baked Alaska
DISCOVERY LAB

Is it possible to bake ice cream without its melting? If you put a bowl of ice cream in a hot oven, you know what you'll get—ice cream soup! But what do you suppose would happen if you covered the ice cream with another food and then baked it? Let's find out.

MATERIALS
- conventional oven
- small bowl
- fork or wire whisk
- egg
- large spoonful of sugar (about 15 mL)
- pinch of salt
- electric mixer
- 2 large slices of sponge cake, pound cake, or angel food cake (10 cm square bread slices are also acceptable)
- cookie sheet covered with aluminum foil
- your favorite jam
- large spoon
- ice
- watch or clock
- oven mitts

Objective
To investigate the insulating property of meringue

Putting It Together
1. Preheat the oven to 250°C (475°F).
2. Prepare the meringue by cracking the egg and carefully separating the white from the yolk into a bowl. Discard the yolk. Beat the egg white with the fork or whisk until it holds its shape. Add the sugar and a pinch of salt, and then beat the mixture rapidly until it becomes very stiff. This is your meringue.
3. Put the two slices of cake on the cookie sheet. Spread a spoonful of jam over each slice of cake.
4. Get the ice cream from the freezer. Put a scoop of ice cream about 3 cm in diameter in the center of each slice of cake. Smooth the meringue over a scoop of ice cream, covering it completely. Check all sides to make sure the ice cream is well covered. Do not cover the other scoop of ice cream so that you can compare what happens to a covered scoop and an uncovered scoop.
5. While wearing the oven mitts, place the cookie sheet in the oven on the middle rack. Bake the cakes for 3 to 5 minutes, until the meringue turns light brown.
6. Remove the cakes from the oven, and serve them immediately.

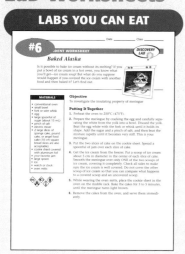

ECOLABS & FIELD ACTIVITIES

#6 STUDENT WORKSHEET
Energy-Efficient Home
DESIGN YOUR OWN

You are applying for a position with Sun Homes, a firm that builds attractive and energy-efficient houses in your area. To get the job, you must show Sun Homes that you know about insulation and their efficiency. As part of the interview process, you must build a model of an energy-efficient home with your insulator of choice. Sun Homes will choose the applicant with the most efficient model. Good luck!

MATERIALS
- large coffee can with plastic lid
- smaller can with a volume of at least 200 mL

Ask a Question
Which insulating materials provide the most efficient home insulation?

Make a Prediction

LONG-TERM PROJECTS & RESEARCH IDEAS

#6 STUDENT WORKSHEET
Firewalking Exposed
DESIGN YOUR OWN

Randolph Atkinson eyed the glowing pit of red coals that lay before him. His bare feet twitched in anticipation. "Am I crazy?" he asked himself. "Why am I doing this?" Before his doubts got the better of him, he took a deep breath and stepped forward. His mind raced. "I'm walking on fire! I can't believe this!"
    Believe it. Firewalking is real. The earliest stories of firewalking probably came from India around 1200 B.C. Since then, it has been an organized event in many different cultures and religions. In the 1930s, scientists began paying closer attention to this phenomenon and began to study how it is possible to walk across a bed of hot coals (around 425°C) without burning one's feet. In the interest of science, some of these scientists even took the walk of fire themselves!

SAFETY ALERT!
You shouldn't do this at home! Firewalking requires expert knowledge and preparation.

Hot Stuff
1. Using the library and the Internet, investigate the history and physics of firewalking. How has it been explained in other cultures? What is science's explanation for why firewalking is possible? Are there any tricks that firewalkers

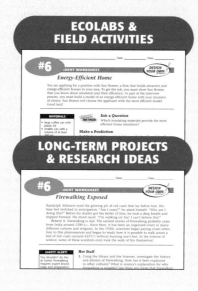

WHIZ-BANG DEMONSTRATIONS

#6 TEACHER-LED DEMONSTRATION
Cool It
DISCOVERY LAB

Purpose
Students explore the concepts of temperature and evaporation.

Time Required
10–15 minutes

Lab Ratings
TEACHER PREP
CONCEPT LEVEL
CLEAN UP

MATERIALS
- 2 identical indoor thermometers
- portable fan

What to Do
1. Place one thermometer 0.5 to 1 m in front of the fan, and place the other thermometer in the center of the room, out of the path of the fan. Do not turn on the fan.
2. Ask a student to record the temperature on each of the thermometers. The

thermometers should give the same temperature reading.
3. Turn on the fan. Ask students to predict what will happen to the reading on the thermometer in front of the fan. (Expected answer: The reading of the thermometer in front of the fan will be lower than the reading on the other thermometer.)
4. After a few minutes, have the student read the thermometers again. Both thermometers should read roughly the same temperature as before you turned on the fan.

Discussion
Use the following questions as a guide to encourage class discussion:
- How does a fan create a breeze? (As the blades turn, more air molecules are directed away from the fan, creating an air current.)
- Why didn't the breeze lower the temperature of the air? (The increased movement of air molecules does not lower the temperature of the air. In fact, an extremely sensitive thermometer might read a slightly higher temperature due to the increased movement of the air molecules.)
- Why does the breeze feel cool? (The breeze from the fan cools the skin by increasing the evaporation of sweat from the skin's surface. The evaporation cools the body.)

Michael E. Kral
West Hardin Middle School
Cecilia, Kentucky

DATASHEETS FOR LABBOOK

DATASHEET

#6 **Feel the Heat**

#6 **Save the Cube!**

#6 **Counting Calories**

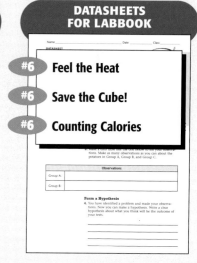

Write a third statement on the line for your observations. Make as many observations as you can about the potatoes in Group A, Group B, and Group C.

Observations	
Group A	
Group B	

Form a Hypothesis
4. You have identified a problem and made your observations. Now you can make a hypothesis. Write a clear hypothesis about what you think will be the outcome of your tests.

Applications & Extensions

CRITICAL THINKING & PROBLEM SOLVING

#6 CRITICAL THINKING WORKSHEET
Try and Try Again

While surfing the Internet, you find the following Web site:

The Recent History of Failed Inventions
Part IX

Hello, culture lovers. I'm Rex Sophist, here to bring you the latest update on inventions that did not quite work. That's right, here's a new list from the people who showed you such blunders as the metal basketball and the waterbed car seat!
- A man in Hapablatt, UT, has invented a frying-pan sleeve made of lead. This lead sleeve fits over the metal handles of iron frying pans.
- A woman in Salisbury, SD, designed a thermostat strip made of thick, solid aluminum.
- A man in Dry Cheeks, AZ, built a house in the desert with thin copper walls.
    Well, folks, that's the report for this week. Make sure you log on to our Web site next week for The Recent History of Failed Inventions, Part X, when we will feature the inventor of the wooden car engine.

Understanding Concepts
1. Why is a lead frying-pan sleeve a bad idea?

2. What materials would work better than lead as a sleeve for a frying-pan handle? Explain.

EYE ON THE ENVIRONMENT

#22 Science in the News: Critical Thinking Worksheets

Geothermal Energy
1. Identify the primary cost-efficient aspect of a geothermal energy system.

2. Is a backup energy source needed to supplement the geothermal energy source? Why or why not?

3. What are the environmentally friendly aspects of geothermal energy?

4. Identify two limitations of geothermal energy.

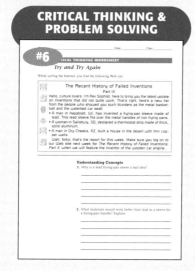

Chapter Background

SECTION 1

Temperature

▶ Temperature Scales

Daniel Gabriel Fahrenheit (1686–1736) developed the first mercury thermometer in 1714. His scale used the temperature of a brine solution of ice and salt as 0°. He chose 30° for the freezing temperature of water and 90° for the temperature of the human body. These were later adjusted to 32° and 98.6°.

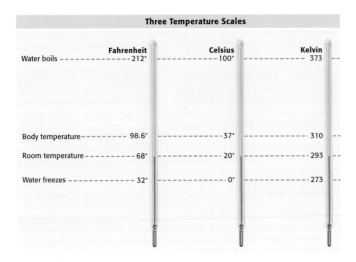

Three Temperature Scales

	Fahrenheit	Celsius	Kelvin
Water boils	212°	100°	373
Body temperature	98.6°	37°	310
Room temperature	68°	20°	293
Water freezes	32°	0°	273

- Anders Celsius (1701–1744) developed the centigrade temperature scale using two physical properties of pure water as his standards. The modern Celsius scale assigns 0° to the freezing point of pure water and 100° to the boiling point of pure water. The Celsius scale has been adopted for use by the scientific community.

- In 1848, British physicist and mathematician William Thomson (1824–1907), later Lord Kelvin, developed the absolute temperature scale. Using J.A.C. Charles's (1746–1823) work with gases, Kelvin realized that a gas decreased by $\frac{1}{273}$ of its volume for each Celsius-degree decrease in temperature. Kelvin theorized that a substance would lose all energy at a temperature of −273°C, so he assigned that point a value of zero on his scale.

IS THAT A FACT!

☛ How much energy does the human body radiate in 1 second? It uses as much as a 60 W light bulb.

SECTION 2

What Is Heat?

▶ Benjamin Thompson (1753–1814)

In the eighteenth century, most scientists defined heat as an invisible and weightless fluid that soaked into an object as it was heated and left an object as it cooled.

- Benjamin Thompson, also known as Count von Rumford, an American-born British physicist, noticed that metal became very hot during the process of boring cannons. He set up an experiment to find out why.

- In his experiment, Thompson encased the cannon form in a wooden barrel filled with water. After hours of drilling, the water began to boil. When the drilling stopped, the water stopped boiling. When the drilling began again, the water once again boiled. The water continued to boil for as long as the drill was turned. If heat had been a material substance, it would have run out eventually and the cannon would have become cold—no matter how much drilling was done.

- Because there was no source of heat, Thompson decided that heat was actually a form of energy supplied by the work of the horses turning the drill. Thompson reasoned that the drilling caused the molecules in the cannon to vibrate faster and that the cannon's molecules caused the water molecules to vibrate faster. When the drilling stopped, the source of energy also stopped.

Chapter 6 • Heat and Heat Technology

Review & Assessment

STUDY GUIDE

CHAPTER TESTS WITH PERFORMANCE-BASED ASSESSMENT

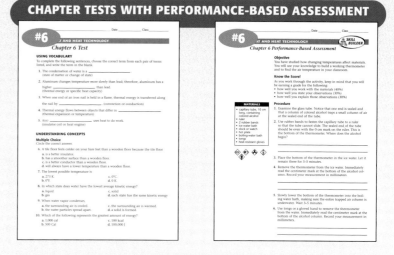

Lab Worksheets

LABS YOU CAN EAT

ECOLABS & FIELD ACTIVITIES

LONG-TERM PROJECTS & RESEARCH IDEAS

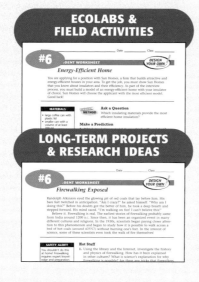

WHIZ-BANG DEMONSTRATIONS

DATASHEETS FOR LABBOOK

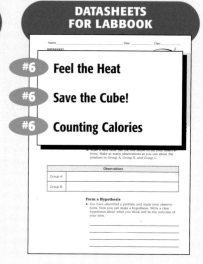

#6 **Feel the Heat**

#6 **Save the Cube!**

#6 **Counting Calories**

Applications & Extensions

CRITICAL THINKING & PROBLEM SOLVING

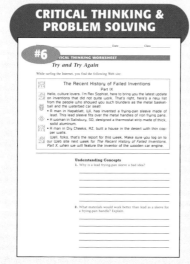

EYE ON THE ENVIRONMENT

Chapter Background

SECTION 1

Temperature

▶ Temperature Scales

Daniel Gabriel Fahrenheit (1686–1736) developed the first mercury thermometer in 1714. His scale used the temperature of a brine solution of ice and salt as 0°. He chose 30° for the freezing temperature of water and 90° for the temperature of the human body. These were later adjusted to 32° and 98.6°.

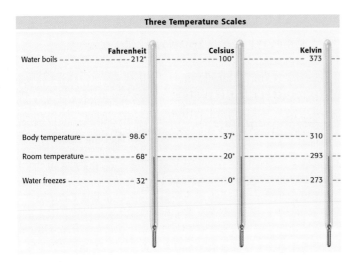

Three Temperature Scales

	Fahrenheit	Celsius	Kelvin
Water boils	212°	100°	373
Body temperature	98.6°	37°	310
Room temperature	68°	20°	293
Water freezes	32°	0°	273

- Anders Celsius (1701–1744) developed the centigrade temperature scale using two physical properties of pure water as his standards. The modern Celsius scale assigns 0° to the freezing point of pure water and 100° to the boiling point of pure water. The Celsius scale has been adopted for use by the scientific community.

- In 1848, British physicist and mathematician William Thomson (1824–1907), later Lord Kelvin, developed the absolute temperature scale. Using J.A.C. Charles's (1746–1823) work with gases, Kelvin realized that a gas decreased by $\frac{1}{273}$ of its volume for each Celsius-degree decrease in temperature. Kelvin theorized that a substance would lose all energy at a temperature of −273°C, so he assigned that point a value of zero on his scale.

IS THAT A FACT!

➤ How much energy does the human body radiate in 1 second? It uses as much as a 60 W light bulb.

SECTION 2

What Is Heat?

▶ Benjamin Thompson (1753–1814)

In the eighteenth century, most scientists defined heat as an invisible and weightless fluid that soaked into an object as it was heated and left an object as it cooled.

- Benjamin Thompson, also known as Count von Rumford, an American-born British physicist, noticed that metal became very hot during the process of boring cannons. He set up an experiment to find out why.

- In his experiment, Thompson encased the cannon form in a wooden barrel filled with water. After hours of drilling, the water began to boil. When the drilling stopped, the water stopped boiling. When the drilling began again, the water once again boiled. The water continued to boil for as long as the drill was turned. If heat had been a material substance, it would have run out eventually and the cannon would have become cold—no matter how much drilling was done.

- Because there was no source of heat, Thompson decided that heat was actually a form of energy supplied by the work of the horses turning the drill. Thompson reasoned that the drilling caused the molecules in the cannon to vibrate faster and that the cannon's molecules caused the water molecules to vibrate faster. When the drilling stopped, the source of energy also stopped.

SECTION 3

Matter and Heat

▶ Water and Heat

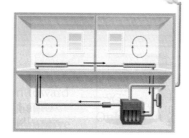

When thermal energy is added to substances, they usually expand. When thermal energy is subtracted, they usually contract. Water behaves this way until it reaches the temperature range between 4°C and 0°C. In this range, water expands as it cools and freezes, making its solid form (ice) less dense than its liquid form.

▶ Latent Heat

The amount of thermal energy that is lost or gained during a phase change is called latent heat. During a phase change, there is no change in temperature. The energy that is absorbed or released is used to break or to recreate physical bonds.

IS THAT A FACT!

- More than 2 million joules of thermal energy are lost from a mammal's body as 1 L of perspiration is evaporated.

SECTION 4

Heat Technology

▶ Central Heating

Central-heating systems that used hot water were developed in the 1800s. The first successful central-heating system, used in 1835, relied on warm air. In 1850, steam heating was developed.

- Radiant heating refers to systems in which floors, walls, and ceilings are used as radiant-heating units. When floors and walls are used, steam or hot-water pipes are placed in the floors or the walls during the construction of the building.

- Radiant heating can be provided by electrical resistance. If electrical resistance is used, the panels containing coils are placed in the baseboard or the ceiling.

▶ Steam Engines

Hero of Alexandria (first century A.D.) invented a type of steam engine, but the French physicist Denis Papin (c. 1647–1712) developed the first piston steam engine in 1690. Thomas Savery (c. 1650–1715) and Thomas Newcomen (1663–1729) made improvements on Papin's design, but it was James Watt (1736–1819) who produced the modern steam engine.

▶ Internal Combustion Engines

Jean Joseph Etienne Lenoir (1822–1900) is given credit for inventing the first practical internal combustion engine. Nikolaus August Otto (1832–1891) and Rudolf Diesel (1858–1913) also did extensive work with internal combustion engines. Gottlieb Daimler (1834–1900) assisted Otto with this engine. Daimler, who developed both two- and four-cycle engines, patented his own engine in 1887.

- Karl Benz (1844–1929), a German engineer, developed a two-cycle internal combustion engine and a light four-cycle engine. In 1886, Benz patented a vehicle that had his engine.

- Benz and Daimler, who worked independently of each other and who never met, were each credited with building the first automobile.

IS THAT A FACT!

- Heating, cooling, and breathing produce hazardous waste gases and vapors. An adequate ventilation system provides about 280 to 850 L of outside air per minute for each person in a room.

> **For background information about teaching strategies and issues, refer to the *Professional Reference for Teachers*.**

CHAPTER 6

Heat and Heat Technology

 Pre-Reading Questions

Students may not know the answers to these questions before reading the chapter, so accept any reasonable response.

Suggested Answers

1. Use a thermometer to measure how hot or cold objects are.

2. An object is hot or cold relative to another object. For example, if an object's temperature is higher than your body temperature, energy transfers from the object to your body and the object feels hot. If an object's temperature is lower than your body temperature, energy transfers from your body to the object and the object feels cold.

3. Central heating systems, such as hot-water or warm-air heating systems, use a combination of conduction and convection to heat the air in the house.

CHAPTER 6

Heat and Heat Technology

 Pre-Reading Questions

1. How do you measure how hot or cold an object is?
2. What makes an object hot or cold?
3. How can heat be used in your home?

148

UP, UP, AND AWAY

A hot-air balloon race is fun to watch. The balloons start out flat, but as they fill with hot air, the balloons grow larger until they are ready to take off. Balloons don't need engines or wings. They rely on heat and thermal expansion to get them off the ground and into the sky. In this chapter, you will learn more about heat and its place in your daily life.

---

internet connect

 HRW On-line Resources

go.hrw.com

For worksheets and other teaching aids, visit the HRW Web site and type in the keyword: **HSTHOT**

 SCiLINKS NSTA

www.scilinks.com

Use the *sci*LINKS numbers at the end of each chapter for additional resources on the **NSTA** Web site.

 Smithsonian Institution

www.si.edu/hrw

Visit the Smithsonian Institution Web site for related on-line resources.

CNNfyi.com

www.cnnfyi.com

Visit the CNN Web site for current events coverage and classroom resources.

Activity

SOME LIKE IT HOT

Sometimes you can tell the relative temperature of something by touching it with your hand. In this activity, you will find out how well your hand works as a thermometer!

Procedure

1. Gather small pieces of the following materials from your teacher: **metal, wood, plastic foam, rock, plastic,** and **cardboard.**

2. Allow the materials to sit untouched on a table for several minutes.

3. Put your hands palms down on each of the various materials. Observe how warm or cool each one feels.

4. In your ScienceLog, list the materials in order from coolest to warmest.

5. Place a **thermometer strip** on the surface of each material. In your ScienceLog, record the temperature of each material.

Analysis

6. Which material felt the warmest?

7. Which material had the highest temperature? Was it the same material as in question 6?

8. Why do you think some materials felt warmer than others?

9. Was your hand a good thermometer? Why or why not?

149

START-UP Activity

SOME LIKE IT HOT

MATERIALS
FOR EACH GROUP: • small pieces of metal, wood, plastic foam, rock, plastic, cardboard   • thermometer strip (You can use bulb thermometers, but liquid crystal thermometer strips or cards, available from a science store or supply house, may measure temperature of the materials more accurately.)

Answers to START-UP Activity

6. Answers will vary, but students may say that the plastic foam felt the warmest.

7. Students should find that the materials were all about the same temperature.

8. Answers will vary, but students may conclude that the material of which something is made determines how warm or cold it feels.

9. Students will probably conclude that their hands were not a good thermometer because some materials felt warmer than others, even though they were all about the same temperature.

Focus

Temperature

This section explains temperature and how it is measured. Students learn how temperature relates to kinetic energy. They will explore thermal expansion and learn how to convert between the three temperature scales.

 Bellringer

Write the following on the board:

The temperature of boiling water is 100° on the Celsius scale and 212° on the Fahrenheit scale.

Look at each of the following temperatures carefully, and decide whether you think that it is hot or cold:

60°F, 60°C, 37°F, 37°C, 0°C, 100°F, 70°F

Write your responses in your ScienceLog.

1 Motivate

DEMONSTRATION

Using a metal ball-and-ring set, demonstrate how the ball easily slips through the ring. Be sure to use tongs or protective gloves. Heat the ball for a minute or two, then try to pass the ball through the ring. Ask students to theorize why the ball no longer passes through the ring. Next heat the ring and pass the ball through it. Ask students to theorize why the ball again passed through the ring. (The ball expanded when it was heated, so it would not fit through the ring. When the ring was heated, the ring expanded enough to allow the ball to pass through.)

Terms to Learn

temperature
thermal expansion
absolute zero

What You'll Do

◆ Describe how temperature relates to kinetic energy.
◆ Give examples of thermal expansion.
◆ Compare temperatures on different temperature scales.

Temperature

You probably put on a sweater or a jacket when it's cold outside. Likewise, you probably wear shorts in the summer when it gets hot. But how hot is hot, and how cold is cold? Think about how the knobs on a water faucet are labeled "H" for hot and "C" for cold. But does only hot water come out when the hot water knob is on? You may have noticed that when you first turn on the water, it is warm or even cool. Are you being misled by the label on the knob? The terms *hot* and *cold* are not very scientific terms. If you really want to specify how hot or cold something is, you must use temperature.

What Is Temperature?

You probably think of temperature as a measure of how hot or cold something is. But scientifically, **temperature** is a measure of the average kinetic energy of the particles in an object. Using *temperature* instead of words like *hot* or *cold* reduces confusion. The scenario below emphasizes the importance of communicating about temperature. You can learn more about hot and cold comparisons by doing the QuickLab on the next page.

 **Directed Reading Worksheet** Section 1

internetconnect

SCLINKS NSTA
TOPIC: What Is Temperature?
GO TO: www.scilinks.org
KEYWORD: HSTP230

MISCONCEPTION ALERT

Students often think that heat and temperature are the same. Stress that temperature is the measure of the average kinetic energy of the molecules in a substance. Heat is the transfer of thermal energy between objects that are at different temperatures. These concepts are covered in Section 2 of this chapter.

Temperature Depends on the Kinetic Energy of Particles

All matter is made of particles—atoms or molecules—that are in constant motion. Because the particles are in motion, they have kinetic energy. The faster the particles are moving, the more kinetic energy they have. What does temperature have to do with kinetic energy? Well, as described in **Figure 1,** the more kinetic energy the particles of an object have, the higher the temperature of the object.

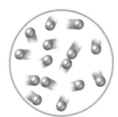 

Figure 1 *The gas particles on the right have more kinetic energy than those on the left. So, the gas on the right is at a higher temperature.*

Temperature Is an Average Measure Particles of matter are constantly moving, but they don't all move at the same speed and in the same direction all the time. Look back at Figure 1. As you can see, the motion of the particles is random. The particles of matter in an object move in different directions, and some particles move faster than others. As a result, some particles have more kinetic energy than others. So what determines an object's temperature? An object's temperature is the best approximation of the kinetic energy of the particles. When you measure an object's temperature, you measure the average kinetic energy of the particles in the object.

The temperature of a substance is not determined by how much of the substance you have. As shown in **Figure 2,** different amounts of the same substance can have the same temperature. However, the total kinetic energy of the particles in each amount is different. You will learn more about total kinetic energy in the next section.

Figure 2 *Even though there is more tea in the teapot than in the mug, the temperature of the tea in the mug is the same as the temperature of the tea in the teapot.*

QuickLab

Hot or Cold?

1. Put both your hands into a **bucket of warm water,** and note how it feels.

2. Now put one hand into a **bucket of cold water** and the other into a **bucket of hot water.**

3. After a minute, take your hands out of the hot and cold water and put them back in the warm water.

4. Can you rely on your hands to determine temperature? In your ScienceLog, explain your observations.

151

Science Bloopers

When Anders Celsius invented his temperature scale, he set the freezing point of water as 100° and the boiling point of water at 0°. Apparently, the person who made thermometers for Celsius got the two numbers reversed, and ever since, 0° has been the freezing point of water and 100° has been the boiling point of water.

IS THAT A FACT!

There are five temperature scales used today: Fahrenheit, Celsius, Kelvin, the international thermodynamic temperature scale, and Rankine. Scientists use the Celsius and Kelvin scales almost exclusively.

Ask students to use the figure of the **Three Temperature Scales** on this page to determine human body temperature on the Kelvin scale (310 K), the Celsius scale (37°C), and the Fahrenheit scale (98.6°F).

At what temperature does water boil on the Celsius scale? (100°C) on the Kelvin scale? (373 K)

DISCUSSION

The Fahrenheit scale defines the freezing point of water as 32°F. By the time 0°F is reached, the temperature is well below the freezing point of water. Human body temperature is 98.6°F. Discuss with the class what would happen if normal human body temperature suddenly shot up to 98.6°C. Would air temperatures of 70–75°C feel comfortable? Why do doctors worry more about a fever of a couple of degrees Celsius than a fever of a couple of degrees Fahrenheit?

Teaching Transparency 238
"Three Temperature Scales"

BRAIN FOOD

The coldest temperature on record occurred in Vostok Station, Antarctica. In 1983, the temperature dropped to –89°C (about –192°F). The hottest temperature on record occurred in 1922 in a Libyan desert. A scorching temperature of 58°C (about 136°F) was recorded—in the shade!

Measuring Temperature

How would you measure the temperature of a steaming cup of hot chocolate? Would you take a sip of it or stick your finger into it? Probably not—you would use a thermometer.

Using a Thermometer Many thermometers are a thin glass tube filled with a liquid. Mercury and alcohol are often used in thermometers because they remain liquids over a large temperature range. Thermometers can measure temperature because of thermal expansion. **Thermal expansion** is the increase in volume of a substance due to an increase in temperature. As a substance gets hotter, its particles move faster. The particles themselves do not expand; they just spread out so that the entire substance expands. Different substances expand by different amounts for a given temperature change. When you insert a thermometer into a hot substance, the liquid inside the thermometer expands and rises. You measure the temperature of a substance by measuring the expansion of the liquid in the thermometer.

Temperature Scales Temperature can be expressed according to different scales. Notice how the same temperatures have different readings on the three temperature scales shown below.

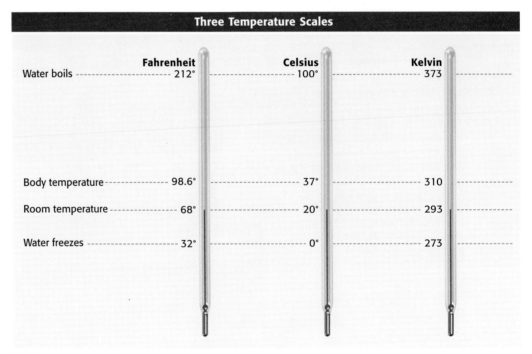

Three Temperature Scales

	Fahrenheit	Celsius	Kelvin
Water boils	212°	100°	373
Body temperature	98.6°	37°	310
Room temperature	68°	20°	293
Water freezes	32°	0°	273

When you hear a weather report that gives the current temperature as 65°, chances are that you are given the temperature in degrees Fahrenheit (°F). In science, the Celsius scale is used more often than the Fahrenheit scale. The Celsius scale is divided into 100 equal parts, called degrees Celsius (°C), between the freezing point and boiling point of water. A third scale, called the Kelvin (or absolute) scale, is the official SI temperature scale. The Kelvin scale is divided into units called kelvins (K)—not degrees kelvin. The lowest temperature on the Kelvin scale is 0 K, which is called **absolute zero.** It is not possible to reach a temperature lower than absolute zero. In fact, temperatures within a few billionths of a kelvin above absolute zero have been achieved in laboratories, but absolute zero itself has never been reached.

Temperature Conversion As shown by the thermometers illustrated on the previous page, a given temperature is represented by different numbers on the three temperature scales. For example, the freezing point of water is 32°F, 0°C, or 273 K. As you can see, 0°C is actually a much higher temperature than 0 K, but a change of 1 K is equal to a change of one Celsius degree. In addition, 0°C is a higher temperature than 0°F, but a change of one Fahrenheit degree is *not* equal to a change of one Celsius degree. You can convert from one scale to another using the simple equations shown below. After reading the examples given, try the MathBreak on this page.

What can you do at temperatures near absolute zero? Turn to page 180 to find out!

To convert	Use this equation:	Example
Celsius to Fahrenheit °C ⟶ °F	$°F = \left(\frac{9}{5} \times °C\right) + 32$	Convert 45°C to °F. $°F = \left(\frac{9}{5} \times 45°C\right) + 32 = 113°F$
Fahrenheit to Celsius °F ⟶ °C	$°C = \frac{5}{9} \times (°F - 32)$	Convert 68°F to °C. $°C = \frac{5}{9} \times (68°F - 32) = 20°C$
Celsius to Kelvin °C ⟶ K	$K = °C + 273$	Convert 45°C to K. $K = 45°C + 273 = 318$ K
Kelvin to Celsius K ⟶ °C	$°C = K - 273$	Convert 32 K to °C. $°C = 32$ K $- 273 = -241°C$

MATH BREAK

Converting Temperatures

Use the equations at left to answer the following questions:

1. What temperature on the Celsius scale is equivalent to 373 K?

2. Absolute zero is 0 K. What is the equivalent temperature on the Celsius scale? on the Fahrenheit scale?

3. Which temperature is colder, 0°F or 200 K?

153

Answers to MATHBREAK

1. 100°C

2. −273°C; −459.4°F

3. 200 K is colder

3) Extend

RESEARCH

Writing Encourage students to research the lives and work of Anders Celsius, Gabriel Fahrenheit, William Rankine, and William Thomson (Lord Kelvin). Students can present their findings on posters, by writing a story or skit, or in a report.

PORTFOLIO

MATH and MORE

When solving equations, it is important to follow the order of operations. Remind students to do what is inside the parentheses first, then multiply or divide from left to right, and finally add or subtract from left to right.

Have students do the following conversion problems:

• Normal body temperature is 98.6°F. Marie has a temperature of 38.5°C. Does Marie have a fever? (yes; 38.5°C = 101.3°F)

• The temperature tonight is supposed to be 265 K. Will water left in a bucket outside freeze? (yes; 265 K = −8°C, which is below water's freezing point, 0°C)

 Math Skills Worksheet "Using Temperature Scales"

Quiz

1. Most substances _____ when they are cooled. (contract)

2. The common temperature scale used by most Americans is the _____ scale. (Fahrenheit)

3. Scientists use either the _____ scale or the _____ scale. (Celsius, Kelvin)

4. Temperature _____ as average kinetic energy decreases. (decreases)

ALTERNATIVE ASSESSMENT

Ask students to theorize why large buildings and sidewalks are constructed with expansion joints. (to allow for thermal expansion)

Ask them to explain what would happen in hot or cold weather if there were no expansion joints.

Homework

Writing Have students explain how they could measure temperature if they were given a thermometer without marks on it. Remind students that water would help them with their measurements.

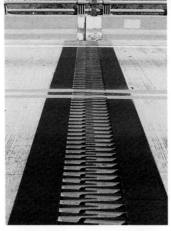

Figure 3 *The concrete segments of a bridge can expand on hot days. When the temperature drops, the segments contract.*

More About Thermal Expansion

Have you ever gone across a highway bridge in a car? You probably heard and felt a *"thuh-thunk"* every couple of seconds as you went over the bridge. That sound occurs when the car goes over small gaps called expansion joints, shown in **Figure 3**. These joints keep the bridge from buckling as a result of thermal expansion. Recall that thermal expansion is the increase in volume of a substance due to an increase in temperature.

Thermal expansion also occurs in a thermostat, the device that controls the heater in your home. Inside a thermostat is a bimetallic strip. A *bimetallic strip* is made of two different metals stacked in a thin strip. Because different materials expand at different rates, one of the metals expands more than the other when the strip gets hot. This makes the strip coil and uncoil in response to changes in temperature. This coiling and uncoiling closes and opens an electric circuit that turns the heater on and off in your home, as shown in **Figure 4.**

Figure 4 How a Thermostat Works

Electrical contacts

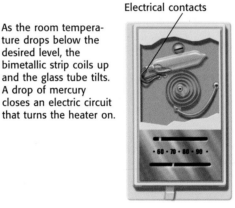

a As the room temperature drops below the desired level, the bimetallic strip coils up and the glass tube tilts. A drop of mercury closes an electric circuit that turns the heater on.

b As the room temperature rises above the desired level, the bimetallic strip uncoils. The drop of mercury rolls back in the tube, opening the electric circuit, and the heater turns off.

---

internet connect

*sci*LINKS.
NSTA

TOPIC: What Is Temperature?
GO TO: www.scilinks.org
*sci*LINKS NUMBER: HSTP230

SECTION REVIEW

1. What is temperature?

2. What is the coldest temperature possible?

3. Convert 35°C to degrees Fahrenheit.

4. **Inferring Conclusions** Why do you think heating a full pot of soup on the stove could cause the soup to overflow?

▼ Answers to Section Review

1. Temperature is a measure of how hot or cold an object is. Specifically, temperature is a direct measure of the average kinetic energy of the particles in an object.

2. The coldest possible temperature is absolute zero (0 K or −273°C).

3. $°F = (\frac{9}{5} × °C) + 32$
   $°F = \frac{9}{5} × 35°C + 32$
   $°F = 95$, or 95°F

4. The soup could overflow its pot as it cooks on the stove because of thermal expansion. The soup will expand in volume as its temperature increases. If the cold soup is too close to the top of a pot, it will likely overflow as it expands.

Terms to Learn

heat	insulator
thermal energy	convection
conduction	radiation
conductor	specific heat capacity

What You'll Do

◆ Define *heat* as the transfer of energy between objects at different temperatures.

◆ Compare conduction, convection, and radiation.

◆ Use specific heat capacity to calculate heat.

◆ Explain the differences between temperature, thermal energy, and heat.

What Is Heat?

It's time for your annual physical. The doctor comes in and begins her exam by looking down your throat using a wooden tongue depressor. Next she listens to your heart and lungs. But when she places a metal stethoscope on your back, as shown in **Figure 5,** you jump a little and say, "Whoa! That's cold!" The doctor apologizes and continues with your checkup.

Why did the metal stethoscope feel cold? After all, it was at the same temperature as the tongue depressor, which didn't make you jump. What is it about the stethoscope that made it feel cold? The answer has to do with how energy is transferred between the metal and your skin. In this section, you'll learn about this kind of energy transfer.

Heat Is a Transfer of Energy

You might think of the word *heat* as having to do with things that feel hot. But heat also has to do with things that feel cold—like the stethoscope. In fact, heat is what causes objects to feel hot or cold or to get hot or cold under the right conditions. You probably use the word *heat* every day to mean different things. However, in this chapter, you will learn a specific meaning for it. **Heat** is the transfer of energy between objects that are at different temperatures.

Why do some things feel hot, while others feel cold? When two objects at different temperatures come in contact, energy is always transferred from the object with the higher temperature to the object with the lower temperature. When the doctor's stethoscope touches your back, energy is transferred from your back to the stethoscope because your back has a higher temperature (37°C) than the stethoscope (probably room temperature, 20°C). So to you, the stethoscope is cold, but compared to the stethoscope, you are hot! You'll learn why the tongue depressor didn't feel cold to you a little later in this section.

Figure 5 *The reason the metal stethoscope feels cold is actually because of heat!*

155

Focus

What Is Heat?

In this section, students learn that heat is the transfer of energy between objects at different temperatures. They also learn the three methods of heating objects and how to calculate heat using specific heat capacity. Finally, they learn about the differences between temperature, thermal energy, and heat.

Bellringer

Have students imagine the following:

You walk into the bathroom in your bare feet. The temperature in there is 23°C. You step onto the tile floor, and it feels very cold. Quickly, you step onto the throw rug in front of the sink, and the rug feels warmer.

Ask students to answer these questions in their ScienceLog:

Is the floor really colder than the rug? Why do they seem to be at different temperatures when your bare feet touch them?

Directed Reading Worksheet Section 2

---

internetconnect

SCI**LINKS**
NSTA

TOPIC: What Is Heat?
GO TO: www.scilinks.org
KEYWORD: HSTP240

MISCONCEPTION
///ALERT\\\

In everyday usage, the word *heat* is used in a variety of ways, such as warmth or the energy contained in a hot object. However, a much narrower definition of *heat* is used in this chapter. Students should understand that heat is a transfer of energy between objects that are at different temperatures. The example described on this page is a useful introduction to this concept.

1 Motivate

DEMONSTRATION

Place three small objects with similar masses, such as a rock, a block of brass, and a block of steel, in boiling water. After 2 minutes, remove each object and place it on a block of wax. When the objects have cooled, remove them from the wax. Measure the depth of the indentation made by each object on the wax. Ask the students to explain the differences. (Each object had a different amount of thermal energy.)

MISCONCEPTION ///ALERT

The thermal energy of a substance is related to the substance's temperature as well as its state. For example, equal masses of liquid water and steam at the same temperature (100°C) have different amounts of thermal energy. Because the steam stores the energy used to separate the particles of liquid water to change it to steam, the steam has more thermal energy than the liquid water.

2 Teach

READING 📖 STRATEGY

Prediction Guide Before students read the section about heat and thermal energy, ask them whether the following statements are true or false.

- Thermal energy depends partly on the temperature of a substance. (true)
- A cup of water at 283 K and a pot of water at 283 K have the same thermal energy. (false)

Figure 6 *Although both soups are at the same temperature, the soup in the pan has more thermal energy than the soup in the bowl.*

Heat and Thermal Energy If heat is a transfer of energy, what form of energy is being transferred? The answer is thermal energy. **Thermal energy** is the total energy of the particles that make up a substance. Thermal energy, which is expressed in joules (J), depends partly on temperature. An object at a high temperature has more thermal energy than it would at a lower temperature. Thermal energy also depends on how much of a substance you have. As described in **Figure 6,** the more moving particles there are in a substance at a given temperature, the greater the thermal energy of the substance.

When you hold an ice cube, thermal energy is transferred from your hand to the ice cube. The ice cube's thermal energy increases, and it starts to melt. But your hand's thermal energy decreases. The particles in the surface of your skin move more slowly, and the surface temperature of your skin drops slightly. So your hand feels cold!

Reaching the Same Temperature Take a look at **Figure 7.** When objects at different temperatures come in contact, energy will always be transferred from the higher-temperature object to the lower-temperature object until both objects reach the same temperature. This point is called *thermal equilibrium* (EE kwi LIB ree uhm). When objects are at thermal equilibrium, no net change in either object's thermal energy occurs. Although one object may have more thermal energy, both objects have the same temperature.

Figure 7
Reaching Thermal Equilibrium

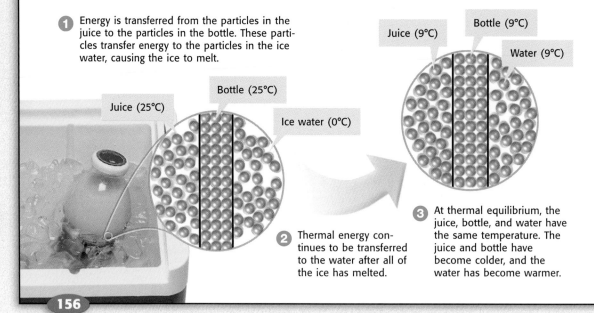

1. Energy is transferred from the particles in the juice to the particles in the bottle. These particles transfer energy to the particles in the ice water, causing the ice to melt.

Juice (25°C)
Bottle (25°C)
Ice water (0°C)

Juice (9°C)
Bottle (9°C)
Water (9°C)

2. Thermal energy continues to be transferred to the water after all of the ice has melted.

3. At thermal equilibrium, the juice, bottle, and water have the same temperature. The juice and bottle have become colder, and the water has become warmer.

Homework

Ask students this question:

When energy has been transferred by heat, what happens to it? Explain your answer. (Energy transferred by heat moves from a higher-temperature object to a lower-temperature object. The thermal energy of the lower-temperature object increases, as does its temperature. The thermal energy of the higher-temperature object decreases, as does its temperature.)

Conduction, Convection, and Radiation

So far you've read about several examples of energy transfer: stoves transfer energy to substances in pots and pans; you can adjust the temperature of your bath water by adding cold or hot water to the tub; and the sun warms your skin. In the next couple of pages you'll learn about three processes involving this type of energy transfer: *conduction*, *convection*, and *radiation*.

Conduction Imagine that you put a cold metal spoon in a bowl of hot soup, as shown in **Figure 8**. Soon the handle of the spoon warms up—even though it is not in the soup! The entire spoon gets warm because of conduction. **Conduction** is the transfer of thermal energy from one substance to another through direct contact. Conduction can also occur within a substance, such as the spoon in Figure 8.

How does conduction work? As substances come in contact, particles collide and thermal energy is transferred from the higher-temperature substance to the lower-temperature substance. Remember that particles of substances at different temperatures have different average kinetic energy. So when particles collide, higher-kinetic-energy particles transfer kinetic energy to lower-kinetic-energy particles. This makes some particles slow down and other particles speed up until all particles have the same average kinetic energy. As a result, the substances have the same temperature.

QuickLab

Heat Exchange

1. Fill a **film canister** with **hot water.** Insert the **thermometer apparatus** prepared by your teacher. Record the temperature.

2. Fill a **250 mL beaker** two-thirds full with **cool water.** Insert **another thermometer** in the cool water, and record its temperature.

3. Place the canister in the cool water. Record the temperature measured by each thermometer every 30 seconds.

4. When the thermometers read nearly the same temperature, stop and graph your data. Plot temperature (*y*-axis) versus time (*x*-axis).

5. In your ScienceLog, describe what happens to the rate of energy transfer as the two temperatures get closer.

Figure 8 *The end of this spoon will warm up because conduction, the transfer of energy through direct contact, occurs all the way up the handle.*

QuickLab

MATERIALS

FOR EACH GROUP:
- film canister
- 2 thermometers
- 250 mL beaker
- hot and cool water
- graph paper

Safety Caution: Remind students to handle thermometers carefully. Caution students to wear safety goggles during this activity.

Teacher Notes: Prepare the film canister lids in advance. Make a hole in each canister lid with an awl or a pair of sharp scissors. The thermometer should fit tightly enough in the lid that water will not drip out when the assembly is turned upside down. (One-hole stoppers can also be used.)

Students should graph both sets of data on the same grid. You may wish to assist students in adjusting the scales of their graph to show all their data.

Answers to QuickLab

5. Answers will vary, but students should see that the rate of energy transfer decreases as the two water samples approach the same temperature.

Teaching Transparency 239
"Reaching Thermal Equilibrium"

Teaching Transparency 240
"Conduction"

SCIENCE HUMOR

Q: Why did the music teacher bring a metal pole to orchestra rehearsal?

A: He wanted the orchestra to have a good conductor.

IS THAT A FACT!

Special ceramic tiles were created for use on the underside of the space shuttle. These tiles transfer so little energy that one side can be exposed to a welder's torch while the other side remains cool to the touch.

157

Answer to APPLY

The drink holder is an insulator because it does not conduct thermal energy very well. It protects the can, which is a conductor, from energy that transfers from the warmer air to the cooler can.

DEMONSTRATION

Convection Currents Fill a 250 mL beaker about two-thirds full of water. Place the beaker on a hot plate turned on low or medium. Roll some very small pieces of aluminum foil into small, tightly packed balls. Drop the foil balls into the water, and direct students to observe what happens to the balls as the water warms up. Ask students what the movement of the foil balls suggests about the movement of water within the beaker. (The circulation of the foil balls suggests that the water in the beaker is circulating too.)

Then ask what method of heating is shown in this demonstration. (convection)

CONNECT TO EARTH SCIENCE

Convection currents caused by the uneven heating of Earth's surface are responsible for Earth's winds, weather patterns, and ocean currents. Without these currents, Earth's climates might be very different and life on Earth might also be greatly changed.

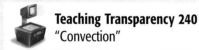

Teaching Transparency 240 "Convection"

Conductors	Insulators
Curling iron	Flannel shirt
Iron skillet	Oven mitt
Cookie sheet	Plastic spatula
Copper pipes	Fiberglass insulation
Stove coils	Ceramic bowl

Conductors and Insulators Substances that conduct thermal energy very well are called **conductors**. For example, the metal in a doctor's stethoscope is a conductor. Energy is transferred rapidly from your higher-temperature skin to the room-temperature stethoscope. That's why the stethoscope feels cold. Substances that do not conduct thermal energy very well are called **insulators**. For example, the doctor's wooden tongue depressor is an insulator. It has the same temperature as the stethoscope, but the tongue depressor doesn't feel cold. That's because thermal energy is transferred very slowly from your tongue to the wood. Compare some typical conductors and insulators in the chart at left.

Keepin' It Cool

The drink holder shown here is made from a foamlike material that helps keep your can of soda cold. How is this drink holder an insulator?

Figure 9 *The repeated rising and sinking of water during boiling is due to convection.*

Convection When you boil a pot of water, like the one shown in **Figure 9**, the water moves in roughly circular patterns because of convection. **Convection** is the transfer of thermal energy by the movement of a liquid or a gas. The water at the bottom of a pot on a stove burner gets hot because of contact with the pot itself (conduction). As a result, the hot water becomes less dense because its higher-energy particles have spread apart. The warmer water rises through the denser, cooler water above it. At the surface, the warm water begins to cool, and the lower-energy particles move closer together, making the water denser. The denser, cooler water sinks back to the bottom, where it will be heated again. This circular motion of liquids or gases due to density differences that result from temperature differences is called a *convection current*.

Science Bloopers

The use of glass fibers goes back to the ancient Egyptians, but making useful fiberglass was hard to do. Then, in 1932, as a researcher was trying to weld glass blocks together, a burst of compressed air accidentally hit some molten glass. The burst blew the molten glass into very fine glass fibers. This accident led to one of today's most common insulating materials, fiberglass.

Radiation Unlike conduction and convection, radiation can involve either an energy transfer between particles of matter or an energy transfer across empty space. **Radiation** is the transfer of energy through matter or space as electromagnetic waves, such as visible light and infrared waves.

All objects, including the heater in **Figure 10,** radiate electromagnetic waves. The sun emits mostly visible light, which you can see and your body can absorb, making you feel warmer. The Earth emits mostly infrared waves, which you cannot see but can still make you feel warmer.

Figure 10 *The coils of this portable heater warm a room by radiating visible light and infrared waves.*

Radiation and the Greenhouse Effect Earth's atmosphere, like the windows of a greenhouse, allows the sun's visible light to pass through it. But like the windows of a greenhouse keep energy inside the greenhouse, the atmosphere traps some reradiated energy. This process, called the *greenhouse effect,* is illustrated in **Figure 11.** Some scientists are concerned that high levels of greenhouse gases (water vapor, carbon dioxide, and methane) in the atmosphere may trap too much energy and make Earth too warm. However, if not for the greenhouse effect, the Earth would be a cold, lifeless planet.

Figure 11 The Greenhouse Effect

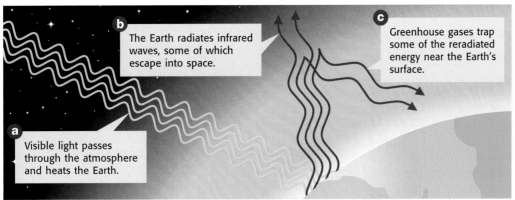

b The Earth radiates infrared waves, some of which escape into space.

c Greenhouse gases trap some of the reradiated energy near the Earth's surface.

a Visible light passes through the atmosphere and heats the Earth.

SECTION REVIEW

1. What is heat?

2. Explain how radiation is different from conduction and convection.

3. **Applying Concepts** Why do many metal cooking utensils have wooden handles?

internetconnect

SC*i*LINKS.
NSTA

TOPIC: What Is Heat?; Conduction, Convection, and Radiation
GO TO: www.scilinks.org
*sci*LINKS NUMBER: HSTP240, HSTP245

LabBook   **PG 200**
Save the Cube!

internetconnect

SC*i*LINKS.
NSTA

TOPIC: Conduction, Convection, and Radiation
GO TO: www.scilinks.org
KEYWORD: HSTP245

USING THE TABLE

Have students study the table of **Specific Heat Capacities of Some Common Substances** found on this page. Then ask the following questions:

- If you have equal masses of each of the following pairs of substances, which will become hotter faster: some silver coins or water (silver coins); a copper pan on a hot stove or its wooden handle (pan); a car's aluminum door handle sitting in the hot summer sun or the windshield (the windshield).

- Explain why water is used as a coolant. (Water has a very high specific heat capacity.)

CROSS-DISCIPLINARY FOCUS

Home Economics When an apple pie is taken from the oven, the crust cools faster than the filling. Ask students to compare the specific heat capacity of the crust with that of the filling.

Figure 12 *On a hot summer day, the metal part of a seat belt feels hotter than the cloth part.*

Meteorology
CONNECTION

Water has a higher specific heat capacity than land. This difference affects the climate of different areas on Earth. Climates in coastal areas are moderated by the ocean. Because of water's high specific heat capacity, the ocean retains a lot of thermal energy. So even in the winter, when inland temperatures drop, coastal areas stay moderately warm. Because water does not heat up as easily as land does, oceans can help to keep coastal areas cool during the summer when inland temperatures soar.

160

Heat and Temperature Change

On a hot summer day, have you ever fastened your seat belt in a car, as shown in **Figure 12**? If so, you may have noticed that the metal buckle felt hotter than the cloth belt. Why? Keep reading to learn more.

Thermal Conductivity Different substances have different thermal conductivities. *Thermal conductivity* is the rate at which a substance conducts thermal energy. Conductors, such as the metal buckle, have higher thermal conductivities than do insulators, such as the cloth belt. Because of the metal's higher thermal conductivity, it transfers energy more rapidly to your hand when you touch it than the cloth does. So even when the cloth and metal are the same temperature, the metal feels hotter.

Specific Heat Capacity Another difference between the metal and the cloth is how easily they change temperature when they absorb or lose energy. When equal amounts of energy are transferred to or from equal masses of different substances, the change in temperature for each substance will differ. **Specific heat capacity** is the amount of energy needed to change the temperature of 1 kg of a substance by 1°C.

Look at the table below. Notice that the specific heat capacity of the cloth of a seat belt is more than twice that of the metal seat belt buckle. This means that for equal masses of metal and cloth, less energy is required to change the temperature of the metal. So the metal buckle gets hot (and cools off) more quickly than an equal mass of the cloth belt.

Different substances have different specific heat capacities. Check out the specific heat capacities for various substances in the table below.

Specific Heat Capacities of Some Common Substances			
Substance	Specific heat capacity (J/kg•°C)	Substance	Specific heat capacity (J/kg•°C)
Lead	128	Metal of seat belt	500
Gold	129	Glass	837
Mercury	138	Aluminum	899
Wood	176	Cloth of seat belt	1,340
Silver	234	Steam	2,010
Copper	387	Ice	2,090
Iron	448	Water	4,184

BRAIN FOOD

Challenge students to explain whether water would be a good insulator for a home with passive solar heating, such as the Earthship that students read about in the chapter opener.

Heat—The Amount of Energy Transferred

Unlike temperature, energy transferred between objects cannot be measured directly—it must be calculated. When calculating energy transferred between objects, it is helpful to define *heat* as the amount of energy that is transferred between two objects that are at different temperatures. Heat can then be expressed in joules (J).

How much energy is required to heat a cup of water to make tea? To answer this question, you have to consider the water's mass, its change in temperature, and its specific heat capacity. In general, if you know an object's mass, its change in temperature, and its specific heat capacity, you can use the equation below to calculate heat (the amount of energy transferred).

Heat (J) = specific heat capacity (J/kg•°C) × mass (kg) × change in temperature (°C)

Mass of water = 0.2 kg
Temperature (before) = 25°C
Temperature (after) = 80°C
Specific heat capacity of water = 4,184 J/kg•°C

Figure 13 *Information used to calculate heat, the amount of energy transferred to the water, is shown above.*

Calculating Heat Using the equation above and the data in **Figure 13,** you can follow the steps below to calculate the heat added to the water. Because the water's temperature increases, the value of heat is positive. You can also use this equation to calculate the heat removed from an object when it cools down. The value for heat would then be negative because the temperature decreases.

① Write down what you know.

Specific heat capacity of water = 4,184 J/kg•°C
Mass of water = 0.2 kg
Change in temperature = 80°C − 25°C = 55°C

② Substitute the values into the equation.

Heat = specific heat capacity × mass × change in temperature
= 4,184 J/kg•°C × 0.2 kg × 55°C

③ Solve and cancel units.

Heat = 4,184 J/kg•°C × 0.2 kg × 55°C
= 4,184 J × 0.2 × 55
= 46,024 J

MATH BREAK

Calculating Energy Transfer

Use the equation at left to solve the following problems:

1. Imagine that you heat 2 L of water to make pasta. The temperature of the water before is 40°C, and the temperature after is 100°C. What is the heat involved? (Hint: 1 L of water = 1 kg of water)

2. Suppose you put a glass filled with 180 mL of water into the refrigerator. The temperature of the water before is 25°C, and the temperature after is 10°C. How much energy was transferred away from the water as it became colder?

WEIRD SCIENCE

A paper cup can be used to boil water. The water removes the thermal energy—water boils at 100°C—from the paper before the cup reaches its kindling temperature (more than 230°C).

Homework

Concept Mapping Have students use the concept of specific heat capacity to explain in a concept map why coastal cities have milder temperatures year-round than inland cities do.

RESEARCH

Have students find out how insulating materials are rated. Ask them to research what the R-values are based on and what R-values are recommended for homes in your geographic area. Students can present their results on a poster or with a model.

GOING FURTHER

A typical use of calorimetery is to figure out how much energy is transferred in a chemical reaction. When acids and bases react with each other, there is less chemical potential energy in the products than in the reacting acid and base molecules. Because energy is conserved, energy will be transferred to the reaction's environment.

Water is used in calorimeters because its specific heat capacity is well known. Have students propose a way to use water to calculate the change in chemical potential energy. (Perform the reaction in water. Measure the mass of the water and the temperature increase to calculate the amount of energy transferred to the water.)

PG 201

Counting Calories

Critical Thinking Worksheet
"Try and Try Again"

Math Skills Worksheet
"Knowing Nutrition"

Build your own calorimeter! Try the lab on page 201 of the LabBook.

Calorimeters When one object transfers thermal energy to another object, the energy lost by one object is gained by the other object. This is the key to how a *calorimeter* (KAL uh RIM uh ter) works. Inside a calorimeter, shown in **Figure 14,** thermal energy is transferred from a known mass of a test substance to a known mass of another substance, usually water.

Using a Calorimeter If a hot test substance is placed inside the calorimeter's inner container of water, the substance transfers energy to the water until thermal equilibrium is reached. By measuring the temperature change of the water and using water's specific heat capacity, you can determine the exact amount of energy transferred by the test substance to the water. You can then use this amount of energy (heat), the change in the test substance's temperature, and the mass of the test substance to calculate that substance's specific heat capacity.

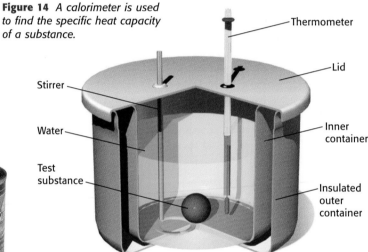

Figure 14 *A calorimeter is used to find the specific heat capacity of a substance.*

Thermometer

Lid

Stirrer

Water

Inner container

Test substance

Insulated outer container

Figure 15 *A serving of this fruit contains 120 Cal (502,080 J) of energy that becomes available when it is eaten and digested.*

Calories and Kilocalories Heat can also be expressed in units called calories. A *calorie (cal)* is the amount of energy needed to change the temperature of 0.001 kg of water by 1°C. Therefore, 1,000 calories are required to change the temperature of 1 kg of water by 1°C. One calorie is equivalent to 4.184 J. Another unit used to express heat is the *kilocalorie (kcal)*, which is equivalent to 1,000 calories. The kilocalorie is also known as a *Calorie* (with a capital C). These are the Calories listed on food labels, such as the label shown in **Figure 15.**

CROSS-DISCIPLINARY FOCUS

Health Have students examine the nutrition information labels from several packages of prepared foods or snacks to determine the number of kilocalories (Calories, with a capital C) contained in one serving. One Calorie is 1,000 calories. One calorie (lowercase c) can also be defined as the amount of energy needed to change the temperature of 1 g of water by 1°C. Then have students calculate the joules of energy that would be transferred to their body by eating one serving of each of the foods.

The Differences Between Temperature, Thermal Energy, and Heat

So far in this chapter, you have been learning about some concepts that are closely related: temperature, heat, and thermal energy. But the differences between these concepts are very important.

Temperature Versus Thermal Energy Temperature is a measure of the average kinetic energy of an object's particles, and thermal energy is the total energy of an object's particles. While thermal energy varies with the mass of an object, temperature does not. A drop of boiling water has the same temperature as a pot of boiling water, but the pot has more thermal energy because there are more particles.

Thermal Energy Versus Heat Heat and thermal energy are not the same thing; heat is a transfer of thermal energy. In addition, heat can refer to the amount of energy transferred from one object to another. Objects contain thermal energy, but they do not contain heat. The table below summarizes the differences between temperature, thermal energy, and heat.

Self-Check

How can two substances have the same temperature but different amounts of thermal energy? *(See page 232 to check your answer.)*

Temperature	Thermal energy	Heat
A measure of the average kinetic energy of the particles in a substance	The total energy of the particles in a substance	The transfer of energy between objects that are at different temperatures
Expressed in degrees Fahrenheit, degrees Celsius, or kelvins	Expressed in joules	Amount of energy transferred expressed in joules or calories
Does not vary with the mass of a substance	Varies with the mass and temperature of a substance	Varies with the mass, specific heat capacity, and temperature change of a substance

SECTION REVIEW

1. Some objects get hot more quickly than others. Why?

2. How are temperature and heat different?

3. **Applying Concepts** Examine the photo at right. How do you think the specific heat capacities for water and air influence the temperature of a swimming pool and the area around it?

163

▼ *Answers to Section Review*

1. It depends on an object's thermal conductivity. An object with a low thermal conductivity gets hotter (and cooler) more slowly than one with a high thermal conductivity.

2. Temperature is a measure of the average kinetic energy of particles in a substance. Heat is the transfer of energy between

objects that are at different temperatures (or the amount of energy transferred) and must be calculated, not measured.

3. Sample answer: Water has a higher specific heat capacity than air. The water must absorb more energy to increase its temperature than does the surrounding air, so water may feel cool even when it is hot outdoors.

4) Close

Answer to Self-Check

Two substances can have the same temperature but different amounts of thermal energy because temperature, unlike thermal energy, does not depend on mass. A small amount of a substance at a particular temperature will have less thermal energy than a large amount of the substance at the same temperature.

Quiz

Ask students whether the following statements are true or false.

1. Heat is the transfer of energy between two objects with different temperatures. (true)

2. Conduction occurs in fluids. (false)

3. Convection currents result from temperature differences in liquids and gases. (true)

4. Radiation is the means by which the energy from the sun is transferred to Earth. (true)

5. Water stays warm or cool longer than land does because water has a lower specific heat capacity than land does. (false)

ALTERNATIVE ASSESSMENT

Concept Mapping Have the students construct a concept map using the following terms:

temperature, thermal energy, heat, conduction, radiation, convection, solids, liquids, gases, vacuum

Reinforcement Worksheet
"Feel the Heat"

Focus

Matter and Heat

In this section, students learn how substances change from state to state and how heat affects matter during changes of state. They also learn how heat affects matter during chemical changes.

 **Bellringer**

Ask students to predict what changes would occur if they added an equal number of ice cubes to a glass of cold water and a glass of warm water. Ask them to explain their answer.

1 Motivate

DEMONSTRATION

On an overhead projector, place a beaker half-full of very hot water. Place a second beaker half-full of very cold water next to the first. Before turning on the projector, ask students to watch the screen. As you drop food coloring into each beaker, have students describe what they see happening in the beaker. Ask them these questions:

From your observations, which beaker contained the hotter water? How did you come to this conclusion? Predict what will happen to the molecules of a liquid if more thermal energy is added.

 Teaching Transparency 241 "Models of a Solid, a Liquid, and a Gas"

 Teaching Transparency 242 "Changes of State for Water"

Terms to Learn

states of matter
change of state

What You'll Do

◆ Identify three states of matter.
◆ Explain how heat affects matter during a change of state.
◆ Describe how heat affects matter during a chemical change.

Matter and Heat

Have you ever eaten a frozen juice bar outside on a hot summer day? It's pretty hard to finish the entire thing before it starts to drip and make a big mess! The juice bar melts because the sun radiates energy to the air, which transfers energy to the frozen juice bar. The energy absorbed by the juice bar increases the kinetic energy of the molecules in the juice bar, which starts to turn to a liquid. In this section, you'll learn more about how heat affects matter.

States of Matter

The matter that makes up a frozen juice bar has the same identity whether the juice bar is frozen or has melted. The matter is just in a different form, or state. The **states of matter** are the physical forms in which a substance can exist. Recall that matter consists of particles—atoms or molecules—that can move around at different speeds. The state a substance is in depends on the speed of its particles and the attraction between them. Three familiar states of matter are solid, liquid, and gas, represented in **Figure 16.** You may recall that thermal energy is the total energy of the particles that make up a substance. Suppose you have equal masses of a substance in its three states, each at a different temperature. The substance will have the most thermal energy as a gas and the least thermal energy as a solid. That's because the particles move around fastest in a gas.

Figure 16 Models of a Solid, a Liquid, and a Gas

Particles of a solid do not move fast enough to overcome the strong attraction between them, so they are held tightly together. The particles vibrate in place.

Particles of a liquid move fast enough to overcome some of the attraction between them. The particles are able to slide past one another.

Particles of a gas move fast enough to overcome nearly all of the attraction between them. The particles move independently of one another.

164

 Directed Reading Worksheet Section 3

```
CONNECT TO
LIFE SCIENCE
```

Life on Earth would end if there were no water. Water occurs in three states—solid, liquid, and gas—and all three are critical to survival. Even though water vapor (a gas) is invisible, it is just as important as the water we can see.

Changes of State

When you melt cheese to make a cheese dip, like that shown in **Figure 17,** the cheese changes from a solid to a thick, gooey liquid. A **change of state** is the conversion of a substance from one physical form to another. A change of state is a *physical change* that affects one or more physical properties of a substance without changing the substance's identity. Changes of state include *freezing* (liquid to solid), *melting* (solid to liquid), *boiling* (liquid to gas), and *condensing* (gas to liquid).

Graphing Changes of State Suppose you put an ice cube in a pan and set the pan on a stove burner. Soon the ice will turn to water and then to steam. If you made a graph of the energy involved versus the temperature of the ice during this process, it would look something like the graph below.

As the ice is heated, its temperature increases from –25°C to 0°C. At 0°C, the ice begins to melt. Notice that the temperature of the ice remains 0°C even as more energy is added. This added energy changes the arrangement of the particles, or molecules, in the ice. The temperature of the ice remains constant until all of the ice has become liquid water. At that point, the water's temperature will start to increase from 0°C to 100°C. At 100°C, the water will begin to turn into steam. Even as more energy is added, the water's temperature stays at 100°C. The energy added at the boiling point changes the arrangement of the particles until the water has entirely changed to a gaseous state. When all of the water has become steam, the temperature again increases.

Figure 17 *When you melt cheese, you change the state of the cheese but not its identity.*

✓ Self-Check

Why do you think you can get a more severe burn from steam than from boiling water? *(See page 232 to check your answer.)*

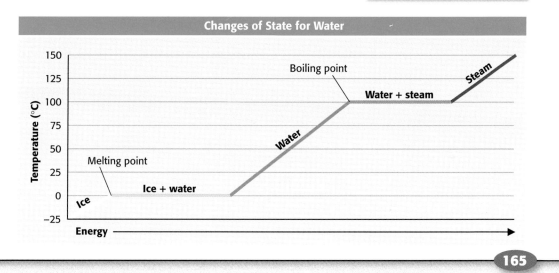

Changes of State for Water

(graph: Temperature (°C) on y-axis from –25 to 150; Energy on x-axis. Labels: Ice, Melting point, Ice + water, Water, Boiling point, Water + steam, Steam)

MISCONCEPTION ///ALERT\\\

The graph at the bottom of the page is not drawn to scale. The slope of the portions where temperature is increasing represents specific heat capacity. If the graph were drawn to scale, the slopes where ice and steam are increasing in temperature would be twice as steep as the slope where water is increasing in temperature. That's because water's specific heat capacity is roughly twice that of ice or steam. In addition, more energy is required for water to vaporize than for ice to melt. If the graph were drawn to scale, the length of the horizontal segment representing ice melting would be shorter than that for water vaporizing.

---

2) Teach

ACTIVITY

MATERIALS

FOR EACH GROUP:
- 3 thermometers
- 3 test tubes
- 10 mL each of water, nail polish remover, and isopropyl alcohol (in the test tubes)

Safety Caution: Caution students to wear safety goggles and gloves for this activity. Nail polish remover and alcohol should be handled with care.

Have students insert the thermometers into the liquids and wait for the temperatures to stabilize before taking readings. Have them record the temperatures on a chart. Then have them remove one thermometer, carefully wave it in the air, and take another temperature reading. Instruct them to record the new temperature, and then repeat the procedure for the other liquids. Ask students what caused the temperature to decrease as the thermometer was waved around. (As it evaporated, the liquid absorbed energy from the thermometer.)

USING THE FIGURE

Draw students' attention to the graph on this page. Discuss where the two plateaus occur. (at 0°C and at 100°C)

Ask students if ice can be warmer than 0°C and if liquid water can be warmer than 100°C. (No, energy added at these temperatures causes a change of state, not a temperature increase.)
Sheltered English

Answer to Self-Check

Steam can cause a more severe burn than boiling water because steam contains more energy per unit mass than does boiling water.

RESEARCH

 Ask students to find out about French chemist Pierre E. M. Berthelot (1827–1907). Have them find out what contributions he made to the study of chemical changes. (He synthesized many organic compounds, including alcohols, methane, benzene, and acetylene.)

Students can display their results in a concept map, on a poster, or by writing a poem or skit.

PORTFOLIO

4) **Close**

Quiz

Ask students whether these statements are true or false.

1. When ice changes to a liquid, it absorbs energy. (true)

2. When a liquid evaporates, it absorbs energy. (true)

3. When a vapor condenses to a liquid, energy is given off. (true)

4. When a liquid boils, energy is absorbed. (true)

ALTERNATIVE ASSESSMENT

Concept Mapping Have students make a concept map showing how heat affects matter during a change of state and during a chemical change.

internet**connect**

SC*i*LINKS

NSTA

TOPIC: Changes of State
GO TO: www.scilinks.org
KEYWORD: HSTP250

Biology
C O N N E C T I O N

The substances your body needs to survive and grow come from food. Carbohydrates, proteins, and fats are major sources of energy for the body. The energy content of food can be found by burning a dry food sample in a special calorimeter. Both carbohydrates and proteins provide 4 Cal of energy per gram, while fats provide 9 Cal of energy per gram.

Figure 18 *In a natural-gas fireplace, the methane in natural gas and the oxygen in air change into carbon dioxide and water. As a result of the change, energy is given off, making a room feel warmer.*

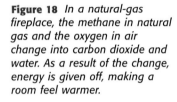

internet**connect**

SC*i*LINKS

NSTA

TOPIC: Changes of State
GO TO: www.scilinks.org
*sci*LINKS NUMBER: HSTP250

Heat and Chemical Changes

Heat is involved not only in changes of state, which are physical changes, but also in *chemical changes*—changes that occur when one or more substances are changed into entirely new substances with different properties. During a chemical change, new substances are formed. For a new substance to form, old bonds between particles must be broken and new bonds must be created. The breaking and creating of bonds between particles involves energy. Sometimes a chemical change requires that thermal energy be absorbed. For example, photosynthesis is a chemical change in which carbon dioxide and water combine to form sugar and oxygen. In order for this change to occur, energy must be absorbed. That energy is radiated by the sun. Other times, a chemical change, such as the one shown in **Figure 18**, will result in energy being released.

SECTION REVIEW

1. During a change of state, why doesn't the temperature of the substance change?

2. Compare the thermal energy of 10 g of ice with the thermal energy of the same amount of water.

3. When water evaporates (changes from a liquid to a gas), the air near the water's surface becomes cooler. Explain why.

4. **Applying Concepts** Many cold packs used for sports injuries are activated by bending the package, causing the substances inside to interact. How is heat involved in this process?

▼ *Answers to Section Review*

1. Energy added to or removed from a substance during a change of state rearranges the particles of the substance rather than raising or lowering the temperature.

2. Particles of water in the liquid state have more kinetic energy than particles of water in the solid state, so 10 mL of water has more thermal energy than 10 g of ice (if the water and ice are not at the same temperature).

3. Sample answer: For water to evaporate, it must absorb energy. The air near the water's surface transfers energy to the water to make it evaporate. Because the air loses energy, it becomes cooler.

4. Sample answer: When you bend the ice pack, the substances inside interact. That interaction absorbs so much energy that the pack feels colder.

Terms to Learn

insulation
heat engine
thermal pollution

What You'll Do

◆ Analyze several kinds of heating systems.
◆ Describe how a heat engine works.
◆ Explain how a refrigerator keeps food cold.
◆ Give examples of some effects of heat technology on the environment.

Heat Technology

You probably wouldn't be surprised to learn that the heater in your home is an example of heat technology. But did you know that automobiles, refrigerators, and air conditioners are also examples of heat technology? It's true! You can travel long distances, you can keep your food cold, and you can feel comfortable indoors during the summer—all because of heat technology.

Heating Systems

Many homes and buildings have a central heating system that controls the temperature in every room. On the next few pages, you will see some different central heating systems.

Hot-Water Heating The high specific heat capacity of water makes it useful for heating systems. In a hot-water heating system, shown in **Figure 19,** water is heated by burning fuel (usually natural gas or fuel oil) in a hot-water heater. The hot water is pumped through pipes that lead to radiators in each room. The hot water heats the radiators, and the radiators then heat the colder air surrounding them. The water returns to the hot-water heater to be heated again. A *steam-heating system* is similar, except that steam is used in place of water.

Figure 19
A Hot-Water Heating System

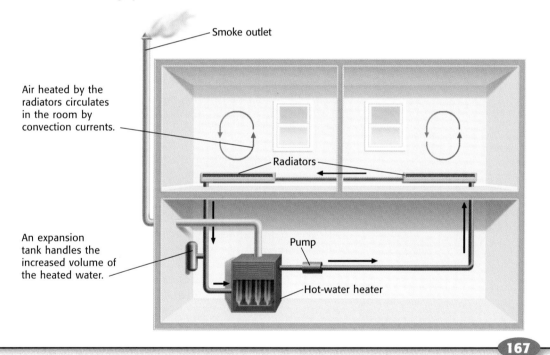

Smoke outlet

Air heated by the radiators circulates in the room by convection currents.

Radiators

An expansion tank handles the increased volume of the heated water.

Pump

Hot-water heater

167

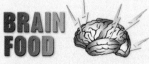
BRAIN FOOD

An advantage to using steam instead of water is that steam has a higher temperature than hot water. However, it is more difficult to regulate room temperature with a steam-heating system than with a hot-water heating system.

CROSS-DISCIPLINARY FOCUS

History The first heating systems developed by people were probably open fires in caves. When people found a way to make a hole in the side or top of the cave to let the smoke out, a type of fireplace was created. Fireplaces with a chimney tall enough to provide adequate draft for fires were first built in the twelfth century.

Focus
Heat Technology

In this section, students learn about different kinds of heating systems, heat engines, and cooling systems. They also learn about some effects of heat on the environment.

🔔 Bellringer

Write the following on the board:

Predict whether leaving the refrigerator door open on a hot summer day will help to cool the kitchen. Explain your answer.

Have students write their responses in their ScienceLog. Review these predictions after students have read pages 171 and 172.

1 Motivate

DISCUSSION

Have students work together to hypothesize about how a refrigerator or an air conditioner works and how heat is involved in an appliance that cools. Have the groups share their hypotheses with the class. Discuss with students some ways people may have cooled their homes before air conditioners were invented, and have them imagine what their lives would be like today without heating or air conditioning.

Directed Reading Worksheet Section 4

READING 📖 STRATEGY

Prediction Before students read this section, have them predict the answers to the following questions about heating and cooling systems:

- Where should a heat register or heating vent be placed for maximum effect? (on the floor)
- Where should the cold-air return be placed? (on the floor)
- If you were cooling a house with central air conditioning, where would you place the cold-air register? (on the ceiling) the warm-air return? (on the ceiling)

MISCONCEPTION //// ALERT

Students often believe that blankets provide thermal energy. Explain that blankets insulate the body; the air pockets in the blanket material slow the escape of thermal energy from the body into the air, and the feeling of warmth results. Electric blankets are an exception.

Homework

Have students investigate the type of heating and cooling systems used in their home. Ask them to draw a diagram of their home showing the placement of the equipment (fireplaces, registers, cold-air intakes, hot-water pipes, radiators, and so on) used to keep their home warm or cool.

Warm-Air Heating Although air has a lower specific heat capacity than water, warm-air heating systems are used in many homes and offices in the United States. In a warm-air heating system, shown in **Figure 20,** air is heated in a separate chamber by burning fuel (usually natural gas) in a furnace. The warm air travels through ducts to different rooms, which it enters through vents. The warm air heats air in the rooms. Cooler air sinks below the warm air and enters a vent near the floor. Then a fan forces the cooler air into the furnace, where the air will be heated and returned to the ducts. An air filter cleans the air as it circulates through the system.

Figure 20
A Warm-Air Heating System

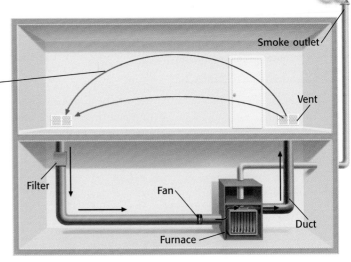

Warm air is circulated in the rooms by convection currents.

Smoke outlet

Vent

Filter

Fan

Duct

Furnace

Figure 21 *Millions of tiny air pockets in this insulation help prevent thermal energy from flowing into or out of a building.*

Heating and Insulation Thermal energy may be transferred out of a house during cold weather and into a house during hot weather. To keep the house comfortable, a heating system must run almost continuously during the winter, and air conditioners often do the same during the summer. This can be wasteful. That's where insulation comes in. **Insulation** is a substance that reduces the transfer of thermal energy. Insulation, such as the fiberglass insulation shown in **Figure 21,** is made of insulators—materials that do not conduct thermal energy very well. Insulation that is used in walls, ceilings, and floors helps a house stay warm in the winter and cool in the summer.

Insulation is made of a variety of materials. The effectiveness of an insulating material is its R-value. The higher the R-value, the greater the insulating effectiveness. The R-value of a material depends on the type of material, its thickness, and its density.

168

Solar Heating The sun radiates an enormous amount of energy. Solar heating systems use this energy to heat houses and buildings. *Passive solar heating* systems do not have moving parts. They rely on a building's structural design and materials to use energy from the sun as a means of heating. *Active solar heating* systems do have moving parts. They use pumps and fans to distribute the sun's energy throughout a building.

Look at the house in **Figure 22.** The large windows on the south side of the house are part of the passive solar heating system. These windows receive maximum sunlight, and energy is radiated through the windows into the rooms. Thick, well-insulated concrete walls absorb energy and heat the house at night or when it is cloudy. In the active solar heating system, water is pumped to the solar collector, where it is heated. The hot water is pumped through pipes and transfers its energy to them. A fan blowing over the pipes helps the pipes transfer their thermal energy to the air. Warm air is then sent into rooms through vents. Cooler water returns to the water storage tank to be pumped back through the solar collector.

Figure 22 *Passive and active solar heating systems work together to use the sun's energy to heat an entire house.*

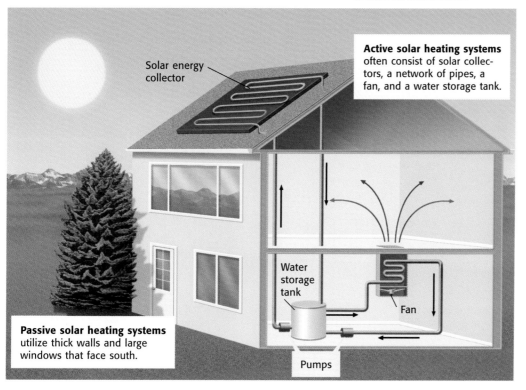

Solar energy collector

Active solar heating systems often consist of solar collectors, a network of pipes, a fan, and a water storage tank.

Water storage tank

Fan

Passive solar heating systems utilize thick walls and large windows that face south.

Pumps

IS THAT A FACT!

Earth receives enough energy from the sun in 1 minute to meet the planet's energy demands for an entire year. If humans could find better ways to capture and use solar energy, dependence on fossil fuels for energy sources could be reduced.

CROSS-DISCIPLINARY FOCUS

History In 1769, Nicolas-Joseph Cugnot (1725–1804), a French Army engineer, built a three-wheeled, steam-powered tractor. It traveled very slowly (3.6 km/h) and had to stop every 20 minutes to build up a fresh head of steam. Cugnot's tractor was hard to drive and not very practical, but his ideas led others to create better self-propelled vehicles.

USING THE FIGURE

Concept Mapping Ask students to study **Figures 23** and **24.** Have them create a concept map that shows the similarities and differences between an external combustion engine and an internal combustion engine. The concept map should show the source of the energy, what the energy does, where the combustion takes place, and any other features of the two types of engines.

Ask students which type of engine is more efficient and why.

Oceanography
CONNECTION

Ocean engineers are developing a new technology known as Ocean Thermal Energy Conversion, or OTEC. OTEC uses temperature differences between surface water and deep water in the ocean to do work like a heat engine does. Warm surface water vaporizes a fluid, such as ammonia, causing it to expand. Then cool water from ocean depths causes the fluid to condense and contract. The continuous cycle of vaporizing and condensing converts thermal energy into kinetic energy that can be used to generate electrical energy.

Heat Engines

Did you know that automobiles work because of heat? A car has a **heat engine,** a machine that uses heat to do work. In a heat engine, fuel combines with oxygen in a chemical change that produces thermal energy. This process, called *combustion,* is how engines burn fuel. Heat engines that burn fuel outside the engine are called *external combustion engines.* Heat engines that burn fuel inside the engine are called *internal combustion engines.* In both types of engines, fuel is burned to produce thermal energy that can be used to do work.

External Combustion Engine A simple steam engine, shown in **Figure 23,** is an example of an external combustion engine. Coal is burned to heat water in a boiler and change the water to steam. When water changes to steam, it expands. The expanding steam is used to drive a piston, which can be attached to other mechanisms that do work, such as a flywheel. Modern steam engines, such as those used to generate electrical energy at a power plant, drive turbines instead of pistons.

Figure 23 An External Combustion Engine

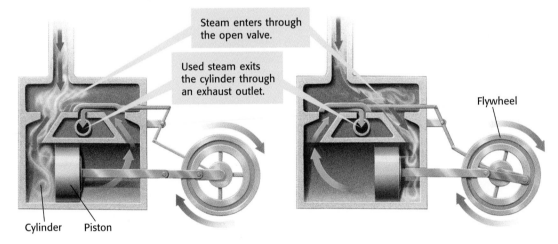

Steam enters through the open valve.

Used steam exits the cylinder through an exhaust outlet.

Flywheel

Cylinder   Piston

a The expanding steam enters the cylinder from one side. The steam does work on the piston, forcing the piston to move.

b As the piston moves to the other side, a second valve opens and steam enters. The steam does work on the piston and moves it back. The motion of the piston turns a flywheel.

170

Science Bloopers

When automobiles were first built, they shared the roads with horses. Horses were often quite frightened by the cars. Uriah Smith, founder of a "horseless carriage" company in Michigan, came up with a solution to this problem: He made an automobile with a wooden, life-size horse head on the front. Unfortunately, this did nothing to quiet the noise of the engine, and horses were still frightened by cars.

Internal Combustion Engine In the six-cylinder car engine shown in **Figure 24,** fuel is burned inside the engine. During the intake stroke, a mixture of gasoline and air enters each cylinder as the piston moves down. Next the crankshaft turns and pushes the piston up, compressing the fuel mixture. This is called the compression stroke. Next comes the power stroke, in which the spark plug uses electrical energy to ignite the compressed fuel mixture, causing the mixture to expand and force the piston down. Finally, during the exhaust stroke, the crankshaft turns and the piston is forced back up, pushing exhaust gases out of the cylinder.

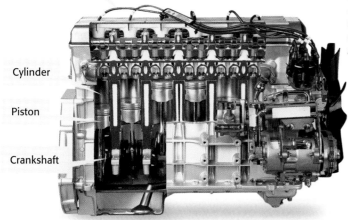

Wire to spark plug

Cylinder

Piston

Crankshaft

Figure 24 *The continuous cycling of the four strokes in the cylinders converts thermal energy into the kinetic energy required to make a car move.*

Cooling Systems

When it gets hot in the summer, an air-conditioned room can feel very refreshing. Cooling systems are used to transfer thermal energy out of a particular area so that it feels cooler. An air conditioner, shown in **Figure 25,** is a cooling system that transfers thermal energy from a warm area inside a building or car to an area outside, where it is often even warmer. But wait a minute—doesn't that go against the natural direction of heat—from higher temperatures to lower temperatures? Well, yes. A cooling system moves thermal energy from cooler temperatures to warmer temperatures. But in order to do that, the cooling system must do work.

Figure 25 *This air conditioning unit keeps a building cool by moving thermal energy from inside the building to the outside.*

171

USING THE FIGURE

After students have studied **Figure 26,** discuss with them how refrigeration has affected food storage and the kinds of foods we eat. What did refrigeration allow that had never been possible before?

GOING FURTHER

Have interested students investigate the controversy about the effect of Freon™ on the environment. Students should also research the alternatives to Freon. Explain that Freon used to be a commonly used refrigerant in the United States.

CROSS-DISCIPLINARY FOCUS

History The air conditioning systems we use today evolved from commercial refrigeration systems. In 1902, a young engineer named Willis Carrier helped a printing company that was having a problem with its color printing. Humidity caused the paper to expand or shrink. The colored inks would not align correctly, which caused fuzzy pictures. Carrier intended to control humidity with his device. To his surprise, the air was not only drier but also cooler. Carrier patented his machine in 1906 and made his first international sale to a silk mill in Japan in 1907. In this country, textile mills in the southern states were among the first to use Carrier's machines. The Carrier Corporation still manufactures air conditioners for homes and businesses today.

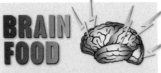

BRAIN FOOD

If you had a refrigerator in Antarctica, you would have to heat it to keep it running. Otherwise, the refrigerator would transfer energy to its surroundings until it reached the same temperature as its surroundings. It would freeze!

Cooling Takes Energy Most cooling systems require electrical energy to do the work of cooling. The electrical energy is used by a device called a compressor. The compressor does the work of compressing the refrigerant, a gas that has a boiling point below room temperature. This property of the refrigerant allows it to condense easily.

To keep many foods fresh, you store them in a refrigerator. A refrigerator is another example of a cooling system. **Figure 26** shows how a refrigerator continuously transfers thermal energy from inside the refrigerator to the condenser coils on the outside of the refrigerator. That's why the area near the back of a refrigerator feels warm.

Figure 26 How a Refrigerator Works

③ When the liquid passes through the expansion valve, it goes from a high-pressure area to a low-pressure area. As a result, the temperature of the liquid decreases.

Low pressure

High pressure

④ As the cold liquid refrigerant moves through the evaporating coils, it absorbs thermal energy from the refrigerator compartment, making the inside of the refrigerator cold. As a result, the temperature of the refrigerant increases, and it changes into a gas.

⑤ The gas is then returned to the compressor, and the cycle repeats.

② The hot gas flows through the condenser coils on the outside of the refrigerator. The gas condenses into a liquid, transferring some of its thermal energy to the coils.

① The compressor uses electrical energy to compress the refrigerant gas; this compression increases the pressure and temperature of the gas.

IS THAT A FACT!

A German scientist named Karl von Linde (1842–1934) made the first practical refrigerator, which used ammonia as the refrigerant.

Heat Technology and Thermal Pollution

Heating systems, car engines, and cooling systems all transfer thermal energy to the environment. Unfortunately, too much thermal energy can have a negative effect on the environment.

One of the negative effects of excess thermal energy is **thermal pollution,** the excessive heating of a body of water. Thermal pollution can occur near large power plants, which are often located near a body of water. Electric power plants burn fuel to produce thermal energy that is used to generate electrical energy. Unfortunately, it is not possible for all of that thermal energy to do work, so some waste thermal energy results. **Figure 27** shows how a cooling tower helps remove this waste thermal energy in order to keep the power plants operating smoothly. In extreme cases, the increase in temperature downstream from a power plant can adversely affect the ecosystem of the river or lake. Some power plants reduce thermal pollution by reducing the temperature of the water before it is returned to the river.

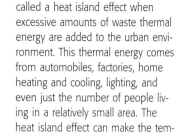

Environment CONNECTION

Large cities can exhibit something called a heat island effect when excessive amounts of waste thermal energy are added to the urban environment. This thermal energy comes from automobiles, factories, home heating and cooling, lighting, and even just the number of people living in a relatively small area. The heat island effect can make the temperature of the air in a city higher than that of the air in the surrounding countryside.

Figure 27 *Cool water is circulated through a power plant to absorb waste thermal energy.*

Cool water

Warm water

SECTION REVIEW

1. Compare a hot-water heating system with a warm-air heating system.

2. What is the difference between an external combustion engine and an internal combustion engine?

3. **Analyzing Relationships** How are changes of state an important part of the way a refrigerator works?

internet**connect**

*sci*LINKS
NSTA

TOPIC: Heating Systems
GO TO: www.scilinks.org
*sci*LINKS NUMBER: HSTP252

173

Feel the Heat
Teacher's Notes

Time Required

One or two 45-minute class periods

Lab Ratings

EASY —————— HARD

TEACHER PREP 🍼🍼🍼
STUDENT SET-UP 🍼🍼
CONCEPT LEVEL 🍼🍼🍼
CLEAN UP 🍼🍼

MATERIALS

Materials listed are for each group of 2–4 students.

Safety Caution

Caution students to review all safety cautions and icons before beginning this activity. Remind students that a thermometer should never be used for stirring. The container of hot water should be located where it cannot spill on students. Caution students to handle the nails carefully.

Procedure Notes

Heat water before class. Do not let the water temperature exceed 60°C. You may want to keep a large container of water heating on a hot plate. For step 4, the nails are set aside for about 5 minutes so that they will warm up to the same temperature as the water.

Answer

1. Accept all reasonable predictions.

Discovery Lab

USING SCIENTIFIC METHODS

Feel the Heat

Heat is the transfer of energy between objects at different temperatures. Energy moves from objects at higher temperatures to objects at lower temperatures. If two objects are left in contact for a while, the warmer object will cool down and the cooler object will warm up until they eventually reach the same temperature. In this activity, you will combine equal masses of water and iron nails at different temperatures to determine which has a greater effect on the final temperature.

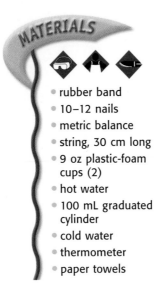

MATERIALS

- rubber band
- 10–12 nails
- metric balance
- string, 30 cm long
- 9 oz plastic-foam cups (2)
- hot water
- 100 mL graduated cylinder
- cold water
- thermometer
- paper towels

174

Datasheets for LabBook

Make a Prediction

1 When you combine substances at different temperatures, will the final temperature be closer to the initial temperature of the warmer substance or the colder substance, or halfway in between? Write your prediction in your ScienceLog.

Conduct an Experiment/Collect Data

2 Copy the table on the next page into your ScienceLog.

3 Use the rubber band to bundle the nails together. Find and record the mass of the bundle. Tie a length of string around the bundle, leaving one end of the string 15 cm long.

4 Put the bundle of nails into one of the cups. Hang the string outside the cup. Fill the cup with enough hot water to cover the nails, and set it aside for at least 5 minutes.

5 In the graduated cylinder, measure cold water exactly equal to the mass of the nails (1 mL of water = 1 g). Record this volume in the table.

6 Measure and record the temperature of the hot water with the nails, and the temperature of the cold water.

7 Use the string to move the bundle of nails to the cup of cold water. Use the thermometer to monitor the temperature of this water-nail mixture. When the temperature stops changing, record this final temperature in the table.

8 Empty the cups, and dry the nails.

CLASSROOM TESTED & APPROVED

Dennis Hanson
Big Bear Middle School
Big Bear Lake, California

Data Collection Table

Trial	Mass of nails (g)	Volume of water that equals mass of nails (mL)	Initial temp. of water and nails (°C)	Initial temp. of water to which nails will be transferred (°C)	Final temp. of water and nails combined (°C)
1					
2					

DO NOT WRITE IN BOOK

9 For Trial 2, repeat steps 3 through 8, but switch the order of the hot and cold water. Record all of your measurements.

Analyze the Results

10 In Trial 1, you used equal masses of cold water and nails. Did the final temperature support your initial prediction? Explain.

11 In Trial 2, you used equal masses of hot water and nails. Did the final temperature support your initial prediction? Explain.

12 In Trial 1, which substance—the water or the nails—changed temperature the most after you transferred the nails? What about in Trial 2? Explain your answers.

Draw Conclusions

13 The cold water in Trial 1 gained energy. Infer where the energy came from.

14 Evaluate how the energy gained by the nails in Trial 2 compares with the energy lost by the hot water in Trial 2. Explain.

15 Which material seems to be able to hold energy better? Explain your answer.

16 Specific heat capacity is a property of matter that indicates how much energy is required to change the temperature of 1 kg of a material by 1°C. Which material in this activity has a higher specific heat

capacity (changes temperature less for the same amount of energy)—the nails or the water?

17 Would it be better to have pots and pans made from a material with a high specific heat capacity or a low specific heat capacity? Explain your answer.

Communicate Results

18 Discuss with classmates how you would change your initial prediction to include specific heat capacity.

175

Chapter Highlights

Chapter Highlights

VOCABULARY DEFINITIONS

SECTION 1

temperature a measure of how hot (or cold) something is; specifically, a measure of the average kinetic energy of the particles in an object

thermal expansion the increase in volume of a substance due to an increase in temperature

absolute zero the lowest possible temperature (0 K, −273°C)

SECTION 2

heat the transfer of energy between objects that are at different temperatures; the amount of energy that is transferred between objects that are at different temperatures; energy is always transferred from higher-temperature objects to lower-temperature objects until thermal equilibrium is reached

thermal energy the total energy of the particles that make up an object

conduction the transfer of thermal energy from one substance to another through direct contact; conduction can also occur within a substance

conductor a substance that conducts thermal energy very well

insulator a substance that does not conduct thermal energy very well

convection the transfer of thermal energy by the movement of a liquid or a gas

radiation the transfer of energy through matter or space as electromagnetic waves, such as visible light and infrared waves

specific heat capacity the amount of energy needed to change the temperature of 1 kg of a substance by 1°C; specific heat capacity is a characteristic property of a substance

---

SECTION 1

Vocabulary

temperature (p. 150)
thermal expansion (p. 152)
absolute zero (p. 153)

Section Notes

- Temperature is a measure of the average kinetic energy of the particles of a substance. It is a specific measurement of how hot or cold a substance is.

- Thermal expansion is the increase in volume of a substance due to an increase in temperature. Temperature is measured according to the expansion of the liquid in a thermometer.

- Fahrenheit, Celsius, and Kelvin are three temperature scales.

- Absolute zero—0 K, or −273°C— is the lowest possible temperature.

- A thermostat works according to the thermal expansion of a bimetallic strip.

SECTION 2

Vocabulary

heat (p. 155)
thermal energy (p. 156)
conduction (p. 157)
conductor (p. 158)
insulator (p. 158)
convection (p. 158)
radiation (p. 159)
specific heat capacity (p. 160)

Section Notes

- Heat is the transfer of energy between objects that are at different temperatures.

- Thermal energy is the total energy of the particles that make up a substance.

- Energy transfer will always occur from higher temperatures to lower temperatures until thermal equilibrium is reached.

☑ Skills Check

Math Concepts

TEMPERATURE CONVERSION To convert between different temperature scales, you can use the equations found on page 153. The example below shows you how to convert a Fahrenheit temperature to a Celsius temperature.

Convert 41°F to °C.

$$°C = \frac{5}{9} \times (°F - 32)$$

$$°C = \frac{5}{9} \times (41°F - 32)$$

$$°C = \frac{5}{9} \times 9 = 5°C$$

Visual Understanding

HEAT—A TRANSFER OF ENERGY Remember that thermal energy is transferred between objects at different temperatures until both objects reach the same temperature. Look back at Figure 7, on page 156, to review what you've learned about heat.

176

Lab and Activity Highlights

Feel the Heat `PG 174`

Save the Cube! `PG 200`

Counting Calories `PG 201`

Datasheets for LabBook
(blackline masters for these labs)

SECTION 2

- Conduction, convection, and radiation are three methods of energy transfer.

- Specific heat capacity is the amount of energy needed to change the temperature of 1 kg of a substance by 1°C. Different substances have different specific heat capacities.

- Energy transferred by heat cannot be measured directly. It must be calculated using specific heat capacity, mass, and change in temperature.

- A calorimeter is used to determine the specific heat capacity of a substance.

Labs

Save the Cube! (*p. 200*)
Counting Calories (*p. 201*)

SECTION 3

Vocabulary
states of matter (*p. 164*)
change of state (*p. 165*)

Section Notes

- A substance's state is determined by the speed of its particles and the attraction between them.

- Thermal energy transferred during a change of state does not change a substance's temperature. Rather, it causes a substance's particles to be rearranged.

- Chemical changes can cause thermal energy to be absorbed or released.

SECTION 4

Vocabulary
insulation (*p. 168*)
heat engine (*p. 170*)
thermal pollution (*p. 173*)

Section Notes

- Central heating systems include hot-water heating systems and warm-air heating systems.

- Solar heating systems can be passive or active.

- Heat engines use heat to do work. External combustion engines burn fuel outside the engine. Internal combustion engines burn fuel inside the engine.

- A cooling system transfers thermal energy from cooler temperatures to warmer temperatures by doing work.

- Transferring excess thermal energy to lakes and rivers can result in thermal pollution.

SECTION 3

states of matter the physical forms in which a substance can exist

change of state the conversion of a substance from one physical form to another

SECTION 4

insulation a substance that reduces the transfer of thermal energy

heat engine a machine that uses heat to do work

thermal pollution the excessive heating of a body of water

 Vocabulary Review Worksheet

 Blackline masters of these Chapter Highlights can be found in the **Study Guide**.

---

internet connect

GO TO: go.hrw.com

*SCI*LINKS_{sm}
N S T A

GO TO: www.scilinks.org

Visit the **HRW** Web site for a variety of learning tools related to this chapter. Just type in the keyword:

KEYWORD: HSTHOT

Visit the **National Science Teachers Association** on-line Web site for Internet resources related to this chapter. Just type in the *sci*LINKS number for more information about the topic:

TOPIC: What Is Temperature?   **sciLINKS NUMBER:** HSTP230
TOPIC: What Is Heat?   **sciLINKS NUMBER:** HSTP240
TOPIC: Conduction, Convection, and Radiation   **sciLINKS NUMBER:** HSTP245
TOPIC: Changes of State   **sciLINKS NUMBER:** HSTP250
TOPIC: Heating Systems   **sciLINKS NUMBER:** HSTP252

177

Lab and Activity Highlights

LabBank

 Whiz-Bang Demonstrations, Cool It

Calculator-Based Labs
- How Low Can You Go?
- Counting Calories
- Feel the Heat

 Labs You Can Eat, Baked Alaska

EcoLabs & Field Activities, Energy-Efficient Home

Long-Term Projects & Research Ideas, Firewalking Exposed

1. Temperature is a direct measure of the average kinetic energy of the particles of a substance; thermal energy is the total kinetic energy of the particles of the substance.

2. Heat is the transfer of energy between objects at different temperatures. Thermal energy is energy transferred by heat.

3. A conductor is a material that conducts energy easily. An insulator is a material that does not conduct energy easily.

4. Conduction is the transfer of energy from one substance to another through direct contact. Convection is the transfer of energy by the movement of a gas or a liquid.

5. The states of matter are the physical forms in which a substance can exist. A change of state occurs when a substance changes from one state to another.

UNDERSTANDING CONCEPTS

Multiple Choice

6. c	**10.** d
7. b	**11.** a
8. b	**12.** b
9. c	

Short Answer

13. Temperature is a direct measure of the average kinetic energy of the particles in a substance. The more kinetic energy the particles have, the higher the temperature of the substance.

14. Specific heat capacity is the amount of energy needed to change the temperature of 1 kg of a substance by 1°C. Specific heat capacity determines the rate at which a substance changes temperature. Every substance has a unique specific heat capacity.

USING VOCABULARY

For each pair of terms, explain the difference in their meanings.

1. temperature/thermal energy

2. heat/thermal energy

3. conductor/insulator

4. conduction/convection

5. states of matter/change of state

UNDERSTANDING CONCEPTS

Multiple Choice

6. Which of the following temperatures is the lowest?
- **a.** 100°C
- **b.** 100°F
- **c.** 100 K
- **d.** They are the same.

7. Compared with the Pacific Ocean, a cup of hot chocolate has
- **a.** more thermal energy and a higher temperature.
- **b.** less thermal energy and a higher temperature.
- **c.** more thermal energy and a lower temperature.
- **d.** less thermal energy and a lower temperature.

8. The energy units on a food label are
- **a.** degrees.
- **b.** Calories.
- **c.** calories.
- **d.** joules.

9. Which of the following materials would not be a good insulator?
- **a.** wood
- **b.** cloth
- **c.** metal
- **d.** rubber

---

10. The engine in a car is a(n)
- **a.** heat engine.
- **b.** external combustion engine.
- **c.** internal combustion engine.
- **d.** Both (a) and (c)

11. Materials that warm up or cool down very quickly have a
- **a.** low specific heat capacity.
- **b.** high specific heat capacity.
- **c.** low temperature.
- **d.** high temperature.

12. In an air conditioner, thermal energy is
- **a.** transferred from higher to lower temperatures.
- **b.** transferred from lower to higher temperatures.
- **c.** used to do work.
- **d.** taken from air outside a building and transferred to air inside the building.

Short Answer

13. How does temperature relate to kinetic energy?

14. What is specific heat capacity?

15. Explain how heat affects matter during a change of state.

16. Describe how a bimetallic strip works in a thermostat.

---

15. During a change of state, the thermal energy transferred to or from the matter is used to rearrange the particles of the matter. This rearranging involves overcoming the attraction between particles (as when a solid changes to a liquid) or increasing the attraction between particles (as when a liquid changes to a solid).

16. A bimetallic strip is made of two metals that expand and contract at different rates with changes in temperature. If the temperature drops below the thermostat setting, the strip coils up. This causes a glass tube to tilt, and a drop of mercury rolls down the tube to close an electric circuit that turns on the heater. When the temperature rises, the process is reversed.

Concept Mapping

17. Use the following terms to create a concept map: thermal energy, temperature, radiation, heat, conduction, convection.

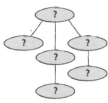

18. Why does placing a jar under warm running water help loosen the lid on the jar?

19. Why do you think a down-filled jacket keeps you so warm? (Hint: Think about what insulation does.)

20. Would opening the refrigerator cool a room in a house? Why or why not?

21. In a hot-air balloon, air is heated by a flame. Explain how this enables the balloon to float in the air.

MATH IN SCIENCE

22. The weather forecast calls for a temperature of 86°F. What is the corresponding temperature in degrees Celsius? in kelvins?

23. Suppose 1,300 mL of water are heated from 20°C to 100°C. How much energy was transferred to the water? (Hint: Water's specific heat capacity is 4,184 J/kg•°C.)

INTERPRETING GRAPHICS

Examine the graph below, and then answer the questions that follow.

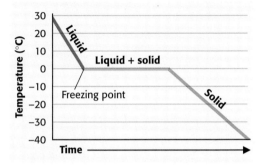

24. What physical change does this graph illustrate?

25. What is the freezing point of this liquid?

26. What is happening at the point where the line is horizontal?

Reading Check-up

Take a minute to review your answers to the Pre-Reading Questions found at the bottom of page 148. Have your answers changed? If necessary, revise your answers based on what you have learned since you began this chapter.

179

Concept Mapping

17. An answer to this exercise can be found at the front of this book.

CRITICAL THINKING AND PROBLEM SOLVING

18. The water warms the lid, causing it to expand so that it can be removed more easily.

19. Inside a down-filled jacket are thousands of air pockets between the feathers. You stay warm because these air pockets slow the transfer of energy from your body to the cooler air outside the jacket.

20. No; a refrigerator transfers thermal energy from its interior into the room. If you open the refrigerator door, its interior warms up, and it has to transfer even more thermal energy away from its interior.

21. Heating the air increases the kinetic energy of the air particles, causing them to move faster and spread apart. As a result, the warmer air rises and the balloon floats.

MATH IN SCIENCE

22. 30°C; 303 K
23. Energy transferred = 4,184 J/kg•°C × 1.3 kg × 80°C = 435,136 J

INTERPRETING GRAPHICS

24. freezing; a change of state from liquid to a solid
25. 0°C
26. a change of state; Energy is being transferred away from the substance and the attraction between particles is increasing.

Concept Mapping Transparency 10

Blackline masters of this Chapter Review can be found in the **Study Guide.**

Background

Scientists know that as gases approach absolute zero, they condense into a state of matter called a Bose-Einstein condensate. This state is named for physicists Satyendra Nath Bose and Albert Einstein. At these very low temperatures, almost all particle motion ceases and the particles overlap one another. In 1999, scientists used a thick Bose-Einstein condensate of sodium atoms to slow the speed of a beam of light to 61 km/h.

Discussion

Why is cryogenics useful to biological researchers? (Scientists can preserve tissues and test the effects of extremely low temperatures on living tissue.)

Science, Technology, and Society
The Deep Freeze

In the dark reaches of outer space, temperatures can drop below −270°C. Perhaps the only place colder is a laboratory here on Earth!

The Quest for Zero

All matter is made up of tiny, constantly vibrating particles. Temperature is a measure of the average kinetic energy of these particles. The colder a substance gets, the less kinetic energy its particles have and the slower the particles move. In theory, at absolute zero (−273°C), all movement of matter should stop. Scientists are working in laboratories to slow down matter so much that the temperature approaches absolute zero.

How Low Can They Go?

Using lasers, along with magnets, mirrors, and supercold chemicals, scientists have cooled matter to within a few billionths of a degree of absolute zero. In one method, scientists aim lasers at tiny gas particles inside a special chamber. The lasers hold the particles so still that their temperature approaches −272.999998°C.

To get an idea of what takes place, imagine turning on several garden hoses as high as they can go. Then direct the streams of water at a soccer ball so that each stream pushes the ball from a different angle. If the hoses are aimed properly, the ball won't roll in any direction. That's similar to what happens to the particles in the scientists' experiment.

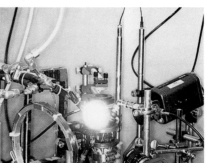

▲ *This laser device is used to cool matter to nearly absolute zero.*

Cryogenics—Cold Temperature Technology

Supercold temperatures have led to some super-cool technology. Cryosurgery, which is surgery that uses extremely low temperatures, allows doctors to seal off tiny blood vessels during an operation or to freeze diseased cells and destroy them.

Cooling materials to near absolute zero has also led to the discovery of superconductors. Superconductors are materials that lose all of their electrical resistance when they are cooled to a low enough temperature. Imagine the possibilities for materials that could conduct electricity indefinitely without any energy loss. Unfortunately, it takes a great deal of energy to cool such materials. Right now, applications for superconductors are still just the stuff of dreams.

Freezing Fun on Your Own

▶ You can try your hand at cryoinvestigation. Place 50 mL of tap water, 50 mL of salt water (50 mL of water plus 15 g of salt), and 50 mL of rubbing alcohol (isopropanol) in three separate plastic containers. Then put all three containers in your freezer at the same time. Check the containers every 5 minutes for 40 minutes. Which liquid freezes first? How can you explain any differences?

180

Answers to Freezing Fun on Your Own

The tap water should freeze first. The salt water should freeze second. The alcohol should not freeze at all because alcohol's freezing point (−117.3°C) is below the temperature of the freezer. Different liquids freeze at different temperatures. (Remind students not to ingest these substances.)

DiAPLEX®: The Intelligent Fabric

Wouldn't it be great if you had a winter coat that could automatically adjust to keep you cozy regardless of the outside temperature? Well, scientists have developed a new fabric, called DiAPLEX, that can be used to make such a coat!

With Pores or Without?

Winter adventurers usually wear nylon fabrics to keep warm. These nylon fabrics are laminated with a thin coating that contains thousands of tiny pores, or openings. The pores allow moisture, such as sweat from your body, and excess thermal energy to escape. You might think the pores would let moisture and cold air into the fabric, but that's not the case. Because the pores are so small, the nylon fabric is windproof and waterproof.

DiAPLEX is also made from laminated nylon, but the coating is different. DiAPLEX doesn't have pores; it is a solid film. This film makes DiAPLEX even more waterproof and breathable than other laminated nylon fabrics. So how does it work?

Moving Particles

DiAPLEX keeps you warm by taking advantage of how particles move. When the air outside is cold, the particles of DiAPLEX arrange themselves into a solid sheet, forming an insulator and preventing the transfer of thermal energy from your body to colder surroundings. As your body gets warm, such as after exercising, the fabric's particles respond to your body's increased thermal energy. Their kinetic energy increases, and they rearrange to create millions of tiny openings that allow excess thermal energy and moisture to escape.

Donning DiAPLEX

DiAPLEX has a number of important advantages over traditional nylon fabrics. Salts in perspiration and ice can clog the pores of traditional nylon fabrics, decreasing their ability to keep you warm and dry. But DiAPLEX does not have this problem because it contains no pores. Because DiAPLEX is unaffected by UV light and is machine washable, it is also a durable fabric that is easy to care for.

Anatomy Connection

▶ Do some research to find out how your skin lets thermal energy and moisture escape.

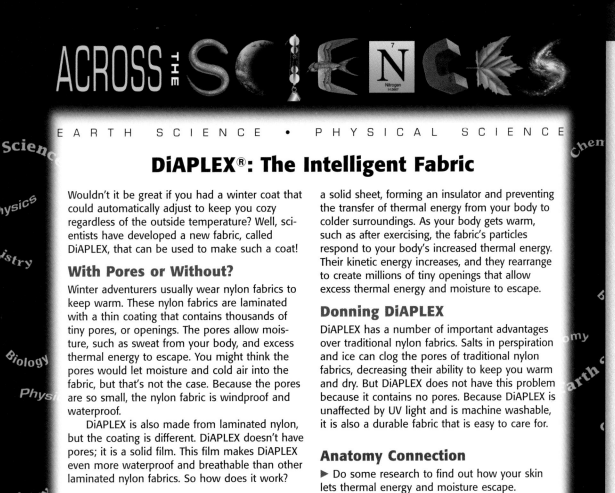

▶ *When your body is cold, the DiAPLEX garment adjusts to prevent the transfer of thermal energy from your body to its surroundings, and you feel warmer.*

▶ *When your body gets too warm, the DiAPLEX garment adjusts to allow your body to transfer excess thermal energy and moisture to your surroundings, and you feel cooler.*

Thermal energy

Moisture

181

Background

DiAPLEX® fabric allows moisture to escape twice as fast as regular microporous fabrics do, and it maintains a constant internal temperature of 0°C.

This may sound cold, but at temperatures above 0°C, skiers begin to leave their microporous jackets on the slopes. The jackets don't allow enough body heat to escape, and the skiers start to sweat. People who wear DiAPLEX garments, however, remove layers of clothing far less frequently.

DiAPLEX works on the principles of micro-Brownian motion, the random, zigzag motion of particles in solution. This phenomenon was first observed by the British botanist Robert Brown in 1827.

Students may find DiAPLEX intriguing because the molecules of this solid fabric are capable of moving and reconfiguring, properties usually believed to occur only in liquids and gases. As the temperature rises, the molecules of DiAPLEX become more excited and move more rapidly. Although DiAPLEX is a solid fabric, the temperature range over which its molecules are active is conveniently the temperature range where we change our clothes most often.

Answer to Anatomy Connection

Sweat is one way our bodies remove excess thermal energy. Our skin contains about 100 sweat glands per square centimeter. The evaporation of sweat from the skin's surface removes thermal energy from the body much more efficiently than simply radiating thermal energy from the blood into the air. Without sweat, we would have great difficulty cooling our bodies on a hot day or after exercising. Most sweat is about 99 percent water, mixed with small amounts of salts, acids, and waste products.

SAFETY FIRST!

Exploring, inventing, and investigating are essential to the study of science. However, these activities can also be dangerous. To make sure that your experiments and explorations are safe, you must be aware of a variety of safety guidelines.

You have probably heard of the saying, "It is better to be safe than sorry." This is particularly true in a science classroom where experiments and explorations are being performed. Being uninformed and careless can result in serious injuries. Don't take chances with your own safety or with anyone else's.

Following are important guidelines for staying safe in the science classroom. Your teacher may also have safety guidelines and tips that are specific to your classroom and laboratory. Take the time to be safe.

Safety Rules!

Start Out Right

Always get your teacher's permission before attempting any laboratory exploration. Read the procedures carefully, and pay particular attention to safety information and caution statements. If you are unsure about what a safety symbol means, look it up or ask your teacher. You cannot be too careful when it comes to safety. If an accident does occur, inform your teacher immediately, regardless of how minor you think the accident is.

Safety Symbols

All of the experiments and investigations in this book and their related worksheets include important safety symbols to alert you to particular safety concerns. Become familiar with these symbols so that when you see them, you will know what they mean and what to do. It is important that you read this entire safety section to learn about specific dangers in the laboratory.

If you are instructed to note the odor of a substance, wave the fumes toward your nose with your hand. Never put your nose close to the source.

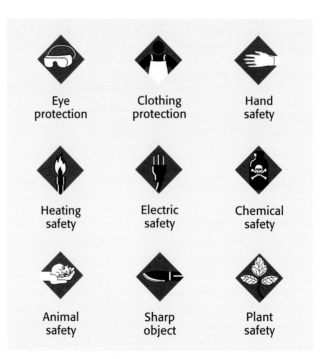

Eye protection

Clothing protection

Hand safety

Heating safety

Electric safety

Chemical safety

Animal safety

Sharp object

Plant safety

Eye Safety

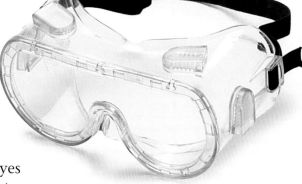

Wear safety goggles when working around chemicals, acids, bases, or any type of flame or heating device. Wear safety goggles any time there is even the slightest chance that harm could come to your eyes. If any substance gets into your eyes, notify your teacher immediately, and flush your eyes with running water for at least 15 minutes. Treat any unknown chemical as if it were a dangerous chemical. Never look directly into the sun. Doing so could cause permanent blindness.

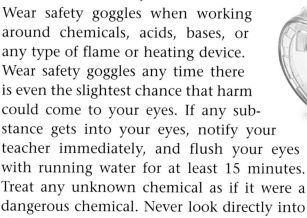

Avoid wearing contact lenses in a laboratory situation. Even if you are wearing safety goggles, chemicals can get between the contact lenses and your eyes. If your doctor requires that you wear contact lenses instead of glasses, wear eye-cup safety goggles in the lab.

Safety Equipment

Know the locations of the nearest fire alarms and any other safety equipment, such as fire blankets and eyewash fountains, as identified by your teacher, and know the procedures for using them.

Be extra careful when using any glassware. When adding a heavy object to a graduated cylinder, tilt the cylinder so the object slides slowly to the bottom.

Neatness

Keep your work area free of all unnecessary books and papers. Tie back long hair, and secure loose sleeves or other loose articles of clothing, such as ties and bows. Remove dangling jewelry. Don't wear open-toed shoes or sandals in the laboratory. Never eat, drink, or apply cosmetics in a laboratory setting. Food, drink, and cosmetics can easily become contaminated with dangerous materials.

Certain hair products (such as aerosol hair spray) are flammable and should not be worn while working near an open flame. Avoid wearing hair spray or hair gel on lab days.

Sharp/Pointed Objects

Use knives and other sharp instruments with extreme care. Never cut objects while holding them in your hands. Place objects on a suitable work surface for cutting.

Heat

Wear safety goggles when using a heating device or a flame. Whenever possible, use an electric hot plate as a heat source instead of an open flame. When heating materials in a test tube, always angle the test tube away from yourself and others. In order to avoid burns, wear heat-resistant gloves whenever instructed to do so.

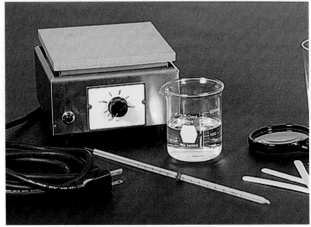

Electricity

Be careful with electrical cords. When using a microscope with a lamp, do not place the cord where it could trip someone. Do not let cords hang over a table edge in a way that could cause equipment to fall if the cord is accidentally pulled. Do not use equipment with damaged cords. Be sure your hands are dry and that the electrical equipment is in the "off" position before plugging it in. Turn off and unplug electrical equipment when you are finished.

Chemicals

Wear safety goggles when handling any potentially dangerous chemicals, acids, or bases. If a chemical is unknown, handle it as you would a dangerous chemical. Wear an apron and safety gloves when working with acids or bases or whenever you are told to do so. If a spill gets on your skin or clothing, rinse it off immediately with water for at least 5 minutes while calling to your teacher.

Never mix chemicals unless your teacher tells you to do so. Never taste, touch, or smell chemicals unless you are specifically directed to do so. Before working with a flammable liquid or gas, check for the presence of any source of flame, spark, or heat.

Animal Safety

Always obtain your teacher's permission before bringing any animal into the school building. Handle animals only as your teacher directs. Always treat animals carefully and with respect. Wash your hands thoroughly after handling any animal.

Plant Safety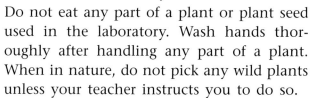

Do not eat any part of a plant or plant seed used in the laboratory. Wash hands thoroughly after handling any part of a plant. When in nature, do not pick any wild plants unless your teacher instructs you to do so.

Glassware

Examine all glassware before use. Be sure that glassware is clean and free of chips and cracks. Report damaged glassware to your teacher. Glass containers used for heating should be made of heat-resistant glass.

Built for Speed
Teacher's Notes

Time Required

One or two 45-minute class periods

Lab Ratings

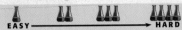

EASY ——————————→ HARD

TEACHER PREP ♫
STUDENT SET-UP ♫
CONCEPT LEVEL ♫♫
CLEAN UP ♫

MATERIALS

Students may be able to supply toy vehicles from home. The toy vehicles should be self-propelled, either battery-operated or wind-up.

Preparation Notes

If you are using battery-operated cars, ensure that the batteries are fresh and that spare batteries are available. You may wish to discuss the use of correct units (m/s) before students begin.

Answers

1. Goals and procedures will vary, but students should outline a procedure for measuring their car's speed.

4. Answers will vary.

5. Answers will vary. Students should show some critical analysis of their procedure and that of others.

6. Answers will vary. Students should consider factors such as battery life and the age of the spring in wind-up vehicles. They may mention other factors, such as the testing surface or the wheels of the vehicle.

Built for Speed

Imagine that you are an engineer at GoCarCo, a toy-vehicle company. GoCarCo is trying to beat the competition by building a new toy vehicle. Several new designs are being tested. Your boss has given you one of the new toy vehicles and instructed you to measure its speed as accurately as possible with the tools you have. Other engineers (your classmates) are testing the other designs. Your results could decide the fate of the company!

Materials

- toy vehicle
- meterstick
- masking tape
- stopwatch

Procedure

1. How will you accomplish your goal? Write a paragraph in your ScienceLog to describe your goal and your procedure for this experiment. Be sure that your procedure includes several trials.

2. Show your plan to your boss (teacher). Get his or her approval to carry out your procedure.

3. Perform your stated procedure. Record all data in your ScienceLog. Be sure to express all data in the correct units.

Analysis

4. What was the average speed of your vehicle? How does your result compare with the results of the other engineers?

5. Compare your technique for determining the speed of your vehicle with the techniques of the other engineers. Which technique do you think is the most effective?

6. Was your toy vehicle the fastest? Explain why or why not.

Going Further

Think of several conditions that could affect your vehicle's speed. Design an experiment to test your vehicle under one of those conditions. Write a paragraph in your ScienceLog to explain your procedure. Be sure to include an explanation of how that condition changes your vehicle's speed.

186

Going Further

Procedures will vary but should show a clear understanding of how the condition could affect the vehicle's speed.

 Datasheets for LabBook

Elsie Waynes
Terrell Junior High
Washington, D.C.

Relating Mass and Weight

Why do objects with more mass weigh more than objects with less mass? All objects have weight on Earth because their mass is affected by Earth's gravitational force. Because the mass of an object on Earth is constant, the relationship between the mass of an object and its weight is also constant. You will measure the mass and weight of several objects to verify the relationship between mass and weight on the surface of Earth.

Materials

- metric balance
- small classroom objects
- spring scale (force meter)
- string
- scissors
- graph paper

Collect Data

1. Copy the table below into your ScienceLog.

Mass and Weight Measurements		
Object	Mass (g)	Weight (N)

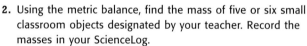
DO NOT WRITE IN BOOK

2. Using the metric balance, find the mass of five or six small classroom objects designated by your teacher. Record the masses in your ScienceLog.

3. Using the spring scale, find the weight of each object. Record the weights in your ScienceLog. (You may need to use the string to create a hook with which to hang some objects from the spring scale, as shown at right.)

Analyze the Results

4. Using your data, construct a graph of weight (y-axis) versus mass (x-axis). Draw a line that best fits all your data points.

5. Does the graph confirm the relationship between mass and weight on Earth? Explain your answer.

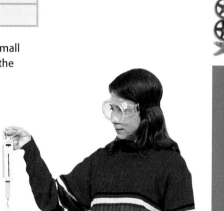

187

Answers

4. The graph should be a straight or almost straight line. (If the line is not straight, encourage students to check their data or remeasure the weights and masses of the objects.)

5. Weight is a measure of the gravitational force on an object. Weight depends on mass. Because an object's mass never changes, its weight on Earth never changes. The straight line of the graph illustrates the direct relationship between mass and weight.

 Datasheets for LabBook

Relating Mass and Weight
Teacher's Notes

Time Required

One 45-minute class period

Lab Ratings

EASY ———————→ HARD

TEACHER PREP	🧪
STUDENT SET-UP	🧪
CONCEPT LEVEL	🧪🧪
CLEAN UP	🧪

MATERIALS

The materials listed are for each group of 2–3 students. A set of metric masses may be used as objects, but at least one random object should be included. Objects must be measurable with the spring scales and metric balances.

Safety Caution

Remind students to review all safety cautions and icons before beginning this lab activity.

Preparation Notes

If metric masses are used, put a small piece of opaque tape over the stamped value for mass. Ensure all objects are easily picked up with the spring scales. Use string to create a "handle." Choose at least five objects for each group.

Barry L. Bishop
San Rafael Junior High
Ferron, Utah

A Marshmallow Catapult
Teacher's Notes

Time Required

One or two 45-minute classes

Lab Ratings

EASY ————————→ HARD

TEACHER PREP 🧪🧪
STUDENT SET-UP 🧪
CONCEPT LEVEL 🧪🧪
CLEAN UP 🧪

MATERIALS

The materials listed are for each group of 1–3 students. Marshmallows may be dusted with alum (a harmless but bitter kitchen spice) to discourage students from eating all the supplies. You may wish to leave the marshmallows out overnight to harden, so they will be easier to launch.

Safety Caution

Remind students to review all safety cautions and icons before beginning this lab activity.

Preparation Notes

Some ceilings may be too low and some classrooms too crowded for this lab. Move to the hallway or outdoors to give students plenty of room.

Answers

1. Accept all reasonable hypotheses.

8. The catapult should launch farthest at a 40–50° angle.

9. The path of the projectile does depend on the angle because different angles resulted in different distances.

A Marshmallow Catapult

Catapults use projectile motion to launch objects across distances. A variety of factors can affect the distance an object can be launched, such as the weight of the object, how far the catapult is pulled back, and the catapult's strength. In this lab, you will build a simple catapult and determine the angle at which the catapult will launch an object the farthest.

Materials

- plastic spoon
- block of wood, 3.5 cm × 3.5 cm × 1 cm
- duct tape
- miniature marshmallows
- protractor
- meterstick

Form a Hypothesis

1. At what angle, from 10° to 90°, will a catapult launch a marshmallow the farthest?

Test the Hypothesis

2. Copy the table below into your ScienceLog. In your table, add one row each for 20°, 30°, 40°, 50°, 60°, 70°, 80°, and 90° angles.

Angle	Distance 1 (cm)	Distance 2 (cm)	Average distance (cm)
10°	DO NOT WRITE IN BOOK		

3. Attach the plastic spoon to the 1 cm side of the block with duct tape. Use enough tape so that the spoon is attached securely.

4. Place one marshmallow in the center of the spoon, and tape it to the spoon. This serves as a ledge to hold the marshmallow that will be launched.

5. Line up the bottom corner of the block with the bottom center of the protractor, as shown in the photograph. Start with the block at 10°.

6. Place a marshmallow in the spoon, on top of the taped marshmallow. Pull back lightly, and let go. Measure and record the distance from the catapult that the marshmallow lands. Repeat the measurement, and calculate an average.

7. Repeat step 6 for each angle up to 90°.

Analyze the Results

8. At what angle did the catapult launch the marshmallow the farthest? Compare this with your hypothesis. Explain any differences.

Draw Conclusions

9. Does the path of an object's projectile motion depend on the catapult's angle? Support your answer with your data.

10. At what angle should you throw a ball or shoot an arrow so that it will fly the farthest? Why? Support your answer with your data.

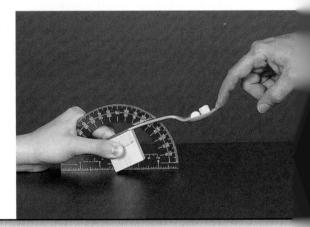

10. An angle of approximately 45° is best because it gives the best combination of distance and height. The evidence is that the marshmallow traveled farthest at 40–50°.

Datasheets for LabBook

CLASSROOM TESTED & APPROVED

Vicky Farland
Crane Junior High
Yuma, Arizona

Blast Off!

You have been hired as a rocket scientist for NASA. Your job is to design a rocket that will have a controlled flight while carrying a payload. Keep in mind that Newton's laws will have a powerful influence on your rocket.

Procedure

1. When you begin your experiment, your teacher will tape one end of the fishing line to the ceiling.

2. Use a pencil to poke a small hole in each side of the cup near the top. Place a 15 cm piece of string through each hole, and tape down the ends inside.

3. Inflate the balloon, and use the twist tie to hold it closed.

4. Tape the free ends of the strings to the sides of the balloon near the bottom. The cup should hang below the balloon. Your model rocket should look like a hot-air balloon.

5. Thread the fishing line that is hanging from the ceiling through the straw. Tape the balloon securely to the straw.

6. Tape the loose end of the fishing line to the floor.

Collect Data

7. Untie the twist tie while holding the end of the balloon closed. When you are ready, release the end of the balloon. Mark and record the maximum height of the rocket.

8. Repeat the procedure, adding a penny to the cup each time until your rocket cannot lift any more pennies.

Analysis

9. In a paragraph, describe how all three of Newton's laws influenced the flight of your rocket.

10. Draw a diagram of your rocket. Label the action and reaction forces.

Going Further

Brainstorm ways to modify your rocket so that it will carry the most pennies to the maximum height. Select the best design. When your teacher has approved all the designs, each team will build and launch their rocket. Which variable did you modify? How did this variable affect your rocket's flight?

Materials

- tape
- 3 m fishing line
- pencil
- small paper cup
- 15 cm pieces of string (2)
- long, thin balloon
- twist tie
- drinking straw
- meterstick
- pennies

Blast Off!
Teacher's Notes

Time Required

One or two 45-minute class periods

Lab Ratings

EASY ———————→ HARD

TEACHER PREP	▲▲
STUDENT SET-UP	▲▲▲
CONCEPT LEVEL	▲▲▲▲
CLEAN UP	▲

MATERIALS

You need 100 pennies per group. Use two balloons for more force.

Answers

9. Newton's first law: The rocket remains at rest until a force is exerted on it. Newton's second law: The rocket's acceleration depends on the force (which is constant) and the mass (which increases with each penny). Newton's third law: The force of the air leaving the balloon on the rocket is equal and opposite to the force of the balloon on the air.

10. See the sample diagram at left. You may wish to point out the less obvious force pairs.

Going Further

Answers will vary but should show a clear understanding of how the variable affects the rocket's flight.

 Datasheets for LabBook

Vicky Farland
Crane Junior High
Yuma, Arizona

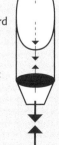

Reaction: upward force of released air pushing balloon

Action: downward force of air being squeezed out of balloon

Action: downward force of pennies

Reaction: upward force of balloon

Action: downward gravitational force of the Earth on the rocket (rocket's weight)

Reaction: upward gravitational force of the rocket on Earth.

Quite a Reaction
Teacher's Notes

Time Required

One to two 45-minute class periods

Lab Ratings

EASY ——————→ HARD

TEACHER PREP 🧪🧪
STUDENT SET-UP 🧪🧪
CONCEPT LEVEL 🧪🧪🧪
CLEAN UP 🧪

MATERIALS

The materials listed are for groups of 1–3 students. Thick pieces of poster board work well. One piece of corrugated cardboard will work as a substitute. A large marble will produce more-dramatic results than a small marble. Also, be sure to give students enough time for the glue to dry.

Safety Caution

Remind students to review all safety cautions and icons before beginning this lab activity.

Pick up any marbles, pins, or other materials that fall on uncarpeted floors immediately. This helps prevent slips and falls. Give students plenty of space to do this lab.

Vicky Farland
Crane Junior High
Yuma, Arizona

Quite a Reaction

Catapults have been used for centuries to throw objects great distances. You may already be familiar with catapults after doing the marshmallow catapult lab. According to Newton's third law of motion (whenever one object exerts a force on a second object, the second object exerts an equal and opposite force on the first), when an object is launched, something must also happen to the catapult. In this activity, you will build a kind of catapult that will allow you to observe the effects of Newton's third law of motion and the law of conservation of momentum.

Conduct an Experiment

1. Glue the cardboard rectangles together to make a stack of three.

2. Push two of the pushpins into the cardboard stack near the corners at one end, as shown below. These will be the anchors for the rubber band.

3. Make a small loop of string.

4. Put the rubber band through the loop of string, and then place the rubber band over the two pushpin anchors. The rubber band should be stretched between the two anchors with the string loop in the middle.

5. Pull the string loop toward the end of the cardboard stack opposite the end with the anchors, and fasten the loop in place with the third pushpin.

6. Place the six straws about 1 cm apart on a tabletop or on the floor. Then carefully center the catapult on top of the straws.

7. Put the marble in the closed end of the V formed by the rubber band.

Materials

- glue
- 10 cm × 15 cm rectangles of cardboard (3)
- 3 pushpins
- string
- rubber band
- 6 plastic straws
- marble
- scissors
- meterstick

 Datasheets for LabBook

8. Use scissors to cut the string holding the rubber band, and observe what happens. (Be careful not to let the scissors touch the cardboard catapult when you cut the string.)

9. Reset the catapult with a new piece of string. Try launching the marble several times to be sure that you have observed everything that happens during a launch. Record all your observations in your ScienceLog.

Analyze the Results

10. Which has more mass, the marble or the catapult?

11. What happened to the catapult when the marble was launched?

12. How far did the marble fly before it landed?

13. Did the catapult move as far as the marble did?

Draw Conclusions

14. Explain why the catapult moved backward.

15. If the forces that made the marble and the catapult move apart are equal, why didn't the marble and the catapult move apart the same distance? (Hint: The fact that the marble can roll after it lands is not the answer.)

16. The momentum of an object depends on the mass and velocity of the object. What is the momentum of the marble before it is launched? What is the momentum of the catapult? Explain your answers.

17. Using the law of conservation of momentum, explain why the marble and the catapult move in opposite directions after the launch.

Going Further
How would you modify the catapult if you wanted to keep it from moving backward as far as it did? (It still has to rest on the straws.) Using items that you can find in the classroom, design a catapult that will move backward less than the original design.

Answers

10. Answers will depend on the type of marble and the type of cardboard. It is likely that the catapult will have more mass.

11. The catapult moved backward.

12. Answers will vary depending on the mass of the marble, the type of cardboard, and the size of the straws.

13. Answers will vary, but the marble will likely go farther than the catapult.

14. The catapult moved backward due to Newton's third law. The catapult exerted a force on the marble that made it move forward. The marble exerted an equal and opposite force on the catapult, making it move backward.

15. More friction acts on the cardboard because it is in contact with the straws. Some students may also note that the marble and the cardboard have different masses. The acceleration (and, therefore, the velocity) of each is different as a result of Newton's second law, $F = ma$.

16. The momentum of both the marble and the catapult is zero because both have zero velocity.

17. Because the initial momentum of the system is zero, the catapult has to move backward with a momentum equal to that of the marble moving forward. The momenta of the catapult and marble have to be in opposite directions so they will cancel out.

Going Further
Accept all reasonable designs.

Density Diver
Teacher's Notes

Time Required

One 45-minute class period

Lab Ratings

EASY ————————→ HARD

TEACHER PREP
STUDENT SET-UP
CONCEPT LEVEL
CLEAN UP

Lab Notes

If there is any air in the bottle, students will have to squeeze harder to make the diver move.

Answers

1. Accept all reasonable hypotheses.

7. When the water level inside the diver rises, the diver starts sinking. When the level decreases, the diver floats.

8. Higher water level corresponds to higher density. Adding more water to the diver results in more mass in the same volume, so the density is greater.

9. When the density is higher, the diver starts to sink. When it is low, the diver floats. When it is just right, the diver hovers without sinking or rising.

10. Controlling the water level inside the diver is similar to controlling the water level inside a submarine.

11. Squeezing the bottle increases the water pressure. This increase is transmitted equally throughout the bottle to the diver (Pascal's principle). The air inside the diver is compressed and water enters the diver. This increases the density of the diver.

Using Scientific Methods

DISCOVERY LAB

Density Diver

Crew members of a submarine can control the submarine's density underwater by allowing water to flow into and out of special tanks. These changes in density affect the submarine's position in the water. In this lab, you'll control a "density diver" to learn for yourself how the density of an object affects its position in a fluid.

Materials

- 2 L plastic bottle with screw-on cap
- water
- medicine dropper

Form a Hypothesis

1. How does the density of an object determine whether the object floats, sinks, or maintains its position in a fluid? Write your hypothesis in your ScienceLog.

Test the Hypothesis

2. Completely fill the 2 L plastic bottle with water.

3. Fill the diver (medicine dropper) approximately halfway with water, and place it in the bottle. The diver should float with only part of the rubber bulb above the surface of the water. If the diver floats too high, carefully remove it from the bottle and add a small amount of water to the diver. Place the diver back in the bottle. If you add too much water and the diver sinks, empty out the bottle and diver and go back to step 2.

4. Put the cap on the bottle tightly so that no water leaks out.

5. Apply various pressures to the bottle. Carefully watch the water level inside the diver as you squeeze and release the bottle. Record what happens in your ScienceLog.

6. Try to make the diver rise, sink, or stop at any level. Record your technique and your results.

Analyze the Results

7. How do the changes inside the diver affect its position in the surrounding fluid?

8. What is the relationship between the water level inside the diver and the diver's density? Explain.

Draw Conclusions

9. What relationship did you observe between the diver's density and the diver's position in the fluid?

10. Explain how your density diver is like a submarine.

11. Explain how pressure on the bottle is related to the diver's density. Be sure to include Pascal's principle in your explanation.

12. What was the variable in this experiment? What factors were controlled?

12. The variable is the amount of pressure put on the bottle by squeezing. Factors controlled include the amount of water, the type of bottle, and the size of the medicine droppers.

 Datasheets for LabBook

CLASSROOM TESTED & APPROVED

C. John Graves
Monforton Middle School
Bozeman, Montana

Out the Spouts

Although many undersea vessels explore the ocean depths, few are able to descend to the deepest parts of the ocean. The reason? Water exerts tremendous pressure at these depths. In this activity you'll witness one of the effects of this pressure firsthand.

Procedure

1. With a sharp pencil, punch a small hole in the center of one side of an empty cardboard milk container.

2. Make another hole 4 cm above the center hole. Then make another hole 8 cm above the center hole.

3. With a single piece of masking tape, carefully cover the holes. Leave a little tape free at the bottom for easy removal.

4. Fill the container with water, and place it in a large plastic tray or sink.

5. Quickly pull the tape off the container.

6. Record your observations in your ScienceLog.

Analysis

7. Did the same thing happen at each hole after you removed the tape? If not, what do you think caused the different results? Record your answers in your ScienceLog.

Materials

- pencil
- cardboard milk container
- masking tape
- water
- large plastic tray or sink

Out the Spouts
Teacher's Notes

Time Required

One 45-minute class period

Lab Ratings

EASY ————————→ HARD

TEACHER PREP
STUDENT SET-UP
CONCEPT LEVEL
CLEAN UP

MATERIALS

FOR EACH GROUP:
- pencil
- empty cardboard milk container
- metric ruler
- masking tape
- water
- large plastic tray or sink

Safety Caution

Make sure students wear safety goggles and an apron when doing this activity

Answers

7. The same thing does not happen at each hole after the tape is removed. Water spurts out farther from the middle hole than from the top hole, and even farther out of the bottom hole than out of the top two holes. The difference in how far each stream of water travels is due to the difference in water pressure. Water pressure increases with depth. More pressure is pushing on the bottom of the column, so the water is pushed out with greater force and travels further.

193

Inclined to Move
Teacher's Notes

Time Required

One 45-minute class period

Lab Ratings

EASY ——————————→ HARD

TEACHER PREP 🍶🍶
STUDENT SET-UP 🍶🍶
CONCEPT LEVEL 🍶🍶🍶
CLEAN UP 🍶

Safety Caution

Remind students to review all safety cautions and icons before beginning this lab activity.

Answers

6. The amount of work done should increase as ramp height increases (line A).

7. The amount of work done should increase as ramp height increases (line B).

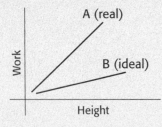

8. It requires less force but more work to raise the book using the ramp. At each height, more work must be done to overcome friction between the book and the ramp.

9. The higher the inclined plane is, the greater the input force.

10. The slope of ideal work versus height will always be less than the slope of real work versus height. That's because there is no friction in ideal work, but

Inclined to Move

In this lab, you will examine a simple machine—an inclined plane. Your task is to compare the work done with and without the inclined plane and to analyze the effects of friction.

Collect Data

1. Copy the table below into your ScienceLog.

2. Tie a piece of string around a book. Attach the spring scale to the string. Use the spring scale to slowly lift the book to a height of 50 cm. Record the output force (the force needed to lift the book). The output force is constant throughout the lab.

3. Use the board and blocks to make a ramp 10 cm high at the highest point. Measure and record the ramp length.

4. Keeping the spring scale parallel to the ramp, as shown below, slowly raise the book. Record the input force (the force needed to pull the book up the ramp).

5. Increase the height of the ramp by 10 cm. Repeat step 4. Repeat this step for each ramp height up to 50 cm.

Analyze the Results

6. The *real* work done includes the work done to overcome friction. Calculate the real work at each height by multiplying the ramp length (converted to meters) by the input force. Graph your results, plotting work (*y*-axis) versus height (*x*-axis).

7. The *ideal* work is the work you would do if there were no friction. Calculate the ideal work at each height by multiplying the ramp height (m) by the output force. Plot the data on your graph.

Materials

- string
- small book
- spring scale
- meterstick
- wooden board
- blocks
- graph paper

Force vs. Height			
Ramp height (cm)	Output force (N)	Ramp length (cm)	Input force (N)
10			
20			
30		*DO NOT WRITE IN BOOK*	
40			
50			

Draw Conclusions

8. Does it require more or less force and work to raise the book using the ramp? Explain, using your calculations and graphs.

9. What is the relationship between the height of the inclined plane and the input force?

10. Write a statement that summarizes why the slopes of the two graphs are different.

real work includes the work done to overcome the friction between the book and the ramp.

Datasheets for LabBook

Jennifer Ford
North Ridge Middle School
North Richland Hills, Texas

194

Building Machines

You are surrounded by machines. Some are simple machines, such as ramps for wheelchair access to a building. Others are compound machines, like elevators and escalators, that are made of two or more simple machines. In this lab, you will design and build several simple machines and a compound machine.

Procedure

1. Use the listed materials to build a model of each simple machine: inclined plane, lever, wheel and axle, pulley, screw, and wedge. Describe and draw each model in your ScienceLog.

2. In your ScienceLog, design a compound machine using the materials listed. You may design a machine that already exists, or you may invent your own machine—be creative!

3. After your teacher approves your design, build your compound machine.

Analysis

4. List a possible use for each of your simple machines.

5. Compare your simple machines with those created by your classmates.

6. How many simple machines are in your compound machine? List them.

7. Compare your compound machine with those created by your classmates.

8. What is a possible use for your compound machine? Why did you design it as you did?

9. A compound machine is listed in the Materials list. What is it?

Going Further

Design a compound machine that has all the simple machines in it. Explain what the machine will do and how it will make work easier. With your teacher's approval, build your machine.

Materials

- bottle caps
- cardboard
- craft sticks
- empty thread spools
- glue
- modeling clay
- paper
- pencils
- rubber bands
- scissors
- shoe boxes
- stones
- straws
- string
- tape
- other materials available in your classroom that are approved by your teacher

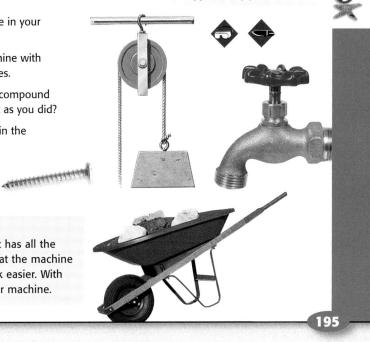

195

Norman Holcomb
Marion Elementary School
Maria Stein, Ohio

Datasheets for LabBook

Answer to Going Further

Accept all reasonable designs. Check all materials for safety and availability.

Building Machines
Teacher's Notes

Time Required

One or two 45-minute class periods

Lab Ratings

EASY ——————→ HARD

TEACHER PREP   🧪🧪
STUDENT SET-UP   🧪🧪
CONCEPT LEVEL   🧪🧪
CLEAN UP   🧪

MATERIALS

The materials listed for this lab should be available in quantities sufficient for the entire class. You may provide different materials for students to use. Be sure students work carefully with the supplied materials. Students should work in groups of 2–4. Be sure to approve designs before students begin building their compound machines.

Safety Caution

Remind students to review all safety cautions and icons before beginning this lab activity.

Answers

4. Accept all reasonable answers.

5. Accept all reasonable answers.

6. Answers will vary, based on machine design.

7. Accept all reasonable answers.

8. Accept all reasonable answers.

9. The compound machine listed in the Materials List is the pair of scissors.

Wheeling and Dealing
Teacher's Notes

Time Required

Two 45-minute class periods

Lab Ratings

EASY ———————————→ HARD

TEACHER PREP   🧪🧪🧪🧪

STUDENT SET-UP   🧪🧪

CONCEPT LEVEL   🧪🧪🧪🧪

CLEAN UP   🧪

MATERIALS

The materials listed in this lab are for each group of 2–4 students. The materials listed below are what you will need in order to prepare each wheel and axle assembly.

• 30 cm of 1 in. dowel
• 70 cm of 0.5 in. dowel for handles (cut into 4 pieces of 10 cm, 15 cm, 20 cm, and 25 cm)
• wheel
• small screw
• 1.5 in. PVC pipe

Safety Caution

Remind students to review all safety cautions and icons before beginning this lab activity.

Lab Notes

The wheel and axle assembly must be constructed before class. Use a marker to number the handles 1 through 4 (shortest to longest). Drill a 0.5 in. diameter hole half way through the large dowel near one end. The handles will be inserted into the hole. A small screw should be inserted into the large dowel near the handle attachment point, on the side away from

Wheeling and Dealing

A wheel and axle is one type of simple machine. A crank handle, such as that used in pencil sharpeners, ice-cream makers, and water wells is one kind of wheel and axle. In this lab, you will use a crank handle to find out how a wheel and axle helps you do work. You will also determine what effect the length of the handle has on the operation of the machine.

Materials

• wheel and axle assembly
• meterstick
• large mass
• spring scale
• handles
• 0.5 m string
• 2 C-clamps

Procedure

1. Copy Table 1 into your ScienceLog.

2. Measure the radius (in meters) of the large dowel in the wheel and axle assembly. Record this in Table 1 as the axle radius, which remains constant throughout the lab. (Hint: Measure the diameter and divide by two.)

3. Using the spring scale, measure the weight of the large mass. Record this in Table 1 as the output force, which remains constant throughout the lab.

4. Use two C-clamps to secure the wheel and axle assembly to the table, as shown at right.

Collect Data

5. Measure the length (in meters) of handle 1. Record this as a wheel radius in Table 1.

6. Insert the handle into the hole in the axle. Attach one end of the string to the large mass and the other end to the screw in the axle. The mass should hang down and the handle should turn freely.

7. Turn the handle to lift the mass off the floor. Hold the spring scale upside down, and attach it to the end of the handle. Measure the force (in newtons) as the handle pulls up on the spring scale. Record this as the input force.

Table 1 Data Collection				
Handle	Axle radius (m)	Output force (N)	Wheel radius (m)	Input force (N)
1				
2				
3				
4				

DO NOT WRITE IN BOOK

the end. This will be the attachment point for the string. The 1.5 in. PVC pipe should have an inside diameter slightly larger than the large dowel. The clamps are the most expensive pieces and are optional. If students work in groups, one student may act as the clamp and hold the PVC pipe firmly against the tabletop. Use a 500 g or 1 kg mass for the large mass.

It takes a fair amount of time and materials to build the wheel and axle assemblies,

but once you have built them, they will be available to use in subsequent years.

Students should review the sections on work input, work output, mechanical efficiency, mechanical advantage, and a wheel and axle before beginning this lab. Demonstrate the assembly for students. Remind students that they can measure the axle radius and the wheel radius in centimeters and then convert to meters.

8. Remove the spring scale, and lower the mass to the floor. Remove the handle.

9. Repeat steps 5 through 8 with the other three handles. Record all data in Table 1.

Analyze the Results

10. Copy Table 2 into your ScienceLog.

Table 2 Calculations

Handle	Axle distance (m)	Wheel distance (m)	Work input (J)	Work output (J)	Mechanical efficiency (%)	Mechanical advantage
1						
2						
3						
4						

DO NOT WRITE IN BOOK

11. Calculate the following for each handle using the equations given. Record your answers in Table 2.

   a. Distance axle rotates = $2 \times \pi \times$ axle radius

   Distance wheel rotates = $2 \times \pi \times$ wheel radius

   (Use 3.14 for the value of π.)

   b. Work input = input force $\times$ wheel distance

   Work output = output force $\times$ axle distance

   c. Mechanical efficiency = $\dfrac{\text{work output}}{\text{work input}} \times 100$

   d. Mechanical advantage = $\dfrac{\text{wheel radius}}{\text{axle radius}}$

Draw Conclusions

12. What happens to work output and work input as the handle length increases? Why?

13. What happens to mechanical efficiency as the handle length increases? Why?

14. What happens to mechanical advantage as the handle length increases? Why?

15. What will happen to mechanical advantage if the handle length is kept constant and the axle radius gets larger?

16. What factors were controlled in this experiment? What was the variable?

Larry Tackett
Andrew Jackson Middle School
Cross Lanes, West Virginia

 Datasheets for LabBook

197

Safety Caution

Remind students not to stand too close to the handle after the string is wound on the axle. If the spring scale comes off the handle, the handle may spin around and hit someone.

Answers

11a. Axle distance = 2π (0.012 m) = 0.075 m

   Wheel distance = $2 \pi \times$ (handle length: 0.10 m, 0.15 m, 0.20 m, 0.25 m) = 0.63 m, 0.94 m, 1.3 m, 1.6 m

   b. Answers will depend on the mass used. Check calculations for accuracy.

   c. Mechanical efficiency will depend on the materials used. Check calculations for accuracy.

   d. Mechanical advantages are 8.3, 12.5, 16.7, and 20.8 for the handles (10 cm, 15 cm, 20 cm, and 25 cm).

12. As the handle length increases, work output stays the same, but work input gets slightly larger because the machine becomes less efficient.

13. The mechanical efficiency decreases as the handle length increases because the large dowel rotates within the PVC pipe more, creating more friction. More friction leads to lower mechanical efficiency.

14. Mechanical advantage increases as handle length increases because the input force for a large handle (wheel) is less.

15. The mechanical advantage will decrease.

16. Controlled factors include the axle radius and the mass used. The variable was the wheel radius (the length of the handle).

Energy of a Pendulum
Teacher's Notes

Time Required

One 45-minute class period

Lab Ratings

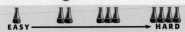

EASY ———————→ HARD

TEACHER PREP   🧪
STUDENT SET-UP   🧪
CONCEPT LEVEL   🧪🧪
CLEAN UP   🧪

MATERIALS

The materials listed are for each student.

Safety Caution

Caution students to swing the pendulum gently. Students should be a reasonable distance from one another and from classroom equipment. Students should wear safety goggles.

Answers

5. Accept all reasonable answers.

6. slowest when it is first released and when it is at the top of the opposite side; fastest at the bottom of its swing during each trial

7. greatest potential energy at the greatest height on either side; smallest potential energy at the bottom of its swing

8. greatest kinetic energy at the bottom of its swing (moving fastest); smallest kinetic energy at the top of its swing (moving slowest)

9. The pendulum's kinetic energy increases on its way down (as the pendulum speeds up). As

---

Energy of a Pendulum

A pendulum clock is a compound machine that uses stored energy to do work. A spring stores energy, and with each swing of the pendulum, some of that stored energy is used to move the hands of the clock. In this lab you will take a close look at the energy conversions that occur as a pendulum swings.

Materials

- 1 m of string
- 100 g hooked mass
- marker
- meterstick

Collect Data

1. Make a pendulum by tying the string around the hook of the mass. Use the marker and the meterstick to mark points on the string that are 50 cm, 70 cm, and 90 cm away from the mass.

2. Hold the string at the 50 cm mark. Gently pull the mass to the side, and release it without pushing it. Observe at least 10 swings of the pendulum.

3. In your ScienceLog, record your observations. Be sure to note how fast and how high the pendulum swings.

4. Repeat steps 2 and 3 while holding the string at the 70 cm mark and again while holding the string at the 90 cm mark.

Analyze the Results

5. In your ScienceLog, list similarities and differences in the motion of the pendulum during all three trials.

6. At which point (or points) of the swing was the pendulum moving the slowest? the fastest?

Draw Conclusions

7. In each trial, at which point (or points) of the swing did the pendulum have the greatest potential energy? the smallest potential energy? (Hint: Think about your answers to question 6.)

8. At which point (or points) of the swing did the pendulum have the greatest kinetic energy? the smallest kinetic energy? Explain your answers.

9. Describe the relationship between the pendulum's potential energy and its kinetic energy on its way down. Explain.

10. What improvements might reduce the amount of energy used to overcome friction so that the pendulum would swing for a longer period of time?

the pendulum moves from its highest point to its lowest point, potential energy decreases.

10. Accept all reasonable answers.

Datasheets for LabBook

Edith C. McAlanis
Socorro Middle School
El Paso, Texas

Eggstremely Fragile

All moving objects have kinetic energy. The faster an object is moving, the more kinetic energy it has. When a falling object hits the floor, the law of conservation of energy requires that the energy be transferred to another object or changed into another form of energy.

When an unprotected egg hits the ground from a height of 1 m, most of the kinetic energy of the falling egg is transferred to the pieces of the shell—with messy results. In this lab you will design a protection system for an egg.

Conduct an Experiment

1. Using the materials provided by your teacher, design a protection system that will prevent the egg from breaking when it is dropped from heights of 1, 2, and 3 m. Keep the following points in mind while developing your egg-protection system:

   a. The egg and its protection system must fit inside the closed milk carton. (Note: The milk carton will not be dropped with the egg.)

   b. The protective materials don't have to be soft.

   c. The protective materials can surround the egg or can be attached to the egg at various points.

2. In your ScienceLog, explain why you chose your materials.

3. You will perform the three trials at a time and location specified by your teacher. Record your results for each trial in your ScienceLog.

Analyze the Results

4. Did your egg survive all three trials? If it did not, why did your egg-protection system fail? If your egg did survive, what features of your egg-protecting system transferred or absorbed the energy?

Draw Conclusions

5. How do egg cartons like those you find in a grocery store protect eggs from mishandling?

Materials

- raw egg
- empty half-pint milk carton
- assorted materials provided by your teacher

Eggstremely Fragile
Teacher's Notes

Time Required
One or two 45-minute class periods

Lab Ratings

EASY ———————→ HARD

TEACHER PREP 🧪🧪
STUDENT SET-UP 🧪🧪
CONCEPT LEVEL 🧪🧪🧪
CLEAN UP 🧪🧪🧪

Safety Caution
Students should wear safety goggles and an apron when doing this lab. Caution students not to throw the eggs. Students should wash their hands thoroughly after handling the eggs.

Procedure Notes
The more types of materials you provide, the more creative students' solutions will be. Good materials include cotton balls, plastic straws, modeling clay, wooden craft sticks, newspaper, glue, and Silly Putty™. Try to provide both hard and soft materials. Place the egg and protection system in a plastic bag; wrap the egg and protective system in plastic wrap; or spread a large plastic sheet on the ground at the drop point.

199

Answers

4. Answers will depend on the results of the trials. Possible reasons for failure include thin protection or the protection falling off. Features that enable the egg to survive might include those that slow the egg down so that it lands gently or those that pad the egg so that the protective material, rather than the egg, absorbs the energy of the impact.

5. The cardboard or plastic foam provides padding, and the shape of the carton directs energy away from the egg instead of into the shell.

 Datasheets for LabBook

John Zambo
E. Ustach Middle School
Modesto, California

Save the Cube!
Teacher's Notes

Time Required

One or two 45-minute class periods

Lab Ratings

EASY ————————————→ HARD

TEACHER PREP 🧪🧪🧪
STUDENT SET-UP 🧪🧪
CONCEPT LEVEL 🧪🧪🧪
CLEAN UP 🧪

MATERIALS

Use incandescent lights, a hair dryer, or hot plates (low setting) to prepare a "thermal zone." Use the lowest setting on the hot plate so the plastic bags do not melt. Provide a large assortment of materials to protect the ice cubes, including white paper, cotton balls, plastic-foam packing peanuts, bubble wrap, tape, aluminum foil, and rubber bands.

Safety Caution

Caution students to wear heat-resistant gloves if working near a hot plate.

Procedure Notes

Set up the thermal zone before class. Have students find and record the masses of the empty cup and empty bag before they obtain their ice cubes.

 Datasheets for LabBook

Save the Cube!

The biggest enemy of an ice cube is the transfer of thermal energy—heat. Energy can be transferred to an ice cube in three ways: conduction (the transfer of energy through direct contact), convection (the transfer of energy by the movement of a liquid or gas), and radiation (the transfer of energy through matter or space). Your challenge in this activity is to design a way to protect an ice cube as much as possible from all three types of energy transfer.

DESIGN YOUR OWN !

Materials

- small plastic bag
- ice cube
- assorted materials provided by your teacher
- empty half-pint milk carton
- metric balance
- small plastic or paper cup

Procedure

1. Follow these guidelines: Use a plastic bag to hold the ice cube and any water from its melting. You may use any of the materials to protect the ice cube. The ice cube, bag, and protection must all fit inside the milk carton.

2. Describe your proposed design in your ScienceLog. Explain how your design protects against each type of energy transfer.

3. Find the mass of the empty cup, and record it in your ScienceLog. Then find and record the mass of an empty plastic bag.

4. Place an ice cube in the bag. Quickly find and record their mass together.

5. Quickly wrap the bag (and the ice cube inside) in its protection. Remember that the package must fit in the milk carton.

6. Place your protected ice cube in the "thermal zone" set up by your teacher. After 10 minutes, remove the package from the zone and remove the protective material from the plastic bag and ice cube.

7. Open the bag. Pour any water into the cup. Find and record the mass of the cup and water together.

8. Find and record the mass of the water by subtracting the mass of the empty cup from the mass of the cup and water.

9. Use the same method to find and record the mass of the ice cube.

10. Find the percentage of the ice cube that melted using the following equation:

$$\% \text{ melted} = \frac{\text{mass of water}}{\text{mass of ice cube}} \times 100$$

11. Record this percentage in your ScienceLog and on the board.

Analysis

12. Compared with other designs in your class, how well did your design protect against each type of energy transfer? How could you improve your design?

13. Why is a white plastic-foam cooler so useful for keeping ice frozen?

200

Answers

12. Answers will vary but should provide an accurate assessment of results and reasonable ideas for design improvement.

13. Answers should address how the cooler minimizes the effects of all three types of energy transfer (radiation, convection, and conduction).

CLASSROOM TESTED & APPROVED

David Sparks
Redwater Junior High
Redwater, Texas

Counting Calories

Energy transferred by heat is often expressed in units called calories. In this lab, you will build a model of a device called a calorimeter. Scientists often use calorimeters to measure the amount of energy that can be transferred by a substance. In this experiment, you will construct your own calorimeter and test it by measuring the energy released by a hot penny.

Procedure

1. Copy the table below into your ScienceLog.

Data Collection Table									
Seconds	0	15	30	45	60	75	90	105	120
Water temp. (°C)									

DO NOT WRITE IN BOOK

2. Place the lid on the small plastic-foam cup, and insert a thermometer through the hole in the top of the lid. (The thermometer should not touch the bottom of the cup.) Place the small cup inside the large cup to complete the calorimeter.

3. Remove the lid from the small cup, and add 50 mL of room-temperature water to the cup. Measure the water's temperature, and record the value in the first column (0 seconds) of the table.

4. Using tongs, heat the penny carefully. Add the penny to the water in the small cup, and replace the lid. Start your stopwatch.

5. Every 15 seconds, measure and record the temperature. Gently swirl the large cup to stir the water, and continue recording temperatures for 2 minutes (120 seconds).

Analysis

6. What was the total temperature change of the water after 2 minutes?

7. The number of calories absorbed by the water is the mass of the water (in grams) multiplied by the temperature change (in °C) of the water. How many calories were absorbed by the water? (Hint: 1 mL of water = 1 g of water)

8. In terms of heat, explain where the calories to change the water temperature came from.

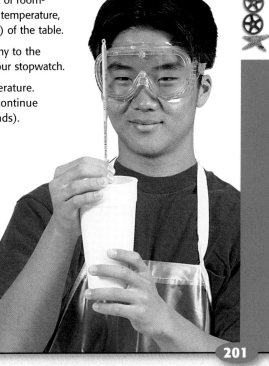

201

John Zambo
E. Ustach Middle School
Modesto, California

Materials

- small plastic-foam cup with lid
- thermometer
- large plastic-foam cup
- water
- 100 mL graduated cylinder
- tongs
- heat source
- penny
- stopwatch

Counting Calories
Teacher's Notes

Time Required

One 45-minute class period

Lab Ratings

EASY ———————→ HARD

TEACHER PREP 🧪🧪
STUDENT SET-UP 🧪
CONCEPT LEVEL 🧪🧪
CLEAN UP 🧪

MATERIALS

The materials listed are for each group of 2–3 students.

Safety Caution

Caution students to wear goggles and an apron and to use care when working near the heat source. Remind students never to use a thermometer for stirring.

Preparation Notes

You may wish to model the procedure for making the calorimeter and the proper method of heating the penny before students begin the lab. Remind students that a calorie is the amount of energy needed to raise the temperature of 1 g of water by 1°C. All students should heat the penny for the same amount of time.

Datasheets for LabBook

Answers

6. Answers should be the final temperature (at 120 seconds) minus the initial temperature (at 0 seconds).

7. The number of calories absorbed by the water equals temperature change (step 6) times the mass of the water (50 g).

8. The calories came from the penny. The penny increased the temperature of the water by transferring energy to it.

Concept Mapping: A Way to Bring Ideas Together

What Is a Concept Map?

Have you ever tried to tell someone about a book or a chapter you've just read and found that you can remember only a few isolated words and ideas? Or maybe you've memorized facts for a test and then weeks later discovered you're not even sure what topics those facts covered.

In both cases, you may have understood the ideas or concepts by themselves but not in relation to one another. If you could somehow link the ideas together, you would probably understand them better and remember them longer. This is something a concept map can help you do. A concept map is a way to see how ideas or concepts fit together. It can help you see the "big picture."

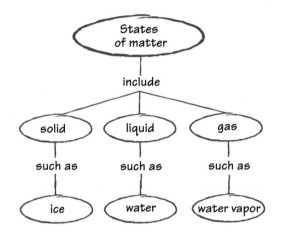

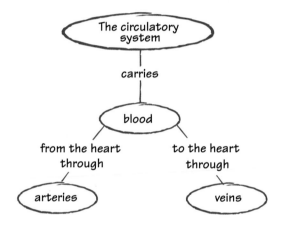

How to Make a Concept Map

1 **Make a list of the main ideas or concepts.**

It might help to write each concept on its own slip of paper. This will make it easier to rearrange the concepts as many times as necessary to make sense of how the concepts are connected. After you've made a few concept maps this way, you can go directly from writing your list to actually making the map.

2 **Arrange the concepts in order from the most general to the most specific.**

Put the most general concept at the top and circle it. Ask yourself, "How does this concept relate to the remaining concepts?" As you see the relationships, arrange the concepts in order from general to specific.

3 **Connect the related concepts with lines.**

4 **On each line, write an action word or short phrase that shows how the concepts are related.**

Look at the concept maps on this page, and then see if you can make one for the following terms:

plants, water, photosynthesis, carbon dioxide, sun's energy

One possible answer is provided at right, but don't look at it until you try the concept map yourself.

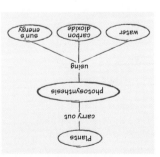

SI Measurement

The International System of Units, or SI, is the standard system of measurement used by many scientists. Using the same standards of measurement makes it easier for scientists to communicate with one another.

SI works by combining prefixes and base units. Each base unit can be used with different prefixes to define smaller and larger quantities. The table below lists common SI prefixes.

SI Prefixes			
Prefix	**Abbreviation**	**Factor**	**Example**
kilo-	k	1,000	kilogram, 1 kg = 1,000 g
hecto-	h	100	hectoliter, 1 hL = 100 L
deka-	da	10	dekameter, 1 dam = 10 m
		1	meter, liter
deci-	d	0.1	decigram, 1 dg = 0.1 g
centi-	c	0.01	centimeter, 1 cm = 0.01 m
milli-	m	0.001	milliliter, 1 mL = 0.001 L
micro-	μ	0.000 001	micrometer, 1 μm = 0.000 001 m

SI Conversion Table		
SI units	**From SI to English**	**From English to SI**
Length		
kilometer (km) = 1,000 m	1 km = 0.621 mi	1 mi = 1.609 km
meter (m) = 100 cm	1 m = 3.281 ft	1 ft = 0.305 m
centimeter (cm) = 0.01 m	1 cm = 0.394 in.	1 in. = 2.540 cm
millimeter (mm) = 0.001 m	1 mm = 0.039 in.	
micrometer (μm) = 0.000 001 m		
nanometer (nm) = 0.000 000 001 m		
Area		
square kilometer (km^2) = 100 hectares	$1\ km^2 = 0.386\ mi^2$	$1\ mi^2 = 2.590\ km^2$
hectare (ha) = 10,000 m^2	1 ha = 2.471 acres	1 acre = 0.405 ha
square meter (m^2) = 10,000 cm^2	$1\ m^2 = 10.765\ ft^2$	$1\ ft^2 = 0.093\ m^2$
square centimeter (cm^2) = 100 mm^2	$1\ cm^2 = 0.155\ in.^2$	$1\ in.^2 = 6.452\ cm^2$
Volume		
liter (L) = 1,000 mL = 1 dm^3	1 L = 1.057 fl qt	1 fl qt = 0.946 L
milliliter (mL) = 0.001 L = 1 cm^3	1 mL = 0.034 fl oz	1 fl oz = 29.575 mL
microliter (μL) = 0.000 001 L		
Mass		
kilogram (kg) = 1,000 g	1 kg = 2.205 lb	1 lb = 0.454 kg
gram (g) = 1,000 mg	1 g = 0.035 oz	1 oz = 28.349 g
milligram (mg) = 0.001 g		
microgram (μg) = 0.000 001 g		

Temperature Scales

Temperature can be expressed using three different scales: Fahrenheit, Celsius, and Kelvin. The SI unit for temperature is the kelvin (K).

Although 0 K is much colder than 0°C, a change of 1 K is equal to a change of 1°C.

Three Temperature Scales

	Fahrenheit	Celsius	Kelvin
Water boils	212°	100°	373
Body temperature	98.6°	37°	310
Room temperature	68°	20°	293
Water freezes	32°	0°	273

Temperature Conversions Table

To convert	Use this equation:	Example
Celsius to Fahrenheit °C $\longrightarrow$ °F	$°F = \left(\dfrac{9}{5} \times °C\right) + 32$	Convert 45°C to °F. $°F = \left(\dfrac{9}{5} \times 45°C\right) + 32 = 113°F$
Fahrenheit to Celsius °F $\longrightarrow$ °C	$°C = \dfrac{5}{9} \times (°F - 32)$	Convert 68°F to °C. $°C = \dfrac{5}{9} \times (68°F - 32) = 20°C$
Celsius to Kelvin °C $\longrightarrow$ K	$K = °C + 273$	Convert 45°C to K. $K = 45°C + 273 = 318\ K$
Kelvin to Celsius K $\longrightarrow$ °C	$°C = K - 273$	Convert 32 K to °C. $°C = 32\ K - 273 = -241°C$

Measuring Skills

Using a Graduated Cylinder

When using a graduated cylinder to measure volume, keep the following procedures in mind:

1 Make sure the cylinder is on a flat, level surface.

2 Move your head so that your eye is level with the surface of the liquid.

3 Read the mark closest to the liquid level. On glass graduated cylinders, read the mark closest to the center of the curve in the liquid's surface.

Using a Meterstick or Metric Ruler

When using a meterstick or metric ruler to measure length, keep the following procedures in mind:

1 Place the ruler firmly against the object you are measuring.

2 Align one edge of the object exactly with the zero end of the ruler.

3 Look at the other edge of the object to see which of the marks on the ruler is closest to that edge. **Note:** Each small slash between the centimeters represents a millimeter, which is one-tenth of a centimeter.

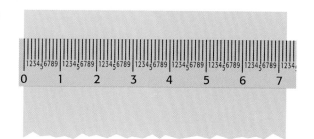

Using a Triple-Beam Balance

When using a triple-beam balance to measure mass, keep the following procedures in mind:

1 Make sure the balance is on a level surface.

2 Place all of the countermasses at zero. Adjust the balancing knob until the pointer rests at zero.

3 Place the object you wish to measure on the pan. **Caution:** Do not place hot objects or chemicals directly on the balance pan.

4 Move the largest countermass along the beam to the right until it is at the last notch that does not tip the balance. Follow the same procedure with the next-largest countermass. Then move the smallest countermass until the pointer rests at zero.

5 Add the readings from the three beams together to determine the mass of the object.

6 When determining the mass of crystals or powders, use a piece of filter paper. First find the mass of the paper. Then add the crystals or powder to the paper and re-measure. The actual mass of the crystals or powder is the total mass minus the mass of the paper. When finding the mass of liquids, first find the mass of the empty container. Then find the mass of the liquid and container together. The mass of the liquid is the total mass minus the mass of the container.

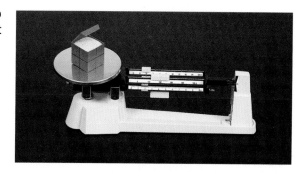

Scientific Method

The series of steps that scientists use to answer questions and solve problems is often called the **scientific method.** The scientific method is not a rigid procedure. Scientists may use all of the steps or just some of the steps of the scientific method. They may even repeat some of the steps. The goal of the scientific method is to come up with reliable answers and solutions.

Six Steps of the Scientific Method

1 **Ask a Question** Good questions come from careful **observations.** You make observations by using your senses to gather information. Sometimes you may use instruments, such as microscopes and telescopes, to extend the range of your senses. As you observe the natural world, you will discover that you have many more questions than answers. These questions drive the scientific method.

Questions beginning with *what, why, how,* and *when* are very important in focusing an investigation, and they often lead to a hypothesis. (You will learn what a hypothesis is in the next step.) Here is an example of a question that could lead to further investigation.

Question: How does acid rain affect plant growth?

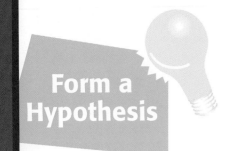

2 **Form a Hypothesis** After you come up with a question, you need to turn the question into a **hypothesis.** A hypothesis is a clear statement of what you expect the answer to your question to be. Your hypothesis will represent your best "educated guess" based on your observations and what you already know. A good hypothesis is testable. If observations and information cannot be gathered or if an experiment cannot be designed to test your hypothesis, it is untestable, and the investigation can go no further.

Here is a hypothesis that could be formed from the question, "How does acid rain affect plant growth?"

Hypothesis: Acid rain causes plants to grow more slowly.

Notice that the hypothesis provides some specifics that lead to methods of testing. The hypothesis can also lead to predictions. A **prediction** is what you think will be the outcome of your experiment or data collection. Predictions are usually stated in an "if . . . then" format. For example, **if** meat is kept at room temperature, **then** it will spoil faster than meat kept in the refrigerator. More than one prediction can be made for a single hypothesis. Here is a sample prediction for the hypothesis that acid rain causes plants to grow more slowly.

Prediction: If a plant is watered with only acid rain (which has a pH of 4), then the plant will grow at half its normal rate.

3 **Test the Hypothesis** After you have formed a hypothesis and made a prediction, you should test your hypothesis. There are different ways to do this. Perhaps the most familiar way is to conduct a **controlled experiment.** A controlled experiment tests only one factor at a time. A controlled experiment has a **control group** and one or more **experimental groups.** All the factors for the control and experimental groups are the same except for one factor, which is called the **variable.** By changing only one factor, you can see the results of just that one change.

Sometimes, the nature of an investigation makes a controlled experiment impossible. For example, dinosaurs have been extinct for millions of years, and the Earth's core is surrounded by thousands of meters of rock. It would be difficult, if not impossible, to conduct controlled experiments on such things. Under such circumstances, a hypothesis may be tested by making detailed observations. Taking measurements is one way of making observations.

Test the Hypothesis

4 **Analyze the Results** After you have completed your experiments, made your observations, and collected your data, you must analyze all the information you have gathered. Tables and graphs are often used in this step to organize the data.

Analyze the Results

5 **Draw Conclusions** Based on the analysis of your data, you should conclude whether or not your results support your hypothesis. If your hypothesis is supported, you (or others) might want to repeat the observations or experiments to verify your results. If your hypothesis is not supported by the data, you may have to check your procedure for errors. You may even have to reject your hypothesis and make a new one. If you cannot draw a conclusion from your results, you may have to try the investigation again or carry out further observations or experiments.

Draw Conclusions

Do they support your hypothesis?

No

Yes

6 **Communicate Results** After any scientific investigation, you should report your results. By doing a written or oral report, you let others know what you have learned. They may want to repeat your investigation to see if they get the same results. Your report may even lead to another question, which in turn may lead to another investigation.

Communicate Results

Scientific Method in Action

The scientific method is not a "straight line" of steps. It contains loops in which several steps may be repeated over and over again, while others may not be necessary. For example, sometimes scientists will find that testing one hypothesis raises new questions and new hypotheses to be tested. And sometimes, testing the hypothesis leads directly to a conclusion. Furthermore, the steps in the scientific method are not always used in the same order. Follow the steps in the diagram below, and see how many different directions the scientific method can take you.

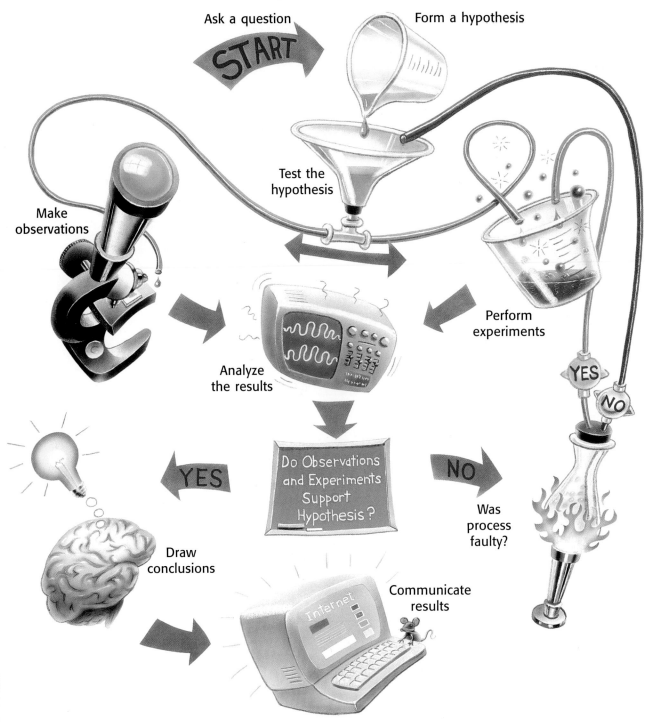

Ask a question

START

Form a hypothesis

Test the hypothesis

Make observations

Perform experiments

Analyze the results

Do Observations and Experiments Support Hypothesis?

YES

NO

Was process faulty?

Draw conclusions

Communicate results

Internet

Making Charts and Graphs

Circle Graphs

A circle graph, or pie chart, shows how each group of data relates to all of the data. Each part of the circle represents a category of the data. The entire circle represents all of the data. For example, a biologist studying a hardwood forest in Wisconsin found that there were five different types of trees. The data table at right summarizes the biologist's findings.

Wisconsin Hardwood Trees	
Type of tree	Number found
Oak	600
Maple	750
Beech	300
Birch	1,200
Hickory	150
Total	3,000

How to Make a Circle Graph

1 In order to make a circle graph of this data, first find the percentage of each type of tree. To do this, divide the number of individual trees by the total number of trees and multiply by 100.

$$\frac{600 \text{ oak}}{3,000 \text{ trees}} \times 100 = 20\%$$

$$\frac{750 \text{ maple}}{3,000 \text{ trees}} \times 100 = 25\%$$

$$\frac{300 \text{ beech}}{3,000 \text{ trees}} \times 100 = 10\%$$

$$\frac{1,200 \text{ birch}}{3,000 \text{ trees}} \times 100 = 40\%$$

$$\frac{150 \text{ hickory}}{3,000 \text{ trees}} \times 100 = 5\%$$

2 Now determine the size of the pie shapes that make up the chart. Do this by multiplying each percentage by 360°. Remember that a circle contains 360°.

$20\% \times 360° = 72°$ $25\% \times 360° = 90°$
$10\% \times 360° = 36°$ $40\% \times 360° = 144°$
$5\% \times 360° = 18°$

3 Then check that the sum of the percentages is 100 and the sum of the degrees is 360.

$20\% + 25\% + 10\% + 40\% + 5\% = 100\%$
$72° + 90° + 36° + 144° + 18° = 360°$

4 Use a compass to draw a circle and mark its center.

5 Then use a protractor to draw angles of 72°, 90°, 36°, 144°, and 18° in the circle.

6 Finally, label each part of the graph, and choose an appropriate title.

A Community of Wisconsin Hardwood Trees

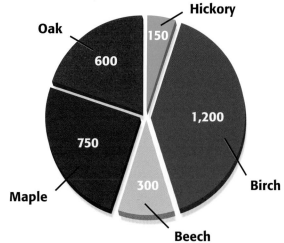

Line Graphs

Line graphs are most often used to demonstrate continuous change. For example, Mr. Smith's science class analyzed the population records for their hometown, Appleton, between 1900 and 2000. Examine the data at left.

Because the year and the population change, they are the *variables*. The population is determined by, or dependent on, the year. Therefore, the population is called the **dependent variable**, and the year is called the **independent variable**. Each set of data is called a **data pair.** To prepare a line graph, data pairs must first be organized in a table like the one at left.

Population of Appleton, 1900–2000	
Year	Population
1900	1,800
1920	2,500
1940	3,200
1960	3,900
1980	4,600
2000	5,300

How to Make a Line Graph

❶ Place the independent variable along the horizontal (*x*) axis. Place the dependent variable along the vertical (*y*) axis.

❷ Label the *x*-axis "Year" and the *y*-axis "Population." Look at your largest and smallest values for the population. Determine a scale for the *y*-axis that will provide enough space to show these values. You must use the same scale for the entire length of the axis. Find an appropriate scale for the *x*-axis too.

❸ Choose reasonable starting points for each axis.

❹ Plot the data pairs as accurately as possible.

❺ Choose a title that accurately represents the data.

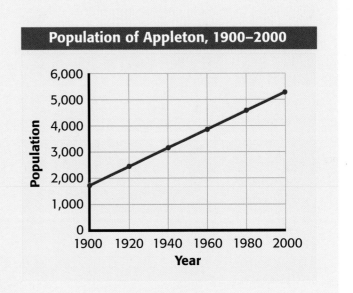

How to Determine Slope

Slope is the ratio of the change in the *y*-axis to the change in the *x*-axis, or "rise over run."

❶ Choose two points on the line graph. For example, the population of Appleton in 2000 was 5,300 people. Therefore, you can define point *a* as (2000, 5,300). In 1900, the population was 1,800 people. Define point *b* as (1900, 1,800).

❷ Find the change in the *y*-axis. (*y* at point *a*) − (*y* at point *b*) 5,300 people − 1,800 people = 3,500 people

❸ Find the change in the *x*-axis. (*x* at point *a*) − (*x* at point *b*) 2000 − 1900 = 100 years

❹ Calculate the slope of the graph by dividing the change in *y* by the change in *x*.

$$slope = \frac{change\ in\ y}{change\ in\ x}$$

$$slope = \frac{3,500\ people}{100\ years}$$

$$slope = 35\ people\ per\ year$$

In this example, the population in Appleton increased by a fixed amount each year. The graph of this data is a straight line. Therefore, the relationship is **linear.** When the graph of a set of data is not a straight line, the relationship is **nonlinear.**

Using Algebra to Determine Slope

The equation in step 4 may also be arranged to be:

$$y = kx$$

where y represents the change in the y-axis, k represents the slope, and x represents the change in the x-axis.

$$\text{slope} = \frac{\text{change in } y}{\text{change in } x}$$

$$k = \frac{y}{x}$$

$$k \times x = \frac{y \times x}{x}$$

$$kx = y$$

Bar Graphs

Bar graphs are used to demonstrate change that is not continuous. These graphs can be used to indicate trends when the data are taken over a long period of time. A meteorologist gathered the precipitation records at right for Hartford, Connecticut, for April 1–15, 1996, and used a bar graph to represent the data.

Precipitation in Hartford, Connecticut April 1–15, 1996

Date	Precipitation (cm)	Date	Precipitation (cm)
April 1	0.5	April 9	0.25
April 2	1.25	April 10	0.0
April 3	0.0	April 11	1.0
April 4	0.0	April 12	0.0
April 5	0.0	April 13	0.25
April 6	0.0	April 14	0.0
April 7	0.0	April 15	6.50
April 8	1.75		

How to Make a Bar Graph

❶ Use an appropriate scale and a reasonable starting point for each axis.

❷ Label the axes, and plot the data.

❸ Choose a title that accurately represents the data.

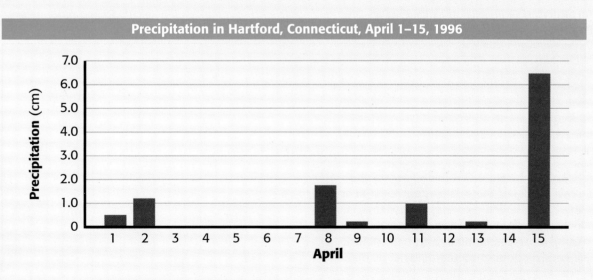

Precipitation in Hartford, Connecticut, April 1–15, 1996

Math Refresher

Science requires an understanding of many math concepts. The following pages will help you review some important math skills.

Averages

An **average,** or **mean,** simplifies a list of numbers into a single number that *approximates* their value.

    Example: Find the average of the following set of numbers: 5, 4, 7, and 8.

Step 1: Find the sum.

$$5 + 4 + 7 + 8 = 24$$

Step 2: Divide the sum by the amount of numbers in your set. Because there are four numbers in this example, divide the sum by 4.

$$\frac{24}{4} = 6$$

The average, or mean, is **6.**

Ratios

A **ratio** is a comparison between numbers, and it is usually written as a fraction.

    Example: Find the ratio of thermometers to students if you have 36 thermometers and 48 students in your class.

Step 1: Make the ratio.

$$\frac{36 \text{ thermometers}}{48 \text{ students}}$$

Step 2: Reduce the fraction to its simplest form.

$$\frac{36}{48} = \frac{36 \div 12}{48 \div 12} = \frac{3}{4}$$

The ratio of thermometers to students is **3 to 4,** or $\frac{3}{4}$. The ratio may also be written in the form 3:4.

Proportions

A **proportion** is an equation that states that two ratios are equal.

$$\frac{3}{1} = \frac{12}{4}$$

To solve a proportion, first multiply across the equal sign. This is called cross-multiplication. If you know three of the quantities in a proportion, you can use cross-multiplication to find the fourth.

    Example: Imagine that you are making a scale model of the solar system for your science project. The diameter of Jupiter is 11.2 times the diameter of the Earth. If you are using a plastic-foam ball with a diameter of 2 cm to represent the Earth, what diameter does the ball representing Jupiter need to be?

$$\frac{11.2}{1} = \frac{x}{2 \text{ cm}}$$

Step 1: Cross-multiply.

$$\frac{11.2}{1} \times \frac{x}{2}$$

$$11.2 \times 2 = x \times 1$$

Step 2: Multiply.

$$22.4 = x \times 1$$

Step 3: Isolate the variable by dividing both sides by 1.

$$x = \frac{22.4}{1}$$

$$x = 22.4 \text{ cm}$$

You will need to use a ball with a diameter of **22.4 cm** to represent Jupiter.

Percentages

A **percentage** is a ratio of a given number to 100.

    Example: What is 85 percent of 40?

Step 1: Rewrite the percentage by moving the decimal point two places to the left.

$$.85$$

Step 2: Multiply the decimal by the number you are calculating the percentage of.

$$0.85 \times 40 = 34$$

85 percent of 40 is **34.**

Decimals

To **add** or **subtract decimals,** line up the digits vertically so that the decimal points line up. Then add or subtract the columns from right to left, carrying or borrowing numbers as necessary.

    Example: Add the following numbers: 3.1415 and 2.96.

Step 1: Line up the digits vertically so that the decimal points line up.

$$\begin{array}{r} 3.1415 \\ + \ 2.96 \\ \hline \end{array}$$

Step 2: Add the columns from right to left, carrying when necessary.

$$\begin{array}{r} {}^{1\ 1} \\ 3.1415 \\ + \ 2.96 \\ \hline 6.1015 \end{array}$$

The sum is **6.1015.**

Fractions

Numbers tell you how many; **fractions** tell you *how much of a whole.*

    Example: Your class has 24 plants. Your teacher instructs you to put 5 in a shady spot. What fraction does this represent?

Step 1: Write a fraction with the total number of parts in the whole as the denominator.

$$\frac{?}{24}$$

Step 2: Write the number of parts of the whole being represented as the numerator.

$$\frac{5}{24}$$

$\frac{5}{24}$ of the plants will be in the shade.

Reducing Fractions

It is usually best to express a fraction in simplest form. This is called *reducing* a fraction.

    Example: Reduce the fraction $\frac{30}{45}$ to its simplest form.

Step 1: Find the largest whole number that will divide evenly into both the numerator and denominator. This number is called the greatest common factor (GCF).

factors of the numerator 30: 1, 2, 3, 5, 6, 10, **15,** 30

factors of the denominator 45: 1, 3, 5, 9, **15,** 45

Step 2: Divide both the numerator and the denominator by the GCF, which in this case is 15.

$$\frac{30}{45} = \frac{30 \div 15}{45 \div 15} = \frac{2}{3}$$

$\frac{30}{45}$ reduced to its simplest form is $\frac{2}{3}$.

Adding and Subtracting Fractions

To **add** or **subtract fractions** that have the **same denominator,** simply add or subtract the numerators.

Examples:

$$\frac{3}{5} + \frac{1}{5} = ? \text{ and } \frac{3}{4} - \frac{1}{4} = ?$$

Step 1: Add or subtract the numerators.

$$\frac{3}{5} + \frac{1}{5} = \frac{4}{} \text{ and } \frac{3}{4} - \frac{1}{4} = \frac{2}{}$$

Step 2: Write the sum or difference over the denominator.

$$\frac{3}{5} + \frac{1}{5} = \frac{4}{5} \text{ and } \frac{3}{4} - \frac{1}{4} = \frac{2}{4}$$

Step 3: If necessary, reduce the fraction to its simplest form.

$\frac{4}{5}$ cannot be reduced, and $\frac{2}{4} = \frac{1}{2}$.

To **add** or **subtract fractions** that have **different denominators,** first find the least common denominator (LCD).

Examples:

$$\frac{1}{2} + \frac{1}{6} = ? \text{ and } \frac{3}{4} - \frac{2}{3} = ?$$

Step 1: Write the equivalent fractions with a common denominator.

$$\frac{3}{6} + \frac{1}{6} = ? \text{ and } \frac{9}{12} - \frac{8}{12} = ?$$

Step 2: Add or subtract.

$$\frac{3}{6} + \frac{1}{6} = \frac{4}{6} \text{ and } \frac{9}{12} - \frac{8}{12} = \frac{1}{12}$$

Step 3: If necessary, reduce the fraction to its simplest form.

$\frac{4}{6} = \frac{2}{3}$, and $\frac{1}{12}$ cannot be reduced.

Multiplying Fractions

To **multiply fractions,** multiply the numerators and the denominators together, and then reduce the fraction to its simplest form.

Example:

$$\frac{5}{9} \times \frac{7}{10} = ?$$

Step 1: Multiply the numerators and denominators.

$$\frac{5}{9} \times \frac{7}{10} = \frac{5 \times 7}{9 \times 10} = \frac{35}{90}$$

Step 2: Reduce.

$$\frac{35}{90} = \frac{35 \div 5}{90 \div 5} = \frac{7}{18}$$

Dividing Fractions

To **divide fractions,** first rewrite the divisor (the number you divide *by*) upside down. This is called the reciprocal of the divisor. Then you can multiply and reduce if necessary.

Example:

$$\frac{5}{8} \div \frac{3}{2} = ?$$

Step 1: Rewrite the divisor as its reciprocal.

$$\frac{3}{2} \rightarrow \frac{2}{3}$$

Step 2: Multiply.

$$\frac{5}{8} \times \frac{2}{3} = \frac{5 \times 2}{8 \times 3} = \frac{10}{24}$$

Step 3: Reduce.

$$\frac{10}{24} = \frac{10 \div 2}{24 \div 2} = \frac{5}{12}$$

Scientific Notation

Scientific notation is a short way of representing very large and very small numbers without writing all of the place-holding zeros.

> **Example:** Write 653,000,000 in scientific notation.

Step 1: Write the number without the place-holding zeros.

$$653$$

Step 2: Place the decimal point after the first digit.

$$6.53$$

Step 3: Find the exponent by counting the number of places that you moved the decimal point.

$$6.53000000$$

The decimal point was moved eight places to the left. Therefore, the exponent of 10 is positive 8. Remember, if the decimal point had moved to the right, the exponent would be negative.

Step 4: Write the number in scientific notation.

$$6.53 \times 10^8$$

Area

Area is the number of square units needed to cover the surface of an object.

> **Formulas:**
> Area of a square = side × side
> Area of a rectangle = length × width
> Area of a triangle = $\frac{1}{2}$ × base × height
>
> **Examples:** Find the areas.

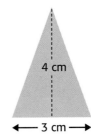

Triangle
Area = $\frac{1}{2}$ × base × height
Area = $\frac{1}{2}$ × 3 cm × 4 cm
Area = **6 cm²**

Rectangle
Area = length × width
Area = 6 cm × 3 cm
Area = **18 cm²**

Square
Area = side × side
Area = 3 cm × 3 cm
Area = **9 cm²**

Volume

Volume is the amount of space something occupies.

> **Formulas:**
> Volume of a cube =
> side × side × side
>
> Volume of a prism =
> area of base × height
>
> **Examples:**
> Find the volume
> of the solids.

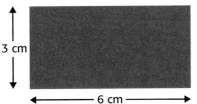
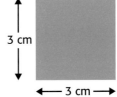
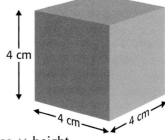

Cube
Volume = side × side × side
Volume = 4 cm × 4 cm × 4 cm
Volume = **64 cm³**

Prism
Volume = area of base × height
Volume = (area of triangle) × height
Volume = $\left(\frac{1}{2} \times 3\ \text{cm} \times 4\ \text{cm} \right) \times 5\ \text{cm}$
Volume = 6 cm² × 5 cm
Volume = **30 cm³**

Periodic Table of the Elements

Each square on the table includes an element's name, chemical symbol, atomic number, and atomic mass.

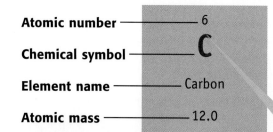

Atomic number ———— 6

Chemical symbol ———— **C**

Element name ———— Carbon

Atomic mass ———— 12.0

The background color indicates the type of element. Carbon is a nonmetal.

The color of the chemical symbol indicates the physical state at room temperature. Carbon is a solid.

Period 1

1
H
Hydrogen
1.0

Background

Metals	▨
Metalloids	▨
Nonmetals	▨

Chemical Symbol

Solid	▨
Liquid	▨
Gas	▨

	Group 1	**Group 2**	**Group 3**	**Group 4**	**Group 5**	**Group 6**	**Group 7**	**Group 8**	**Group 9**
Period 2	3 **Li** Lithium 6.9	4 **Be** Beryllium 9.0							
Period 3	11 **Na** Sodium 23.0	12 **Mg** Magnesium 24.3							
Period 4	19 **K** Potassium 39.1	20 **Ca** Calcium 40.1	21 **Sc** Scandium 45.0	22 **Ti** Titanium 47.9	23 **V** Vanadium 50.9	24 **Cr** Chromium 52.0	25 **Mn** Manganese 54.9	26 **Fe** Iron 55.8	27 **Co** Cobalt 58.9
Period 5	37 **Rb** Rubidium 85.5	38 **Sr** Strontium 87.6	39 **Y** Yttrium 88.9	40 **Zr** Zirconium 91.2	41 **Nb** Niobium 92.9	42 **Mo** Molybdenum 95.9	43 **Tc** Technetium (97.9)	44 **Ru** Ruthenium 101.1	45 **Rh** Rhodium 102.9
Period 6	55 **Cs** Cesium 132.9	56 **Ba** Barium 137.3	57 **La** Lanthanum 138.9	72 **Hf** Hafnium 178.5	73 **Ta** Tantalum 180.9	74 **W** Tungsten 183.8	75 **Re** Rhenium 186.2	76 **Os** Osmium 190.2	77 **Ir** Iridium 192.2
Period 7	87 **Fr** Francium (223.0)	88 **Ra** Radium (226.0)	89 **Ac** Actinium (227.0)	104 **Rf** Rutherfordium (261.1)	105 **Db** Dubnium (262.1)	106 **Sg** Seaborgium (263.1)	107 **Bh** Bohrium (262.1)	108 **Hs** Hassium (265)	109 **Mt** Meitnerium (266)

A row of elements is called a period.

A column of elements is called a group or family.

Lanthanides	58 **Ce** Cerium 140.1	59 **Pr** Praseodymium 140.9	60 **Nd** Neodymium 144.2	61 **Pm** Promethium (144.9)	62 **Sm** Samarium 150.4
Actinides	90 **Th** Thorium 232.0	91 **Pa** Protactinium 231.0	92 **U** Uranium 238.0	93 **Np** Neptunium (237.0)	94 **Pu** Plutonium 244.1

These elements are placed below the table to allow the table to be narrower.

This zigzag line reminds you where the metals, nonmetals, and metalloids are.

						Group 18
						2 **He** Helium 4.0

		Group 13	Group 14	Group 15	Group 16	Group 17	
		5 **B** Boron 10.8	6 **C** Carbon 12.0	7 **N** Nitrogen 14.0	8 **O** Oxygen 16.0	9 **F** Fluorine 19.0	10 **Ne** Neon 20.2
		13 **Al** Aluminum 27.0	14 **Si** Silicon 28.1	15 **P** Phosphorus 31.0	16 **S** Sulfur 32.1	17 **Cl** Chlorine 35.5	18 **Ar** Argon 39.9

Group 10	Group 11	Group 12						
28 **Ni** Nickel 58.7	29 **Cu** Copper 63.5	30 **Zn** Zinc 65.4	31 **Ga** Gallium 69.7	32 **Ge** Germanium 72.6	33 **As** Arsenic 74.9	34 **Se** Selenium 79.0	35 **Br** Bromine 79.9	36 **Kr** Krypton 83.8
46 **Pd** Palladium 106.4	47 **Ag** Silver 107.9	48 **Cd** Cadmium 112.4	49 **In** Indium 114.8	50 **Sn** Tin 118.7	51 **Sb** Antimony 121.8	52 **Te** Tellurium 127.6	53 **I** Iodine 126.9	54 **Xe** Xenon 131.3
78 **Pt** Platinum 195.1	79 **Au** Gold 197.0	80 **Hg** Mercury 200.6	81 **Tl** Thallium 204.4	82 **Pb** Lead 207.2	83 **Bi** Bismuth 209.0	84 **Po** Polonium (209.0)	85 **At** Astatine (210.0)	86 **Rn** Radon (222.0)
110 **Uun*** Ununnilium (271)	111 **Uuu*** Unununium (272)	112 **Uub*** Ununbium (277)		114 **Uuq*** Ununquadium (285)		116 **Uuh*** Ununhexium (289)		118 **Uuo*** Ununoctium (293)

A number in parenthesis is the mass number of the most stable form of that element.

63 **Eu** Europium 152.0	64 **Gd** Gadolinium 157.3	65 **Tb** Terbium 158.9	66 **Dy** Dysprosium 162.5	67 **Ho** Holmium 164.9	68 **Er** Erbium 167.3	69 **Tm** Thulium 168.9	70 **Yb** Ytterbium 173.0	71 **Lu** Lutetium 175.0
95 **Am** Americium (243.1)	96 **Cm** Curium (247.1)	97 **Bk** Berkelium (247.1)	98 **Cf** Californium (251.1)	99 **Es** Einsteinium (252.1)	100 **Fm** Fermium (257.1)	101 **Md** Mendelevium (258.1)	102 **No** Nobelium (259.1)	103 **Lr** Lawrencium (262.1)

*The official names and symbols for the elements greater than 109 will eventually be approved by a committee of scientists.

Physical Science Laws and Principles

Law of Conservation of Energy

The law of conservation of energy states that energy can be neither created nor destroyed.

The total amount of energy in a closed system is always the same. Energy can be changed from one form to another, but all the different forms of energy in a system always add up to the same total amount of energy, no matter how many energy conversions occur.

Law of Universal Gravitation

The law of universal gravitation states that all objects in the universe attract each other by a force called gravity. The size of the force depends on the masses of the objects and the distance between them.

The first part of the law explains why a bowling ball is much harder to lift than a table-tennis ball. Because the bowling ball has a much larger mass than the table-tennis ball, the amount of gravity between the Earth and the bowling ball is greater than the amount of gravity between the Earth and the table-tennis ball.

The second part of the law explains why a satellite can remain in orbit around the Earth. The satellite is carefully placed at a distance great enough to prevent the Earth's gravity from immediately pulling it down but small enough to prevent it from completely escaping the Earth's gravity and wandering off into space.

Newton's Laws of Motion

Newton's first law of motion states that an object at rest remains at rest and an object in motion remains in motion at constant speed and in a straight line unless acted on by an unbalanced force.

The first part of the law explains why a football will remain on a tee until it is kicked off or until a gust of wind blows it off.

The second part of the law explains why a bike's rider will continue moving forward after the bike tire runs into a crack in the sidewalk and the bike comes to an abrupt stop until gravity and the sidewalk stop the rider.

Newton's second law of motion states that the acceleration of an object depends on the mass of the object and the amount of force applied.

The first part of the law explains why the acceleration of a 4 kg bowling ball will be greater than the acceleration of a 6 kg bowling ball if the same force is applied to both.

The second part of the law explains why the acceleration of a bowling ball will be larger if a larger force is applied to it.

The relationship of acceleration (a) to mass (m) and force (F) can be expressed mathematically by the following equation:

$$\text{acceleration} = \frac{\text{force}}{\text{mass}}, \text{ or } a = \frac{F}{m}$$

This equation is often rearranged to the form:

$$\text{force} = \text{mass} \times \text{acceleration},$$
$$\text{or}$$
$$F = m \times a$$

Newton's third law of motion states that whenever one object exerts a force on a second object, the second object exerts an equal and opposite force on the first.

This law explains that a runner is able to move forward because of the equal and opposite force the ground exerts on the runner's foot after each step.

Law of Reflection

The law of reflection states that the angle of incidence is equal to the angle of reflection. This law explains why light reflects off of a surface at the same angle it strikes the surface.

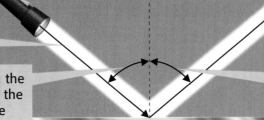

A line perpendicular to the mirror's surface is called the *normal.*

The beam of light reflected off the mirror is called the *reflected beam.*

The beam of light traveling toward the mirror is called the *incident beam.*

The angle between the incident beam and the normal is called the *angle of incidence.*

The angle between the reflected beam and the normal is called the *angle of reflection.*

Charles's Law

Charles's law states that for a fixed amount of gas at a constant pressure, the volume of the gas increases as its temperature increases. Likewise, the volume of the gas decreases as its temperature decreases.

If a basketball that was inflated indoors is left outside on a cold winter day, the air particles inside of the ball will move more slowly. They will hit the sides of the basketball less often and with less force. The ball will get smaller as the volume of the air decreases. If a basketball that was inflated outdoors on a cold winter day is brought indoors, the air particles inside of the ball will move more rapidly. They will hit the sides of the basketball more often and with more force. The ball will get larger as the volume of the air increases.

Boyle's Law

Boyle's law states that for a fixed amount of gas at a constant temperature, the volume of a gas increases as its pressure decreases. Likewise, the volume of a gas decreases as its pressure increases.

This law explains why the pressure of the gas in a helium balloon decreases as the balloon rises from the Earth's surface.

Pascal's Principle

Pascal's principle states that a change in pressure at any point in an enclosed fluid will be transmitted equally to all parts of that fluid.

When a mechanic uses a hydraulic jack to raise an automobile off the ground, he or she increases the pressure on the fluid in the jack by pushing on the jack handle. The pressure is transmitted equally to all parts of the fluid-filled jacking system. The fluid presses the jack plate against the frame of the car, lifting the car off the ground.

Archimedes' Principle

Archimedes' principle states that the buoyant force on an object in a fluid is equal to the weight of the volume of fluid that the object displaces.

A person floating in a swimming pool displaces 20 L of water. The weight of that volume of water is about 200 N. Therefore, the buoyant force on the person is 200 N.

Bernoulli's Principle

Bernoulli's principle states that as the speed of a moving fluid increases, its pressure decreases.

Bernoulli's principle explains how a wing gives lift to an airplane or even how a Frisbee® can fly through the air. Because of the shape of the Frisbee, the air moving over the top of the Frisbee must travel farther than the air below the Frisbee in the same amount of time. In other words, the air above the Frisbee is moving faster than the air below it. This faster-moving air above the Frisbee exerts less pressure than the slower-moving air below it. The resulting increased pressure below exerts an upward force, pushing the Frisbee up.

Useful Equations

Average speed

$$\text{Average speed} = \frac{\text{total distance}}{\text{total time}}$$

Example: A bicycle messenger traveled a distance of 136 km in 8 hours. What was the messenger's average speed?

$$\frac{136 \text{ km}}{8 \text{ h}} = 17 \text{ km/h}$$

The messenger's average speed was **17 km/h.**

Average acceleration

$$\frac{\text{Average}}{\text{acceleration}} = \frac{\text{final velocity} - \text{starting velocity}}{\text{time it takes to change velocity}}$$

Example: Calculate the average acceleration of an Olympic 100 m dash sprinter who reaches a velocity of 15 m/s south at the finish line. The race was in a straight line and lasted 10 s.

$$\frac{15 \text{ m/s} - 0 \text{ m/s}}{10 \text{ s}} = 1.5 \text{ m/s/s}$$

The sprinter's average acceleration is **1.5 m/s/s south.**

Net force

Forces in the Same Direction

When forces are in the same direction, add the forces together to determine the net force.

Example: Calculate the net force on a stalled car that is being pushed by two people. One person is pushing with a force of 13 N north-west and the other person is pushing with a force of 8 N in the same direction.

$$13 \text{ N} + 8 \text{ N} = 21 \text{ N}$$

The net force is **21 N northwest.**

Forces in Opposite Directions

When forces are in opposite directions, subtract the smaller force from the larger force to determine the net force.

Example: Calculate the net force on a rope that is being pulled on each end. One person is pulling on one end of the rope with a force of 12 N south. Another person is pulling on the opposite end of the rope with a force of 7 N north.

$$12 \text{ N} - 7 \text{ N} = 5 \text{ N}$$

The net force is **5 N south.**

Work

Work is done by exerting a force through a distance. Work has units of joules (J), which are equivalent to Newton-meters.

$$W = F \times d$$

Example: Calculate the amount of work done by a man who lifts a 100 N toddler 1.5 m off the floor.

$$W = 100 \text{ N} \times 1.5 \text{ m} = 150 \text{ N•m} = 150 \text{ J}$$

The man did **150 J** of work.

Power

Power is the rate at which work is done. Power is measured in watts (W), which are equivalent to joules per second.

$$P = \frac{W}{t}$$

Example: Calculate the power of a weightlifter who raises a 300 N barbell 2.1 m off the floor in 1.25 s.

$$W = 300 \text{ N} \times 2.1 \text{ m} = 630 \text{ N•m} = 630 \text{ J}$$
$$P = \frac{630 \text{ J}}{1.25 \text{ s}} = 504 \text{ J/s} = 504 \text{ W}$$

The weightlifter has **504 W** of power.

Pressure

Pressure is the force exerted over a given area. The SI unit for pressure is the pascal, which is abbreviated Pa.

$$\text{Pressure} = \frac{\text{force}}{\text{area}}$$

Example: Calculate the pressure of the air in a soccer ball if the air exerts a force of 10 N over an area of 0.5 m².

$$\text{Pressure} = \frac{10 \text{ N}}{0.5 \text{ m}^2} = 20 \text{ N/m}^2 = 20 \text{ Pa}$$

The pressure of the air inside of the soccer ball is **20 Pa.**

Density

$$\text{Density} = \frac{\text{mass}}{\text{volume}}$$

Example: Calculate the density of a sponge with a mass of 10 g and a volume of 40 mL.

$$\frac{10 \text{ g}}{40 \text{ mL}} = 0.25 \text{ g/mL}$$

The density of the sponge is **0.25 g/mL.**

Concentration

$$\text{Concentration} = \frac{\text{mass of solute}}{\text{volume of solvent}}$$

Example: Calculate the concentration of a solution in which 10 g of sugar is dissolved in 125 mL of water.

$$\frac{10 \text{ g of sugar}}{125 \text{ mL of water}} = 0.08 \text{ g/mL}$$

The concentration of this solution is **0.08 g/mL.**

Glossary

A

absolute zero the lowest possible temperature (0 K, −273°C) (153)

acceleration (ak SEL uhr AY shuhn) the rate at which velocity changes; an object accelerates if its speed changes, if its direction changes, or if both its speed and its direction change (8)

active solar heating a solar-heating system consisting of solar collectors and a network of pipes that distributes energy from the sun throughout a building (169)

Archimedes' (ahr kuh MEE deez) **principle** the principle that states that the buoyant force on an object in a fluid is an upward force equal to the weight of the volume of fluid that the object displaces (68)

atmospheric pressure the pressure caused by the weight of the atmosphere (63)

average speed the overall rate at which an object moves; average speed can be calculated by dividing total distance by total time (5)

B

balanced forces forces on an object that cause the net force to be zero; balanced forces do not cause a change in motion or acceleration (14)

Bernoulli's (buhr NOO leez) **principle** the principle that states that as the speed of a moving fluid increases, its pressure decreases (73)

bimetallic (BIE muh TAL ik) **strip** a strip made by stacking two different metals in a long thin strip; because the different metals expand at different rates, a bimetallic strip can coil and uncoil with changes in temperature; bimetallic strips are used in devices such as thermostats (154)

biomass organic matter, such as plants, wood, and waste, that contains stored energy (138)

block and tackle a fixed pulley and a movable pulley used together; it can have a large mechanical advantage if several pulleys are used (104)

Boyle's law the law that states that for a fixed amount of gas at a constant temperature, the volume of a gas increases as its pressure decreases (219)

buoyant force the upward force that fluids exert on all matter; buoyant force opposes gravitational force (68)

C

calorie the amount of energy needed to change the temperature of 0.001 kg of water by 1°C; 1 calorie is equivalent to 4.184 J (162)

calorimeter (KAL uh RIM uht uhr) a device used to determine the specific heat capacity of a substance (162)

centripetal (sen TRIP uht uhl) **acceleration** the acceleration that occurs in circular motion; an object traveling in a circle is constantly changing directions, so acceleration occurs continuously (10)

change of state the conversion of a substance from one physical form to another (165)

Charles's law the law that states that for a fixed amount of gas at a constant pressure, the volume of a gas increases as its temperature increases (219)

chemical change a change that occurs when one or more substances are changed into entirely new substances with different properties; cannot be reversed using physical means (166)

chemical energy the energy of a compound that changes as its atoms are rearranged to form a new compound; chemical energy is a form of potential energy (120)

combustion the burning of fuel; specifically, the process in which fuel combines with oxygen in a chemical change that produces thermal energy (170)

compound machine a machine that is made of two or more simple machines (104)

conduction (thermal) the transfer of thermal energy from one substance to another through direct contact; conduction can also occur within a substance (157)

conductor (thermal) a substance that conducts thermal energy well (158)

convection the transfer of thermal energy by the movement of a liquid or a gas (158)

convection current the circular motion of liquids or gases due to density differences that result from temperature differences (158)

D

density the amount of matter in a given space; mass per unit volume (65)

drag the force that opposes or restricts motion in a fluid; drag opposes thrust (76)

E

energy the ability to do work (116)

energy conversion a change from one form of energy into another (124)

energy efficiency (e FISH uhn see) a comparison of the amount of energy before a conversion and the amount of useful energy after a conversion (130)

energy resource a natural resource that can be converted by humans into other forms of energy in order to do useful work (134)

external combustion engine a heat engine that burns fuel outside the engine, such as a steam engine (170)

F

fixed pulley a pulley that is attached to something that does not move; fixed pulleys change the direction of a force but do not increase the force (103)

fluid any material that can flow and that takes the shape of its container (62)

force a push or a pull; all forces have both size and direction (11)

fossil fuels nonrenewable energy resources that form in the Earth's crust over millions of years from the buried remains of once-living organisms (134)

free fall the condition an object is in when gravity is the only force acting on it (39)

friction a force that opposes motion between two surfaces that are touching (15, 131)

fulcrum the fixed point about which a lever pivots (98)

G

geothermal energy energy resulting from the heating of the Earth's crust (138)

gravitational potential energy energy due to an object's position above the Earth's surface (118)

gravity a force of attraction between objects that is due to their masses (21)

greenhouse effect the natural heating process of a planet, such as the Earth, by which gases in the atmosphere trap thermal energy (159)

H

heat the transfer of energy between objects that are at different temperatures; energy is always transferred from higher-temperature objects to lower-temperature objects until thermal equilibrium is reached (155); *also* the amount of energy that is transferred between objects that are at different temperatures (161)

heat engine a machine that uses heat to do work (170)

hydraulic (hie DRAW lik) **device** a device that uses liquids to transmit pressure from one point to another (67)

I

ideal machine a machine that has 100 percent mechanical efficiency (97)

inertia the tendency of all objects to resist any change in motion (45)

input force the force applied to a machine (93)

insulation a substance that reduces the transfer of thermal energy (168)

insulator (thermal) a substance that does not conduct thermal energy well (158)

internal combustion engine a heat engine that burns fuel inside the engine; for example, an automobile engine (171)

J

joule (J) the unit used to express work and energy; equivalent to the newton-meter (N•m) (90)

K

kilocalorie the unit of energy equal to 1,000 calories; the kilocalorie can also be referred to as the Calorie, which is the unit of energy listed on food labels (162)

kinetic (ki NET ik) **energy** the energy of motion; kinetic energy depends on speed and mass (117)

L

law of conservation of energy the law that states that energy is neither created nor destroyed (132)

law of universal gravitation the law that states that all objects in the universe attract each other through gravitational force; the size of the force depends on the masses of the objects and the distance between them (22)

lever a simple machine consisting of a bar that pivots at a fixed point, called a fulcrum; there are three classes of levers, based on where the input force, output force, and fulcrum are placed in relation to the load: first class levers, second class levers, and third class levers (98)

lift an upward force on an object (such as a wing) caused by differences in pressure above and below the object (74)

light energy the energy produced by the vibrations of electrically charged particles (122)

lubricant (LOO bri kuhnt) a substance applied to surfaces to reduce the friction between them (19)

M

machine a device that helps make work easier by changing the size or direction (or both) of a force (92)

mass the amount of matter that something is made of (25)

mechanical advantage a number that tells how many times a machine multiplies force; can be calculated by dividing the output force by the input force (96)

mechanical efficiency (e FISH uhn see) a comparison—expressed as a percentage—of a machine's work output with the work input; can be calculated by dividing work output by work input and then multiplying by 100 (97)

mechanical energy the total energy of motion and position of an object (119)

momentum a property of a moving object that depends on the object's mass and velocity (50)

motion an object's change in position over time when compared with a reference point (4)

movable pulley a pulley attached to the object being moved; movable pulleys increase force (103)

N

negative acceleration acceleration in which velocity decreases; also called deceleration (9)

net force the force that results from combining all the forces exerted on an object (12)

newton (N) the SI unit of force (11)

nonrenewable resource a natural resource that cannot be replaced or that can be replaced only over thousands or millions of years (134)

nuclear energy the form of energy associated with changes in the nucleus of an atom (123)

nuclear fission the process in which a large nucleus splits into two smaller nuclei (137)

nuclear fusion the process in which two or more nuclei with small masses join together, or fuse, to form a larger, more massive nucleus (123)

O

output force the force applied by a machine (93)

P

pascal (Pa) the SI unit of pressure; equal to the force of 1 N exerted over an area of one square meter (62)

Pascal's principle the principle that states that a change in pressure at any point in an enclosed fluid is transmitted equally to all parts of that fluid (67)

passive solar heating a solar-heating system that relies on thick walls and large windows to use energy from the sun as a means of heating (169)

perpetual (puhr PECH oo uhl) **motion machine** a machine that runs forever without any additional energy input; perpetual motion machines are impossible to create (133)

physical change a change that affects one or more physical properties of a substance; many physical changes are easy to undo (165)

positive acceleration acceleration in which velocity increases (9)

potential energy the energy of position or shape (118)

power the rate at which work is done (91)

pressure the amount of force exerted on a given area; expressed in pascals (Pa) (62)

projectile (proh JEK tuhl) **motion** the curved path an object follows when thrown or propelled near the surface of the Earth (41)

pulley a simple machine consisting of a grooved wheel that holds a rope or a cable (103)

R

radiation the transfer of energy through matter or space as electromagnetic waves, such as visible light and infrared waves (159)

reference point an object that appears to stay in place in relation to an object being observed for motion (4)

renewable resource a natural resource that can be used and replaced over a relatively short time (137)

resultant velocity the combination of two or more velocities (7)

S

screw a simple machine that is an inclined plane wrapped in a spiral (101)

simple machines the six machines from which all other machines are constructed: a lever, an inclined plane, a wedge, a screw, a wheel and axle, and a pulley (98)

sound energy the energy caused by an object's vibrations (122)

specific heat capacity the amount of energy needed to change the temperature of 1 kg of a substance by 1°C (160)

speed the rate at which an object moves; speed depends on the distance traveled and the time taken to travel that distance (5)

states of matter the physical forms in which a substance can exist; states include solid, liquid, gas, and plasma (164)

T

temperature a measure of how hot (or cold) something is; specifically, a measure of the average kinetic energy of the particles in an object (150)

terminal velocity the constant velocity of a falling object when the size of the upward force of air resistance matches the size of the downward force of gravity (38)

thermal energy the total energy of the particles that make up an object (120, 156)

thermal equilibrium the point at which two objects reach the same temperature (156)

thermal expansion the increase in volume of a substance due to an increase in temperature (152)

thermal pollution the excessive heating of a body of water (173)

thrust the forward force produced by an airplane's engines; thrust opposes drag (75)

turbulence an irregular or unpredictable flow of fluids that can cause drag; lift is often reduced by turbulence (76)

U

unbalanced forces forces on an object that cause the net force to be other than zero; unbalanced forces produce a change in motion or acceleration (13)

V

velocity (vuh LAHS uh tee) the speed of an object in a particular direction (6)

W

watt (W) the unit used to express power; equivalent to joules per second (J/s) (91)

wedge a simple machine that is a double inclined plane that moves; a wedge is often used for cutting (101)

weight a measure of the gravitational force exerted on an object, usually by the Earth (24)

wheel and axle a simple machine consisting of two circular objects of different sizes; the wheel is the larger of the two circular objects (102)

work the action that results when a force causes an object to move in the direction of the force (88)

work input the work done on a machine; the product of the input force and the distance through which it is exerted (93)

work output the work done by a machine; the product of the output force and the distance through which it is exerted (93)

Index

A **boldface** number refers to an illustration on that page.

Self-Check Answers

Chapter 1—Matter in Motion

Page 6: Numbers 1 and 3 are examples of velocity.

Page 13: 2 N north

Page 18: sliding friction

Page 22: Gravity is a force of attraction between objects that is due to the masses of the objects.

Chapter 2—Forces in Motion

Page 38: A leaf is more affected by air resistance.

Page 45: This can be answered in terms of either Newton's first law or inertia.

Newton's first law: When the bus is still, both you and the bus are at rest. The bus started moving, but no unbalanced force acted on your body, so your body stayed at rest.

Inertia: You have inertia, and that makes you difficult to move. As a result, when the bus started to move, you didn't move with it.

Chapter 3—Forces in Fluids

Page 75: Air travels faster over the top of a wing.

Chapter 4—Work and Machines

Page 89: Pulling a wheeled suitcase is doing work because the force applied and the motion of the suitcase are in the same direction.

Chapter 5—Energy and Energy Resources

Page 125: A roller coaster has the greatest potential energy at the top of the highest hill (usually the first hill) and the greatest kinetic energy at the bottom of the highest hill.

Chapter 6—Heat and Heat Technology

Page 163: Two substances can have the same temperature but different amounts of thermal energy because temperature, unlike thermal energy, does not depend on mass. A small amount of a substance at a particular temperature will have less thermal energy than a large amount of the substance at the same temperature.

Page 165: Steam can cause a more severe burn than boiling water because steam contains more energy per unit mass than does boiling water.